Democracy, human rights and regional co-operation in Southern Africa

Edited by
Dominic Milazi, Munyae Mulinge
and Elizabeth Mukamaambo

D1581195

Africa Institute of South Africa
in collaboration with SAUSSC

African Century Publications Series No. 9

Series Editor: Elizabeth le Roux

First published in 2002 by the
Africa Institute of South Africa
PO Box 630
Pretoria 0001
South Africa

ISBN 0 7983 0150 3

Typeset and designed by A1 Graphics, Pretoria.
Printed and bound by MC Printers, Pretoria.
Cover by Dayv van der Merwe, Dayv Labour, Pretoria.

The Africa Institute of South Africa is a think tank and research organisation, focusing on political, socio-economic, international and development issues in contemporary Africa. The Institute conducts research,
publishes books, monographs and a quarterly journal, and holds regular
seminars on issues of topical interest. It is also home to one of the best
library and documentation centres world-wide, with materials on every
African country.

For more information, contact the Africa Institute at PO Box 630,
Pretoria 0001, South Africa; email ai@ai.org.za; or visit our website at
http://www.ai.org.za.

Contents

Acknowledgements

The Southern African Universities Social Sciences Conference (SAUSSC) would like to thank the GTZ, UNESCO, SIDA (SAREC) and the IDRC for their generous financial support, as well as Chancellor College, University of Malawi, Centre for Social Research and the following private businesses in Malawi: Adsoms Hardware, Jaydee Furnishings and Fargo Limited. SAUSSC would also like to thank the local organising committee at the University of Malawi for their good work in planning and coordinating the hosting of the 21st SAUSSC.

We acknowledge with thanks the contribution made by SAUSSC towards the publication of this volume.

Many thanks, too, to Dominic Milazi, who sadly passed away during the production of this volume. The organisation recognises his invaluable service as SAUSSC President from 1999–2001 and as a very active member of the organisation from its inception.

Introduction

The papers appearing in this book were written by scholars of the Southern African Universities Social Sciences Conference (SAUSSC). Since its establishment in the 1970s, SAUSSC has served as a platform for discussions on issues affecting Southern African Societies, and remains dedicated to academic research and the dissemination of information among universities in the region.

The 21st Conference held in Mangochi, Malawi from 29 November to 4 December 1999 debated the issue of Democracy, Human Rights and Regional Co-operation. This book comprises a selection of papers presented at the conference. Topics include sustainable democratic governance, challenges to regional integration, globalisation and regional integration, regional integration and sustainable development, regional conflict and the quest for peace, and regional economic co-operation. The SAUSSC hopes that this book will enhance public awareness and promote positive change in the region.

The one pre-eminent research interest covered by most writers centres on the regional challenges of sustainable democracy and development and associated problems of the region's capacity building for democracy, simultaneous democratisation and the respect for human rights.

Other issues besetting Southern Africa from the perspective of African scholars are, perhaps, more analytically separate though interrelated aspects of the development problematique. Among these are issues of civil conflict and management, peace and security, civil society and social development, citizenship and information technology.

The third category of development issues covered are those that are, by and large, country-specific and less regional in scope. These include youth development, domestic violence, political language as threat to democracy, women's rights, and so forth.

Overall, the contributions are diverse with different theoretical viewpoints, but there are also cross-currents, particularly in the conceptual analysis of democracy, human rights, socio-economic development and regional co-operation.

The Duty of Government to Citizens on the Road to Democracy

Tommy Fényes and Charles Freysen

This chapter explores the relation of the functions of government to the rights of individuals in fledgling democracies. According to Shapiro, democracy has been a flawed hegemony since the fall of communism.[1] Its flexibility, its commitment to equality of representation, and its recognition of the legitimacy of opposition politics are all positive features for political institutions. But democracy has many deficiencies: it is all too easily held hostage by powerful interests, it often fails to deliver social justice, and it does not cope well with a number of aspects of today's political landscape, such as political identities, boundary disputes, and environmental crises.

Today the most common form of democracy is representative democracy, in which citizens elect officials to make political decisions, formulate laws and administer programmes on behalf of the population at large. On the road to democracy in many countries of the world, and especially Africa, governments have a duty to citizenry to perform well in the execution of tasks to ensure the advancement of democratic values, basic human rights and the rule of law.

We will now address these issues in general terms and then turn to the challenges for the 21st century, which are pertinent for the SADC region.

The Functions of Governments

In an authoritarian society, interest groups such as charitable organisations, churches, environmental and neighbourhood groups, business associations, and labour unions, are controlled, licensed, watched or otherwise accountable to the government.

In a democracy, the powers of the government are, by law, clearly defined and sharply limited. According to the dictionary, democracy is defined as government by the people in which the supreme power is vested in the people and exercised directly by them or by their elected agents under a free electoral system. In this institutionalisation of freedom it is possible to identify time-tested fundamentals of constitutional government, human rights and equality before the law that is the duty of the government to ensure.

Whatever the method used, public officials in a representative democracy hold office in the name of the people and remain accountable to the people for their actions.

Majority rule and minority rights

In a democratic society it is the duty of the government to ensure that majority rule must be coupled with guarantees of individual human rights that, in turn, serve to protect the rights of minorities – whether ethnic, religious or political, or simply the losers in the debate over a piece of controversial legislation. The rights of minorities should not depend upon the goodwill of the majority but are protected because democratic laws and institutions protect the rights of all citizens.[2]

The rights to life, liberty and the pursuit of happiness

To secure these rights, governments are instituted among men, deriving their just powers from the consent of the governed, said Thomas Jefferson in the American Declaration of Independence.

Democratic governments are created to protect the freedoms that every individual possesses by virtue of his or her existence. Such inalienable rights include the freedom of speech, which is the lifeblood of any democracy. Another right is the freedom of faith, which means that no person should be required to profess any religion or other belief against his or her desires.

Citizenship

Democracies rest upon the principle that governments exist to serve the people rather than the people existing to serve governments. On the other hand, a healthy democracy depends on the continuing, informed participation of a broad range of the citizens.

Human rights

As a principle, the protection of basic human rights is widely accepted. It is embodied in written constitutions throughout the world as well as in the Charter of the United Nations and in international agreements. Governments in general have the duty to protect inalienable rights, such as freedom of speech, through restraint, by limiting their own actions. Funding of education, providing health care or guaranteeing employment demand the opposite – that is, the active involvement of the government in policy formulation and implementation.

Equality and the law

It is also the duty of the government to ensure the right to equality before the law. Frank points out that in every society throughout history, those who administer the criminal justice system hold power with the potential for abuse and tyranny.[3]

It is the duty of the state to have the power to maintain order and punish criminal acts, and the rules and procedures by which the state enforces its laws must be public and explicit, not secret, arbitrary or subject to political manipulation by the state.

Constitutions

The foundation upon which a democratic government rests is its constitution – the formal statement of its fundamental obligation, limitations, procedures and institutions. It is the supreme law of the land and all citizens, from presidents to commoners alike, are subject to its provisions. At a minimum, the constitution establishes the authority of government, provides guarantees for fundamental human rights and sets forth the government's basic operating procedures.

Elections

To hold free and fair elections is a fundamental duty of any democratic representative government. It translates the consent of the governed into governmental authority. Democratic elections are competitive, periodic, inclusive, definitive elections in which the chief decision-makers in a government are selected by citizens who enjoy broad freedom to criticise government, to publish their criticism and to present alternatives.[4] It is a duty of the government to ensure that citizens can cast a free ballot, while, to minimise the opportunities for intimidation, voters must be permitted to cast their ballots in secret.

A more difficult duty is the advancement and acceptance of the concept of loyal opposition. It means that all sides in a democracy share a common commitment to its basic values. The state must promote this idea and the ground rules of the society must encourage tolerance and civility in public debate.

Democracy and economics

Democracy implies no specific doctrine of economics. Democratic governments have embraced committed socialists and free marketers alike. Indeed, a good deal of the debate in any modern democracy concerns the proper role of the government in the economy. Based on South Africa's

short democratic experience we can analyse the process of economic policy-making for the well-being of its citizens.

Policy-making challenges in South Africa

The first democratic government in South Africa has established the principles of equality of opportunity and social citizenship. The second post-
apartheid government's duty is to form a new comprehensive strategy for
economic growth. According to Bernstein, this will require new social and
political alliances.[5] The result of the 1999 elections gave the government a
strong mandate for bold action. In the interests of the country, the region
and all its citizens, the government's duty is to act decisively, formulate and
implement a comprehensive economic strategy and build the political
growth coalition necessary to sustain it.

The country's comparative advantage must be exploited. Bernstein
includes the following factors:

* democratic constitution and bill of rights protecting citizens and foreign
  investors;
* powerful political leadership;
* multi-cultural and tolerant population;
* well-developed infrastructure and urban system;
* a relatively highly skilled middle-class;
* a strong and vibrant business community;
* a highly developed financial sector that works well and is managed independently of state influences.[6]

A report by the Centre for Development and Enterprises (CDE) also
stresses the need for South Africa's human capital to be preserved and nurtured. All policy should recognise that the growing and racially diverse middle and professional class has a huge contribution to make to the transformation of the whole society.

Furthermore the trade-offs between different social and development
priorities must be carefully considered to complete the growth strategy. It
is also a duty of the government to shift itself towards strategic management practices, to make itself more efficient and coherent. According to
Bernstein, the new president, Thabo Mbeki, should play to the centre of
South African politics. It is the broad majority of people who are not
racists, who are reasonable in their expectations of government, who
would support measures against crime and corruption, and who are in
favour of opening up opportunities and economic possibilities in a massive
way for all South Africans.

Conclusion

With globalisation and regional integration increasing tremendously, if the government of South Africa performs the duties and executes policies discussed above, the whole SADC region should benefit substantially. Democracy is considered a necessary pre-requisite in the region for stability and economic prosperity.

Notes and References

1   I Shapiro (ed), *Democracy's Value*, New York: Yale University Press, 1999.
2   H Cincotta (ed), *What is Democracy?*, Washington DC: US Information Agency, 1991.
3   JP Frank, *Models of Democratic Government*, Washington DC: American Federation of Teachers, Education for Democracy International, 1991.
4   J Kirkpatrick, 'What are Democratic Elections?', in H Cincotta (ed), *What is Democracy?*, Washington DC: US Information Agency, 1991.
5   A Bernstein (ed), *Policy-making in a New Democracy: South Africa's Challenges for the 21st Century*, Johannesburg: Centre for Development and Enterprise, 1999.
6   *Ibid*.

Negotiating Democracy in Swaziland, 1960s to 1990s

Ackson M Kanduza

A growing concern among scholars of politics and governance in Africa is the issue of consolidating democracy. There is no fixed or pure form of democracy and this raises serious questions about what essentials may lead to the consolidation of democracy in Africa. Therefore, the various forms and stages reached in the process of democratisation create considerable anxiety about what democracy is and how long the emerging democracies will last. There is a significant feeling that the second 'de-colonisation' in Africa will inevitably fail because of Africa's recent political record and because African leaders often claim their systems are democratic, but this is not in fact the case.

African democracies range from situations of non-party politics, such as in Swaziland and Uganda, to situations in which multi-party politics are actively promoted and entrenched as in South Africa, Botswana, Mauritius and Malawi. The "range and extent of political attributes encompassed by democracy" lead to a great deal of confusion about what constitutes basic democracy and therefore what should be consolidated.[1] In turn, this confusion leads to what are often conflicting and destructive national claims about the extent of democratisation. Africa has not significantly moved away from traditions of single-party regimes which also claimed to be democracies because of periodic elections.

The central argument of this chapter is that the existence of several political parties and periodic elections are but minor essentials for democracy. This is the case because multi-party politics in Africa has not sustained the principle of widening political participation which is one of the essential demands when negotiating transition to multiparty politics. This is particularly well-documented in the Zambian case, which was accorded the status of 'torch-bearer' following the apparently successful elections of October 1991.[2] The discussion explores negotiations for multi-party politics as a process in which the seed for democracy is sown and subsequently watered and nurtured.

Swaziland is a case study of how different stakeholders have negotiated political participation and governance in the country since the 1960s. The term 'negotiation' is broadly used to denote two forms of political contestation. First, it refers to formal discussions seeking a modus operandi. Common examples are the national conferences in former French colonies in Africa or the Lancaster House talks which produced an agreement for the first democratic elections in Zimbabwe. Second, the term negotiation is used to portray contending and contrasting perspectives on governance. In this sense negotiation is a long process of struggle which takes a diachronic perspective.

The primary purpose of the discussion is to demonstrate that understanding how democratisation is negotiated contributes to the consolidation of tolerance and the expectation that citizens have open political choices. It is important to recognise the experiences and institutions that emerge in the course of negotiating broadening political participation in the politics and economy of a nation. To take the Zambian case again, the negotiations for transition to multi-party politics in 1990 and 1991 and the constitutional review between 1994-1995, gave the impression that the whole process was about getting rid of one-party stalwarts from public office instead of promoting real participatory politics.

Transition and negotiation

Experiences of significant political transitions in Africa have involved highly contested negotiations. Negotiation reduces the distance between stakeholders. Strong rivals finally agree on a modus vivendi to guide a transition and to create a new dispensation. The parties develop a greater understanding of each other's strengths and weaknesses. Understanding, and sometimes acceptance, emerges as a product of strong consultation and tolerance of differences; and it is generally understood that the difference will form part of future negotiations which are at the core of any democracy. In the process of negotiating the transition to democracy, the ultimate goal is to promote tolerance towards plurality and the principle that the governed must have a choice in the selection of their leaders.

South Africa is easily the most relevant example of prolonged negotiations for a transition to democracy leading to institutionalised mechanisms for political plurality. The Government of National Unity in which the African National Congress (ANC), National Party (NP) and Inkatha Freedom Party (IFP) shared ministerial responsibilities is one example demonstrating tolerance for difference. The ANC, as the overwhelming stakeholder, valued building democracy rather than grabbing political power – to which the party was entitled because of commanding majority support from the South African population. It was also a commitment to sustain democratic change. Indeed, when the National Party withdrew from the

Government of National Unity, the basic agreement on how to handle party differences in the course of promoting democracy was not adversely affected. South Africa's negotiations towards transition from a fascist form of governance to democracy introduced and entrenched a unique form of political inclusiveness. Instead of a winner-takes-all parliamentary system, South Africa's negotiation accepted the principle of proportional represen-tation. This is a principle of inclusiveness which facilitated the representa-tion in parliament of political parties which would not have entered parlia-ment under the system of winner-takes-all. The South African negotiations for transition and two national elections which followed in 1994 and 1999 assured the consolidation of democratic governance.

This is not to argue that negotiations in and of themselves create insti-tutions which guarantee or sustain democratic governance. The Zambian case is a tragic contrast to the South African one. It may be argued that the Zambian tragedy is the same as that of Kenya: Machiavellian politics in both Kenya and Zambia have undermined democracy.[3] There were sever-al highlights in Zambia between 1989 and the elections of October 1991. One of these highlights was an agreement that a national referendum was not necessary despite an earlier announcement from the government to hold a referendum. This was an acknowledgement of the fact that there was overwhelming support for multi-party politics. Some sections of pro-democracy forces went so far as to argue that the one-party political sys-tem had become illegitimate. Another highlight in Zambia's negotiations towards transition was an agreement for a fundamental review of the con-stitution after elections involving many political parties. This stopped the process of constitutional review which the incumbent government of the United National Independence Party (UNIP) under President Kenneth Kaunda's leadership had started.

The new government of the Movement for Multiparty Democracy (MMD) under President Frederick Chiluba initially approached the issue of reviewing the constitution as if they were writing a totally new law. The overwhelming support which the MMD received in the 1991 elections (out of a small voter turnout) led to extreme and rapid nullification of democrat-ic practices. The majority of those who voted in 1991 influenced this subse-quent authoritarianism. The MMD was completely uninterested in the fact that, despite an apparent overwhelming demand for political change between 1989 and 1991, only 43% of registered voters took part in the elec-tions of October 1991.[4] This turnout was lower than in 1983 or 1988 under the one-party political law. The turnout of voters in the 1996 elections was even lower than in 1991. The new constitution was a monstrous step towards building a fascist state in Zambia. Social and economic policies since

November 1991 have persistently pointed in the direction of consolidating fascist tendencies rather than strengthening democracy, although the December 2001 elections may have given some renewed cause for hope.

Regular commentators on political changes in Africa have drawn attention to serious inadequacies in democratic practice in Africa. Larry Diamond, for instance, expresses concern about the undemocratic dominance of ruling parties.[5] Zambia is one case in point because, despite its initial optimism, there have been subsequent early signs that democracy was "slowly dying".[6] Kenya is another case where the dominance of the ruling party since independence is often cited as an impediment to democratisation.[7]

Richard Joseph recently examined how an upsurge in political violence accompanied the transition to multiparty politics in many African states. He notes that this brought about a "complex pattern of regime change". Joseph is, however, resolute that there is no need for "democratic pessimism", rather "… these circumstances should invite a renewed commitment to investigate their essential features as a prelude to devising more appropriate theories of democratic development".[8] Marina Ottaway notes that the political changes of the 1990s were a "complex and at times stormy process", and raised questions about "… whether African countries will enjoy lasting political transformation or revert to authoritarianism".[9]

The struggle for democracy in Swaziland

A study of the protracted struggle for multi-party politics, and subsequently democracy, in Swaziland should yield insights on how to consolidate democracy in Africa. In retrospect, a study of de-colonisation politics between 1960 and 1964 in Swaziland demonstrates that multi-party politics were destined to fail. Support for party politics came from two sources: the British colonial administration supported politics based on organised political parties, while an incipient Swazi middle-class grouped themselves into a number of political parties between 1960 and 1964. By the end of 1964 most of the leaders had reluctantly but realistically abandoned their parties and joined the Swazi traditional rulers.[10] The British colonial administration in Swaziland and the Swazi educated elite shared the belief that political parties were a cardinal feature of liberal democracy. They also advocated for a constitutional monarchy.

This political awakening was partly in response to the 'winds of change' statement of Harold Macmillan, British Prime Minister, to the South African Parliament in February 1960. But the Swazi rulers also wanted to put their stamp on the pace of change. They rejected the idea of political parties, arguing that parties would turn one Swazi against another. At the same time, they embraced non-racialism by concluding an alliance with politically minded white settlers. The white settlers were afraid of the socialist and nationalisation rhetoric of the political parties formed by the educated elite. Then, the labour unrest of May and June 1963 influenced Swazi traditional leaders to devise strategies which were common in Africa, strategies of subordinating the labour movement to the cause of nation-building. The battle lines were drawn between two camps. One camp comprised the Swazi aristocracy and white settlers, and the other camp was made up of colonial officials and the Swazi educated (middle) class who advocated a liberal democracy and a constitutional monarchy.

The names of these political organisations demonstrate considerable ideological contrast. The Swaziland Progressive Party, led by JJ Nquku, was initially formed as a non-political organisation through British paternalism in 1930. It was in reality a tea club for the new Swazi elite; under the watchful eye of the colonial administration, King Sobhuza II and the Swazi National Council. Nquku, President since 1948, influenced its becoming a political party in 1960 in opposition to an agreed proposal between Swazi settlers and the aristocracy for equal racial representation in the legislature despite the preponderance of the Swazi population. By 1964, the SPP had split into no less than three factions. One of the breakaway leaders was Dr Ambrose Zwane, who founded the Ngwane National Liberatory Congress (NNLC). However, this intellectual failed to impress the Swazi peasants.[11] He also found that it was not easy to dislodge the king's party, the Imbokodvo National Movement (INM). The Swaziland Democratic Party, led by Dr Allen Nxumalo and Simon Sishayi Nxumalo, and with the support of some white settlers, sought to promote liberal democracy. It was opposed to the radical African Nationalism of NNLC and the ultra-conservative agenda of the INM. But all of these parties fragmented under pressure from the Swazi aristocracy.[12] Efforts to unite them through the Joint Council of Swaziland Political Parties failed miserably.

Thus, a traditional monarchy led Swaziland to independence in 1968. In the elections of May 1972, the NNLC appeared to strengthen and thus provided the basis to have all political parties included in the King's decree of 12 April 1973.

This royal decree to ban political parties left the Swazi aristocracy virtually alone in the political field. The decree created auspicious conditions to play political games without legal competitors. However, the NNLC and its leadership refused to be cowed. Its president and some of its leaders spent considerable time in detention or in exile during the 1970s. Although it was clear that the party lacked a significant political base among Swazi peasants and the middle class, several features helped the

Swazi aristocracy to entrench itself and to promote its idea of politics. First, they were part of a trend throughout Africa in the 1970s to develop one-party political systems. Second, the government effectively used a draconian law of detaining political activists for sixty days. This law was extensively used into the 1980s.[13] Third, the Swazi rulers received much support from the South African apartheid government which supported reactionary regimes and groups in order to destroy anti-apartheid forces in Southern Africa. Finally, and probably the most critical factor, the 1970s and early 1980s witnessed general economic prosperity in which a Swazi middle-class was formed because of economic expansion and educational development.[14] This is not to argue that economic prosperity necessarily freezes political opposition. While this was the case in Swaziland, it also reflected the absence of history of successful mass mobilisation of the people during the nationalist phase. Major political leaders of the early 1960s had joined the Swazi ruling class.

Thus, there was not much continuity in the development of forces which supported and sought liberal democracy. The Swazi educated elite had limited support for party politics. The Swazi ruling class also silenced the labour movement. During the labour strikes of May and June 1963, emerging political parties found favourable circumstances for recruiting members. In the elections of early 1972, the Swazi working class, especially in the sugar plantation industry, appeared to be an important source of support for political parties seeking liberal democracy. For some time the 1973 decree was understood to have also banned trade union organisations. For this reason, a trade union among teachers transformed itself into an association of professional practitioners. At the same time, the Swazi ruling class attempted to promote labour organisations which approached labour issues using traditional Swazi systems of representation. Appointees of the King and the Swazi National Council were deployed in many industries to help workers to deal with industrial grievances.

This retrogressive development did little to galvanise political parties against the entrenchment of a centralist conservative but complex state. In 1977 a teachers' strike with sympathy activities from their students petered out because they were warned against being influenced by radical tendencies from the South African labour movement. The forces fighting for liberal democracy were also not jerked out of slumber by the failure to carry through a promise to review the constitution between 1974 and 1978. Following a royal command, a commission was set up to review the constitutional status in the country following the King's decree of 1973. A cynical, but critically important view was that with the King having more power than had been provided for in the independence constitution, there was not much justification for the Constitutional Review Commission to carry out its mandate.

Instead, the Tinkhundla system of government was introduced in 1978. The system combined, and at the times also abused, Swazi and Western forms of political organisation. A committee of seven supervised the election of an Electoral College which in turn elected members of parliament. The Swazi aristocratic government reformed itself despite limited direct pressure from pro-democracy forces. Ironically, however, these palace reforms masked intense rivalries within the aristocracy. These burst into the open following the death of King Sobhuza II in August 1982. Kuper, Macmillan and Levin share the view that Sobhuza II's political power was based on his effective use and manipulation of popular Swazi traditions.[15] However, it is clear that the absence of an alternative ideology gave further strength to traditionalist governance. The Swazi traditionalist ideologies monopolised the political forums without organised and systematic opposition.

This deepened the crisis of political groups seeking multi-party politics. These groups did not evolve a vision informed by sustained experiences in the struggle. In part, but substantially so, the groups seeking liberal democracy had lost direction so badly that they saved their sworn enemy from collapse. Much instability followed the aftermath of King Sobhuza II's death. Palace power strugglers are always expected, and are part of Swazi traditions of succession.[16] These palace struggles dominated the 1980s. The youth of Swaziland upheld the stability of succession in supporting Queen Regent Dzeliwe in the struggles leading to the deposition. Even these struggles caught the pro-democracy forces off-guard.

However, the palace crisis created an opportunity for pro-democracy forces to coalesce. In July 1983 the People's United Democratic Movement (PUDEMO) was formed. Richard Levin has written the most detailed history of PUDEMO based on his first-hand experiences in Swaziland and close relations with those at the centre.[17] The authoritative nature of the account is impressive but Levin fails to present a balanced evaluation of PUDEMO, emphasising PUDEMO's dominance of Swazi opposition politics in the late 1980s and 1990s. While it is clear that the overall strength of the Swazi ruling elite surpassed that of PUDEMO and popular opposition in the 1980s and 1990s, it is necessary to be sensitive to weakness within popular opposition. This leads to an understanding why PUDEMO and the youth of Swaziland failed to position themselves appropriately in the struggles for the Swazi monarchy in the 1980s.

Even more critical is the failure of organised Swazi political elites to transcend their own social class. This comes out clearly in Richard Levin's interview with Mandla Hlatshwako, one of the leading figures in PUDE-

MO. Levin concedes that PUDEMO's major challenge is how to organise the peasants. Hlatshwako commented:

> The land question is an area where we need a lot of debate ... because I feel we have not fully refined our own approach to it. But it is the most central issue in the political question of Swaziland. I think its going to dominate the future political direction of this country, our relationship with our land.[18]

Clearly, this interview of April 1992 implies that PUDEMO had no lessons to learn from the parties of the 1960s on the peasantry and the land question. For anyone living in Swaziland from the late 1980s and the early 1990s, it was surprising that the political parties failed to stand up when the Swazi state attacked the peasants. Many peasants who failed to pay back loans that they received from the Swaziland Savings and Development Bank had property confiscated in a ruthless and brutal manner, reminiscent of mass evictions in apartheid South Africa. In a subsequent government investigation in 1996 about how the Bank recovered what it was owed, there is no evidence that pro-democracy groups attempted to mobilise the peasants.[19] Instead, Hlatshwako lamented that "... rural people have been exposed to a lot of propaganda over the years, to the extent that some of them can see no other option than the one imposed on them by the powers that be".[20]

What is most revealing is how fragmented the political groups are. When Mario Masuku, the current President of PUDEMO, was re-elected to that position, the election did not reveal internal democratic practices in the Movement. Leadership struggles and party fragmentation are still disturbing characteristics of Swaziland's only surviving political party from the 1960s, the NNLC. Since the death of its founding president in 1998, the NNLC has fragmented into two opposing factions. These tendencies are absent in many political parties in Swaziland which appear to have a single membership, which is that of the party's president. These separatist tendencies are transmitted to umbrella organisations. The Swaziland Democratic Alliance (SDA), for instance, has suffered from ineffective leadership and mobilisation. These separatist tendencies foster authoritarianism even when political parties are in formal existence. Such authoritarian practices become a hallmark of the government of such a political organisation. The threat to democracy becomes real and the population becomes silenced.

The Swaziland ruling class reacted with increasing sophistication to the growing demands for participatory politics. The palace intrigues were overcome through an early installation of Sobhuza's successor, King Mswati III, who was then still in his teens. Leading figures in the intrigues were detained or sentenced to long periods of imprisonment. Political activists, including those that had supported the installation of King Mswati

III, were not spared from restrictions. The ruling class asserted itself wide-ly and effectively. It further attempted to consolidate its legitimacy through the general election of 1988 and frequent public meetings at the Main National Cattle Byre. In these meetings, there was much open comment and criticism. These tended to demonstrate, to the Swazi rulers, democ-racy in the context of Swazi traditions and traditional institutions.

The Swazi ruling class was guided by this vision of a traditional context for democracy. From the late 1980s and throughout the 1990s, Swaziland followed its vision in responding to growing pressure for a multi-party based democracy by effecting two broad strategies. The first strategy was a cocktail of political activities and the second was an economic pro-gramme. To begin with the political front, the Swazi government reformed the Tinkhundla system for the general elections. In 1990 and 1992, two commissions gathered views about political attitudes among the Swazi. The first, headed by a senior prince, Prince Masitsela, appears to have started its work without a clear designation. It subsequently dubbed itself a *Vusela* (greetings) commission. Consistent with Swazi tradition the com-mission carried greetings from the King and the Queen Mother, to all parts of the country. The next commission, headed by another Senior Prince, Prince Mahlalengangeni, surveyed Swazi opinions about what form of gov-ernment they wanted and was appropriate for the kingdom. Press reports indicated widespread preference for multi-party governance.

The commission made two fundamental recommendations. The first was a rejection of political parties on the questionable grounds that Swazis were not ready for political parties. In general terms, political leaders in Swaziland often argue that the political education of the vast majority of the people in the kingdom is not sufficiently high to make political parties viable. Therefore, demands for political parties are associated only with a small group of educated Swazis. The essence of this line of thinking is that Swazis prefer what they understand and that is the traditional form of gov-ernance. However, this would be reformed in the light of what Swazis selected from global trends as appropriate for their traditional system of government.

In line with this approach, direct elections were introduced in 1993. The second such elections were held in 1998. Swazi leaders are aware that "the system of governance together with the quality of public management define the overall environment within which production and the general con-duct of human affairs take place".[21] Thus, reform of the traditional system of government and avoidance of political parties are seen to meet that goal.

A dual system of government based on traditional Swazi institutions and contemporary forms of governance is essentially what Swazi rulers protect. However, they are also acutely aware that "the duality of government has had an adverse impact on the activity of governance in the country".[22] They are also keenly aware that the decree of 1973 which banned political parties affected governance adversely. In a document projecting government vision for 25 years, it is acknowledged that "all legislative, executive and judicial powers were vested in the king; thus compromising one of the principles of good governance (namely, the separation of powers between the three arms of government)".

These sensitivities have not been allowed into open maturity. They have not been allowed to grow because the guiding principle of Swazi rulers is to maintain a government that mixes traditional and modern forms of governance. However, traditional institutions still dominate. Thus, as of now, political parties are not likely to be allowed in Swaziland. There is a view among sections of Swazi society that commissions of inquiry have dominated Swazi politics in the 1990s in order to deflect political demands. On the other hand, the commissions are cited as evidence of rulers consulting the Swazis.

This interpretation has been used in economic matters. In 1993 Prince Guduza headed an Economic Review Commission which reported in 1995. On the basis of its recommendations, short and long-term economic strategies have been designed. They reflect government thinking and draw on changes in approaches for the economic development of Swaziland going as far back as 1988. The short-term strategy is called the Economic and Social Reform Agenda (ESRA). This Agenda constitutes building blocks making up the long-term project called the National Development Strategy (NDS), covering the period 1997 to 2022.

These have been comprehensive responses covering both the political and economic concerns of the Swazi people. These commissions and frequent reference to commission reports in public statements from government leaders and senior civil servants clearly demonstrate how the Swazi ruling class is negotiating political change. The strategies are also responses to declining economic performance. The economy, which grew at about 6% throughout the 1980s, slowed down to around 3% in the 1990s. Employment growth declined to about 1% in the late 1990s with occasional negative growth. The country has also embarked on an extensive programme of tarring the roads. Besides obvious economic justifications, one reason is to enable the King to visit and consult with his people directly and frequently. Thus, the Swazi rulers have diverse political and economic strategies with which they are negotiating their particular form of democratic governance.

However, they do not compromise on the principles key to traditional governance. Two examples will suffice to elaborate this point. First, when a Constitutional Review Commission was appointed in 1996, headed by Prince Mangaliso (a Professor of Law), it was expected that it would report before the elections at the end of 1998. Another expectation was that the elections would be postponed if the work on the constitution was not completed. However, elections took place within the framework recognising the primacy of Swazi traditions. Within the context of these traditions, the king scored high marks for openly showing that while the Constitutional Review Commission was given much autonomy to ensure that it presented a constitution that would last, it is high time that the CRC completed its work.

A second example relates to the censoring of the National Development Strategy. This document came out of extensive consultations with private business, the international community, Swazi chiefs and various non-government organisations. The consultations started in 1997. When the Prime Minister's Office prepared a document to be launched by the King, traditionalists would have none of the event until a section anticipating political reform, and probably political parties, was removed. This was complied with. Thus, negotiating democratisation in Swaziland is a complex matter. The present rulers of Swaziland seek their particular understanding of democracy while there are groups in Swaziland which see democracy, at a minimum, to be based on political parties. Political parties are a global trend in developing democracies but Swazi rulers want these trends to be grounded in the Swazi tradition of governance.

The debate on democracy and democratisation in Africa has focused on tensions between national perspectives and globalisation of governance and also on celebrating how pro-democracy groups dislodged dictatorships from political power. Difficulties in sustaining the initial advances in democratic practice have generally been discussed in the broad context just outlined. There is a simplistic notion that a failure to dislodge one-party leaders and their parties such as in Kenya means the failure of democracy in such countries. A closely related interpretation is that the tendency of new successors to one-party rule to manipulate constitutions has perpetuated authoritarian rule rather than promoted democracy.

Conclusion

This chapter has attempted to understand the process in which democracy is negotiated. This was done to explore a hypothesis that understanding the relative strength of stakeholders negotiating democracy and how they position themselves in the process of creating democratic conditions illuminates the process of democratisation. Negotiation is initiation into democracy. At a minimum, African intellectuals should undertake such studies as political education and their contribution to democratisation in Africa. In safeguarding democracy, a well-informed civil society is essential.

In drawing illustrative data from Swaziland, the chapter explores the nature of pro-democracy formations in Swaziland from the 1960s to the 1990s. The preliminary picture, one which calls for critical analysis, is that while pressure for multi-party politics has increased and become both complex and subtle over the years, the ruling class has responded with a diversified programme of new political initiatives and numerous economic development projects. These appear calculated to stifle a political party-based democracy and consolidate the current political power structure. A democratic game appears to be in play in Swaziland in the process of negotiating broader democratic governance. Through its various political and economic development programmes, the Swazi aristocracy has defined its commitment to democracy in terms of improving the socio-economic and living standards of the Swazi people. The Swazi aristocracy is acutely aware that their failure to deliver in economic terms will destroy their brand of democracy.

Notes and References

1   L Diamond, 'Is the Third Wave over?', *Journal of Democracy*, vol 7, 1996, p 21.

2   B Chikulo, 'Parliamentary by-elections in Zambia: Implications for 1966 Poll', *Review of African Political Economy*, vol 23, 1996, pp 447–453.

3   SM Makinda, 'Democracy and Multiparty Politics in Africa', *Journal of Modern African Studies*, vol 34, 1996.

4   Chikulo 1996, p 450.

5   Diamond 1996, pp 20–37.

6   M Bratton, 'Second Elections in Africa', *Journal of Democracy*, vol 9, 1998, p 65.

7   ES Atieno-Odhiambo, 'Democracy and the ideology of order in Kenya', in MG Schatberg (ed), *The Political Economy of Kenya*, New York: Praeger, 1987; Makinda 1996, pp 560–561.

8   R Joseph, 'Africa, 1990–1997: from Abertura to Closure', *Journal of Democracy*, vol 9, 1998, pp 3–17.

9   M Ottaway, 'From political opening to democratization', in M Ottaway, *Democracy in Africa: The Hard Road Ahead*, Bouder: Lynne Rienner, 1997.

10   CP Potholom, 'Changing African political configurations in Swaziland', *Journal of Modern African Studies*, vol 4, 1996.

11   H Macmillan, 'Swaziland: Decolonisation and the triumph of tradition', in

J Daniel and MF Stephen (eds), *Historical Perspectives on the Political Economy of Swaziland*, Mbabane: UNISWA, 1986.

12   RP Stevens, 'Swaziland Political Development', *Journal of Modern African Studies*, no 1, 1963; Potholom 1996.

13   R Levin, *'No more tears': Struggles for Land in Mpumalanga, South Africa*, Trenton: Africa World Press, 1997.

14   AM Kanduza, 'Political Economy of Democratisation in Swaziland', Paper presented at an OSSREA Congress, 1996.

15   H Kuper, *Sobhuza II, Ngwenyama and King of Swaziland: The Story of an Hereditary Ruler and his Country*, London: Duckworth, 1978; H Kuper, *An African Aristocracy: Rank among the Swazi*, London: Oxford University Press; Macmillan 1986; Levin 1997.

16   Levin 1997.

17   *Ibid*.

18   *Ibid*., p 229–230.

19   B Fine, *The Political Economy of South Africa: From Minerals-energy Complex to Industrialisation*, London: Hurst, 1996.

20   Levin 1997, p 230.

21   Swaziland Government, *National Development Strategy (NDS): A Twenty-five Year Vision*, Mbabane: Government Printers, 1997, p 7.

22   *Ibid*., p 8.

Participatory National Development Planning: Lessons of Experience from Malawi Vision 2020

Naomi Ngwira

Beginning in the middle of the 1990s there have been a number of planning efforts in some African countries that are called Visions, which are based on the African Futures methodology, or National Long-term Perspective Studies (NLTPS).[1] The list of countries involved includes Ghana, Côte d'Ivoire, Zambia, Zimbabwe, Mauritius and Senegal. This chapter examines and evaluates Malawi's experience in implementing the NLTPS. To talk about planning is to tread on very controversial ground in economics, because of the role of government in the economy. To elucidate our position on planning and the role of government in the economy, we will first summarise the debate on the need for development planning and for participatory development planning, and how it can be introduced into the development planning process in Malawi.

National Development Planning: Retrospect and Prospect

National development planning is the process concerned with making anticipatory decisions with reference to the future evaluation of a country, and deriving present-day decisions from them.[2] The basic elements of a development plan include development objectives, strategy and priorities, development policies, and a scheme of resource allocation. Annual budgets and medium-term plans gird together these elements.

In the 1950s-1970s developing countries were exhorted to plan their economies based on the findings and models of economists like Rosensten-Rodan, Todaro, Harrod and Domar. The hallmark of these models and views which together constitute development economics is that standard neo-classical economic theory has little validity in the developing world.[3] Governments therefore need to intervene into markets through planning. Planning was understood to be a quantitative programming exercise to determine the resource allocation to sectors or projects.

National development planning fell into disrepute at the end of the

1970s. It was denounced by those from western democratic countries as an exercise in futility and merely a tool for autocratic policy-making as epitomised by its use – and failure – in communist governance. This was because the policy prescription of the *dirigisme* which attended planning led to serious distortions in economic incentives. The main argument against *dirigisme* is that no general rule of second best welfare economics permits government failures, which may be worse than market failures.[4]

Governments have a history of failure in attempting to manage directly the production of private goods and services, as epitomised by the record of public enterprise management which is replete with disasters. Reasons for failure include difficulty in shading labour in order to be cost effective, and treating procurement as a way of enriching contractors and procurement officers rather than producing efficiently.

Other arguments against planning are that there is no empirical evidence that planning leads to development; and that African countries are in any case uncontrollable – they are exposed to too much external influence to be planned effectively.

The paragons of this critical view of planning are the Bretton Woods institutions, who at the beginning of the 1980s proclaimed a new era of capitalistic market economics in which the role of government and hence planning in the economy is minimised. Their main view is that government's responsibility for directing the production and distribution of goods and services should be reduced and left to the private sector. Governments should be active in those areas where markets prove inadequate or fail altogether, such as investing in education, health and physical infrastructure. In addition, governments should offer a competitive climate for enterprise development, and macro-economic management. Government should support and not supplant markets by making market-friendly interventions.[5]

Critics of these views (known collectively as the "Washington Consensus") have noted, first, that Structural Adjustment Programmes (SAPs) are actually predicated on extensive government involvement in the economy: to regulate markets in the face of strong capitalistic interests requires strong government intervention. Thus the question is not one of intervention versus *laissez-faire*, a popular dichotomy but a false one. The question is rather one of the proper division of responsibilities and roles, and efficiency in those roles. A basic premise of this chapter is that participatory development planning is crucial to engendering the proper division and effectiveness in discharging these roles. Second, the critics note that the virtues of the market have been over-emphasised and its benefits over-advertised in developing countries which, they argue, still have economic structures racked by market imperfections and failures.

In recent years, the World Bank has softened its views in light of the experience in ASEAN countries.[6] There is now recognition that the role of government can go beyond providing physical and social infrastructure, to actually guide the market. The term used to describe this kind of intervention, *market-friendly interventions*, shows the bias of the Bretton Woods institutions towards market economics instead of describing the phenomenon accurately.

Planning of state intervention of one type or another is a prerequisite for creating significant economic structural transformation and growth in an economy.[7] Development that is left to the laws of the market is a danger to social justice, national cohesion and regional integration. Planning may have failed in the past but there were reasons; weak institutions and capabilities and external influences played their part. The lack of real strategic choice demoralised implementers. Thus, planning is not dead – what is dead is a type of planning.[8] SAPs are evidence of the need for planning, but they have failed too.[9] There are examples of successful planning like the Asian countries, which engage in long-term strategic planning, and where the government gets involved with the private sector. Planning has to take cognisance of three things. First, the turbulent times: the reasons which necessitated planning must be strategic. Second, the democratic wind of political change: the current SAPs are plans that are not negotiated with stakeholders, and they lack a political mandate. Third, the dispensation of liberal economic governance: the new type of planning must recognise the ascendancy of the private sector in economic governance. Thus the new planning must be a blend of indicative and co-operative planning as practised in Japan, Korea and Singapore.

National Development Planning in Malawi

The key elements of the economic planning machinery in Malawi are the economic committee of the cabinet; the National Economic Council (NEC – but previously Ministry of Economic Planning and Development), responsible for co-ordinating development management activities; the Ministry of Finance, responsible for budget policy; the Reserve Bank of Malawi, responsible for monetary policy; the National Statistical Office (NSO), responsible for the collection and dissemination of statistics; the planning departments in line ministries who formulate and implement the government's sectoral policies; and the district development committees which serve as the highest decision-making bodies in the districts' development planning issues. The core development planning functions are carried out by economists operating either in the NEC or in line ministry planning units. In the line ministries, the planning units carry out sector functions, such as analysis of economic trends and developments in the sector, policy analysis, developing the government's programmes for the sector, programme co-ordination, and monitoring and evaluation.

The main document used in co-ordinating planning activities from 1971 until 1996 was the Statement of Development Policies (DEVPOL). However, attention in the recent past has focused on the Public Sector Investment Programme. Most recently, the Medium Expenditure Framework has been more prominent. This trend fits in with the adoption of Structural Adjustment Programmes, which have a medium-term outlook.

Civil society also has its part to play in development planning. And, what Steinberg noted about Korea a decade ago is also largely true of Malawi. That is:

> A new set of forces will affect Korean economic policy making in the next decade. These are a product of the most significant change ... and the proliferation of intermediary institutions between the family or clan and the state. These institutions are ... a growing force for pluralism in society ... [and] result in a context in which economic policy formulation will no longer be insulated. The result will be a process less economically efficient but more responsive to popular needs.[10]

A prerequisite for effective participatory national development planning which aims to reduce poverty is the existence of a vibrant civil society. There is no agreed upon definition of the term civil society, as it is perceived and experienced differently by different societies. However, the common thread in all definitions is that civil society is the realm of organised social life standing between the individual and the state.[11] It can also be defined as the "aggregate of institutions whose members are engaged primarily in a complex of non-state activities – economic and cultural production, voluntary associations and household life – and who in this way preserve and transform their identity by exercising all sorts of pressures or controls upon state institutions".[12] Civil society is thus a "vast array of both formal and informal community organisations, religious institutions and movements, voluntary associations, trade unions and guilds, cultural institutions, co-operatives, fraternal and ethnic associations and human services delivery systems".[13]

The involvement of civil society in economic planning can be at macro, meso or micro levels. In the past, civil society has not participated in macro-level planning in Malawi, neither in articulating broad policy goals nor providing technical input into the structuring of plans. There are two major reasons for this. In the pre-democracy era, the leadership assumed that it knew exactly what the people wanted: defeating the "three enemies" of ignorance, poverty and disease. The assumption of the leadership was also that the civil service through the DEVPOL and sectoral activities was adequately translating this into action.

Towards the end of the 1980s there was progress made towards the involvement of some sections of civil society in planning. This was effected through involving NGOs and civil society leaders in workshops to review sector policies within government departments; there was also substantial liberalisation of the process of making cost estimates and work plans. However, only a few government departments effectively involved people at the local level, most notably the National Environmental Action Plan (NEAP) process, where the country was divided into eight zones in which systematic stakeholder consultations were held to generate information and ideas.[14]

Since the early 1990s, the emergence of economic institutions and organisations of civil society has provided an opportunity for participation in policy making which has not been fully utilised. The Malawi Chamber of Commerce and Industry and the government are engaged in consultations to form a Business Council to plan policies and programmes jointly rather than have the private sector simply reacting to government action. But the culture of allowing civil society to participate in policy-making has to be cultivated. At the macro-policy level, the Malawi Institute of Democratic and Economic Affairs has tried to influence the formulation of the budget. Its major limitations have been an inadequate capacity to analyse the budgets, and also gain legitimacy.

But civil society can also participate in national development planning by forming interest groups to maintain their welfare through more efficient and effective organisation or through advocating for change in the policies that affect them. Among the micro-level organisations of civil society with the potential to deal directly with policy issues are producers and marketing associations, and credit institutions. These have a long history in Malawi, going back to the colonial period. These associations are for the most part ineffective because they are constrained by a lack of skills. The situation is made worse by the self-interest of many leaders of these organisations.

With the changes in the country's politics, and as a way of implementing the poverty alleviation policy, the government facilitated the emergence of a number of 'economic' NGOs. Notable examples include the National Association for Business Women (NABW), Women's World Banking (WWB), and the National Association for Small and Medium Enterprises (NASME). These organisations have clubs operating at community level. The main objectives are to facilitate access to cheaper credit, provide training and skills in business enterprise management, and marketing. They have been perceived by most Malawians as the most effective way to empower the population in efforts towards poverty reduction. However, the performance of most of the credit associations and their clubs and NGOs has not been impressive. They have failed to achieve their objectives due to inadequate funding, poor managerial skills, lack of focus, inadequate market research, and an absence of good business values and ethics among the clientele.

The National Long Term Perspective Study

Apart from the NEAP process, the only other planning activity that has had extensive civil society participation is the NLTPS. The NLTPS conceptualises national development planning as a multidisciplinary exercise that involves strategic reflection and national dialogue between the government, the private sector and civil society for the purpose of formulating a long-term national development strategy that acts as a framework for short and medium-term policy making.

A major difference between the NLTPS process and the traditional process of developing long-term or medium-term plans is that in the latter planners were tied to a country's comparative economic advantage. The NLTPS entails peering into the future to see what prospects lie there for countries to create an economic competitive advantage that can lead to significant economic growth, and consequently improve the material well-being of the people. Another difference is that in developing the Vision, the private sector is included and consulted, as well as the general public through its interested groups. The Vision is not put together by only government technocrats.

The NLTPS has several conceptual elements and procedural steps. The first of these, long-term strategic thinking, is important for two reasons: to undergird development projects of a country so that it goes in the right direction, and to create opportunities for the country rather than leave it to be victim of international economic forces. The future becomes an opportunity rather than a destiny. This is the antithesis of SAPs which encourage countries to put all their energies into the short-term, and implicitly deny the existence of real choice for most poor countries.

Moreover, a worthwhile vision is one that is widely shared and becomes a force that motivates everyone towards greater achievements. Visionary leadership is forward-looking, creative and strategic, and in the context of NLTPS energises the populace to rally around the Vision.

Evidence indicates that the lack of popular debate over national development policies imposes severe constraints on motivation for high productivity. The NLTPS process is intended to enlist the people's active input as well as sustained support in the resultant Vision. The role of technocrats is to enhance this participation and make the citizens aware of which aspirations are technically feasible given the permutations of public, private, and community resources. This avoids creating a 'wish list' for which the citizens hope that the government is their benefactor.

In addition, long-term strategic thinking requires forecasting. The concept of scenarios planning is based on the recognition of two approaches: predictive foresight and creative foresight. While the former aims to identify the key forces that will shape the future and predict their outcomes, the latter involves people in creating an imagined future they would ideally have and then planning effective means to make it happen.[15] The first type of foresight is a step to the second. It will produce the kind of scenario for a country that can be rejected, and needs improvement.

Strategic management involves the adoption of appropriate action to achieve long-term goals. The concept of strategic management treats planning and implementation as complementary activities. In the course of implementing the activities, there is a need to learn from mistakes and to steer the course in line with the Vision.

The phases of the NLTPS process are issues identification; basic studies; scenario planning; strategy formulation; and development planning, implementation, monitoring and evaluation. Issues identification refers to the identification of the aspirations of a country: what the people want to have or achieve by some future date. These are integrated into themes or issues to facilitate in-depth analysis. Basic studies are then carried out on the themes and sectors identified. The aim is to gather information to construct alternative future scenarios, which are summarised in a Strategic Intelligence Matrix (SIM). The information in the SIM pertains to future events, actors, trends, strengths and weaknesses of past and present strategies, as well as threats and opportunities.

Once the information has been collected through basic studies, scenarios are made as alternative futures that highlight key uncertainties. These constitute narratives of what could happen if certain things happen or do not happen. The results of the SIM are used to construct several alternative scenarios of a country's future to enable public debate and identification of a shared Vision. This is followed by strategy formulation, which involves the identification of strategic issues, options and actions to realise the Vision. These are the critical variables to be tackled before the Vision can be realised. Using the SIM a strategic action matrix (SAM) is constructed: for each aspiration the planner derives the most appropriate action to achieve it based on the strengths and weaknesses to be exploited, and the weaknesses and threats to be managed.

Lastly, Development planning, implementation, monitoring and evaluation involves making medium-term plans that are consistent with the realisation of the Vision. In this process, SAPs, public sector investment programs, and government annual budgets, as well as private sector plans are formulated within the context of the Vision.

The Need for a Vision

When the democratically elected government came to power, it within a short time felt the need to conduct a process in which the people of Malawi could articulate their aspirations, and a perception of how these aspirations can be achieved. The leadership was partly responding to public outcry over lack of a vision.

A request was made to UNDP for funding, which was coincidentally helping African governments to formulate a method for long-term planning, in response to a request of heads of state that met in Maastricht, Holland in 1993. Thus the simple request of government evolved into what became a rather technical project. This, in the author's view, is partly responsible for some of the problems that have dogged the Malawi Vision 2020 Vision process and implementation.

There are several advantages to a country having a Vision. The first use of a Vision like any other long-term development plan, is to provide a framework for formulating, implementing and evaluating short and medium-term plans. Without a coherent long-term plan development efforts can degenerate into a list of confusing and incompatible projects which take the country nowhere or in the wrong direction. In the same vein, a Vision provides a realistic time frame in which to plan and implement some of the most important development issues, such as population and environmental issues or changing the structure of an economy, which cannot be achieved in the context of the short-term outlook of, say, structural adjustment programmes.

Secondly, through the participatory process of development, a Shared Vision is an instrument for harnessing the energies of the people into a material force for economic growth and development, and complements the political process of articulating the needs and choices of the people.

A Vision is also needed to provide a strategic framework for how a country can take advantage of long-term prospects offered by the world economic environment. There are several scenarios for the future of a country and not all of them are desirable. A Vision provides a way of taking the future as an opportunity rather than as destiny through consciously creating and controlling the forces that contribute to achieving the desired scenario.

Implementation

The steps that led to the creation of the Vision were the training of a National Core Team in the concept and methodology for developing the Vision; conducting nation-wide consultations with Malawians to solicit their aspirations and perspectives on how to attain them; implementing various information, education and communication activities to increase the people's awareness of the Vision process; facilitating discussion networks of Malawian experts on the various strategic issues and actions which were identified during the First Vision Workshop and consultations; conducting the Second Vision Workshop to review the findings; presenting the findings to a national Conference; and launching the Vision.

The First Vision Workshop used the SIM to produce a Draft Vision and identified nine strategic issues to be addressed in order to realise the Vision. The aim of the nation-wide consultations was to understand the aspirations of diverse groups of Malawians and to get views on the ideas that emerged from the First Workshop. All districts in Malawi were visited. Consultations were made with groups such as students in primary schools, the general population in urban and rural areas, specific interest groups such as the judiciary, the police, trade unions, lending institutions, people with disabilities, women's groups, youth groups, district development committees and district executive committees (DECs), political parties and many others. As expected, the consultations broadened the Visioning process. New aspirations and strategies emerged under each of the nine strategic issues.

Throughout the Visioning process, information, education and communication (IEC) activities were relied upon to solicit contributions of views and ideas from Malawians. These activities took the forms of radio announcements, advertisements, and programmes, some of them phone-ins, jingles, and drama skits. Other IEC activities involved the print media through newspaper articles and commentary as well as articles on Vision 2020 by the general public. The outcome of the NLTPs was a Vision which was summarised as follows:

> By the Year 2020, Malawi as a God-fearing nation will be secure, democratically mature, environmentally sustainable, self reliant with equal opportunities and active participation by all, having social services, vibrant cultural and religious values, and being a technologically driven middle income country.[16]

It was agreed that Malawi cannot achieve this Vision until strategies are found to address the following challenges. Achieving good governance; creating sustainable economic growth and development, developing a vibrant culture, expanding the development infrastructure, developing the social sector, science and technology, achieving a fair and equitable distribution of income and wealth, food security and nutrition, and managing natural and environmental resources sustainably.

Evaluation of the NLTPS

The Evaluation of the NLTPS in Malawi can be done at three levels. The NLTPS can be assessed in terms of whether its conceptual elements are implementable or pre-existing in Malawi. The process of implementing the NLTPS can be evaluated in terms of whether it fulfilled the conceptual requirements of the methodology; and what the ramifications of any divergence from the methodology could be in terms of the quality of output. The outcome of the NLTPS, the Vision documents, can also be assessed in terms of their usefulness, and the likelihood of implementation.

The conceptual elements of the NLTPS are citizens' participation; long-term strategic thinking and scenario planning; shared vision and visionary leadership; and strategic management and national learning. A robust vision should be born of long-term thinking and strategic reflection on what prospects there are for Malawi to take advantage of and what threats and weakness it must manage in order to meet its aspirations. Malawi has no institutional technical experience in long-term strategic reflection. Thus the NCT was expected to learn this skill or identify people who had it, and do it for the Vision process, while at the same time consulting about aspirations. During the process, the latter got more attention, such that the outcome was lop-sided being strong on aspirations and the challenges to be met and weak on strategic solutions.

The result is that not much strategic thinking went into the NLTPS process and its outcome, the Vision documents. The documents have no strategy, but a profusion of flatulent strategic options. Others have argued that producing a lead strategy was not the intention of the Vision. What this means then is that some other organisation should fill in on this part. This was being done by the Strategic Unit of the NEC.[17] However its output still lacks the elements of thinking strategically. Most of what was done concerned running simulation models of scenarios which are not really based on ground-breaking strategic choices. The question remains unanswered: does Malawi have strategic choices?

The requirement for visionary leadership is probably the major weakness of the NLTPS in Malawi. Although the request for a Vision came from politicians, the manner in which the process was handled showed a lack of foresight in both political and technocratic ranks. It appears there was a failure on the part of the NCT and NEC to harmonise with politicians on their requirements whilst keeping in mind what the technocrats would need. The popular version of the Vision, which suits the needs of the politicians, was not produced.

Secondly, political leaders misconstrued the views of the people articulated in the Vision as political activism. Far-sighted leaders would possibly have appropriated these aspirations to their advantage. The manifestos of political parties are conspicuously silent about the Vision.

The analytical tools of SWOT, SIM and SAM were a step in the right direction. But they were not fully implemented, especially with respect to the external environment. There is a need to carry these studies further and embellish the scenarios based on the information scanned.

Thus the NLTPS process went ahead on the assumption of pre-existing conditions that in fact were not there. The NCT faced an uphill battle in creating or simulating some of these as the process went on. One of the weakest areas was citizen participation. Participation is more than being consulted. Despite the advent of multiparty democracy, people were not ready to participate because there were few effective frameworks and institutional arrangements for participation.

Apart from these difficulties, a major problem in the implementation of the NLTPS in Malawi was the institutionalisation of the NCT. Whereas there were many advantages to be had from locating the process in the Ministry of Economic Planning and Development, very few gains were derived in practice, especially as the role of the Ministry was questioned and eroded by institutional re-arrangement at that time. In order to create the kind of impact that was expected, there was a need for the NCT to be located strategically in an institution that has a strong influence on macro-economic policy making.

The issue of whether the NCT was part of the ministry or independent created much negative feeling, to the detriment of the spirit of camaraderie required for effective interface between the Ministry and the NCT. The independence of the NCT meant that it had the formidable task of legitimating the undertaking of the NLTPS process with the public on its own. But being linked to the ministry had the usual bureaucratic problems. More importantly, it created the image that the Vision was being created by and for the government in power. This view undermined the goodwill needed to implement the Vision once it had been developed.

The NLTPS implementation process was dogged by many problems which compromised the quality of the process and its outcomes. Because of the lack of *a priori* agreement on the output of the process, there was some discontinuity between the process and production of output. Once the process had been set in motion, it assumed a momentum of its own which alienated politicians, who for much of the process did not give it adequate support. The incumbent government felt that the Vision was contradicting or exposing its weak positions. The Vision did expose issues of bad governance, many of which were not of the current government's making but which were exacerbated by a lack of coherent positions on many economic and social issues. Towards the end of the Visioning process, when the contracts of the NCT expired, and the process had to be completed in the NEC, the question arose as to who would be the champion of the Vision. There were recommendations made to keep the NCT as part of the NEC to oversee the implementation of the Vision. This raises the question of whether a people's Vision can be carried out by a few leaders. The experience of ASEAN countries seem to be that the leaders were visionaries and they sold their visions to the people.[18]

The NLTPS was thus implemented in the context of derisive and hostile attitudes towards planning. Some donors were scornful of the usefulness of the outcome of generating economic growth – the World Bank initiated its own study of 'Growth Options for Malawi'. As much of Malawi's budget and economic activities in the public sector are donor-financed, this negative attitude eroded the capacity to articulate a credible Vision. There was also a vote of no confidence in the outcome of the process as it was not based on quantitative models of growth.

The NCT also had problems interfacing effectively with civil society. Institutions of civil society are weak, for many reasons. The process of consultation with stakeholders was improvised along the way because of this. Some civil society groups, lacking a tradition of wanting to participate, saw the consultations as a way of deriving pecuniary gains; they had to be consulted at fee. The experience of the NCT showed that participatory national development planning in the absence of strong civil society is an empty process. Time and again the NCT was asked in the consultation meetings who will make sure that the Vision will be implemented. This revealed very clearly the lack of perception by the civil society and their institutions that they are responsible for demanding accountability of the leaders to the Vision. Many people feel powerless to do this. And indeed if the people cannot do this, then the Visioning process is a mockery.

One of the outcomes of the NLTPS that is nebulous to quantify, is the experience in conducting nation-wide participatory processes. A lesson from this experience was that we can never fully anticipate the spectrum of ideas, experiences and knowledge of the people. The second lesson was that to be able to process this information into consistent, but also impartial planning documents, is a challenge which needs a fully-fledged organisation with the skill to produce documents for various audiences in a timely and coherent manner. The current tendency is to bias the output to the needs of technocrats.

In the course of time, the outcomes of the NLTPS process were under-stood to be for politicians, civil society, and technocrats. This means that several different products should have been produced. Since one of the objectives of the NLTPS process is to increase the participation of people in development planning, implementation, monitoring and evaluation, politicians needed a general summary of the Vision for themselves, in the languages of their constituencies. Although a good amount of effort was spent on translating some of the versions of the Vision documents into ver-nacular languages, the task was never brought to completion.

The process of producing the documents has been so slow that some of the momentum generated by the anticipation of the documents has been lost. Various institutions started writing complementary, substitute or bet-ter documents. Many people still do not perceive the Vision documents as useful. Some of the blame can be put on the poor style of presentation of the findings of the process, and part of the blame goes to a lack of under-standing of the Vision process.

A major weakness of the Shared Vision as it has been adopted and is being implemented in Malawi is that it lacks a central message of intent and therefore lacks punch. There is a need to isolate the lead development strategy so that everybody identifies it with Vision 2020. This could be elaborated in a sequel to the current Vision 2020 documents.

One expected outcome of the NLTPS is people's ownership of the Vision, and readiness to demand accountability. We have already discussed that citizen participation as a conceptual element of the NLTPS was not pre-existing in Malawi despite the advent of multiparty democracy. But inadequate understanding of the need and funding of post Visioning IEC activities has contributed to lack of ownership. Another reason is lack of institutional mechanisms for the involvement of civil society in monitoring the implementation of the Vision.

Roadblocks to the Implementation of Vision 2020

At a meeting held in July 1998 to jump-start the Vision, participants iden-tified several potential roadblocks to its implementation. The most perti-nent of these include the following:

• Donor attitudes which continue to be competitive and unco-ordinated, disregarding and even disparaging the efforts of government to carry through the Vision;
• Absence of an institutional framework or co-ordination mechanism for implementing and evaluating the Vision;
• Scepticism of some people in the general populace as to the legitimacy of the Vision as well as government commitment to implement it;

- Problems and constraints in mobilising resources for realising the Vision;
- Inadequate awareness of Vision 2020 and lack of continued information and communication activities on the Vision;
- Lack of mechanism to make politicians committed or accountable to the Vision.

According to the NLTPS methodology, one of the strongest ways to com-municate the Vision to the people and persuade them of its merit is the use of alternative scenarios. Stories about the alternative futures are supposed to be used as moral lessons of what can happen to a country if the chosen scenario is not followed. These were developed during consultations, but they have not been used as intended. There was a need to fully develop communication materials from the scenarios so that they could be distrib-uted, and channelled continuously through the popular media.[19]

Enhancing Participation in Development Planning in Malawi

We can conclude that the main impediments to the effective participation in National Development planning are weak institutions of civil society, and inappropriate institutional arrangements to channel that participation.

Strong civil society institutions dealing with economic issues are vital for the smooth running of the national economy because good economic poli-cies do not always fit into the election cycle. Malawi needs independent and committed groups of civil society who will bring continuity to eco-nomic policy-making and implementation. In Malawi there are several problems that need to be dealt with before civil society can be more effec-tive for developmental work. The first threat to civil society is the author-itarian political legacy of the one-party state. This is still very evident in the way current political leaders perceive civil society institutions: as a threat to their policies and political agenda. Often, the politicians react to state-ments from the institutions of civil society with irritation, anger and ridicule rather than reflective analysis. There is a need to inculcate the values that would lead to the perception of civil society institutions as a necessary part of the configuration of democratic institutions.

The second, the political and social apathy of the general populace, is a corollary to the first. The praxis of Malawians is to keep quiet when dis-turbing political or economic issues happen; or they may only respond in spurts. The reasons include ignorance, conceit, and pessimism. Such pes-simism is partly a result of witnessing failure of their actions to influence government activities. Thus immediately after the advent of multiparty democracy there were many labour strikes, caused by raised expectations of the people. There is now a decline in strikes. This experience leads to lack of an assertive spirit.

Third, there is general lack of understanding of the need for a vibrant civil society and its institutions. The Malawian modern elite lacks a solid vision of the type of society the country should have. They tend to be involved in civil society politics only when there is immediate financial gain, or when they can enhance their individual status in society, rather than thinking of the long-term common good. The majority of the technocrats and professionals will shrug off politics or social activism as a career for the unenlightened.

Moreover, even when people understand the need for action, their actions are generally ineffective, partly due to lack of skills to organise. In addition, there is a general lack of the values, ethics and discipline to under-gird their actions. Much of the failure to organise stems from the misunderstandings of democracy and freedom – which are often interpreted to mean 'free for all', 'freedom to do whatever one wants', or 'every man for himself'. The concept of the common good and the need to consolidate the democratic transition into a self-sustaining and self-regenerating social process are not well grasped.

Fifth, civil society is not always civil. There is the presumption that the government is bad (corrupt, inefficient or oppressive) and that civil society is good. This may not be the case in many circumstances. There is a need for the re-orientation of civil society to balance the need to allow the democratic process to take its course, and not to make unreasonable demands on it, but at the same time put due pressure on the process for it to yield the expected benefits.

Sixth, most institutions of civil society in the country are over-dependent on donor funding. They have limited capacity to generate resources internally or on their own. This affects their flexibility in the allocation of resources and the provision of services. It also makes them vulnerable to manipulation and control by donor or funding agencies.

Seventh, the political changes taking place in the country have resulted in the institutions of civil society concentrating on political issues. Little attention has been given to advocacy on economic planning and policy issues. Most NGOs deal with implementing social and economic development programmes at the community level, and human rights, not with advocacy for economic policy making. The only exceptions are CAMA and the Malawi Institute of Democratic Affairs.[20]

Eighth, inadequate flow of usable information and failure to use it also constrains the effectiveness of civil society institutions. For example, the daily newspapers, which are the widest sources of information on economics, have only about 10% economics content.[21] This is partly due to low numbers of economic journalists, but also the fact that newspapers are used primarily to support political views, whose content is 33% in the dailies.

As a result of the above factors, issues of national importance, and those that affect the everyday life of people, are mostly discussed in bars and taverns, and the discussion ends there. With some luck, they may get into newspapers where they are either satirised or 'misanalysed' to ludicrousness. Very rarely do newspapers do justice to the current topical issues and debates on the country's political, social and economic development. When they do so, as in comment columns, they usually have apparent political leanings rather than clear and incisive technical analysis.

Institutional Innovations

The experience of planning in Malawi and the weaknesses of the current system for engendering participation show that in future the national planning machinery should have the following characteristics to respond to the demand of democracy, and to be strategic enough.

Firstly, a strong semi-autonomous Central Planning Unit (CPU) is needed, which has technical staff capable of conducting periodic qualitative analysis of people's aspirations as well as quantitative analysis of the consistency and financial implications of those aspirations. This CPU needs to be supervised by a governing council of members of civil society and it should be legitimated by parliament. It will be the job of the CPU to see to it that there are timely and adequately guidance procedures for translating any policies into sectoral plans, and to advise political leaders if there are conflicts between what they want and an optimal economic growth and development pattern. The requirements to be timely and do a lot of information-gathering for strategic planning will be difficult to achieve in the context of the ordinary civil service.

An institutional arrangement for co-ordinating the participation of national and micro level civil society institutions in policy-making, and the evaluation of the implementation of policy, is also needed. This is to avoid relying on networks, which are closely linked to opportunism. What are needed are definite mechanisms for involving all interests, not just those with clever or strong leaders.

Another requirement is a system of distributing information to all levels of society about the plans and progress in implementing them, as well as feedback to government. The economic report, reports on sectoral programmes, and broadcasts of parliamentary debates are not adequate. The circulation of vernacular newspapers like *Boma Lathu* can be used for this purpose provided the content is made more functional. There is a need to raise civil society institutions which can do environmental scanning to generate information independently for various types of clientele. Some of these institutions could be contracted by government to supply various kinds of information for policy-making. These institutions could be poll takers, talk shows, or centres for research or intelligence gathering. Some of these already exist with varying strengths and weaknesses. The roles of the National Statistical Office would have to be redefined in this light, to be more responsive to the needs for a participatory rather than just technocrat-centred approach to planning.

Lastly, some guidelines and policy on how documents like the Vision should be used for public sectoral planning, and also in the private sector, need to be drawn up. Some studies have already been done which make recommendations on this.[22]

The central premise of this chapter is that there is a lot to be gained from bringing the idealism, knowledge and experience of civil society into a constructive mechanism of elected government. Civil society institutions are the main instrument for articulating the needs of various stakeholders for their inclusion in national development plans. In Malawi, weak civil society, inappropriate planning institutions and arrangements for garnering participation, and lack of far-sighted leadership still impose severe constraints on effective participation in national development planning.

Notes and References

1   African Futures, *Notes on Environmental Scanning*, NLTPS Methodological Working Paper Series, MES/93/003, 1993.

2   PK Quarcoo, 'Is Planning Dead?: View of a Panel of Experts', African Institute for Economic Development and Planning Working Papers no 2, 1992.

3   D Lal, *The Poverty of Development Economics*, London: Institute of Economic Affairs, 1983.

4   *Ibid*.; A Krueger, 'Government Failures in Development', *Journal of Economic Perspectives*, vol 4, no 3, 1990.

5   *The Asian Miracle*, New York: World Bank, 1994.

6   *Ibid*.

7   J Attali, 'A New Political Future', *Times Magazine*, Golden Anniversary Issue, 1996.

8   Quarcoo 1992.

9   S Lall, 'Structural Adjustment and African Industry', *World Development*, vol 23, no 12, 1995; P Mosley, T Subasat and J Weeks, 'Assessing Adjustment in Africa', *World Development*, vol 23, no 9, 1995.

10   D Steinberg, 'Socio-political Factors and Korea's Future Economic Policies',
     World Development, vol 16, no 1, 1988, p 19.
11   G Hyden, 'The challenge of analysing and building civil society', *Africa
     Insight*, vol 26, no 2, 1996.
12   L Sachikonye, *Democracy, Civil Society and Social Movements in Southern
     Africa*, Harare: SAPES Books, 1995, p 7.
13   AM Simone, 'Between the lines: African civil societies and the remaking of
     urban communities', *Africa Insight*, vol 22, no 3, 1992, p 15.
14   Government of Malawi, *The Social Dimensions of Adjustment Initiative in
     Malawi*, Lilongwe: Department of Economic Planning and Development,
     1994.
15   P Raimond, 'Two styles of foresight: Are we predicting the future or invent-
     ing it?', *Long Range Planning*, vol 29, no 2, 1993.
16   *Vision 2020: National Long-term Respective Study, Vol I*, Lilongwe:
     Government of Malawi, 1998a.
17   *Reaching the Vision: Alternative Strategies*, Lilongwe: Government of Malawi,
     1998b.
18   Malaysian Government, 'The way forward: A Vision 2020 Working Paper',
     Presented by the Prime Minister at the inaugural meeting of the Malaysian
     Business Council, 1991.
19   N Ngwira, *The Role of the Media in Malawi Vision 2020*, Lilongwe: National
     Economic Council, 1997.
20   N Ngwira, *Report on Gender Analysis of the Government Budget in Malawi*,
     Harare: UNIFEM, 1999.
21   M Chimombo, 'Government Journalism: From Totalitarianism to
     Democracy?', in KM Phiri and KR Ross (eds), *Democratisation in Malawi: A
     Stocktaking*, Blantyre: CLAIM Books, 1998.
22   B Caiquo, *Report on Mainstreaming Vision 2020 into the National
     Development Process*, Lilongwe: National Economic Council, 1997.

National Capacity Building for Democracy

Fewdays Miyanda

The subject of democracy is a widely discussed one. Every politician and every Head of State is talking about democracy and being democratic. A democratic government is one that is founded on the consent of the governed, that enjoys the consent of its subjects, possesses rightful authority and can legitimately demand or expect obedience from them. Thus, not surprisingly, in the most recent history of political thought "government with the consent of the governed" has become one of the commonly used slogans to specify the nature of a democratic system and distinguish it from those that are non-democratic. What then is democracy?

Democracy refers to knowing how to listen and how to explain in a clear and simple language.[1] It is thus also

> the legal freedom to formulate and advocate political alternatives with the concomitant rights to free association, free speech, and other basic freedoms of person; free and non-violent competition among leaders with periodic validation of their claim to rule; inclusion of all political offices in the democratic process; and provision for the participation of all members of the political community, whatever their political preferences. Practically, this means the freedom to create political parties and to conduct free and honest elections at regular intervals without excluding any effective political office from direct or indirect electoral accountability.[2]

Communication is one of the very important aspects of the democratic process. Africa needs this communication to create truly democratic states. As the scale and scope of state action increases, the importance of communication becomes greater. Communication comes from the Latin verb *communicare*, to share; and this sharing is necessary both between and within the organs of government, and between public authorities and the public. The promotion of democracy requires all those involved in politics to learn to accommodate diverse ideas and ideological orientations. They should also be able to explain their ideas in a clear and simple language so that others can grasp them, and thus afford them an opportunity to make informed decisions and choices concerning the parties they would like to belong to and activities they would take part in. Politicians should use clear and simple language that can be understood by all, and not language that can only be understood by them alone. Being unable to explain simply and clearly is not only a consequence of intoxication by jargon, it corresponds to a more serious weakness which is in fact contempt. Today the things that need to be shared have increased immensely in complexity and technicality. This has made communication even more difficult.

Capacity building for democracy

National capacity building for democracy refers to the developing in every citizen of the ability to exercise and practise democracy, so that everyone works in the same direction for the enhancement of democracy. This means that all stakeholders must understand their role in the enhancement and promotion of democracy in any given country. Every citizen should also understand what democracy is and also what it means to be democratic.

The 19th century theory of democracy – that postulated a legislature to make laws, an executive to carry these laws out, and a judiciary to see to it that the rule of law obtains – is no longer generally acceptable. In this simple scheme of things the body of citizens plays a passive role except on rare occasions when they exercise their right to vote. For most of the time, the citizens are represented in the legislature and administered by the executive. It is now realised that this is insufficient in a democracy to ensure mutual understanding between the governors and governed.[3] We also realise that without such understanding a high degree of popular participation is difficult to achieve. A widespread knowledge of the aims and purposes of government is necessary to secure consciousness of consent and popular support by the governed. Moreover, knowledge by the people of what government wants them to do is essential for the success of public administration. Knowledge about the people by government is one of the pillars of the democratic process. Government must know about such things as age and sex groups and family structure, about infant mortality and incidences of sickness and disability, about occupations and skills, employment and unemployment, incomes and savings, housing conditions, and about many other issues required in connection with education, housing, taxation and other services, if it is to serve the people better. All this can only be achieved through communication.[4]

Knowledge by the people about their government is indispensable if democracy is to succeed in our region. A government cannot operate successfully if its activities are veiled in ignorance, misunderstanding and mystery. If our governments are to make their activities and policies understood by the masses, their public authorities must come into the market places and tell the people simply and clearly what they are trying to do and why; anything short of this can lead to misunderstandings between the governors and governed. They should explain and justify their methods. The authorities should be frank about the difficulties encountered and their own shortcomings. In this way, the governed are more likely to be sympathetic towards government and even be willing to help find solutions. Only by a deliberate effort of this kind can prejudice and ignorant criticism be avoided, and a discriminating body of public opinion built up.

Without such a body of informed opinion in our countries, our governments are unlikely to be judged fairly. The governments will not be praised for their successes or blamed for their failures. And if the public cannot judge the government with some discrimination, the quality of judgement is unlikely to be high. Hence, in a democratic country, part of the task of government is to enlighten the people about its purposes and programmes. More often than not, if the masses do not understand and appreciate the purposes and programmes of government, they will often vandalise the projects that the government is trying to put up, even if they are for the good of the masses. More often than not, members of government think that they are doing fine by using the language of their civil servants and the jargon in fashion, but this is usually unclear language. The outcome is that the gap between those in power and the masses (the governed) widens, and power remains with this mysterious "they", as if they are from a different planet.

What does the inflation differential mean for a family that is listening to the television as they lay the table for dinner or take the children to bed? What do the terms balance of payments, nationalisation, and the Third World mean to them? Politicians, in government and the opposition, should use clear and simple language that the masses understand. Various stakeholders in politics should put in place mechanisms for the sensitisation of the masses about public issues and problems that affect the nation. Also, there should be put in place a large structure for dialogue where the various stakeholders could discuss the problems affecting the nation and try to work together towards solutions rather than stand aloof as if the problems did not concern or affect them.[5]

Moreover, true democracy must always have a counter-power, that is to say the opposition, in order to check the power of those in government. This is because power without counter-power becomes out of control. Government in a truly democratic country should not suppress the opposition because it is only the opposition that can check the activities of the government so that it does not go out of its way. By checking the activities of government, the opposition actually aids it (the government) to govern better.

There should also be freedom in a truly democratic country because it is only freedom that allows the stakeholders to correct the weaknesses of freedom. There should also be a respect for and tolerance of human rights. The protection of human rights is the best guarantee against dictatorship, and where there is tolerance of human rights, there is rule of law that leads to harmonious living among all the citizens. Human rights means protecting victims more than their aggressors. Human rights should not only be evoked when aggressors are being tortured and not caring about those they have aggressed.

In a truly democratic country, people should be able to choose, because democracy is the right to choose. People should be able to choose the school they want to attend, their Member of Parliament, their government, the newspaper they would like to read, the television programmes they would like to watch, their job and their place of residence. Democracy should be understood as putting at our disposal different, balanced solutions. This can only be possible if government works hand in hand with all its citizens so that they are self-reliant, hardworking and co-operative. For us to have different balanced solutions, we must take part in the creation of these alternatives and not only wait for government alone to do everything. When all citizens take part in the development of their country, there is likely to be a lot of development and progress to the extent that it will be easy for government to provide for its people. People must be willing to contribute towards the services they enjoy.

The current tendency in many countries in the region appears to consist in offering the individual the opportunity to acquire goods and services more easily than ever before while at the same time narrowing his range of choice. Thus the individual consumer is usually deprived of any real choice beyond a narrow range of alternatives and his or her personal judgement is not taken into consideration.

Citizens are more likely to take part in government programmes if their individual freedom, initiative and spontaneity are enhanced. After all, progress for democracy lies in the enhancing of these. What matters for individual citizens is that the opportunity for genuine activity be restored to them, and that their individual purposes and those of society as a whole coincide, not only ideologically but in reality.

Every thoughtful person will agree that there is a need to increase citizen participation at all levels of government in the various countries in the sub-region if we are to experience sustainable democracy. There are many possible ways of doing this. For instance, consultation between public authorities and bodies representing special interests can help to secure popular understanding of, and support for, a city or regional plan. For example, women's organisations should be consulted about the location of shopping centres, as it is women who are usually expected to do the shopping. Parents' and teachers' organisations should be consulted about the location of schools, and labour unions and business organisations about the zoning of industrial areas. This kind of consultation involves the initiation of proposals by the planning body in accordance with some general overriding concept, followed by genuine discussion with representative bodies aimed at showing whether the proposals will satisfy the reasonable needs of their members in respect of particular functions. In this way, government is sure to always have the support of its citizens and to be judged fairly as a democratic government.

When we talk about the need for enlarging the freedom and increasing the participation of individual citizens in all countries in the region in order to enhance democracy, this proposition should not be understood to apply only to the state. The state is only one of several modern institutions that contribute to the sense of insignificance and impotence that afflicts the individual in many modern societies.[6]

Political parties, for instance, are today often huge and highly organised institutions in which it is increasingly difficult for a rank and file member to exercise any great influence. A political party can also be very undemocratic in its actions and activities. It can be undemocratic towards government or even its own members. Indeed, some large, entrenched parties are today confronting the same problems of communication, integration and citizen participation as the state itself, and they are seldom more democratic in any genuine sense of the term. Let us take the example of the Movement for Multiparty Democracy (MMD) in Zambia. This party expelled one of its Cabinet Ministers from government and the party for having expressed his desire to stand as the Party President when President Frederick Chiluba stepped down, as he had promised to do, after his second term of office. A good number of Members of Parliament who were in support of this Cabinet Minister becoming the next Party President were also expelled from the party. Even other party members who thought the Cabinet Minister would be a suitable candidate for the position of Party President were also expelled from the party. The Cabinet Minister simply expressed his intention, which was genuine. Why did he have to be expelled from the party if the President was going to step down? Did the ruling party intend not to have another president after the incumbent? Was this democratic? Certainly not. Party members should be allowed to express their opinions and intentions as a way of contributing to the party. After all, this Cabinet Minister was not going to become Party President if he was not voted for at the Party Convention. What the party could have done was to allow him to stand and then if they did not like him, they should have voted for another candidate of their choice. This would have been a more democratic way of doing things.

If countries in the region are to attain and maintain sustainable democracy, they must learn to democratise at all levels of their societies. Democracy should also be interpreted in a normal way through the alternation of all major political parties. No one party or Head of State should remain in power forever. In a democratic country, the masses should also be willing to choose. For instance, when it is time for elections, citizens must be willing to register for elections and vote. They should not show apathy towards elections and when things go wrong begin complaining, when they did not want to elect people they thought could represent them better.[7] Various political parties should also learn to accept the results of the elections and consider the elections to have been free and fair even if their party has lost. The tendency of considering elections as having been rigged and unfair when a political party loses elections should come to an end if we are to have true democracy on the continent. This mentality has led to many conflicts and even civil wars in Africa. To avoid this, politicians must learn to co-exist and live in harmony with each other. It is also important to note that during election campaigns, various political parties should concentrate on telling the electorate what they will do for them when they come to power, and not concentrate on mud-slinging and condemning those in power. The electorate is interested in hearing what any given political party will do for them and not the failures of other parties.

Good democratic leaders are those who honour their promises and transform them into action. They fulfil their promises. Any idea that is not transformed into words is a useless idea; and any word that is not transformed into action is a useless word. Any democracy that no longer believes in the words it uses is dead. Democratic leaders (and specifically politicians) should be prepared to bear the consequences, take risks and make personal sacrifices in the name of the words they use, because if they do not do this, they cease to be democratic and become liars.

Another problem that renders our state presidents a bit undemocratic is the issue of changing the constitution just when the term of office of the serving president is about to expire, so that he can be eligible for another term, as happened in Namibia. This is actually a very bad practice, and it is in fact encouraging dictatorship – even tyranny – in the region. This practice should be stopped if we are to experience true democracy in our various countries.[8]

In order to promote democracy in the Southern African region, in particular, then, government leaders must show courage in their daily life. They must also show honour. They must try to surpass themselves, that is sacrifice and avoid doing things for personal benefits. For instance, any government member who tells lies and misleads others should be brave enough to resign immediately, for the sake of honour. Government should not only be efficient or effective, but also morally respectable. It is not sufficient only to be skillful, because when government is only skillful and the skillfulness becomes defective, there is nothing more left, if not feelings of shame. Political rule can end up in disappointment. It can also end up in contempt.

To promote democracy, we should condemn wrong things as such, whether or not they affect us closely and directly. We should not only condemn things that happen farther away from us and keep quiet when we are closely affected; this would be hypocrisy. Protecting perpetrators more than victims in the name of human rights, in a neighbouring country, should be condemned as much as it should be in our own country.

In democracy, there should be no uncertainty. Each individual in the society should be sure and clear about his or her role, place and state. For example, teachers should know that they are there to teach, students to study, policemen to police, soldiers to defend the motherland, and priests to conduct prayers and accompany mourners to the cemetery. Each one must play their role to the fullest and do their utmost. Hence there should be rule of law and order. If people begin confusing their roles, democracy ceases to exist in the country; you begin hearing of riots and military takeovers. People should understand where they are in this world and also where they are going. This is what is true democracy that is desirable for our sub-region – Southern Africa – and Africa as a whole.

Democracy should also be promoted through education. Education is one of the most important elements in the construction and consolidation of peace in any country. The education and training of soldiers, the military and police is very important if there is to be peace in a country. The idea of a code of conduct for relations between civilians and the military calls for the training of administrators, legislators, journalists and leaders of the civil society.

Today, education is not only a vector for the transmission of theoretical knowledge. It also concerns values: those that are related to peace, Human Rights and democracy. Education should allow people to "learn to live together". It should also teach people the values of tolerance, respect for others and sharing. It helps to promote a spirit of dialogue, non-violence and openness towards others. Nevertheless, education for peace is not an affair of only one part of the society. It calls for the participation of all stakeholders.

Notes and References

1   J-F Denial, *Ce que je crois*, Paris: Bernard Grasset, 1992, p 10. Also see
     J-F Denial, *Mémoires de sept vies*, Paris: PLON, 1994.

2   JJ Linz and A Stepan (eds), *The Dreakdown of Democratic Regimes: Latin America*, Baltimore: Johns Hopkins University Press, 1978, p 5.
3   AD Lindsay, *The Modern Democratic State*, New York: Agalaxy Books, 1962.
4   T Butler, R Elphick and D Welsh (eds), *Democratic Liberalism in South Africa: Its History and Prospects*, Middletown: Wesleyan University Press, 1987.
5   L Diamond, JJ Linz and SM Lipset (eds), *Democracy in Developing Countries: Africa*, Boulder: Lynne Rienner, 1988.
6   Y Shain and A Klieman (eds), *Democracy: The Challenge Ahead*, Basingstoke: Macmillan, 1997.
7   C Pateman, *Participation and Democratic Theory*, Cambridge: Cambridge University Press, 1970.
8   J Cartwright, *Political Leadership in Africa*, London: St Martin's Press, 1983.

Impediments to Simultaneous Democratisation and the Respect for Human Rights in Africa

Munyae M Mulinge

Soon after independence, the potential for good governance in Africa was promising. But as nations progressed in their efforts to build young democracies, the abrogation of good governance by political leaders began to escalate. However, the end of the Cold War, as marked by the disintegration of the USSR, ignited a push for representative democracy in the developing countries. This was fronted by Western countries, especially the USA and the UK, donor and financial aid agencies or institutions, and by political reformers in the developing countries themselves. As a result, the African continent has been experiencing a considerable movement towards democratisation since the early 1990s.[1] Single party or no-party systems, military regimes and personal rule began to give way to multi-party democracy, characterised by competitive presidential and parliamentary elections. This process of democratisation, it was assumed, would proceed hand in hand with improvements in the respect of human rights. This assumption was pegged on the fact that the abuse of human rights was a key feature underlining all autocratic or repressive regimes all over the continent.

This chapter focuses on the democratisation process and the protection of human rights in Africa, with a view to assessing the capacity for the African continent to attain fully-fledged multi-party democracies characterised by a simultaneous respect for human rights. To do so, the major obstacles to the co-existence of democratic governance and respect for human rights are explored. The chapter advances the basic view that the attainment of fully-pledged multi-party democracies in Africa that combine good governance with acceptable levels of respect for individual rights is going to be a bumpy and winding road that will require time to realise. In addition, the link between democracy and respect for human rights should not be assumed to be automatic. While democracy may provide an opportunity to promote human rights, in Africa initially the two need not proceed simultaneously. That is, the view that democracy and human rights are opposite sides of the same coin, with the latter being an indicator of the levels of the former, may not necessarily obtain. In fact, unlike in Western

Europe and North America, in Africa multi-party democracy and the protection of human rights may initially be incompatible.

The concepts of democracy and human rights

As a process, democratisation refers to the act or process of becoming democratic. A democratic government supports a form of governance in which the supreme power is vested in the people and exercised by them indirectly through a system of representation and delegated authority in which the people choose officials and representatives at free and fair elections from time to time. In a truly participatory and representative democracy, a humane society is created through the efforts of the people themselves. A democratic regime should be chosen through competitive elections held on a regular basis.[2] The government must observe the political and social rights of the vast majority of the population. That is, it should be characterised by the absence of arbitrary arrests, tortures and executions; freedom from costly decisions taken by arrogant rulers; equality before the law for all citizens and constitutional safeguards protecting the rights of the citizenry.

Democracy means participation as well as civil and human rights and liberties.[3] The Universal Declaration of Human Rights which is officially recognised by most countries includes within its delineation of individual rights a threefold typology that encompasses civil rights, political rights and social and economic rights.[4] Civil rights refer to freedom from slavery and servitude, torture and inhuman punishment and arbitrary arrest and imprisonment; freedom of speech, faith, opinion, and expression; and the right to life, security, justice, ownership and assembly. Political rights, on the other hand, include the right to vote and nominate for public office and the right to form and join political parties. Finally, social and economic rights include the right to education, work, food, clothing, housing, and medical care. The reference to human rights in this chapter will span all three types of rights but with a bias towards the first two categories.

The 1990s movement towards democratisation in Africa is not the first attempt by the continent to transform democratically. The majority of African countries established some form of pluralism upon the attainment of independence, but these proved to be false dawns and only incipient democracies. A few years into their existence, authoritarianism and repressive regimes superseded these either in the form of military rule or one-party dictatorships, characterised by extensive abuse of citizens' human rights. Others remained democracies only in name. That is, they held multi-party elections every so often but these were never competitive, and their governance practices ran counter to those associated with democratic rule. The same factors which accounted for this eclipse of democracy continue to prevail against the fruition of true democracies and the respect for human rights in Africa today.

Impediments to democratisation and respect for human rights

Setbacks in the democratisation process and respect for human rights across most of Africa can be understood within the context of a variety of political and socio-economic factors. Chief among these are the lack of a democratic culture, the lack of strong democratic institutions, persistent ethnicity and tribalism, economic crises and increased poverty, and inconsistent support and articulation from external players.

Lack of a Democratic Culture

The first major setback in the development of democracy and respect for human rights in Africa is the lack of a democratic culture or tradition. While the ideological climate of the 1990s may have been favourable to democracy, this lack of a strong democratic culture will continue to hamper the flowering of democracy. One clear pointer to the lack of a democratic culture in most African countries is the total misunderstanding of the concept of free and fair elections. Nearly everywhere, political parties consider elections to be free and fair only if they emerge victorious. This means that in Africa political losers are more often than not bad losers. The basis for this attitude is the belief that a political party can only be judged successful if it forms the government. Because of this fact, political parties, and especially ruling parties, will pull out every trick in the hat to guarantee themselves a victory, including engaging in massive rigging of national elections. Rigging could take the form of denying other parties access to public resources and institutions to create unfair and uneven playing fields during electioneering. Since free and fair elections are central to the democratisation process, the rigging of elections is the ultimate defeat of the ideas of democracy.

One may also cite the intolerance of opposition politics by ruling parties that is entrenched in African politics as another indication of the lack of a democratic tradition. Opposition parties are viewed as enemies of ruling parties and are never given the opportunity to thrive. Often they are denied access to public resources and institutions that ruling parties utilise to their own advantage during electioneering periods. Indeed, it appears that opposition parties can only thrive when they are not construed as a real threat to ruling parties. In such circumstances they are allowed to exist because they stand no chance of ever taking over the government from the ruling party. To illustrate, in Botswana, the intolerance of the ruling party to opposition parties appears to have increased after the 1994 elections during which the Botswana National Front (BNF) made significant gains and demonstrated the potential to take over as the ruling party. As the 1999 elections approached, the ruling Botswana Democratic Party (BDP) accorded differential treatment to opposition parties, including denying them equal access to important state-controlled resources.

Several factors account for the absence of a democratic tradition across most of Africa. First, is the cruel, dehumanising, degrading and undemocratic nature of the colonial process. Although it was an unnatural situation, the colonial process was the only experience with Western rule which African people had and it appears to have created the illusion among them that this was the only way things could be done. Second, is the brutality associated with the struggle for independence in most African countries. The independence wars inculcated a belief that those who fought for independence own the government and should do everything to keep it under their control. Born out of this belief is what may be termed the politics of entitlement. This is the feeling by most leaders who fought for independence that their countries owe them something. Unfortunately, the ultimate reward for these leaders appears to be their extended control of the state machinery and, by implication, of national resources. The use of undemocratic and extremely repressive methods that constitute the near total abuse of human rights (such as detention without trial, political murders and unleashing of security forces on disaffected citizenry) to maintain power that has been exercised in countries such as Kenya and Zimbabwe are pointers this way. The converse would be countries like Botswana where independence came through limited conflict with the colonisers and some measure of democratic rule has been observed.

A third explanation for the lack of a democratic tradition in most African countries is the failure of colonial regimes to orient would-be African leaders towards democratic governance and respect for human rights. African leaders, particularly those who took over immediately after independence, had not been schooled in the rule of law that they were expected to uphold. Thus, it was not surprising that "most of the leaders of the newly independent states insisted on the need to rule free from the 'shackles' of written constitutions".[5] To aggravate this, the constitutions that were imposed on the newly emerging nations gave unlimited powers to these leaders.

Lack of Strong Democratic Institutions

Successful democracies depend on effective institutions. Most African countries attained self-rule under some form of democratic governance but lacked the type of democratic institutions that are essential for democracy to thrive.[6] The political and legal systems inherited from their colonial mentors were more concerned with creating a sound administration than with democracy. These undermined the very essence of democracy, thus rendering it untenable. The same problem continues to plague the rebirth and sustenance of democratisation that was ignited in the 1990s. The strength of democratic institutions such as constitutions, civil society, parliaments, the judiciary, political parties, and the military and other security agencies will be assessed to illustrate how these curtail the flourishing of democracy across most of Africa.

Constitutional Frameworks

The constitutions drafted under the guidance of the former colonial powers to usher former colonies to independence retarded the permeation of democracy. They created a class of leaders who were highly unlikely to cultivate and further democratic governance. First, the constitutions vested enormous, even absolute, power in the hands of a single office, institution or individual – usually the presidency – backed by undemocratic laws that muzzled individual freedoms and rights. This created demeaning personality cults which encouraged sycophancy instead of informed debate.[7] The concentration of power stands opposed to the birth and subsequent nurturing of popular participatory democracy and protection against human rights abuses. The laws facilitated a continuity of colonial-type repression in most countries by creating overly powerful states (and heads of state) that are imbued with boundless economic and political power and reigned supreme over civil society. The failure by the new constitutions to cap the length of time one individual could be president allowed for the existence of life-long presidents. Lengthy and uninterrupted stints in power by African presidents have been punctuated with the declining rule of law and increased human rights abuses as political leaders strive to shield political and economic crimes committed against society.

The rebirth of democracy in Africa in the 1990s did not proceed hand in hand with the making of new constitutions that facilitate the respect of human rights. The same oppressive constitutions inherited at independence and watered down through amendments rushed through lame-duck parliaments to suit the whims of individual dictators still remain the pillars of democracy. A typical example of amendments to a constitution that are effected to serve the interests of those in power is the 1996 changes to the Zambian constitution presided over by the ruling Movement for Multiparty Democracy (MMD). The Amendment Bill of the Constitution of Zambia stated that "A Person shall be qualified to be a candidate for president if: a) he is a Zambian citizen; b) both his parents are Zambians by birth; (c) he has attained the age of thirty-five years". Given the events surrounding this amendment, it was very clear that the amendment was the ruling party's weapon for shutting out Kenneth Kaunda, whose parents originally came from neighbouring Malawi, from the November 1996 presidential elections.

In light of the above, virtually everywhere what are supposedly demo-cratically elected presidents and freely chosen governments rule in contra-vention of the wishes of the populace. However, having recognised the damage caused by inherently dysfunctional constitutions to the democrati-sation process, civil society has turned to agitating for comprehensive con-stitutional reforms. Kenya and Zimbabwe are cases in mind. Nevertheless, the clamouring for constitutional reform to speed up the democratisation process has gone unheeded by ruling parties. To cite the case of Kenya, civil society, opposition parties and the citizenry have been calling for a new and more democratic, people-driven constitution since 1992. But the Moi-led Kenya African National Union (KANU) government, using vacuous and vague reasons, has constantly stood in the way of such constitutional reform. According to KANU, changing the constitution should be a pre-rogative of Parliament since it is the institution that represents the people. The truth, however, is that the ruling KANU party members know that only a constitutional review through parliament can serve to prolong its grasp of power in the country. Although a breakthrough was made early in 2001 with the setting up of the Ghai Constitutional Reform Commission, Moi's KANU government appears to be determined to wreck the constitu-tional review process before it takes off properly.

Civil Society and the Citizenry

As Dahl points out, the democratic contest is a struggle between the capacities of authoritarian incumbents and the vigour of political chal-lengers.[8] Democratic rule and respect for human rights will only emerge when dissidence and popular participation exceed the stamina of the restrictive state. A strong civil society or private organisations that are engaged, either co-operatively or adversarially, with the state over nomi-nally public issues, is a necessary precondition for democratisation.[9] It acts to strengthen the political role of the population and to provide a voice for the disparate interests that are not represented by political parties.[10] Civil society organisations affect the nature of opposition to authoritarian rule that can be garnered by a particular society. Indeed, the recent global chal-lenges to authoritarian rule have emerged mainly from elements within civil society such as circles of intellectual dissidents, alliances of labour unions or militant organisations of students.[11] Alliances between the various ele-ments of civil society would bolster the resistance to authoritarian rule.

Another key dimension in the attainment of a successful democratic transition and protection of human rights is concerted popular mobilisation.[12] For democracy to thrive, a politically conscious citizenry that can participate in the political process beyond the ballot box is imperative. Grassroots democracy demands that the character of political development be infused into the consciousness of the people, their cultural outlook and ethical codes of conduct. There should occur a mass conscientisation of the people about politics that would ingrain in them the realisation that politics is an integral part of their lives. Unfortunately, most African democracies could be termed 'democracies without democrats' in the sense that they lack well-informed civil society organisations capable of objectively subjecting governing regimes to any critical assessment.

In most of Africa civil society and the citizenry remain isolated from the process through which political power is generated. According to Ottaway, Africa's civil society today is not any stronger than it was thirty years ago.[13] While civil society organisations remain segmented, the citizenry appear to have heeded the call to "leave politics to the politicians". Almost everywhere, including countries where democratic governance has long existed, such as Botswana, the citizenry are mainly characterised by immense political apathy. Not only do they remain oblivious to their rights as enshrined in the constitution; they also tend to treat the government with an aura of sacredness. As such, they generally fail to interrogate government policies and practices even where they deny them basic democratic and human rights. Because of the weakness of civil society and the political apathy of the citizenry, the responsibility for championing democracy and human rights has become the exclusive preoccupation of a small elite, complemented by international human rights groups. The former are often dismissed by governments as driven by ulterior motives or dancing to whims of their foreign masters, whilst the latter are accused of meddling in the internal affairs of sovereign nation states.

Political Parties

Another indicator of the existence of democracies without democrats in Africa is the political parties themselves. The strength of these forms an integral part of the transition to democracy. Only well-organised, democratic political parties that articulate societal interests can guarantee good governance.[14] Strong, cohesive parties increase the capacity of government to carry out policies that are necessary for the enhancement of the democratic process. Also, effective multi-party coalitions as opposed to splintered groups foster democratisation. Without democratic parties the envisaged benefits from the multi-party system of democracy are unlikely to be realised. An integral element in the strength of political parties is the nature of opposition parties. Strong opposition parties are necessary to provide checks and balances and limit the power (or excesses) of the governing party. They should play a major role in the politics of any democratising nation even between elections. As a general rule, democracy is likely to work more smoothly if key opposition parties are willing to work together rather than fight.[15]

But the political parties that are entrusted with the cultivation of democracy at the national level do not have the championing of democracy as their primary agenda. Most political parties in Africa are driven by the desire to remain in power rather than to guarantee democratic governance. For instance, ruling parties will do everything undemocratic to deny opposition parties the chance to ascend to the governing role. Opposition parties, on the other hand, will sing the democratic song mainly as a reflection of opportunism rather than the principles of democracy. Most of them appear not to understand the importance of the role they play in the cultivation of democratic governance. Rather than play their role as the watchdog for society with diligence and keep the government of the day on its toes, they tend to lose hope as soon as they fail to become the ruling parties and relapse into dormancy as they wait for the next election period. They forget that to move the democratisation process forward they need not be in the government itself. Unless opposition parties can re-evaluate their stance, the democratisation process will remain slow in most of the continent.

Political parties in Africa also suffer a crisis of internal democracy that should set the stage for the wider national democracy. This is evident from the leadership wrangles and splintering of both ruling and opposition political parties even in those countries credited with having good records of democratic governance such as Botswana. Party leaders run the show and control everything including elections and the formulation of policies and members who do not play along are branded dissidents and risk being expelled. Opposition parties may appear to be more vulnerable to splits but ruling parties are often held together through arm-twisting strategies and blackmail by the party leadership and by the sheer desire to maintain their hold on power. A relegation of the seemingly stable and democratic ruling parties to opposition positions would, in fact, lead to their disintegration if not total collapse. The absence of internal democracy among political parties is also reflected in the failure to hold party elections. In Kenya the ruling KANU party has not held proper branch and national elections for over a decade. The party has instead opted for piecemeal branch elections in a bid by the national chairman to tightly control the poll process. Finally, there is the unfair process of nominating parliamentary and local authority candidates. The tendency is for the leadership of political parties to impose candidates on the electorate. This is often done through a flawed nomination process that is characterised by massive rigging or that relies on appointments made by a few people perched at the top of the party power machinery. Sometimes popular candidates are persuaded to withdraw their candidature in favour of a candidate who does not appeal to the electorate.

Finally, most political parties in Africa tend to form along ethnic lines. Ethnic politics fragment the political class and weaken the advocacy for democracy. This has been witnessed in countries such as Kenya and Cameroon where the democratisation process has failed to remove authoritarian regimes from power. Where political parties are tribally based, governance structures that allow ruling parties to monopolise state machinery create conditions that are anti-democracy and promote human rights abuses. Not only are tribal divisions and consciousness solidified, but the majority of stakeholders are disallowed from participating in governance practices and the management of public affairs. This is both a slap in the face of democracy and a dangerous political trend that, in some cases, has deteriorated into political chaos and turmoil.

Parliament and the Judiciary

Democracy also requires strong and autonomous formal bureaucratic organisations such as the civil service, legislature and judiciary.[16] An efficient bureaucracy should provide, without favouritism, the services needed for the functioning of the state. The legislature and the judiciary, on the other hand, are necessary to curb the ever-threatening authoritarian tendencies of the executive. While the legislature is the maker of laws, the judiciary is both an interpreter and a defender of the same and the custodian of individual freedoms and human rights. In most African countries these important pillars of democracy, good governance and the protection of human rights abuse have been hijacked by the executive.[17] As such, they have lost their independence and cannot function as "the bastions of individual liberty and the protector of human rights".

The functioning and independence of the bureaucracy and judiciary has been undermined by the fact that Presidents enjoy unfettered constitutional authority to appoint whomever they please into positions of power and influence. In Kenya it is the President's sole prerogative to appoint, not just Cabinet Ministers and Permanent Secretaries, but just about everybody else who matters for the rule of law to prevail including the Attorney-General, judges, ambassadors, service chiefs, provincial and district commissioners. The same obtains in most African countries, including some that are credited with having been consistently democratic.

The Military and other Security Agencies

Another key element of democracy is a professional army and other security agencies. The control and functioning of the military is an important determinant of the future of democracy in Africa. In the past the military has played an active political role in the governing of most African countries. It has participated in politics either directly by being the government or indirectly by being the disguised (silent) partner in what were essentially coalition governments of civilians and top military officers. The democratisation process must thus entail a de-politicisation, or subordination to democratic control by civilians, of the armed forces and the security and intelligence agencies. As Ottaway put it, for democracy to thrive these should be willing to remain under civilian control without taking advantage of their monopoly on the means of coercion to impose themselves over other institutions.[18] The military and other security agencies should obey orders from the government without becoming the militia of the ruling party.

Persistent Ethnicity and Tribalism

Ethnicity has become the bane of most states and a major stumbling block to democratic governance in Africa. The term represents a consciousness of belonging to a distinctive ethnic category or a feeling of "we-ness" among members of a single ethnic group that enables them to consider themselves as having a distinct identity.[19] The terms ethnicity and tribalism – or the consciousness of belonging to a particular tribe – are often used interchangeably.[20] The entrenchment of tribalism is associated with the emergence of an in-group versus an out-group feeling or the existence of a distinction between "us" and "them". Such distinctions tend to stir up ethnic conflict, foster violence and disintegrate nation states even where at one time people of different ethnic groups may well have co-existed peacefully. This, in turn, creates conditions which are not conducive to democratic rule and the respect for human rights.[21]

Although the existence of ethnicity could be traced to the colonisation of Africa, its continued existence, heightening and resurgence today is mainly caused by the socio-economic and political practices of the postcolonial African ruling elite.[22] The nationalist sentiments they held before independence withered away as soon as they ascended to power. Post-colonial African leaders have moved to perfect and exploit the administrative technique of divide and rule inherited from the colonisers, by using tribalism as "an instrument of power politics and as a useful outlet for the discontent of the masses".[23] They single out one ethnic group – usually the one of their origin – for preferential treatment in the allocation of important, and often scarce, socio-economic and political resources.[24] Whichever tribe occupies the presidency generally enjoys tremendous advantages over other tribes. It has access to better jobs in the government sector, more powerful cabinet posts for its politicians, better infrastructural and educational facilities, better access to government-controlled resources (e.g. scholarships and credit facilities) and generally high status and privilege for its members. This has created an unending fear of political, economic and social domination of one group or several groups by another group or a coalition of other groups. The outcome has been unprecedented ethnic consciousness and conflict even in what once appeared to be relatively stable states.

In countries such as Cameroon, Kenya, Congo, Togo, Niger, Rwanda and Burundi where tribalism has been allowed to sprout, it has caused irredeemable divisions to the country's population and seriously undermined the capacity for democracy and the protection of human rights to flourish. Tribalism defeats the emergence of national unity which is essential for democracy to thrive. It undermines the commitment to democratic ideals and principles by creating a situation in which different groups "pull the nation along in different directions" rather than focus on a national goal.[25] The legalisation of opposition parties in situations where ethnicity is strong has induced ethnic, regional, or clientelist fragmentation as political parties have tended to coalesce along ethnic lines rather than political-ideological lines.[26] In Kenya, for example, the struggle for ethnic dominance through party politics that was witnessed at independence resurfaced again with the introduction of multi-party politics in 1991 to become a major determinant of party membership and the outcome of presidential contests.[27] This trend intensified in the period preceding the 1998 elections as most tribes rushed to consolidate their support around a party headed by one of their own. Leaders of ethnically based parties have little latitude for diversifying their base of support. This produces instability and the politics of threat instead of compromise.[28]

Some African political leaders have opposed Western-type democracy on the grounds that multi-party politics tends to unleash the politics of ethnic identity. According to them, it neither fits the African tradition of solidarity and consensus building, nor satisfies the need for unity and nation building of African states.[29] These have, nevertheless, failed to build the so-called reconciliation systems based on African traditions. Instead they have opted to entrench authoritarian regimes based on personal power, military control or a centralised single party, and more interested in repressing opposition than cultivating consensus.

Economic Crisis and Increased Poverty

The long-standing severe economic uncertainty facing most African countries further weakens the prospects for democratic transition and the consolidation of democracy.[30] The same economic collapse that was the major
factor in the demise of authoritarian rule in the continent remains a stumbling block to democratisation. The new democratic elite in most African
countries inherited economies that are the by-products of about two
decades of economic mismanagement and inappropriate policies. These
economies in most cases have been worsened by the large economic costs
occasioned by the democratic transition itself in terms of civil unrest
and/or violence or the fiscal recklessness of authoritarian regimes fighting
to cling onto power.[31]

Accompanying the deteriorating economies in Africa has been increased
poverty. In some countries, poverty has been compounded by the transitional costs of Structural Adjustment Programmes (SAPs) imposed through
the International Monetary Fund (IMF) and World Bank conditions for economic revival. Where introduced, these have sharply exacerbated the economic stress facing the African populations. SAPs have been accompanied
by declining expenditure on the part of government on social welfare programmes such as food, education, housing and health, coupled with reduc-
tions in the public sector – the dominant employment sector. The trimming
of the public sector has taken the form of early retirements, redundancies,
retrenchments and the freezing of hiring practices. The current levels of
poverty in Africa do not augur well for the fruition of an all-inclusive and
participatory democracy.

Poverty creates citizenry for sale during electioneering processes.
Because of this, democratic governance, the rule of law and respect for
human rights are not the major guiding principles in deciding who is voted
for. The party that has resources – usually the ruling party – to buy voters
in most cases emerges victorious even when it is not capable of entrench-
ing democratic governance. Poverty also creates a feeling of despair, apathy and a sense of fatalism. In the wake of it, the ordinary citizenry does
not see the value of democracy when the real problem confronting them is
the lack of basic needs, especially food and clothing. The poor are likely to
view democratic processes such as voting as a waste of time and to dismiss
them as inconsequential while blaming themselves for their plight. Rather
than become active custodians of democracy they adopt a passive stance
to it. Given that silence is often taken to manifest consent, this gives legitimacy to undemocratic practices such as the abuse of human rights and the
violation of the rule of law.

Inconsistent External Support and Articulation

The push for the democratisation of Africa has not been without external players. Any evaluation of the capacity for the attainment of fully-fledged democracies and respect for human rights in Africa must therefore delve into the external factor. There are two possible sources of external influence. First, is the influence emanating from other African countries acting either individually or collectively through regional bodies such as the Southern African Development Community (SADC) and the Economic Organisation of West African Societies (ECOWAS) or through the Organisation of African Unity (OAU). African leaders who are supportive of the democratisation movement have at times had to adopt a multilateral stance against undemocratic regimes that in certain instances has entailed the imposition of sanctions on such governments or the shunning of their leaders.

The second source of external influence is the international community outside of the African continent. Of significance is the role played by Western nations and international financial institutions such as the IMF and the World Bank. During the early 1990s, for example, countries such as the United States, France and the UK made the promotion of democracy an important consideration in their African policies. To advance the course of democracy, these countries have relied on policy instruments such as policy "sticks" and "carrots", instruments of traditional democracy, and democracy promotion programmes.[32] While policy "sticks" have comprised aid reduction, diplomatic isolation, public condemnation, and visa restrictions, among other things, policy "carrots" have entailed increases in foreign aid, enhanced military co-operation, and trade and investment missions. Instruments of traditional diplomacy, on the other hand, have involved persuasion and consultation. Finally, democracy promotion programmes have included short-term electoral support and long-term institution-building efforts. With respect to international financial institutions, they have moved towards a more explicitly political stance under the rubric of 'governance'. As a result, the political conditionality of 'good governance' has joined the economic conditionality 'transparency and accountability' in international aid and development loans negotiations as foreign-funded democracy projects have become part of the African landscape.[33]

Sustaining multilateral commitment to the promotion of democracy in Africa has proven difficult or impossible. A closer examination of the nature of external influence reveals a considerable lack of consistency on the part of African leaders themselves and the international community. Both sides have been unable to condemn undemocratic leadership in unison and remain divided over the issue. They have also failed to develop a multilateral consensus on the application of even modest economic sanctions against authoritarian regimes in Africa. In particular, the overseas crusaders for democracy in Africa have demonstrated an unwillingness to articulate their support for the democratic agenda in a consistent manner and engage more extensively with local protagonists. As Ottaway puts it, "Western governments have been strong advocates of democracy on paper".[34] While stressing democratisation and respect for humans right as conditions for financial aid and loans, these governments are often inclined to support "governments with dubious democratic credentials rather than risk the instability and unpredictability that accompanies far reaching change". This conveys mixed signals to authoritarian (undemocratic) regimes and encourages them to continue thwarting the democratisation process and upholding their poor human rights records. It has also given some regimes the courage to dismiss those who impose such conditionalities as meddling with the internal affairs of sovereign states.

Several factors account for the limited ability by the international community to facilitate democracy in Africa. First is the wide range of conflicting interests of the international community. For major international watchdog organisations safeguarding other vested interests, both economic and strategic, has made it impossible for them to sustain democracy as the central organising theme of African policy.[35] More often than not the desire to protect such interests takes precedence. For instance, British economic interests and the presence of large numbers of UK passport holders in many of their former colonies have complicated UK efforts to facilitate democracy. In Kenya, for example, the large number of British citizens of Indian descent has made the British government soften their stance with respect to the democratisation process including declaring flawed elections as free and fair.

Closely tied to the pursuit of strategic and economic interests is the issue of political order. As Gordon points out, the quest for political order sometimes eclipses both the democratisation and market reform concerns of the international community in Africa.[36] In particular, the fear of the proliferation of conflicts and crises in the continent may persuade the international community to retreat from their democratisation crusade. The hesitancy evident in the international policy toward Kenya is illustrative. Between 1990 and 1992 external pressure pushed Daniel arap Moi to legalise opposition parties and to hold multi-party elections. Although Kenya held its second multiparty elections in 1998, the prospects for sustained democratic rule have deteriorated since 1992 but the international response has been inconsistent and sometimes totally lacking. It has been speculated that fear by the West that Kenya may descend into anarchy if the push for democratisation is sustained is responsible for this.

Discussion and Conclusion

The push for democratisation in Africa dating from the 1990s aims to create liberal democracies in the continent characterised by free competition for elective office, complemented by a free market (capitalist) economy. This chapter analyses the factors that impede the realisation of fully-fledged democracies and the simultaneous existence of democracy and human rights in sub-Saharan Africa. It advances the view that democratisation is a complex and stormy process that transcends the introduction of multiple political parties to involve the consolidation of institutions and a change in the political culture.[37] As such, true democracies will take time to thrive in Africa. The chapter identifies factors such as the lack of a democratic culture, the lack of strong democratic institutions, entrenched ethnicity, economic crisis and increased poverty and inconsistent support from external players, to be responsible for the slow progress towards democratic governance and respect for human rights.

Certain basic observations can be made. First, the transformation to democracy does not simply require leaders of goodwill assisted by international experts working for Western governments and newly organised non-governmental organisations (NGOs). A vibrant civil society and citizenry is also a necessary precondition for democracy to thrive. For the citizenry to contribute significantly to the democratisation process there is a dire need to politicise it or make it more politically aware. The leadership of organisations such as churches and other religious groups, workers unions, and NGOs should unschool the citizenry from the "leave politics to the politicians" mentality that they have been socialised into over the years. This calls for the intensification of political education to teach our citizenry not just how to vote well but also about the democratic and human rights and freedoms that are guaranteed to them and how to demand these from those who govern them.

Second, one impediment to democratisation that African leaders can easily overcome is the destructive effects of ethnicity. It is the view of this chapter that the existence of ethnic diversity need not inevitably lead to ethnic tensions and conflict or community destruction and hamper development of democratic governance. Furthermore, ethnicity or modern tribalism can be eliminated. To echo Nkrumah, tribes are likely to remain a characteristic of African countries, but tribalism need not persist in these countries; it can be fought and destroyed. What is lacking is serious commitment and political will on the part of the postcolonial African elite to pursue economic, social and political policies that will suppress and eventually end ethnic suspicions, animosities, tensions and conflicts. The Western concept of democracy does not ideally combine tribal societies but accountable leaders could reconcile societies.

The existence of a united Tanzania relatively devoid of tribalism under Julius Nyerere is an indication that tribalism need not be a hindrance to democracy. Nyerere, who led Tanzania to independence in 1961 and ruled until 1985 before becoming the first African leader to step down voluntarily, left his country impoverished materially after the dismal performance of his socialist *ujamaa* policies, but created a united country where tribalism did not feature prominently. He is credited with never having appointed any official or allowing one to be appointed on any basis other than qualifications and experience. Even with the re-emergence of multi-party politics in the country, political parties did not coalesce along tribal lines as has been the case in Kenya.

In addition, pluralist democracies have the capacity to thrive in multi-ethnic societies. The demise of ethnic conflict in Africa may, in fact, lie with the birth of truly democratic multi-party nation states. In such states the use of force and coercion to suppress dissent and conflict deriving from ethnicity would give way to the emergence of conditions that would foster co-operation rather than competition among groups. For true democracy to thrive and produce the desired effects on ethnic tensions and conflicts, however, several steps are necessary. First, a redefinition of the presidency to check the kinds of economic, political and social gains it bestows on the ethnic group occupying it must occur. This way it is possible to reduce the level of ownership of the presidency experienced by the group occupying it. In addition, there is a need to transform the manner in which important, and often scarce, resources are allocated. All ethnic groups must perceive their lot to have some meaningful access to important, and often scarce, resources. This calls for a shift from the reliance on ethnic affiliations to allocate resources to an emphasis on need and merit. Finally, respect for especially numerical minority ethnic groups is a necessary ingredient in the minimisation of disintegrative ethnicity under a multiparty state.

Third, the argument presented by some African political leaders that Western-type democracy is not ideal for Africa because it fosters ethnic divisions has lacked vision. With the exception of Yoweri Museveni of Uganda who has advocated for a democracy without political parties, those who crusade for non-Western types of democracy are yet to specify the forms these should take. This has created a situation of would-be democrats without a democratic vision. Most such leaders still lean on one-party rule. But history has proven that this type of rule is overly flawed and tends to endanger the rule of law and basic democratic principles by becoming dictatorial, authoritarian, and a source of violations of human rights and individual freedoms. It also promotes corruption and nepotism that undermine the potentials for economic development.

Fourth, if the process of democratisation in Africa is to be sustained now, it will have to be under unfavourable economic conditions.[38] The greatest challenge that will continue to plague most of the emerging democracies in Africa is one of sustaining democratic governance and restoring economic stability. In fact, there is every indication that economic recovery and democratisation may initially impede each other. As long as most African nations continue to experience economic crisis, their day-to-day politics "will continue to tolerate, if not engender, tremendous social inequalities, abuses of power and weak pluralist institutions".[39] On the one hand, deteriorating economic conditions will put the young democracies at the risk of losing legitimacy. At the same time, harsh economic policies such as those initiated through the requirements of the IMF and the World Bank, are likely to be met with actions (e.g. mass demonstrations and riots) that may require the violation of the basic principles of democracy and human rights to quell. This suggests that in Africa, unlike in the West and in South-East Asia, democratic change will initially have to be purely political rather than all-inclusive or incorporating socio-economic change.

Finally, external support remains essential for true democracies to flourish in Africa. While other nations may not interfere with internal affairs of sovereign states, nations owe it to each other to champion democratisation the world over. A rule of thumb should be that no nation should recognise or accord hospitality to any leader who has betrayed the course of democracy in his or her country. The OAU should be in the forefront in championing democracy in the continent.

To conclude, it should be underlined that the current African democratic transitions constitute significant political openings. But the development of a democratic political culture cannot take place overnight. What is occurring across most of Africa is political liberalisation; that is, getting rid of barriers to political participation. But the process of democratisation – or the creation of institutions, values and patterns of behaviour conducive to respect for human rights and acknowledgement of the rule of law and a vibrant civil society – is lagging behind. As Gordon posits, the consolidation of democracy in Africa will take a long time to achieve.[40]

Notes and References

1   M Ottaway, 'From political opening to democratization?', in M Ottaway (ed), *Democracy in Africa: The Hard Road Ahead*, London: Lynne Rienner, 1997; JA Widner, 'Political parties and civil society in sub-Saharan Africa', in

M Ottaway (ed), *Democracy in Africa: The Hard Road Ahead*, London: Lynne Rienner, 1997.

2   R Pinkney, *Democracy in the Third World*, Buckingham: Open University Press, 1997; N van de Walle, 'Economic Reform and the Consolidation of Democracy', in M Ottaway (ed), *Democracy in Africa: The Hard Road Ahead*, London: Lynne Rienner, 1997.

3   G Sørensen, *Democracy, Dictatorship and Development: Economic development in selected regimes of the Third World*, London: Macmillan, 1991.

4   ZF Arat, *Democracy and Human Rights in Developing Countries*, London: Lynne Rienner, 1991.

5   K Frimpong, 'Some pitfalls in Africa's quest for democratic rule and good governance', in K Frimpong and G Jacques (eds), *Coruption, Democracy and Good Governance in Africa: Essays on Accountability and Ethical Behavior*, Gaborone: Lentswe La Lesedi, 1999, p 32.

6   DF Gordon, 'On promoting democracy in Africa: The international dimension', in M Ottaway (ed), *Democracy in Africa: The Hard Road Ahead*, London: Lynne Rienner, 1997; Pinkney 1997.

7   Pinkney 1997.

8   R Dahl, *Polyarchy: Participation and Opposition*, New Haven: Yale University Press, 1971.

9   PM Lewis, 'Civil society, political society, and democratic failure in Nigeria', in M Ottaway (ed), *Democracy in Africa: The Hard Road Ahead*, London: Lynne Rienner, 1997.

10   G O'Donnell and P Schmitter, *Transition from Authoritarian Rule: Tentative conclusions about uncertain democracies*, Baltimore: Johns Hopkins University Press, 1986; Dahl 1971.

11   Lewis 1997.

12   O'Donnell and Schmitter 1986; Dahl 1971.

13   Ottaway 1997.

14   *Ibid*.

15   Pinkney 1997.

16   Ottaway 1997; KR Hope, Sr, *African Political Economy: Contemporary issues in development*, London: ME Sharpe, 1997.

17   Frimpong 1999; Hope 1997.

18   Ottaway 1997.

19   G Maré, *Ethnicity and Politics in South Africa*, London: Cambridge University Press, 1993.

20   C Leys, *Underdevelopment in Kenya: The political economy of neocolonialism, 1964–1971*, London: Heinemann, 1975.

21   MM Munyae and MM Mulinge, '"The centrality of a historical perspective in the study of modern social problems in sub-Saharan Africa: A tale from two

case studies', *Journal of Social Development in Africa*, vol 14, no 2, 1999.

22 WC Cockerham, *The Global Society: An Introduction to Sociology*, New York: McGraw-hill, 1995; DH Krymkowski and RL Hall, 'The African development dilemma revisited: Theoretical and empirical exploration', *Ethnic and Racial Studies*, vol 13, no 3, 1990; P Brass, 'Ethnicity and the Colonial and Post-colonial Africa: Abstract', in P Brass, *Ethnic Groups and the State*, London: Croom Helm, 1985; OJM Kalinga, 'Colonial Rule, missionaries and ethnicity in the North Nyasa District, 1891–1938', *African Studies Review*, vol 28, no 1, 1985; K Nkrumah, *Class Struggle in Africa*, London: Panaf Books, 1980; Leys 1975.

23 Nkrumah 1980, p 59. Colonial administrators, particularly those of British descent, tended to favour one tribe over others with the objective of securing loyalty to the administration and encouraging rivalry between different tribes to prevent a sense of unity from evolving to threaten colonial rule. This created paramount and subordinate groups. To illustrate, supremacy was enjoyed by the Ngonde in British Nyasaland (see Kalinga 1985), the Baganda in British Uganda (see C Roberts, 'The Sub-Imperialism of the Baganda', *Journal of African History*, vol 3, no 3, 1962); the Tutsi in Belgian Rwanda and Burundi (see AA Mazrui and M Tidy, *Nationalism and new states in Africa from about 1935 to the present*', New Hampshire: Heinemann, 1984), the Ibo in British Nigeria (see CL Hunt and L Walker, *Ethnic Dynamics: Patterns of intergroup relations in various societies*, Illinois: Dorsey Press, 1974) and the Shona in present-day Zimbabwe (see J Day, 'The insignificance of the tribe in the African politics of Zimbabwe Rhodesia', in WH Morris-Jones (ed), *From Rhodesia to Zimbabwe*, London: Frank Cass, 1980).

24 RM Burkey, *Ethnic and Racial Groups: The Dynamics of Dominance*, Menlo Park: Cummings, 1978; Leys 1975; Cockerham 1995.

25 Frimpong 1999, p 34.

26 Widner 1997.

27 JJ Duran, 'The ecology of ethnic groups from a Kenyan perspective', *Ethnicity*, no 1, 1974.

28 DL Horowitz, *Ethnic Groups in Conflict*, Berkeley: University of California Press, 1985.

29 Ottaway 1997.

30 Gordon 1997.

31 Van de Walle 1997.

32 Gordon 1997.

33 *Ibid*.

34 Ottaway 1997, p 2.

35 MM Mulinge and GN Lesetedi, 'Interrogating our past: Colonialism and the birth and entrenchment of corruption in sub-Saharan Africa', *African Journal of Political Science*, vol 3, no 2, 1998; MM Mulinge and GN Lesetedi, 'The

genesis and entrenchment of corruption in sub-Saharan Africa: A historical and international contextualization', in K Frimpong and G Jacques (eds), *Corruption, Democracy and Good Governance in Africa: Essays on Accountability and Ethical Behavior*, Gaborone: Lentswe La Lesedi, 1999; Gordon 1997.

36   Gordon 1997.
37   Ottaway 1997.
38   *Ibid*.
39   Van de Walle 1997, p 16.
40   Gordon 1997.

Democracy and Development: The Problem of Africa

Mamane Nxumalo

Democracy is a system of government in which citizens have the right to participate in the decision-making process and in which the rulers acknowledge that their power derives from the consent of the governed.[1] In this system there are institutionalised procedures for periodically choosing among contenders for public office. This is referred to as a representative democracy. Political thinker Gaetano Mosca, however, maintains that forms of government are often camouflages for the real rulers of a state. Whatever the form, be it monarchical, aristocratic, or democratic, there is always one political ruling group or elite that holds power in its own hands. Generally, the mass of people has little voice in politics. States are always ruled by the few; they can all be summarised as oligarchies of some kind. This is evident from the disparities that are found in urban and rural development. Urban development tends by far to outstrip rural development even in the most democratic states, particularly in developing countries where the majority of the population lives in rural areas. The nation's wealth in these countries is inequitably distributed with the urban elite receiving the larger share of the economic resources. The large numbers of diametrically opposed interest groups thwart efforts toward rational development further.

Although democracy may be considered to be the best form of government to date, it is not necessarily the only good tool for promoting development. The relationship between democracy and development in Africa remains blurred.

The basic argument presented by this chapter is that the major reason for the false application of democracy and development's failure in many developing countries in Africa is that the social realities of these countries often do not reflect the grandiose expectations of either the rulers or the masses. For instance, democracy and development often come cloaked in foreign norms and values, with no ability to control resources, which eventually leads to an inability to guide and control their destinies. It has been suggested elsewhere that perhaps what these countries need to have now is a benevolent type of dictatorship which will protect the disadvantaged in society by enabling them to access clean running water, good housing, health facilities and improved communication and transport systems, among other things.

One of the most important aspects of the development of the modern state is its association with democracy. The word has its roots in the Greek term *democratia*, the parts of which are *demos* (people) and *kratos* (rule), and its basic meaning is therefore a political system in which the people, not monarchs or aristocracies, rule. Most African leaders in the early days immediately after independence adopted representative one-party democracies. The proponents of the one-party state, however, argued that there was no need to have many political parties in one country, because there was one common enemy – the former colonialists – and that the socio-political problems of each nation were therefore similar. They also argued that the multi-party system of government is divisive, especially in those countries with more than one ethnic group. Other arguments put forth were that multi-partyism was a strategy of the former colonial powers to undermine and destabilise the newly emerging states of Africa for their own socio-economic benefit. The principle underlying representative one-party democracy is that the single party expresses the overall will of the community.[2]

To most African leaders, power automatically translates into personal ownership of the nations' public funds, property and all other national assets and resources. The leader is answerable to no-one, not even to the electorate in cases where there might have been so-called democratic elections to put him (or her) into power. His decision is always final and non-negotiable. Anyone who dares to challenge or even simply question any seemingly undemocratic decision or action by the leader or any of his cronies, receives a permanent negative label of being a dissident, uncooperative and a danger to the status quo. He or she has to be closely watched! Where does such an attitude and behaviour leave the understanding and practice of democracy as is generally understood and practised in Western countries, one might ask?

The Colonial Legacy

It is important to understand and appreciate the reasons and the source of the seeming inability of most countries in Africa to practice democracy as is generally expected of any country that calls itself democratic. First of all, the colonialists took over vast areas of African land, subjugated its peoples under the barrel of a gun, a process which left them completely docile as they surrendered with their knobkerries facing down and feeling totally defenseless under such inhumane and humiliating circumstances. All of this was done under duress and Africans observed that with the use of a gun under your control, all things are possible and almost always the almighty God seems to be on the side of the powerful in society. With the presence

of the army under one's control, absolute military power and control is possible. Is it any wonder then that civil wars, coups d'état and social disor-
ganisation and political instability have been a common feature of the
African political landscape ever since the colonial authorities unwillingly
surrendered political and economic power to the indigenous peoples?

Secondly, it is common knowledge that almost without exception, none
of these colonial powers ever attempted to teach their subjects the practice and processes of Western democracy. They also failed to teach the
Africans how to participate in democratic government, let alone participation in their own governance. The colonial governors ruled by proclamation
and all the laws were made in London, Paris, Berlin, Brussels or Lisbon.[3]
The thought that the African could one day be in a position to govern him
or herself was too remote and removed from the mind that was occupied
with more important things to contemplate. Hence, it is no surprise that at
independence, none of the African countries had been properly prepared
or trained for participatory democracy. They inherited the colonial constitution which they were not schooled in or given sufficient time to mimic.
This form of governance was new to the African since none of the colonial governors had ever practised it in the colonies. No wonder, therefore,
that well into the fifth decade since gaining political independence, none of
the African countries can claim economic independence. The majority of
these are still plagued by civil strife, instability, and political repression.

One should not be misunderstood here to be defending the failure of
African governments to establish democratic political systems. What is
being said is that with all the due criticisms for such failure, it is nevertheless important to understand and appreciate the socio-political background
from which African leaders are coming from. It takes time for attitudes to
change, especially those that have taken centuries to internalise.

What is Development?

Development in human society is a many-sided process. At the level of the
individual, it implies increased skill and capacity, greater freedom, creativi-
ty, self-discipline, responsibility, and material well-being. Some of these are
virtually moral categories and are difficult to evaluate – depending as they
do on the age in which one lives, one's class origins, and one's personal code
of what is wrong. However, what is indisputable is that the achievement of
any of those aspects of personal development is very much tied in with the
state of the society as a whole.[4] It is evident from the above broad definition that to achieve any of these aspects of development, one needs to be
in a relatively free and democratic socio-economic and political environ-

ment. Clearly this ideal is almost impossible to achieve in many of the Third World countries, particularly those in Africa. To many of the leaders democracy in the Western sense is rarely practised since all powers are vested in one man who often uses it arbitrarily and at the expense of all. Here, personal development, community development as well as national development all suffer since the use of arbitrary powers in any form tends to breed a non-conducive environment. Hence the commonly held belief that democracy and development in Africa are strange bedfellows.[5]

Democracy and Stability

There can be no development in the absence of democracy, and stability is the key to democracy and development. However, stability is the godchild of good governance so that these are complementary factors and one without the other is mercilessly doomed to failure. The common denominator of kleptocracy practised by most of Africa's dictators has in most instances led to both political and economic instability in these countries. Power hungry army generals replace the new so-called democratic governments as soon as they are elected into power. The pathetic electorate feeling powerless and weary of many years of political and economic deprivation and civil wars, fearing for their security and that of their loved ones, often lacks the will to effectively challenge any government's seeming undemocratic actions at any level.

In Swaziland for example, the *Tinkhundla* structure of governance allows for the House of Senate to have twenty appointed members and only ten elected members. These twenty appointees are appointed at the pleasure of His Majesty the King; and the same applies to the position of Prime Minister. Clearly, such a system is much more open to corrupt practices of bribery and extortion compared to other systems of government. In Swaziland, it is common for most of the Cabinet Ministers to be semi-illiterate and these are all appointed by the Head of State who is surrounded by traditional leaders, members of the royal family and a few influential figures in society as his advisors. These are the people who actually run the country and hence have great influence in the final choice of who gets what position, yet the criteria used are never clearly defined – in fact, no-one is ever expected to challenge such choices and appointments. Clearly here, the concept of Western democracy is bound to conflict with the local norms and values of how a democratic government should function.[6]

The general public has always viewed the composition of Cabinet with suspicion coupled with a feeling of discontent. Corruption cannot be completely ruled out in this selection and appointment process. For example,

there is the ongoing outcry by the general public concerning the unneces-
sarily large delegations that usually accompany the King when he travels
outside the country. These people travel free of charge with all expenses
paid including huge per diem allowances using hard-earned tax payer's
money. In the late 1990s, the *Times of Swaziland* ran a detailed profile of
each member of these delegations and concluded that many of them had
absolutely no business accompanying the King during most of his trips
abroad.[7] Most of them could not, by any stretch of imagination, contribute
much towards soliciting foreign investors to the country as was the main
reason given for that particular trip by His Majesty. These people had no
legitimate function to serve or contribute except to enjoy the fun-filled,
once in a lifetime, all-expenses-paid luxury trip around the world. It can be
reasonably concluded here that the bureaucracy is fearful, and the powers
that be are selfish and insensitive to the cries and complaints of the taxpayer. The bureaucrats are reluctant to deny their masters the pleasures
they seek lest they lose their jobs while the authorities care little about the
financial and economic state of the nation. In their arrogance they actually believe that they are not only entitled to these luxuries, but that it is their
inalienable right to be granted whatever they wish and demand. Here, it is
the citizen who is being exploited by the powerful, selfish and greedy officials simply because they have the power to do so; meanwhile much-needed development projects and programmes suffer, and people become disil-
lusioned hearing the same popular song from government entitled "government has no money"!

It is now public knowledge that many politicians in developing countries
have been discovered to have secret bank accounts in Switzerland and
other overseas countries. Such huge sums are usually siphoned from public funds. In Swaziland, the main source of illegal income for public servants
comes from kickbacks for awarding contracts and liquor licences, police
receiving bribes for ignoring parking or speed limit violations, illegal sales of
local brews by women who bribe the police, and so on. National courts
have been accused of being "havens" of corruption, nepotism and inefficiency. It was revealed by the *Times of Swaziland* that some high-ranking
officials in the National Courts have been offered bribes for providing
employment.[8] For instance, a cow is usually demanded for each employment position. Questions have been raised regarding the handling of fines
paid by convicted persons in these courts. The report revealed that one
clerk conceded that the temptation to accept bribes in the establishment is
always there. The same report showed that some court presidents rent out
government houses and pocket the rent. Despite these serious allegations,
government has not been able to commission an inquiry because Swazi

courts are untouchable since they fall under traditional authority – the king's office. Here the king always has the last word in every national decision. Many of the heads of state in Africa tend to behave like dictators whilst such behaviour undoubtedly undermines all development efforts, especially as enveloped in the whole process of these corrupt practices as well as lack of transparency.

Illiteracy

The relatively high rate of illiteracy in most of Africa can be said to have contributed to the many coups d'état that the continent has experienced over the years. To the illiterate in urban and rural Africa, democracy means immediate and prompt delivery of the goods soon after the government comes into power. They are not concerned about the intricate processes through which such deliveries have to go, especially if the government concerned seeks to be truly democratic and stable over time. In Africa, democracy and development are often retarded and delayed by the fact that the leaders themselves are not much more literate than the people they are supposed to lead. The literate minority of the population which should be making informed choices at the ballot box often does not bother to vote. They justify their apathy by claiming that voting is "meaningless" when the same elite groups are merely going to be recycled back into the system without any fundamental structural changes in the organisation of government rule taking place.

Such leaders also have a tendency to allocate cabinet posts and other high leadership positions not on merit or the capability to perform in that particular portfolio, but on the basis of favouritism. In many such cases, development projects have suffered and government and donor funds have been misdirected or abused because of lack of foresight and direction on how such projects should be managed and proper decisions made. The pitfall here is that the project manager or technical advisor has no autonomy in making decisions because the minister concerned believes in poking his hands and nose into every little decision even if he is not an expert on the type of project in question. A good and wise leader in Africa is thought to be one who is feared and autocratic in his rule. Many development projects have failed in Africa simply because inappropriate decisions have been made and most of all, the people to be affected by such a project have not been sufficiently involved in the planning stages and in the implementation process. As a result, the project remains "theirs" (the outsiders) and not "ours" (the members of the community). It is at this stage that alienation from the project and other development programmes sets in.

Lack of democratic governance in developing Africa has also led to qualified subordinates in the public service feeling justified in supplementing
their salaries through unethical means. This is because they feel resentment
that their unqualified and hence undeserving seniors earn higher salaries and
other benefits that complement their positions. They feel exploited and
hence see nothing wrong in employing the same unethical means to get
even with the corrupt system. A related factor of such corruption is that
the organisational integrity of government is greatly undermined. For example, directives are carried out half-heartedly or are completely ignored. All
of this results in organisational goals and objectives not being achieved at all,
and the expected professionalism of the public service is undermined and
weakened. The question to be asked is who suffers most as a result of all
this, and the answer is obvious – it is the ordinary taxpayer more than the
public official (who probably has the means to even evade paying tax). This
situation also leads to a false belief that to strive for efficiency and professionalism is worthless and a waste of time. It is therefore more worthwhile
and expedient to pursue success through unconventional means.

In addition, corruption, particularly in a developing country, diverts
national development resources to individual gain or benefit to the detriment of the collective. When airport officers for example demand to be
paid a fee for providing a service already included in the air-ticket fare,
there is reason to believe that the economy of the country is on its way to
economic decay. Widespread corruption in a society leads to the general
public losing faith in the system, with the result that a rather dangerous
cynicism sets in which further hinders development and the implementation of various short, medium and long-term development programmes
and strategies. Community as well as national programmes suffer, especially those aimed at improving the living standards of the population such
as the rural folk.[9]

In many developing countries governments are run by a group of new
power elites who cannot be voted out of office because, once in power,
they believe that they are indispensable leaders who know best and have
the interests of the nation at heart. This they do by clinging onto power at
all costs while at the same time amassing a great deal of wealth for themselves and their friends. This tendency has contributed to general alienation and discontentment among the governed; a situation which has in
many cases resulted in a coup d'état by a small group of soldiers.

Then, when military governments take over, they make promises of
"returning to the barracks" as soon as a new civilian government is ready
to take over from them. However, it would seem that once soldiers have
tasted political power, they too see themselves as the only group that can

steer the country to prosperity, good governance. They become even more corrupt than their predecessors were and hence social, economic and political instability – a situation which greatly hinders development – becomes rife in these countries. A glaring example of this is the situation of the Congo (formerly Zaire) of Mobutu sese Seko, who came to power through a coup d'état and stayed in power for almost 30 years before being forcefully removed from office. Another example of corruption and the concept of life presidency in Africa could be found in the person of Hastings Banda of Malawi. Although Banda's government was a civilian one, it had the same characteristics of those of Zaire. These are two examples of governments – one a military government and the other a civilian government and supposedly democratic but with all the trappings of a totalitarian government – which assumed all powers of state and were ready and willing to regulate all aspects of social life in that country. Robert Michels first raised the problem of oligarchy in 1911. He concluded that the very nature of large-scale organisations makes oligarchy inevitable. This raises the core question as to whether the world will ever run out of power-hungry dictators?

Conclusion

The chapter has attempted to show that democracy and development as practised in African states are difficult to achieve. This is mainly due to the colonial legacy whereby these countries were ruled by colonialists whose governments at home practised democratic governance whereas their colonial subjects were ruled under undemocratic principles; and they never had the opportunity to participate in their own governance. Africans really neither participated in elections nor in a parliamentary system. Their role was to serve the interests of their colonial masters with no questions asked. They were never exposed or trained or involved in any administrative or executive decision-making role. What these Africans learned very well from their colonial masters was that if you have a gun at your disposal you can control and hold the entire population at your command and will.

It is also important to note that at the time of independence of most African states subjugated under colonial rule, none had been adequately prepared through practical training in for example participatory democracy. When they finally took over the reins of power they were given a foreign document with which to govern themselves – their constitution. Here they were not even given enough time to practise and internalise the contents or to properly mimic these. It should therefore not surprise anybody that Africa has celebrated the millennium still being ruled by unflinching dictators who refuse to face the ballot box for fear of being removed from power. Is it any wonder that Africa is still plagued by civil wars, coups d'état, economic and political instability and dependence, border disputes and lack of democratic governance for the majority of the population?

One fact is clear: there can be no development in the absence of democracy, and stability is the key to democracy and development. However, stability is borne out of good governance, and these two factors are complementary, hence one without the other is doomed to failure. African countries have a common denominator of kleptocracy which has led to the undermining of the state's economy and retardation of general development. Corruption, especially in a developing country, diverts national development resources to individual benefit to the detriment of the collective. It also undermines the professionalism of the public service sector and this has the inevitable tendency of leading to widespread social, political and economic instability.

Given all the constraints, one solution would be for these African governments to revisit their education systems, to include the subject of democracy in the primary school curriculum. This would probably at some point weaken or even break the cycle of the violation of democratic principles. Hopefully a new generation of African leaders better equipped and with a new leadership perspective would eventually emerge.

Notes and References

1   I Robertson, *Sociology*, New York: World Publishers, 1977, p 7.

2   A Giddens, *Sociology*, Oxford: Polity Press, 1989, pp 305–307.

3   B Dlamini, *Times of Swaziland*, 7 November 1999, p 17.

4   W Rodney, *How Europe Underdeveloped Africa*, New York: Howard University Press, 1972, p 3; T Barnett, *Sociology and Development*, New York: Routledge, 1988.

5   JE Goldthorpe, *The Sociology of the Third World: Disparity and Development*, Cambridge: Cambridge University Press, 1984.

6   A de Grazia, *Political Organisation*, London: The Free Press, 1962.

7   *Times of Swaziland*, 25 September 1997, p 23.

8   *Times of Swaziland*, 5 September 1997, p 1.

9   AMM Hoogvelt, *The Third World in Global Development*, London: Macmillan, 1983.

The Challenges of Sustainable Democracy: Southern Africa in the 21st Century

John K Akokpari

It is now apparent that the democratic wave that swept across Africa following the collapse of the erstwhile Soviet Union has produced mixed results. While a few countries have made successful transitions from authoritarian to more pluralist systems and have since held second and third leagues of multi-party elections, others have oscillated between constitutional and military rule. In other countries, the results have either been deepening state-society tensions or a complete relapse into full-scale wars, in the process compounding the crisis in governance. In Southern Africa, the picture has not been different. The wars in Angola and the Democratic Republic of Congo (DRC), and the rebel insurgency in Namibia, have either threatened or subverted these countries' democratic experimentation. These developments have not only undercut the initial optimism that greeted what was widely thought to be Africa's "second independence", but have also underscored the potential difficulties of the path to durable and sustainable democracy.

This chapter attempts to expatiate on these dynamics. It unravels and analyses the formidable challenges to sustainable democracy. It opines that these challenges are spawned by the confluence of internally and externally unleashed factors and contradictions, arguing that in contrast to Eastern and Western Africa, Southern Africa has a greater chance of meeting the challenges of democracy because of a convergence of factors, including the hegemonic role of South Africa.

Conceptualising Sustainable Democracy

In placing sustainable democracy in perspective, it is imperative to clarify two central concepts: democracy on the one hand and sustainability on the other. This is germane given the wide gap between instituting democratic practices and ensuring the longevity of those practices without reversals to authoritarian tendencies.

Since its introduction by the Greeks, democracy has been subjected to various competing interpretations. Until the demise of the Soviet Union, it remained a controversial terminology precisely because few governments wanted to be labelled undemocratic. With a universal appeal, democracy was loved both by its friends and foes. Thus, indomitable dictatorial regimes such as those of Saddam Hussein and Fidel Castro, under which grotesque human rights abuses occurred, all claimed to be democratic. Such competing claims on democracy, however, represented attempts to contexualise the concept in given situations. Thus, there have been at various times characterisations such as African democracy, socialist democracy, liberal democracy, guided democracy, developmental democracy and consociational democracy, just to mention a few.[1] The curious irony was that each version claimed to represent the best form of government, meeting the total aspirations of the citizens. However, since the collapse of the Soviet bloc and the concomitant rise to dominance of the United States and the liberal ideology, there has been a policy convergence on the meaning of democracy, perceived largely in liberal terms. According to Huntington, a political system is democratic to the extent that its most powerful collective decision-makers are selected through fair, honest and periodic elections in which candidates freely compete for votes, and in which virtually all the adult population is eligible to vote.[2]

From the above definition one can make an objective characterisation of some of the principal indices of democracy, namely competitive multiparty politics; free, fair and regular elections and; by implication, space for civil society; and respect for human rights and the rule of law. Generally, most observers concentrate on the criteria of electoral process and fundamental freedoms as the central defining features of democracy. Dahl, for example, perceives of democratic regimes as those that hold elections in which the opposition has some chances of winning and taking office.[3] However, others are sceptical about such election-focused definitions and seek to expand the frontiers of democracy's definition.[4] They argue that defining democracy solely in terms of electoral processes and rights is too formal and tends to suggest that elections are the principal indices of democracy. The import of the critique reflects concerns that electoral or human rights-based definitions tend to treat elections as ends in themselves and consequently de-emphasise other equally salient components of democracy, such as the control of the elected by the electors. It is now generally recognised that democracy has little meaning if elected officials remain unaccountable. Thus, a holistic definition of democracy must encapsulate the holding of regular, free and fair elections; respect for human rights; and the institution of probity and accountability on the part of the elected. A truly democratic regime will exhibit all of the above characteristics.[5]

At a formal level, many African states, at the behest of the dominant international credit agencies, have embarked upon processes of democratisation or re-democratisation, albeit reluctantly by some, since the late 1980s. Most of these countries have either inserted human right provisions into their constitutions or have completely re-written them to reflect shifts towards democratic politics. All too soon, however, a gap emerged between the adoption of such flamboyant constitutions on the one hand, and the practical enjoyment of these rights by citizens on the other. In countries such Kenya, Ghana and Cameroon, where the pre-election leaders, mostly dictators, managed the electoral processes and transformed themselves overnight into "democrats", post-election rights were enjoyed at the discretion of the presidents. In these countries, authoritarian tendencies remained, although in a rather muted form, after the multiparty elections, as evidenced by the continued intimidation and harassment of opposition elements and anti-government press houses.[6] This disconcerting scenario of half-baked democratic systems is what Nzongola-Ntalaja describes as "democratic formalism".[7] That is, democracy in form rather than in content or what Diamond aptly characterises as "pseudo-democracies"; meaning regimes which are formally democratic but in which there are no real chances that the incumbents and their parties would be turned out of office.[8] Yet, even granting that formal democracies have been established, the question still remains as to how long they can be sustained before full-scale authoritarian tendencies re-emerge.

Sustainability

The transition from authoritarian to democratic politics, though difficult in some cases, is generally far less easy than the arduous process of sustaining the gains. When the democratic wave passed over Africa, not a few observers were concerned about the possible ephemerality of the process. Many sceptics were concerned that the democratisation process would fit Huntington's metaphorical analogy of a tidal wave in which more established democracies are left on the beach while others are rolled back with the tide.[9] This concern is pertinent particularly in Southern Africa, where a myriad factors seem poised to either subvert or pose major challenges to democracy. As a rule not all countries which attempt or make successful democratic transitions are able to sustain them. Nigeria made an attempted transition from authoritarian to democratic rule but slipped back almost immediately into old-style authoritarian practices in 1993. Similarly, both Angola and Sierra Leone slipped back into seemingly intractable anarchy after holding democratic elections in 1992 and 1995 respectively, and although the people of Lesotho went to the polls in 1998, the aftermath of the elections was marked by violent conflicts between government and opposition. Given the truism that a democratic transition is not automatically followed by its sustainability, it is essential to place the latter in perspective.

What, then, is democratic consolidation or sustainability? How do we recognise a consolidated democracy? In other words, when can a democracy be judged to have been sustainable? The literature is replete with a variety of criteria for determining democratic consolidation. Two of the most popular ones are reviewed here. The first is the "two-election" test, which is often referred to as the "transfer of power" test. Associated with Huntington, this posits that democracy is consolidated when a country holds two successive multi-party elections without interruptions or when a government is defeated in a free and fair election and the results are accepted by the vanquished.[10] In this test, emphasis is placed on the incumbent losing and accepting defeat since this is a hallmark of the political actors' ability to play according to the rules of the game. At a practical level, however, the transfer of power test is suspect, if not flawed, in its inability to provide a persuasive basis for analysis. While by this test Zambia's democracy, for example, will be rated as consolidated, Botswana's, where the dominant Botswana Democratic Party (BDP), has remained in power through competitive elections since independence, will be depicted as fledgling for the simple reason that the BDP has so far not suffered an electoral defeat.[11] Indeed, contrary to the inference of the test, many observers believe that Botswana's democracy has been more sustainable than Zambia's. In fact, some argue that amidst a legion of factors, including ethnic bias, recessionary pressures under SAPs, and state insolvency, the prospects for Zambia consolidating its democracy are limited.[12] Accordingly, the transfer of power test could easily be a misleading index of democratic consolidation if used exclusively without consideration of other factors.

A second criterion for democratic sustainability, which to some extent accommodates the weakness of the transfer of power test, is "the simple longevity or generation" test. Here, about twenty years of regular and competitive elections without turbulence are sufficient to judge a democracy as consolidated. The most distinguishing feature of this test is the emphasis on the holding of regular elections rather than changes in ruling parties. However, like the transfer of power test, the simple longevity test generates questions. First, Africa has seen countless regimes which have consistently organised fraudulent elections that kept them in power for many years. In such political systems, democracy could never be truly said to have been consolidated irrespective of how long they have endured.

Second, historical experience demonstrates that the longer a regime remains in power, the less it becomes distinguishable from the state apparatus. In other words, the tendency for a dominant ruling party to become undemocratic in such situations is high, leading ultimately to the atrophy of human rights and a process of democratic decay rather than consolidation. Third, the simple longevity outlook does not predict the future predisposition of a democratic regime in the face of adversities. Is the regime capable of withstanding shocks and crisis without relapsing into undemocratic practices? In the absence of adequate turbulence to test the capacity of a democratic system to survive, it will be deluding to perceive it as consolidated just because it has endured many years of existence. As Beetham has suggested, "a democracy can best be said to be consolidated when we have good reason to believe that it is capable of withstanding pressures or shocks without abandoning the electoral process or the political freedoms on which it depends, including those of the opposition".[13]

Moreover, by the longevity criteria, nearly all states in Africa will fail the test of democratic sustainability. While this may be valid to some extent, it would probably be unfair to countries like Botswana, Mauritius and Senegal, which have received considerable international accolades for holding regular elections and have so far not witnessed major political disruptions.[14] In this chapter, therefore democratic sustainability is taken to subsume the elements of both the transfer of power and the simple longevity tests. A consolidated democracy, therefore, refers to a system in which free, fair and competitive multi-party elections take place, and in which these practices are sustained for a fairly long period time in spite of disruptive incidence.

Challenges of democratic consolidation in Southern Africa

Factors militating against democratic transitions and consolidation in Africa are varied, and various authors have identified or ranked them according to their style of analysis. For example, Nzongola-Ntalaja and Osaghae have separately suggested that the key obstacles to democratic development in Africa include the political immaturity of democratic forces; weakness of the middle class; monopoly over the public media by incumbent regimes; acts of violence against democracy, including acts of intimidation of opposition constituencies and orchestrated measures to fuel ethnic violence; and the fact that Africa's post-Cold War democratic project was imposed and not home-grown.[15] To the above factors may be added a few more, which are directly relevant to the Southern African region.

Economic crisis and poverty

In a classic study, Prezeworski et al noted that if the per capita income of a country is within the range of $1000-$2000, the probability that democracy will die within a year is 0.06. This rate falls to 0.03 when per capita income is between $2000 and $3000, and declines further to 0.01 when per capita income is between $4000 and $6000. Translated into years, the study notes that when income is under $1000, the average life span of democracy is 8.5 years; for $1000-$2000 the life span is 16 years; for $2-000-$4000 democracy should last for 33 years, and this should rise to 100 years when per capita income is between $4000 and $6000. According to the study, democracies with per capita incomes of $1000 or less are extremely fragile with little likelihood of survival. Thus, the study concluded that "once a country is sufficiently wealthy, with a per capita income of more than $6000 a year, democracy is certain to survive, come hell or winter".[16] In explaining the basis of these conclusions, Lipset argues that the intensity of distributional conflicts is lower at higher income levels and hence tends to facilitate the endurance of democracy.[17]

Going by the conclusions of Prezeworski et al, all Southern African states except the Seychelles (with a per capita income of $7364), will be unable to sustain their democracies because of low per capita incomes and widespread poverty. Most Southern African states have a per capita income of less than $1000, apart from Botswana ($4936), Mauritius ($4-173), Namibia ($2067), South Africa ($2989) and Zambia ($4027).[18] Although the conclusions of Prezeworski et al may sound hyperbolic and extreme in practice, there is little question about the debilitating effect of low incomes on sustainable democracy. In addition to intensifying conflicts related to distribution, low incomes also trigger a chain of inter-connected developments, which undermine governance and stability. Low incomes mean a country must constantly rely on foreign aid and loans, which typically increase the debt burden. In countries like Mozambique, Malawi and Tanzania where per capita income is scarcely above $200, external debt figures are high and amount to over 200% of GNP. In Mozambique, classified as one of the poorest in Southern Africa, the percentage is 444.[19]

Indebtedness in turn has critical implications for democracy. Debt and its ancillary servicing obligations, for example, attenuate governments' capacities to improve upon the quality of life, giving poverty a stronger grip on the population. Impoverished people are as a rule preoccupied with basic economic survival and thus assume an apathetic posture towards politics. To these people, human rights are a luxury, not a necessity. Apathy in turn provides propitious grounds for the pursuit of undemocratic practices by the political elite.[20] Furthermore, impoverished societies are pliable to systematic manipulation by military adventurers, who make vain promises of better economic conditions. Coup-makers therefore manoeuvre the poor into rallying behind them. This, along with the propensity of poverty to ignite protests, which are sometimes sufficiently intense to undermine the authority of the state, and the tendency for the state to be depicted as a channel of accumulation, all underscores the baneful effects of weak economies on sustainable democracy.[21] Thus, in several respects, poverty undermines democratic consolidation. Poverty and unemployment are among the key threats facing most of the nascent democracies of Southern Africa. As a rule, unemployment induces crime, which is inimical to democratic development. Crime creates fear among people and undermines the free exercise of democratic rights. Democracy is surely not anchored on secured foundations where in a theoretically free country people are scared of walking on the streets of their cities. The critical challenge for Southern Africa, therefore, is to revitalise national economies by developing programmes that reduce unemployment, poverty and inequalities and thus avert the threat posed to democratic stability by economic adversities.

Socio-political cleavages

The chemistry of Southern African states, just like those in the rest of Africa, has tremendous potential to circumvent stable governance. With the exception of Lesotho and Swaziland, all Southern African states are heterogeneous, comprising diverse ethnic and, sometimes, racial entities, which constantly look on each other with suspicion. In South Africa, for example, despite rhetoric on reconciliation, racial tensions, particularly between Blacks and Whites, remain high, as is partly exemplified by the rising incidence of farm killings.[4] The reluctance of some predominantly white schools, despite declarations on deracialisation, to admit black students, together with the uneasy calm prevailing in some multi-racial schools, is an indication of the volatile relations between the dominant races in the country.

South Africa's democracy is also threatened by mutual suspicions among black communities. As Osaghae notes, South Africa's previously disadvantaged communities are no longer monolithic.[22] Minority ethnic communities such as the Venda, Sotho and Tswana are increasingly becoming uneasy with what they consider Xhosa domination of the country's post-apartheid politics. Yet, such allegations of domination by particular groups are not only peculiar to South Africa, but are rife in the region. In Botswana, the dominant BDP, composed mainly of Batswana-speaking people who constitute about 95% of the population, is resented by the minority Kalanga, Basarma and Kgalagadi, all of whom together constitute 4% of the population. Similarly, despite the union of the Shona-dominated Zimbabwe African National Union (ZANU) and the pro-Ndebele Zimbabwe Africa People's Union (ZAPU) in April 1988, there are suspicions of Shona domination. This aside, there is a gradual emergence of ethnic factions within the Shona support base of the ZANU-PF. Similarly, the mass mobilisational abilities of the MMD in Zambia have not been sufficient to stem allegations of ethnic bias in favour of the Bemba, which had hitherto constituted the major support base of the UNIP.[23] The incessant conflicts in the DRC are underlaid by persistent Tutsi allegations of being marginalised by other groups in access to the country's politico-economic resources. And communities in the Caprivi Strip in the north of Namibia have, since the independence of the country, been accusing the government in Windhoek of marginalisation and oppression. Such feelings of exclusion are potentially damaging to the spirit of compromise and consensus, which is a key requirement for democratic stability.

This is not to suggest that homogenous countries are absolved from such acrimonious accusations. Indeed, where societies are not fragmented along ethnic lines, such cleavages as religion and political affiliation have proved equally strong in undermining societal cohesion. In Swaziland the polarisation is frequently between the pro-monarchy (royalists) and reformists, i.e. those who support fair and competitive multi-party politics. Tensions between these two ends of the spectrum often flare up in the run-up to national elections. In Lesotho, on the other hand, the political divide has been shaped and sharpened by affiliations to political parties. The main political divisions in turn correspond to the dichotomy between Catholics and Protestants, with the monarchy appearing sympathetic towards the former.[24] These divisions were concretely manifested in the violent conflict that occurred in Lesotho following the general elections of 1998 and which took a peacekeeping force of the Southern African Development Community (SADC) under the leadership of South Africa to contain.[5] Thus, such divisive and centripetal forces as race, tribe, religion and political affiliations are certain to pose immutable challenges to democratic stability in Southern Africa.

Conflicts and wars

As divisive forces threaten to undo Southern Africa's democracies, incessant conflicts and wars, which have become the daily nightmare of some countries, aggravate this threat. The seemingly intractable war between the National Union for the Total Independence of Angola (UNITA) and the ruling Popular Movement for the Liberation of Angola (MPLA) government of Angola, and between rebels and the government of the DRC are well known. These conflicts have periodically assumed horrendous proportions, spawning population displacements, refugees and migration. In other countries, such as Zimbabwe, Zambia, Malawi and Lesotho, low intensity conflicts have flared up intermittently between governments and opposition elements.

The causes of these intra-state conflicts are varied; however, as Matlosa suggests, these reflect contests to control the state and its resources, disputes over territory, lack of openness in the political space, conflicts over unfulfilled expectations in the aftermath of political transitions, and conflicts linked to one-party dominance. He summed up the conflict problematique by noting that "the underlying locomotive of all post-apartheid and post-Cold War conflicts in Southern Africa is no longer ideological contestation, but rather the fierce struggle over the region's abundant resources, including water, diamonds, timber, etc".[25] At a deeper level, however, the causes of such contestations can be reduced to a common denominator, namely, the partisan posture of the state in the distribution of scarce political and economic resources. Specifically, the post-colonial African state has not only failed to accord its numerous and divergent constituencies equal access to the meagre political and economic resources, but has also failed to promote conditions that facilitate fair competition for these resources.[26]

Rather than according equal opportunities to the various constituencies within its boundaries, the state has become a covert, but sometimes an overt, executive instrument for furthering the sectional interests of particular constituencies. This posture sets it and opposition elements on a constant collision course. The genesis of the current conflict in the DRC, for example, lies in the inauspicious politics of exclusion and marginalisation practised by the former strongman, Mobutu Sese Seko. His 32 years of unadulterated kleptocracy showed little inclination to distribute resources fairly among the competing constituencies in the country.[27] Mobutu's successor, Laurent Kabila, seemed to have learnt no lessons from history. Allegations of ethnic Tutsi marginalisation under his reign were rife and disaffection among the aggrieved constituencies culminated in the formation of the Tutsi-dominated Congolese Rally for Democracy (CRD), one of the many rebel groups which fought the Kinshasa government.[28]

In point of fact, wars and insecurity in Southern Africa are no longer the preserve of Angola or the DRC. Some of the previously serene countries like Namibia, Lesotho and Zimbabwe now have the arduous task of stretching resources to foreclose instability and anarchy. In August 1999, rebel insurgency broke out in the Caprivi region in northern Namibia, with protesters demanding autonomous status. The revolt was ignited by the failure of the Namibian government to grant the people of Caprivi the opportunity to determine their own destiny in accordance with a 1964 government pledge. Although the Namibian government has successfully crushed the rebellion, there are no guarantees that it will not resurface since the fundamental concerns of the Caprivi people remain unredressed.

As indicated earlier, an uneasy calm has returned to Lesotho following the mediatory efforts of South Africa and SADC. The post-conflict agreement in 1998 scheduled fresh elections for April 2000, which never took place. The persistent calls by the opposition since April 2000 for fresh general elections and the insistence by government on the absence of auspicious conditions for such polls may be placing Lesotho on, or closer to, a dangerous time bomb. Similarly, since mid-1998, Zimbabwe has been witnessing violent, sometimes bloody, confrontations between supporters of the ruling ZANU-PF and those of the main opposition party, the Movement for Democratic Change (MDC). Resulting from the government's growing unpopularity and its controversial land reform policies, the conflict has shown little sign of abating mainly because of government intransigence and opposition over-exuberance. Zimbabwe's democratic system, once the epitome of stability in Southern Africa, is under serious threat. The central contention here is that conflicts, wars and threats of secession will remain implacable thorns in the flesh of the emerging democracies in Southern Africa in this new millennium.

SAPs and contradictions

As the region battles with the threat of conflict, the strict implementation of the now ubiquitous IMF/World Bank-sponsored structural adjustment programmes (SAPs), which are currently being implemented by nearly all Southern African states, are poised to pose additional challenges to the incipient democracies in the region. This proposition is predicated on the intrinsic contradictions in the SAPs. In the first place, with their decontrolling, downsizing, desubsidisation, devaluation and privatisation packages, SAPs entail pains, which are often the source of resentment among the population. Consequently, the implementation of these reforms requires some degree of authoritarianism. In Ghana, the once acclaimed "star of adjustment" by the international donor community, for example, the Rawlings regime employed wide and unfettered authoritarian powers to suppress popular opposition to the reforms.[29] By contrast, the hesitation of Kenneth Kaunda in resorting to authoritarian powers created difficulties for the Zambian government in the implementation of its adjustment programme. Consequently, sustained protests over the removal of subsidies compelled the Kaunda government to jettison its first reform programme in 1987.[30] The perennial public protests in Zimbabwe since the mid-1990s against the government of Robert Mugabe reflect the impact of the country's economic adjustment policies on the population.

Secondly, and as a corollary to the above, SAPs spawn a fundamental contradiction, which compels the state to balance precariously on a tightwire. On the one hand, adjusting countries are compelled to implement unpopular reforms, which are conditional for aid, and on the other hand, such reforms are distasteful to the majority of the population. The typical adjusting state is thus caught in a perplexing dilemma, between a rock and a hard place, where going forward is a great difficulty and backwards a near impossibility. The crux of the dilemma is how to pursue unpopular austerity programmes while remaining responsive to the concerns of the electorate. Given the apparent incompatibility of the two processes and the difficulty in pursuing them simultaneously, the imperatives to acquire foreign aid and investments may compel the state to sacrifice democracy on the altar of structural adjustment.

Thirdly, adjustment may prove inimical to democracy in the sense that it positions states in a corner where they are made more responsive and accountable to international financial institutions than to their own constituencies. The state is subject to international creditors who dictate the details of economic policies, including financial allocations to departments in the national budget. Some are concerned that this gradual, but real loss of state sovereignty is a harbinger of a benign, yet effective re-colonisation of Africa by multilateral agencies.[31] As economic issues assume centre stage under adjustment, key financially related state establishments such as finance ministries and central banks have come under the unfettered control of the dominant IFIs. Consequently, financial and monetary issues have been insulated from democratic practices such that central banks and finance ministries conduct business with IFIs unencumbered by civil society. In this regard, not only do SAPs truncate democracy, but they also atrophy state sovereignty. A democracy is scarcely genuine, let alone sustainable, when certain key policies are placed beyond discussion. Sadly, this is the grim reality facing Southern African states.

Yet, SAPs do not only emasculate democracy, they also escalate the external indebtedness of countries through the huge structural adjustment-related loans granted by bilateral and multilateral creditors. In general, the debt of developing countries is on the rise. Between 1980 and 1995, for example, total external indebtedness of low income countries rose from US $55 billion to US $215 billion, to more than thrice their export earnings. Africa's share of the debt has continued to rise and now stands at a whopping US $340 billion, paradoxically at a time when the continent's economic fortunes are declining as a result of structural adjustment, globalisation and HIV/AIDS. Commenting on the rapid growth of debt, Ake laments that "the debt burden of Africa is so great and the capacity to repay so limited that it is increasingly necessary to think not in terms of servicing but in terms of debt stock reduction and write-offs".[32] Most heavily indebted countries in Southern Africa such as Zambia, Mozambique and Angola spend 31%, 23% and 20% respectively of their export earnings on debt servicing. The need for fresh loans to service old ones and the competition to remain credit-worthy leads states more towards external agencies than to the internal concerns of citizens.

The imperatives of globalisation

The obtrusive pressures unleashed by SAPs are exacerbated by the imperatives of globalisation, which not only facilitate the erosion of state sovereignty, but also spawn further crises in governance. Under globalisation international public opinion and markets have become the main decision-makers, a development that both circumscribes the freedom of the state and limits its options. The state's circumscription is reinforced by the information superhighway. If news about a country's budgetary difficulties spread, prices and interest rates in other countries both far and near immediately hike. Such fiscal external factors determine the response of the local economy and simultaneously undermine the ability of the state and its constituents to autonomously prescribe solutions for local crisis. In the new world market order, therefore, prescriptions for dealing with a country's internal economic malaise are determined more by conditions in the global market than by local constituencies.

But even more confounding, globalisation has elevated economic issues to undue prominence. For instance, government's important foreign policy decisions are informed more by economic than socio-political considerations. Drowned in debt, and constrained further by the logic of structural adjustment, the major foreign policy concerns of African states are dominated by a desire to receive foreign assistance and to reschedule debts.[33] Consequently foreign ministries, which traditionally ought to be the gatekeepers between domestic and external policy environments, have lost this function, ceding it to finance ministries and central banks. As a further consequence of this shift, there has been a concomitant emergence of new foreign policy makers and advisors who include not only technocrats from the central banks and finance ministries, but also, worryingly, officials from the IFIs. These officials wield considerable influence over foreign policy *vis-à-vis* a country's elected officials, mainly because the threat of aid cuts easily compels African states to conform to the policy dictates of IFIs. Given Africa's continuing need for external aid, the practice of external control of its domestic and foreign policies may not easily abate.

In addition, notions of economic liberalisation and privatisation intrinsic in globalisation may not help the course of the democratisation project in the region. This is precisely because in implementing these largely pau-perising policies, the IFIs prefer to deal with technocrats who lack any political base rather than elected officials who have national constituencies. The reason for this is not far-fetched: technocrats can be trusted to loyal-ly implement externally-generated policies no matter how unpopular they may be, while elected officials will predictably hesitate about implementing such programmes for fear of alienating their supportive constituencies. Such a practice of positioning technocrats rather than elected officials at the centre of governance can potentially undermine democracy, for as Nzongola-Ntalaja correctly notes, "rule by a technocratic elite can only be anti-labour, anti-people and therefore anti-democratic".[34] Thus, the cur-rent wave of globalisation is certain to pose critical challenges to the democratisation projects in Southern Africa. For sure, a trend is emerging where the state and its elected officials are losing effective control over decision-making on domestic, not to mention international issues.

Environmental pressures

The relation between environmental issues and democratic sustainability is generally indirect, unobtrusive and hence scarcely perceptible. This is part-ly due to the tendency for environmental issues to be perceived as com-pletely apolitical and hence with little relevance for governance. This orthodox perception is, however, spurious. It is surmised that environmen-tal issues affect democratic sustainability in at least two ways. First, there is a mutually reinforcing relationship between poverty and environmental degradation. As the World Commission on Environment and Development has noted,

> ... those who are poor and hungry will often destroy their immediate envi-
> ronment in order to survive: they will cut down forests; their live stock will
> overgraze grasslands; they will overuse marginal lands; and in growing num-
> bers they will crowd into congested cities. The cumulative effect of these
> changes is so far-reaching as to make poverty a major global scourge.[35]

As they over-stretch the environment, such environmentally bankrupt communities fall deeper into impoverishment and despondency. This sce-nario is particularly confounding in Africa where the majority of the popu-lation lives in the rural areas and where they depend to a considerable extent on the forest and other natural resources for sustenance. The impact of poverty on democracy has already been noted. It is critical to add, however, that environmental bankruptcy compounds the plight of the poor and makes them even more resigned from politics and the democratic process.

Second, and more poignant, is the fact that faltering democracies in Southern Africa are in part the results of conflicts and wars. But, to be sure, most of the wars in the region are, strictly speaking, environmentally related and can in reality be called eco-wars. In Angola, for example, the struggle between UNITA and MPLA is not only for political control over territory, but also for control over natural resources – the vast deposits of diamond and oil resources. Similarly, the contestations in the DRC are for control over the country's rich mineral fields. The adverse effect of environmental issues on democratic stability is their potential to intensify conflicts, particularly in cases where such natural resources are diminishing. In general, however, environmental issues are subsumed in the more glaring struggle for power such that environmental and politico-economic causes are not easily deciphered. It is surmised, therefore, that Southern Africa is set to confront environmentally related challenges in its march towards democratic stability. However, in contrast to other regions of Africa, Southern Africa still has greater chances of consolidating its emerging democracies.

Optimism for Democratic Sustainability in Southern Africa

Although confronted with challenges, there are still rays of hope for democratic development in Southern Africa. This optimism is premised on a number of factors. Firstly, in terms of economic performance, Southern Africa as a region is doing relatively better than East or West Africa, although some states in the region are still worse off in terms of per capita incomes. Economic indicators in Southern Africa show a promising economic picture, which can boost democratic stability, all things being equal.

Secondly, unlike West Africa where some states showed considerable reluctance and aversion to embark on democratic rule and therefore stage-managed the transitions, Southern African states, with the exception of the DRC (under Mobutu's misrule) and Swaziland, were readily inclined towards formal democratisation. Such enthusiasm provides optimism for democratic consolidation. In every difficult human endeavour the first step to success is the demonstration of an initial commitment. This of course is not to underplay the wars in Angola and the DRC, which along with the incessant violence in Zimbabwe, continue to mar the stability and democratic credentials of the region. It is hoped that ultimately the various protagonists in these countries will embrace the spirit of accommodation and tolerance to plant the seeds of peace.

Third, the role of South Africa as a hegemonic power could facilitate democratisation in the region. Having recently emerged from the debris of apartheid, South Africa seems to have committed itself to democratisation, reflected both in the processes of reconciliation in the country and its desire to export democratic ideals to the region at large. In furtherance of the latter objective, South Africa has been critical of the Swazi monarchy for making slow progress towards political liberalisation. Also, in the pursuit of respect for human rights, Pretoria prevailed, though unsuccessfully, on President Frederick Chiluba in early 1996 to unban former president Kenneth Kaunda from contesting Zambia's second multiparty election. Furthermore, Pretoria appealed for Kaunda's release when the former president was detained on suspicion of complicity in Zambia's failed coup.[36] South Africa has also been an active mediator in regional conflicts. In 1998, it was deeply involved in the resolution of the Lesotho conflict. Some have, however, argued that South Africa's involvement in Lesotho was motivated more by economic and geo-political interests than by a genuine desire to restore democratic rule in that mountain kingdom.[37] Similarly, since the beginning of 1999, South Africa has intensified its efforts at resolving the conflict in the DRC. The conflict on which Pretoria has so far not made any marked impact is the Angolan war. This notwithstanding, the active role of South Africa in the region could be an asset for democratic development.

Fourth, SADC as a regional organisation may also prove functional for democratic stability. Like any regional organisation in the post-Cold War era, SADC has become involved in conflict resolution and the restoration of democratic rule. So far its record in this endeavour has been commendable. In 1994, the organisation intervened to avert a military take-over in Lesotho. It also played a crucial role in the problematic transitions in Swaziland, and Angola. Similarly, under the leadership of South Africa, SADC successfully intervened militarily to end the 1998 Lesotho conflict. But an initial decision of SADC to intervene militarily in the DRC has led to polarisation within the organisation. This division threatens the future of the organisation. However, if, against all odds, SADC succeeds as a peace broker in the DRC, even if diplomatically, its credibility as a peacemaking and democracy-building organisation will be significantly enhanced.

Conclusion

In indicating some of the challenges facing sustainable democracy in Southern Africa, this chapter proceeded with an attempt to show the nuances in the definition of democracy and suggested that there now seems to be a consensus on its definition, that reflects old-neo-liberal thinking. The chapter also stated the importance of extending the frontiers of the definition of democracy by transcending its formal characteristics based on elections and human rights to include the accountability of the rulers to the ruled. If the latter characteristic is downplayed, Southern Africa may face an unpleasant scenario of multi-partyism without real democracy. The chapter also grappled with the rather complex notion of sustainability. It suggests that a democracy is sustainable if, in addition to promoting free, fair and regular elections and upholding the rule of law, the system is also able to protect these processes over a long period of time even in the face of turbulence and adversities.

It also identified and analysed some of the key challenges militating against democratic stability in the region, suggesting that such challenges are both internal and external and include such conjectural factors as economic crisis, socio-political cleavages, conflict and wars, SAPs, globalisation, and environmental pressures. The chapter suggests that these factors can potentially cause democracy in the region to stumble, even tumble. However, as noted, these challenges do not condemn the Southern African region to a perpetual limbo of democratic decadence. On the contrary, there are compelling reasons to be optimistic about democratic development in the region. Among other factors, there is a great deal of political will to sustain democracy in the region. This, along with the roles of South Africa and SADC in defending infant democracies, is basis for optimism about democratic consolidation in the region.

Yet, in general the capacity of Southern Africa to meet the challenges of democracy can be enhanced with the adoption of certain policy measures, such as the following:
• Improving upon the economic situation in the region by formulating credible policies that address the twin conditions of unemployment and poverty;
• Mitigating the effects of socio-political cleavages through the institution of political systems that are accommodative and which promote and protect the rights and interests of minorities and opposition constituencies;
• The assumption by the state of a neutral posture in both mediating among constituencies and in the distribution of resources;
• Instituting policies that arrest the declining trend in the environment;
• Formulating policies that enable Southern Africa to better meet the challenges of globalisation.

Notes and References

1   See, for example, R Sklar, 'Democracy in Africa', *African Studies Review*, vol 26, nos 3–4, September–December 1983.

2   SP Huntington, *The Third Wave: Democratisation in the Late Twentieth Century*, Oklahoma: University of Oklahoma Press, 1991a, pp 7–8.

3   R Dahl, *Polyarchy: Participation and Opposition*, New Haven: Yale University Press, 1971.

4   GJ Schmitz and D Gillies, *The Challenge of Democratic Development: Sustaining democratisation in developing societies*, Ottawa: North-South Institute, 1992, pp 95–96; D Beetham, 'Conditions for Democratic Consolidation', *Review of African Political Economy*, no 60, 1994.

5   R Joseph, 'Africa: The Rebirth of Political Freedom', *Journal of Democracy*, vol 2, no 4, 1991.

6   JK Akokpari, 'Apparent contradictions between economic and political liberalisation: A case study of debates in Ghana', Unpublished PhD thesis, Dalhousie University, Canada, 1996a, pp 173–174.

7   G Nzongola-Ntalaja, 'The State and Democracy in Africa', in G Nzongola-Ntalaja and MC Lee (eds), *The State and Democracy in Africa*, Harare: AAPS, 1997, p 15.

8   L Diamond, *Prospects for Democratic Development in Africa*, Stanford: Hoover Institute, 1997, p 3.

9   SP Huntington, 'Democracy Third Wave', *Journal of Democracy*, vol 2, no 2, 1991b.

10 Huntington 1991a.

11 P du Toit, 'Bridge or Bridgehead? Comparing the party systems of Botswana, Namibia, Zimbabwe, Zambia and Malawi', in H Giliomee and C Simkins (eds), *The Awkward Embrace: One-party domination and democracy*, Cape Town: Tafelberg, 1999, pp 196–197.

12 GF Lungu, 'Zambia: Civil society in the aftermath of political transition', Paper presented at a conference on "Consolidating Democracy: What Role for Civil Society?", Cape Town, 14–15 August 1996.

13 Beetham 1994, pp 160–161.

14 R Sandbrook, 'Liberal Democracy in Africa: A socialist-revisionist perspective', *Canadian Journal of African Studies*, vol 22, no 2, 1988, p 243.

15 E Osaghae, 'Democratisation in Sub-Saharan Africa: Faltering prospects, new hopes', *Journal of Contemporary African Studies*, vol 17, no 1, 1999; Nzongola-Ntalaja 1997, pp 19–20.

16 A Prezeworski, M Alvarez, JA Cheibub and F Limongi, "What makes democracies endure?", *Journal of Democracy*, vol 7, no 1, 1996.

17 SM Lipset, *Political Man*, London: Heinemann, 1960.

18   SADC, *SADC Regional Human Development Report 1998*, Harare: SAPES
     Books, 1998, p 25.
19   *Ibid.*, p 162.
20   JK Akokpari, 'A theoretical perspective on prospects for democratic stability
     in Lesotho', *Lesotho Social Science Review*, vol 4, no 2, 1998a.
21   TP Sevigny, 'From Crisis to Consensus: The United Nations and the challenge
     of development', New York: UN Department of Public Information, 1990;
     D Smith, 'Conflicts and Wars', in S George (ed), *The Debt Boomerang: How
     Third World debt harms us all*, London: Pluto, 1992; MB Brown, *Africa's
     Choices: After thirty years of the World Bank*, Harmondsworth: Penguin, 1995.
22   Osaghae 1999, p 16.
23   Du Toit 1999, p 211.
24   P Sekatle, 'The political dynamics of the 1998 elections in Lesotho', Paper
     presented at the SARIPS Regional Conference on "The Lesotho Crisis",
     Maseru, 5–6 February 1999.
25   K Matlosa, 'Globalisation and Regional Security: Southern Africa at the
     Crossroads', Paper presented at the SARIPS Annual Colloquium on "Peace
     and Security in Southern Africa: Challenges and Opportunities", Harare,
     26–30 September 1999b, p 7.
26   M Doornbos, 'The African state in academic debate: Retrospect and
     prospect', *Journal of Modern African Studies*, vol 28, no 2, June 1990; DA
     Lake and D Rothchild, 'Containing fear: The origins and management of eth-
     nic conflicts', *International Security*, vol 21, no 2, Fall 1996; JK Akokpari,
     'The state, refugees and migration in sub-Saharan Africa', *International
     Migration Review*, vol 36, no 2, 1998b.
27   R Sandbrook, *The Politics of Africa's Economic Stagnation*, Cambridge:
     Cambridge University Press, 1985.
28   *Sunday Times* (Johannesburg), 9 August 1999, p 4.
29   J Haynes, 'Ghana: indebtedness, recovery and the IMF 1977–1987', in TW
     Parfitt and SP Riley (eds), *The African Debt Crisis*, London: Routledge, 1989;
     JK Akokpari, 'Structural adjustments in Africa: Rethinking Ghana's "success
     story"', *International Insights*, vol 12, no 2, 1996b.
30   TM Callaghy, 'Lost between state and market: The politics of economic
     adjustment in Ghana, Zambia and Nigeria', in JM Nelson (ed), *Economic
     Crisis and Policy Choice in the Third World*, Princeton: Princeton University
     Press, 1990.
31   T Mkandawire, 'Adjustment, political conditionality and democratisation in
     Africa', in E Chole and J Ibrahim (eds), *Democratisation Processes in Africa:
     Problems and Prospects*, Dakar: CODESRIA, 1999, p 85.
32   C Ake, *Democracy and Development in Africa*, Washington DC: Brookings
     Institute, 1996, p 106.

33   A Agyeman-Duah and C Daddieh, 'Ghana', in T Shaw and J Okolo (eds), *The Foreign Policies of ECOWAS*, London: Macmillan, 1994; J Kraus, 'The political economy of African regional policies: Marginality and dependence, realism and choice', in T Shaw and J Okolo (eds). *The Foregn Policies of ECOWAS*. London: Macmillan, 1994.

34   Nzongola-Ntalaja 1997, p 17.

35   World Commission on Environment and Development, *Our Common Future*, New York: Oxford University Press, 1990, p 28.

36   *Current UK and Ireland Headlines*, 30 December 1997; *Pretoria News*, 9 September 1997, p 2.

37   F Makoa, 'Election dispute and external military intervention in Lesotho', Paper presented at the SARIPS Regional Conference on "The Lesotho Crisis", Maseru, 5–6 February 1999.

Unhygienic Political Language: A Threat to Democracy in Malawi

Gregory H Kamwendo

Malawi's political history can be divided into three epochs, that is the colonial period (1891–1964), the one-party dictatorial era (1964–1994), and the multi-party, democratic period (1994 to the present). During the dictatorial single party era, the vast majority of Malawians failed to enjoy many of their basic human rights and freedoms due to the dictatorial presidency of Dr Hastings Banda. The culture of democracy, freedom and human rights was ushered in only after the first post-independence general elections were held in 1994. In these elections, Banda's Malawi Congress Party lost its 30-year old grip on Malawi and the United Democratic Front (UDF), led by Bakili Muluzi, came to power. The second post-independence multi-party general elections were held in 1999, and resulted in the UDF retaining power in what the opposition described as controversial polls.

Malawian politics is heavily regulated by ethnic, regional and party affiliations. The voting patterns of the 1994 and 1999 general elections testify to this claim.[1] The question of national unity is certainly of prime importance in this context. Ethnic and political divisions among Malawians have created a culture of intolerance, hostility and in some cases violence. What is observed is that it is political language which reinforces the regionalistic, divisive and intolerant political tendencies. This undesirable political culture has been partly reinforced by politicians' use of foul, inflammatory and intimidatory language. The relationship between political language on the one hand, and political tolerance and national reconciliation on the other hand, has attracted the attention of people of different pursuits in Malawi. These have included academics, human rights activists and election monitors.[2]

This chapter endeavours to demonstrate that such language is a serious threat to Malawi's young democracy. It advances the view that politicians' use of foul, intimidatory or inflammatory language is a serious impediment to the promotion of the culture of democracy in Malawi. To do so, we present an overview of what we term 'unhygienic' political speech, using the Rwandan genocide, which was partly fuelled by political hate speech, as a case study. This is followed by an analysis of political hate speech during Malawi's one-party dictatorship, especially the pro-multi-partyism campaigns in the early 1990s. Unhygienic political speech, however, did not end with the demise of the one-party dictatorship. Rather, it has found its way into the multi-party democracy era. The crucial role the language of the mass media plays in shaping people's political stances, particularly partisan reporting and use of politically unfriendly language, is also noted as having strengthened the culture of political intolerance and violence in Malawi.

Hate speech: an overview

The use of inflammatory, provocative, confrontational or foul language by politicians in Malawi stands out as one of the major threats to Malawi's young and delicate democracy. This type of language has great potential to ignite political violence. For example, during the campaign period in the run-up to Malawi's second post-independence general elections in 1999, and even in the period soon after the announcement of the election results, Malawi witnessed some disturbing waves of politically motivated violence. The most pronounced cases of violence were witnessed in Northern Malawi, where Malawi Congress Party (MCP) and Alliance for Democracy (AFORD) supporters refused to accept the results of the elections, alleging that the electoral system had been rigged by the ruling party, the United Democratic Front (UDF). To this end, UDF supporters and sympathisers were physically harassed or had their property destroyed by members of the opposition parties. Whilst we acknowledge that no single factor is entirely responsible for triggering these waves of violence, we cannot fail to recognise the catalyst role the inflammatory political language factor played. Chimombo claims that "even in the long established democracies, a disturbing rise in hate speech leading to violence has served to emphasise that speech can, and often does, provoke action while in certain particularly troubled areas, discourse has even been linked to genocide".[3] Malawian politicians, from both the ruling and opposition parties, are guilty of using politically inflammatory language which in turn incites or encourages or justifies violence.

Malawi has changed from a 30-year old dictatorship to an open society under the banner of democracy. The current democratic culture has been marred by the abuse of freedom of expression. The end product is that the political arena is full of sour, hate or unfriendly language which, in turn, leads to violence: "Hate speech, as Americans call it, is a troubling matter for people who believe in free speech. It is abusive, insulting, intimidating and harassing and may lead to violence, hatred or discrimination; and it kills." Owen goes on to observe as follows:

> Free speech is thought of as sacred to a democratic society, as the freedom upon which all others depend. But in a world where the effects of speech

that fosters hatred are all too visible, there are two difficult questions that must be asked about the defence of free expression: At whose pain?[4]

There is documented evidence that hate speech incited the Rwanda geno-cide. Nearly a million people were butchered in 1994. The bloody Hutu/Tutsi massacre started after the death, in a plane crash, of President Habriyamana. During the political turmoil following the death of the pres-ident, Hutu extremist politicians who were close to the assassinated pres-ident used a radio station they owned – radio RTLM – to incite ethnic killings. McCullum describes the role of radio RTLM as follows:

> Its pattern of brainwashing in a country where more than 60 percent of adults is illiterate created a climate of mass hysteria. Daily it broadcast a constant stream of hate propaganda and anti-opposition invective, frighteningly remi-niscent of the 'big lie' techniques of Josef Goebeles (sic) in Nazi Germany and the anti-Communist vitriol of the McCarthy era in the US. RTLM's hate dis-semination was constant: hour after hour it referred to opposition politicians as 'enemies' and 'traitors' who 'deserved to die'. The broadcasts were based on the notion of repetition of dehumanising propaganda which referred to all Tutsis as 'cockroaches' (*inyezi* became a code word for crushing Tutsis and moderate Hutus), 'snakes' and 'animals'.[5]

Unhygienic political speech in Malawi

In general, in Malawi some people tend to treat rights and freedoms as if they have no limitations or qualifications. Another often forgotten fact is that rights entail responsibilities. The irresponsible use of freedom of expression in the form of defamation, for example, can attract a legal suit. Freedom of expression is often mistaken to be the freedom to insult oth-ers, thereby making them lose face unjustifiably.

The Single Party Dictatorship Era

A type of hate speech similar to the Rwandan case was noted during Malawi's transition from a one-party to a multi-party state. Supporters of the one-party regime waged vehement verbal attacks on multi-party advo-cates. The latter received a wide range of negative names such as *anyani* or *ankhweri* (Chichewa words for monkeys), or *abongololo* (millipedes).[6] In English, the multi-party advocates were described as disgruntled elements, confusionists, rebels or dissidents who deserved to be dealt with without mercy. The one-party state regarded multi-party advocates as a serious threat to national peace and security. As such, a number of multi-party advocates were detained, tortured or killed, and some lost their jobs or property. The one-party regime used its notorious secret service to silence the multi-party advocates. For a detailed account of how the one-party regime in Malawi brutally silenced multi-party advocates, one can refer to various chapters in Nzunda and Ross.[7]

The MCP leaders, at various levels, used foul language against anyone with a dissenting political view. For example, in 1992 the Catholic Church in Malawi, through its bishops, issued a pastoral letter which exposed and condemned the various injustices and vices of the MCP government. The pastoral letter called for reforms of socio-economic and political policies of the country. In response, the MCP government described the pastoral letter as a seditious document whose ultimate goal was to incite Malawians into rebellion against President Banda. The MCP then castigated the Church and its bishops using foul language. For example, the Bishops were described as *zitsiru* (fools), *agalu* (dogs), *akapirikoni* (rebels) or as *ziboliboli* (curios), among others. One female MCP leader even went to the extent of threatening to *kukodzera ma Bishop mkamwa* (which means to urinate into the Bishops' mouths). As a result of such discourse of threats, denigration, and outright obscenity, some political thugs took the law into their own hands and this led to some of the Catholic Church's structures being subjected to malicious attacks. For example, there was an attempt to set ablaze the Balaka printing press which had printed the pastoral letter. Furthermore, a special MCP convention even resolved to have the bishops killed.

In all these physical and verbal attacks on the Catholic Church, political language played a role as catalyst. Politicians who supported the one-party regime tried as much as possible to use intimidatory political language in order to discourage people from embracing multi-partyism. President Banda joined the verbal warfare against multi-partyism by declaring that there was no room for multi-partyism in Malawi, adding that the "confusionists" behind the multi-party movement deserved to rot in prison or to be thrown into the Shire River as "meat for crocodiles". A number of Malawi Congress Party leaders used Banda's political rallies as forums for waging sour verbal warfare against the multi-party advocates and other political rivals. Even today, in the new political dispensation, politicians from the ruling UDF take advantage of Muluzi's rallies to defame and castigate political rivals.

Due to immense pressure, the MCP government hosted a national referendum in 1993 to decide whether or not Malawi was to change from a one-party state to multi-partyism. Two thirds of the votes went in favour of multi-partyism. The following year witnessed the first post-independence multi-party elections. One of the two major opposition parties, the United Democratic Front, led by Bakili Muluzi, won the elections. Banda,

in turn, honourably accepted defeat. Given that Banda accepted the election results, his supporters did not find any justification for perpetrating any
form of violence. However, history was to repeat itself with the 1999 elections being accompanied by an alarming degree of political violence.

The Multiparty Democracy Era

The first five years of multipartyism (1994–1999) were characterised by
political discourse which was aimed at unwarranted character assassination. Political platforms and the print and electronic media were used as
tools for waging this verbal warfare. Tensions between the ruling party and
the opposition parties grew as time went by. As Malawi approached its
second multi-party elections in 1999, the stage for conflict had been set.
The hate speech which had filled the election campaign period provided
the fuel which finally set off some politically motivated waves of violence.
As Malawians went to the polls in 1999, the country was already divided
along ethnic, party, and regional lines. The Alliance for Democracy was
branded *chipani cha Atumbuka* (a party of the Tumbukas) whilst the UDF
was branded the *chipani cha Achawa* (a party of the Achawas.) Achawa is
a derogatory name for the Yaos. In addition the UDF government was
branded *boma la Aachawa* (government of Achawas), while the Yaos
bragged that *wachiyaowangalusa* (a Yao never loses), and even that they
were *asiyene chilambo* (owners of the land), given that the state president
is a Yao. The opposition was branded as *otsutsa boma*, literally meaning one
who opposed whatever the government side said or did. From 1994 to the
present, the rift between government and the opposition has grown so
wide that in the minds of the ordinary villagers, government and the opposition are natural enemies. The opposition has kept on accusing the ruling
party of being made up of liars, thieves, and corrupt persons who have
"failed to deliver the goods". On its part, the ruling party accuses the
opposition of lacking constructive ideas and working tirelessly to discredit
the ruling party's achievements.

The wish of Malawi's electoral commission and the election monitoring
agencies was to have free and fair elections in 1999. Political leaders were
advised "to be tolerant of each other and [to] avoid abusive, divisive or
inflammatory language which is a great source of violence by their supporters during the campaign period".[8] Diana Cammack advised candidates "not
to use hate speech or threats of war or violence to get people to vote for
them".[9] For example, some of the opposition leaders were reported to have
threatened *kulowa mthengo* (literally meaning to go into the bush) if they
lost the elections. In retaliation, President Muluzi threatened to bring *ndege
zopand' mapiko* (wingless planes) into Malawi to deal with any armed rebels.

Mawaya quotes George Claver as having advised politicians to "use language that will unite, not divide, language that will lead to political tolerance". In the same article, Mawaya quotes Victor Kamanga as having observed that politicians "have used language that lacks respect for individuals, breeds deep trenches of division ... language used by politicians in Malawi has been a language of threats, language that stops at the edge of war".[10]

The political tension and the politically motivated violence, which erupted in some quarters of Malawi soon after the 1999 elections, prompted the Censorship Board to issue a press release in the *Weekly News* as follows:

> Hate songs, violent songs, hate speeches, hate talk, hate articles in papers, hate interviews on the radio or television do not promote peace and love and therefore should not be condoned or promoted by any peace loving Malawian.[11]

President Muluzi, in a move to demonstrate his dislike of hate political language, ordered UDF followers to refrain from castigating or abusing their political rivals through songs. During the 1999 independence celebrations, the president ordered a group of dancers to stop abusing the then leader of the opposition, Gwanda Chakuamba, in their songs. The president advised the dancers to focus their songs on development issues and not character assassination.

The language of the mass media

It is well established globally that the mass media plays a crucial role in shaping the political opinion of people. To this end, in many African countries, governments control the media and the same media is used for destroying the opposition. Under both the one-party state and the newly gained democratic dispensation, the national electronic media in Malawi has never been fully free of government control and is used for supporting the ruling party's agenda.[12]

The print media's coverage of the 1999 general elections was particularly partisan. Articles from 19 press monitoring reports cited by Patel, for example, indicate that:

• *The Chronicle* was identified as a paper with "some sensational and hate provoking reporting";
• *The UDF News* was reported to carry "one-sided and opinionated stories that vilify the opposition parties and their leading personalities. The language used is that of violence and hatred";
• *National Agenda* uses "inflammatory and derogatory language against the UDF and its leaders. It paints a bad image of the government while it supports and promotes the opposition MCP";

- *The Nation*, despite having some problems of lack of neutrality, is "more carefully worded … more professional, factual and sets up a good precedent for a professional culture";
- *Daily Times* was noted to carry "regular attacks on the UDF and its personalities … The general outlook of *Daily Times* during the period under review is that of a strongly anti-government with a posture of troubleshooter in nearly all stories. The paper supports the opposition MCP and its leadership".[13]

Malawi News is not different from the *Daily Times* given that one company, Blantyre Newspapers Company Limited, produces both. After the 1999 elections, these two papers have significantly moved towards more professionalism, thereby striving to present balanced accounts of stories. In fact, in 2000, the *Malawi News* was voted newspaper of the year in a competition organised by the Malawi Broadcasting Corporation.

Conclusion

Consistent with Kayambazinthu and Moyo, this chapter has noted that the culture of hate speech in Malawian politics was in existence even before the birth of the new democratic dispensation.[14] The advent of democracy has not stopped the use of hate speech in politics. Rather, it has strengthened the culture of political hate speech. Hate speech is now being used under the disguise of freedom of expression. This freedom of speech has been grossly abused by both the UDF and the opposition parties.[15] It is unfortunate that in some academic quarters the role played by the UDF in promoting or condoning hate speech or politically unhygienic language has been so magnified that the opposition's own share in this enterprise has been downplayed. For example, Kayambazinthu and Moyo fail to report on the threats of war which were uttered by opposition leaders such as Chakufwa Chihana, Gwanda Chakuamba and Kamlepo Kalua.[16]

We maintain that political discourse has the power to build or destroy a nation's unity. This being the case, politicians have to be careful with the way they handle language. Mdee, writing about Tanzania, describes a situation which is very close to the Malawian context:

> Political opponents are seen as political foes and not as colleagues with different points of view. With this misconception we see every party attempting to destroy one another in public speeches. This is the misuse of freedom of speech. We noted in the introduction that free speech contributes to political freedom which gives one the right to criticise government and other party policies but as we have seen this freedom has been used as the right to

scandalise and insult others. Calling people fools, stupid, parrot, hooligans, evil spirit, power hungry, cheaters is not an appropriate language for politicians to use at public rallies.[17]

The use of derogatory or obscene language against a political rival is obviously a threatening act. The use of threats of war, insults or vulgar language is detrimental to the positive face of both the speaker and the target. The positive face, as used in Brown's and Levinson's politeness theory, represents the human desire to be liked, loved or appreciated by others. By attacking a political rival through the use of foul language, the speaker threatens his victim's positive face (the desire to be appreciated or liked) as well as his own positive face. In other words, by trying to destroy the image of his or her rival, the speaker in the process also destroys his or her own positive face. Thus, the politician needs to care about face saving.[18]

If democracy is to grow well in Malawi, and in other African nations, then the political discourse has to undergo serious changes to reflect a culture of transparency, unity and honesty. The newly gained freedom of expression should not be misused and abused as the right to abuse others. Human rights have to be carefully balanced with responsibilities. The violence in Rwanda, for example, was to some extent fuelled by the use of defamatory, derogatory or profane language against political rivals. It is significant to bear in mind that "politicians' bad reputation concerning their political conduct is to a large extent due to the way they use language".[19]

Notes and References

1   See WC Chirwa, 'The politics of ethnicity and regionalism in contemporary Malawi', *African Rural and Urban Studies*, vol 1, no 2, 1994; KM Phiri and KR Ross (eds), *Democratization in Malawi: A Stocktaking*, Blantyre: CLAIM, 1998; D Kaspin, 'The politics of ethnicity in Malawi's democratic transition', *Journal of Modern African Studies*, vol 33, no 4, 1995.

2   See e.g. G Kamwendo, 'Uses and abuses of language during election campaignss', in M Ott *et al* (eds), *Malawi's Second Democratic Elections: Process, Problems and Prospects*, Blantyre: CLAIM, 2000; N Patel, 'Media in the democratic and electoral process', in M Ott *et al* (eds), *Malawi's Second Democratic Elections: Process, Problems and Prospects*, Blantyre: CLAIM, 2000; E Kayambazinthu and F Moyo, 'Language and violence in Malawian political discourse: A contemporary historical and ethical perspective', Paper presented at the International Conference on Historical and Social Science Research in Malawi, Chancellor College, 26–29 June 2000; P Ngulube-Chinoko, 'Verbal Pollution: A serious impediment to democracy and national reconciliation', *Hope*, vol 1, no 4, 1999; P Mawaya, 'Election jitters face

Malawi', *The Lamp*, no 15, 1999; G Dambula, 'Voting is our duty', *The Lamp*, no 17, 1999; D Cammack, 'Levelling the field for all to play', *The Lamp*, no 17, 1999.

3 M Chimombo, 'Language and Politics', *Applied Linguistics*, vol 19, 1999, p 215.

4 U Owen, 'The speech that kills', *Index on Censorship*, vol 27, no 11, 1998, pp 32–33.

5 H McCullum, 'The angels leave Rwanda', *IAJ Journal for Journalists in Southern Africa*, vol 1, no 1, 1995, p 29.

6 S Chimombo and M Chimombo, *The culture of democracy: Language, literature, the arts and politics in Malawi 1992–94*, Zomba: WASI Publications, 1996; G Kamwendo, 'The impact of democracy on English: The case of vocabulary', *Marang*, Special Issue, 1999; PJ Kishindo, 'Evolution of political terminology in Chichewa and the changing political culture in Malawi', *Nordic Journal of African Studies*, vol 9, no 2.

7 M Nzunda and KR Ross (eds), *Church, law and political transition in Malawi 1992–94*, Gweru: Mambo Press, 1995.

8 Dambula 1999, p 5.

9 Cammack 1999, p 4.

10 Mawaya 1999, p 7.

11 Cited by Kayambazinthu and Moyo 2000, p 1.

12 Patel 2000; Kamwendo 2000.

13 Patel 2000, pp 177–179.

14 Kayambazinthu and Moyo 2000.

15 Kamwendo 2000.

16 Kayambazinthu and Moyo 2000.

17 J Mdee, 'Multiparty democracy and the use of language in political discourse', Paper presented at the 35th Anniversary of the Faculty of Humanities and Social Science, University of Dar es Salaam, Tanzania, 1999, p 12.

18 P Brown and S Levinson, *Politeness: Some universals in language use*, Cambridge: Cambridge University Press, 1987.

19 W Holly, 'Credibility and political language', in R Wodak (ed), *Language, Power and Ideology: Studies in Political Discourse*, Amsterdam: John Benjamins, 1989, p 115.

Anthems, Flags, Symbols and the Spirit of African Nationhood

Kwaku Asante-Darko

The messages presented in national anthems and flags are not comprehensive mission statements. They are, nonetheless, illustrative of the historical experiences as well as the wishes and aspirations of the political
entities concerned. Generally, anthems reveal a nation's conception of
nationhood, ideal governance, socio-economic organisation, and foreign
policy preferences. The anthem is said to be an "official national song honouring the spirit of the native land". The effective role of literary aesthet-
ics in honouring the native land for political, economic, and social purposes
is partly seen in the importance accorded to national anthems as the
embodiment of nationhood. Joseph has noted that:

> ... we should keep in mind that traditionally, Africans do not radically sepa-
> rate art from teaching. Rather than write or sing for beauty, the African writ-
> ers, taking their cue from oral literature, use beauty to communicate impor-
> tant truths and information to society. Indeed, an object is considered beau-
> tiful because of the truths it reveals and the community it helps to build. As
> someone once said, for an African mask to be beautiful, one must believe in
> the being for which it stands.[1]

This is also applicable to the status and role of African national anthems.
This chapter analyses the extent to which the anthems of the newly independent African nations reflect the attempt to address the contradictions
of national consciousness and nation building. We identify and analyse the
contents of these anthems so as to explain the relative abundance of certain themes in relation to others which are virtually absent, such as issues
of gender, race, gratitude, and governance. We also trace the underlying
influence responsible for the overbearing preoccupation with anti-colonial
freedom in these anthems.

The method includes an appreciation of the stylistic significance of the
poetic devices that have gone into the composition of these poems (for that
is what anthems are). The material analysed is a selection of national
anthems from Namibia, Swaziland, Ghana, the Democratic Republic of
Congo, Zimbabwe, Liberia, Sierra Leone and Uganda. We demonstrate
that the themes of these anthems over-emphasise nationalism and freedom

from colonial or racial domination to the neglect of any concrete and pro-found concerns for multi-ethnic inclusiveness, tolerance in matters of governance, and a commitment to democratic traditions in the new states.

We show that the general marginalisation, not to say complete absence, of these vital dimensions of nationhood in African national anthems is indicative of the fact that the new states did not possess enough historical and political commonality to evoke in their anthems and represent in their quest for multi-ethnic nationhood. The chapter further demonstrates that these observations have far-reaching implications for nation-building strategies in Africa, especially in light of the virtual collapse or vacillation of the African state, as demonstrated by the recent experiences of Liberia, Sierra Leone, Somalia, and the DRC. We conclude that a general re-writing of African national anthems to reflect the continent's most recent post-independence experiences and challenges is not only desirable, but also both legitimate and understandable.

Rituals, Poetry and Nationalism

A national anthem is neither a manifesto nor a preamble to a national constitution. It is, by its very structure and content, a symbolic expression of the wishes and aspirations of the nation. Like any other poem, an anthem chants the inner feelings of the persona. There is in this sense a ritualistic dimension to its performance. Many African national anthems indicate simultaneously the dissolution of colonial rule and the (re)appropriation of the post-colonial state, as well as the baptism of the people into one collective whole. In this respect, anthems are poems that do not only try to define the sense and purpose of the national entity but also to arouse emotions intended to impart strength for the nation's endeavour and sustainability.

The appeal of the national anthem is thus closely related to, if not derived from, the creative prowess associated with the practice of poetry. This is because poetry, even in its most secular form, betrays an enterprise susceptible to the seeming invocation of extra-human assistance. It is not surprising therefore if Jacobson notes, concerning the role of poetry in the religious practices in ancient Mesopotamia, that:

> Poetry was another means of invoking the presence of powers for word picture, too, created the corresponding reality. This is clear in the incantation, which often used the form of command to exhort evil forces to go away.[2]

The quest for the strength and resources of holding the new nations together required an emotional element. This element served to enhance the nation's capacity to inculcate its values and ideals into a broad section of the community. The need for the maintenance of the hard-won freedom finds expression in a consecration of the nation to the power of God. Even when the national song marginalises the existence and role of spiritual forces in the nation's development, it is infused with extra power supposedly derived from the new entity/state and the political organisation with whose guidance and backing the will of the people is expected to prevail. This is seen in the anthem of Marxist Mozambique, in particular in these words:

> Long live FRELIMO,
> Guide of the Mozambican people,
> Heroic people who, gun in hand,
> Toppled colonialism.
> All the People united
> From the Rovuma to the Maputo,
> Struggle against imperialism
> And continue, and shall win.[3]

Here, the guidance of the ruling party is evoked as derived from the invincibility or immortality of the force of the people. Guns and a united people are here presented as the fountainhead of the current that sweeps away "imperialism". We equally see from these lines the fact that the unity of the nation is being constructed on a shared hatred for "colonialism". It must be noted however that the appeal to the people's sense of enmity as a source of national mobilisation is not peculiar to African anthems.

The excitement and anxiety that accompanied the advent of independence found expression in the revival of traditional African cultural values. This is partly because the sense of glory associated with nationhood and freedom in the new African states could not be borrowed from the Europeans, who had often looked down on African cultural institutions and treated them with ridicule and contempt. It is obvious that the literary content of these anthems or songs or poems composed to celebrate freedom from foreign oppression contained elements which were authentically African, and specifically framed to oppose or contest European misconceptions about Africans and their history, their past, and their present. An observant commentator has noted that:

> All oral African literature ... is in the final analysis, poetical. It is poetical in the broadest sense of the word, that is to say, if one takes into account the emotive content and the use, nature, frequency, ingeniousness and richness of images and metaphors. These images are often expressed by mean of words that are known as "ideophones", and have no equivalents outside Africa.[4]

The emotive elements of Frelimo uniting an oppressed people of the land between the Rovuma and the Moputo evokes feelings of patriotism and courage in a fight for victory over forces which the persona implicitly underlines as evil by definition. The themes of victory, unity, patriotism, and freedom thus become central to the aesthetic ritual of the anthems of independent African countries.

Ecology

Ecological concern in these anthems has a pan-African inspiration, which the second Pan-African Congress of 1919 noted in the following words:

> The land and its natural resources should be held in trust for the natives ... The investment of capital and the granting of concessions should be regulated so as to prevent the spoliation of the natives and the exhaustion of natural wealth.[5]

Reference to the dependence on nature and the recognition that it is exhaustible and therefore, must be taken good care of is implied in a range of African anthems. The message of African national anthems also embodies an ecological dimension, which is closely linked to the tradition of communal ownership of land, and is consistent with the animistic pantheistic elements of African social organisation and beliefs. The essentially agrarian nature of African economic activity and the consequent primary attachment to the land is consistent with the reference made to the land, resources, and landscape in these anthems. The anthems of Namibia, Malawi, and Guinea Bissau, for instance, make reference to the importance of the land and evoke the nation's dependence on immense resources and vegetation which, they imply, must be exploited for the benefit of their people:

> Our own Malawi, this land so fair,
> Fertile and brave and free.
> With its lakes, refreshing mountain air,
> How greatly blest are we.
> Hills and valleys, soil so rich and rare,
> Give us a bounty free.
> Wood and forest, plains so broad and fair,
> All-beauteous Malawi.[6]

This section of Malawi's national anthem presents, in metaphorical terms, the land as the primary sustenance of the people. The land becomes the symbol of national independence and is made synonymous with the people. That the land is a literal object is demonstrated by the evocation of its fertility. It is personified as land "with its lakes, refreshing mountain air" as can also be seen in the reference to its being "brave and free".

This idea of land as a metaphor of independence is also found in the national anthems of Guinea Bissau and Namibia. In both instances the beauty of the landscape – revealed in references to "sun", "verdure", "fruit", and "flower" – is depicted as the element needed for the continuation of the human lineage. Here, by stating the obvious – that people depend on land for sustenance – the persona acknowledges the ecological importance of land use but more importantly, the centrality of land as a motivation in the struggle for independence is emphasised. The message is that any reckless handling of the environment and its resources could result in unfathomable disaster for the human community, but also that a people dispossessed of their land is worse than the dead who at least own their graves. The anthem of Guinea Bissau depicts this notion in the verse which reads:

> Sun, sweat, verdure and sea,
> Centuries of pain and hope;
> This is the land of our ancestors.
> Fruit of our hands,
> Of the flower of our blood,
> This is our beloved country.[7]

This reference to the land equally brings to mind the ecological concerns which have been evident in the poetry of traditional Africa, with its constant reference to flora and fauna metaphors. Asante-Darko notes in this regard:

> It was the central role of oral literature to create, nurture, and nourish the taboos that protect the environment from human abuse, and avert any reckless acts of abuse that could compromise environmental sustainability and occasion any disaster and human catastrophe.[8]

Nationalism and Pan-Africanism

It is therefore understandable that the identification of land and nation in African thought made the theme of nationalism one of the cardinal themes of African national anthems. It was not only seen as an instrument for anticolonial struggle but also as a means of satisfying the quest for national unity among the multi-ethnic entities of the newly formed nations. It was, thus, intended to cater for a dual motivation. First, it was demonstrative of Africa's quest for self-advancement, which was believed to be feasible only in the context of a new multi-ethnic nationhood. Second, it was a reaction against European degradation of Africans and their culture. It is from this perspective that the claim that African national consciousness is essentially or even initially an European provocation, as Sartre, for instance, does in "Orphée Noir", disregards the fact that this nationalist flavour was in part a form of nostalgic quest for the pre-colonial nations in which Africans had lived for centuries. The commonality of the colonial experience drove home the need for concert among Africans in their endeavour to effect a continental revolution. Kwame Nkrumah, for instance, noted in 1957 that, "The independence of Ghana is meaningless unless it is linked up with the total liberation of the African continent".[9] He proceeded to propose a union of African states which, for want of support, was compromised for an association of African heads of states called the Organisation of African Unity (OAU).

The idea of a unified government for Africa was sometimes miscon- strued as a scheme for the so-called domination of some states by others. As early as 1960 ,Tafawa Balewa had declared that:

> A united States of Africa? Oh, surely it is very premature to start talking about anything like that. Nigeria has not the slightest intention of surrender- ing her sovereignty, no sooner has she gained independence, to anyone else, including other West African countries.[10]

Such views have not completely daunted the pan-African aspiration nor negated the justification that "salvation for Africa lies in unity". Having per- ceived individual national efforts as limited and inadequate to meet the aspi- rations of the continent, several African nations made reference, in their anthems, to the need for a wider concerted effort to conduct their struggle for nation-building and economic development on a continental scale.

The roots of the message of these anthems were really pan-African. They echo the notions and concerns outlined at the 1900 pan-African Congress organised by the Trinidad barrister, H Sylvester Williams. They also present the petitions of several meetings of the African intelligentsia such as those organised at the Sorbonne in Paris in 1956, and in Rome in 1959 under the auspices of the Literary Association, Présence Africaine, whose editorial commented as follows: "The conference elucidated basic truths which can be briefly summarised as follows: 1. No nation without a culture; 2. No culture without a past; 3. No authentic cultural liberation without political liberation first."[11]

It is equally significant to note that the Rome Congress on its part stat- ed in its general resolution that:

> ... Political independence and economic freedom are the indispensable pre- requisites of fecund cultural development in underdeveloped countries in general and in the countries of black Africa in particular.[12]

The anthems of Ghana and Mali in particular illustrate this point and ele- vate post-colonial reconstruction to the status of a concerted continental agenda. Particular mention is made of the Black Star as a symbol of Africa's hope. The symbolism of the Black Star may not correspond to any astronomical reality, unless it is viewed against the background of the symbol of the sunshine, which indicates an instance of complete clarity. It will be understood to mean that when the full truth about human nature is revealed in the eternal light, the Black Star will be seen against "the bright background of the eternal sunshine". The advance and victory of Africa is thus seen to be certain and inevitable. Accordingly, the second stanza of Ghana's national anthem states:

> Raise high the flag of Ghana
> And one with Africa advance;
> Black Star of hope and honour
> To all who thirst for Liberty;
> Where the banner of Ghana freely flies,
> May the way to freedom truly lie;
> Arise, arise, O sons of Ghanaland,
> And under God march on for evermore![13]

The persona's use of the words "high", "advance", "hope", "honour", and "liberty" implies a recognition of the conditions of Africa which is described implicitly as low, dishonoured and dominated.

Mali's anthem reinforces the idea of pan-African advancement by indicating that the "refound dignity" that independence is expected to bring will be achieved when Africans "together arise … to make a united Africa". It is in view of this that the flags of Ghana, Guinea, and Mali have been adopted from the red, yellow, and green colours of Ethiopia.[14] Part of the Malian national anthem, which advocates unity, faith, and hard work towards African unity, goes as follows:

> L'Afrique se lève enfin
> Saluons ce jour nouveau.
> Saluons la liberté,
> Marchons vers l'unité.
> Dignité retrouvée
> Soutient notre combat.
> Fidelès à notre serment
> De faire l'Afrique unie
> Ensemble, debout mes frères
> Tous au rendez-vous de l'honneur.
>
> Africa is at last arising,
> Let us greet this new day.

Let us greet freedom,
Let us march towards unity.
Refound dignity
Supports our struggle.
Faithful to our oath
To make a united Africa,
Together, arise, my brothers,
All to the place where honour calls.[15]

The Ghana-Guinea-Mali Union created in 1958 as a nucleus of a pan-African nation was a concrete but unfruitful realisation of the idea that the messages of anthems often go far beyond wishes, music and ceremony. The disarray that followed the bloc alliances of Casablanca, Brazzaville, and Monrovia, however, demonstrated the frailty of the commitment to unity. There nonetheless remained the astonishing commitment to the conviction that armed struggle was the primary means of Africa's liberation, and on this there was general agreement.

Militarism

African rejection of colonial oppression was done in the knowledge that the fight against colonialism was right. However, this notion of a 'just war' was not enough to give rise to the temerity with which they decided to liberate themselves from the humiliation of the shackles of foreign rule. There was also some reliance on arms as instruments of liberation. Hoffer has noted that:

> For men to plunge headlong into an undertaking of vast change, they must be intensely discontented yet not destitute, and they must have the feeling that by the possession of some potent doctrine, infallible leader or some new technique they have access to a source of irresistible power. They must also have an extravagant conception of the prospects and potentialities of the future. Finally, they must be wholly ignorant of the difficulties involved in their vast undertaking. Experience is a handicap. The men who started the French Revolution were wholly without political experience.[16]

The primacy of power has found expression in the adoration of military might. The anthems of countries where armed struggle was the main means of political liberation contain elements of the adoration of military might. The examples of Mozambique, Angola and Guinea Bissau testify to this. In all these instances there was reliance on military power as a major source of freedom and transformation.

It must also be mentioned that the prominence of the idea of armed struggle is consistent with the position of the 1945 Pan-African Congress in Manchester, where African intellectuals and opinion leaders expressed the idea that: "We are determined to be free, if the Western world is still determined to rule Mankind by force, then Africa, *as a last resort*, may have to appeal to force in the effort to achieve freedom …".[17]

The fact that these anthems uphold violence is indicative of the constant sense of struggle and vigilance that have guided and continue to guide Africa's liberation and reconstruction. The notion of a just war and its psychology of struggle permeate the national psyche of African states in a manner that is virtually indissociable from the songs that express the historical experience of the people. These songs reflect the nature of the general mobilisation, in which gender was not a factor for exclusion.

Gender

In discussing the text of African national anthems one must equally evoke the absence of certain aspects of nation building. In this context gender issues are not given the prominence commensurate with the collective aspiration of a people emerging from oppression. The anthem of Malawi speaks of "… men and women united in the service of Malawi", while the chorus of the anthem of Botswana appeals as follows:

> Awake, awake, O men, awake!
> And women close beside them stand,
> Together we'll work and serve
> This land, this happy land![18]

This statement seems an exception to the realm of African anthems most of which refer to the nation as "fatherland" rather than "motherland". The mention of women in the national anthems of Malawi and Botswana is a refutation of the gross generalisation which presumes that African patriarchal society was unconcerned about the role of its womenfolk. The egalitarian implications thereof serve as a reminder that issues regarding the status of the African woman in post-colonial society have been tabled for debate in the new nations at independence. Some observers have pointed out that:

> Male nationalists frequently argue that colonialism or capitalism has been women's ruin, with patriarchy merely a nasty second cousin destined to wither away when the real villain expires. Yet nowhere has national or socialist revolution brought a full feminist revolution in its train. In many nationalist or socialist countries, women's concerns are at best paid lip service, at worst greeted with hilarity. If women have come to do men's work, men

have not come to share women's work. Nowhere has feminism in its own right been allowed to be more than the maidservant of nationalism.[19]

We will not get into the insinuation or import of a revolution in which men and women swap roles, or where "patriarchy" replaces "matriarchy" as the "maidservant" of nationalism under any economic system. It would be wrong to dismiss the above claims as some whimsical gossip of the male-hating rhetoric. The fact remains that the lot of the African woman has considerably improved in the years after independence. She has made socio-economic strides, which can incontestably be described as irreversible. This is applicable to both matrilineal and patriarchal communities in Africa. This strife for gender parity at the national level had a linguistic counterpart.

Language

Originally, these anthems were generally written in vernacular languages. The exceptions are few and they include Kenya, Lesotho, and Swaziland. The preponderance of foreign languages in the national anthems in many of Africa's new nations can be explained diversely. The reasons range from the need for the mobilisation of multi-lingual ethnic communities to the desire to make their complaints accessible to the coloniser. The borrowing of foreign languages to express African anti-colonial aspirations remains a subject of debate depicting the difficulties associated with national language policies in post-independence Africa. There was the reason of informing the outside world about Africa's agenda for its new-found freedom. The quest for an international audience equally explains why these anthems were in the official or colonial languages.

No Vote of Thanks

There is no implicit acknowledgement of any positive side to the colonial enterprise in these national anthems of Africa. To revolutionary Africa, colonisation was negative and evil. Basil Davidson has well indicated that:

> Contrary to the claims of its prophets, colonial rule did not 'civilise' Africa, or modernise Africa in any meaningful sense of the word, much less leave Africans with the mere job of taking over the prepared positions of a new social structure. ... For while colonial rule built a few roads and railways and opened a few mines and plantations (though for its own convenience and enrichment), dropping here and there a few crumbs of educational and social enlightenment, its central effect was one of dismantlement.[20]

The diabolic dimensions of colonisation had to be highlighted in the purpose of immediate and effective multi-ethnic mobilisation against it. Davidson himself identifies what he calls "Philanthropic individuals and institutions [who] may have worked hard for the good of Africans [but] their saving labour, though often brave and generous, could never be more than palliative and peripheral".[21] But the African revolution and renaissance was not nihilist. It is obvious that among many Africans, voices of gratitude existed on account of the "crumbs" whose effects were "palliative and peripheral" but they were treated as patently minimal and at odds with popular aspirations of the time and hence woefully out of order. For instance, a poet like Dei-Anang lauds the universality of the Commonwealth whose head he honours as "Queen of vast continents and seas/ whose loyal sons/ diverse in race,/ are one in unity,/ the world acclaims/ your majesty".[22] In 1952 Osadebey, on his part, had tempered vitriol with gratitude in his poem "England I love you and I fight for you" when he wrote: "Thank you Sons and daughters of Britannia, You gave me hospitals, You gave me schools ... Yours is the happiness of giving, The joy of doing good."[23]

The dominant voice in the anthems of independence revealed a preference for silence over the issues of colonial blessings. The reason is that these were generally seen to be inadvertent. The nationalist arguments were at best explicitly extenuating as the lines of Aimé Césaire, which draw a balance sheet of colonial deficit in favour of Africa, show. The broad nature of the issue he raised in this poem entitled *Discours sur le colonialisme*, demands extensive reference.[24] Advantages associated with the colonial enterprise such as health, formal education, roads constructed, raw materials exported, etc. are refuted with arguments of cultures that colonialism destroyed, technological potentialities it atrophied and suppressed, the inculcation of an inferiority complex, the institutionalisation of malnutrition, confiscation of lands, and so on. In the euphoria at the threshold of self-rule the strength of the counter-arguments against colonialism benefited from the reality on the ground: "colonial Africa was dying on her feet." All was geared towards the fulfilment of what Nkrumah had called the "political kingdom" in the hope that in seeking such a kingdom, "all the rest shall be added unto it".

Conclusion

The anthems that have been interrogated complement one another in a way which presents a full picture of a continental agenda. Viewed against the background of Africa's current political struggle against economic decline and decay one can hardly ignore the fact that many of the ideals expounded in the anthems of Africa's new nations have not been realised in practice. The scenario is one that demands a rehabilitation, which will transform these songs to restate present continental priorities by reflecting the reasons for the failure of these wishes expressed in the anthems. The long-term answers to the issues raised in these anthems continue to point to the urgency with which some tackle the work of independence. It would seem that until a new and single anthem is created to reflect the current problems, Africans must continue to sing their present national anthems but with new meaning.

Notes and References

1   G Joseph, 'African Literature', in AG April and DL Gordon, *Understanding Contemporary Africa*, Boulder: Lynne Rienner, 1996, p 304.

2   T Jacobsen, *The Treasures of Darkness: A History of Mesopotamian Religion*, New Haven: Yale University Press, 1976, p 25.

3   National Anthem of Mozambique, 1975.

4   G Balandiere and J Maquet, *Dictionary of Black African Civilization*, New York: Leon Amiel Publishers, 1974, p 259.

5   Pan-African Congress, 1919.

6   National Anthem of Malawi, 1964.

7   National Anthem of Guinea Bissau 1975.

8   K Asante-Darko, 'The Flora and Fauna of Negritude poetry: An Ecocritical re-reading', *Mots Pluriels*, no 12, 1999, p 39.

9   K Nkrumah, *Africa Must Unite*, London: Panaf Books, 1963.

10 *The Chronicle*, 1960, p 3.

11 *Présence Africaine*, vol 11, 1956, p 4.

12 *Présence Africaine*, nos 24–25, 1956, p 385.

13 National Anthem of Ghana, 1956.

14 It is the nation associated with the soul of the black race, and which is the only African country that successfully repelled imperial European aggression by the triumph at the Battle of Adowa, 1 March 1896.

15 National Anthem of Mali, 1962.

16 E Hoffer, *The True Believer: Thoughts on the nature of Mass Movements*, New York: Harper & Brothers Publishers, 1951, p 11.

17 PAC 1945.

18 The National Anthem of Botswana, 1966.

19 A MacClintlock, *Imperial Leather: Race, Gender, and Sexuality in the Colonial Context*, New York: Routledge, 1995, p 5.

20 B Davidson, *Which Way Africa: The Search for a New Society*, London: Penguin Publishers, 1964, p 35.

21 *Ibid*.

22 M Dei-Anang, *A Collection of Original Verse*, Accra, 1959, p 60.
23 D Osadebey, *Africa Sings*, Lagos, 1952.
24 "On me parle de progrès, de réalisations, de maladies guéries, de niveaux de
    vie élevé au dessus d'eux-même. Moi, je parle de sociétes vidées
    d'elles-même, de cultures pietinées, d'institution minées, de terres
    confisquées, de religions assassinées, de magnificences artistiques anéanties,
    d'extraordinaires possibilités supprimées. On me lance à la tête des faits, des
    statistiques, des kilométrages de routes, de canaux, de chemins de fer. Moi,
    je parle de millions d'hommes sacrifiés au Congo-Ocean. Je parle de ceux qui
    à l'heure où j'écris, sont en train de creuser à la main le port d'Abidjan. Je
    parle de millions d'hommes arrachés à leurs dieux, à leur terre, à leurs
    habitudes, à leur vie, à la vie, à la danse, à la sagesse. Je parle de millions
    d'hommes à qui on a inculqué savamment la peur, le complexe d'infériorité, le
    tremblement, l'agenouillement, le désespoir, le larbinisme. On me donne plein
    la vue de tonnage de coton ou de cacao exporté, d'hectares d'oliviers ou de
    vigne plantées. Moi, je parle d'économies naturelles, d'économies
    harmonieuses et viables, d'économies à la mesure de l'homme indigène
    désorganisées, de cultures vivrières détruites, de sous-alimentation installée,
    de dévelopment agricole orienté selon le seul bénéfice des métropoles, de
    rafles de produits, de rafles de matières premières." A Césaire, *Discours sur le
    colonialisme*, Paris, 1950.

The Challenges of Globalisation and Regional Integration: The Case of the Southern African Development Community

Blessings Chinsinga

Globalisation and regional integration are arguably the most significant aspects of contemporary international relations. The argument running through the former is that sound national economic policies can no longer be articulated independently of international economic and financial processes since national economic policies are increasingly becoming subsumed into a system of global processes and transactions. It is, for example, argued that unilateral strategic national industrial policies are virtually infeasible. The argument of this chapter, however, is that much as the current wave of globalisation forecasts the diminished role and political agency of the nation state, sound and robust domestic economic policies, especially in the context of viable regional integration, remain quite instrumental in determining its wealth and prosperity.

Regional integration is not so much a recent initiative in international trade relations but has rather assumed particular prominence in the current age of globalisation. The inaugural efforts at regional integration, for instance, on the African continent date back as far as 1958.[1] This was at the time when a fairly good number of countries across the continent had at least attained self-governance after protracted but nonetheless well orchestrated struggles against colonial rule. The drive for regional co-operation at that time was, among other things, in recognition that no country could achieve worthwhile socio-economic development on 'a go it alone frontier'.[2] These sub-regional efforts were held as a prelude to ultimate integration into an African Economic Community by the year 2000. The principles and objectives of regional integration were even embodied in the Organisation of African Unity (OAU) charter. These initiatives have, however, registered a somewhat mixed track record of success.

The reportedly globalising world economy has, however, revived the primacy of regional integration initiatives in contemporary development efforts. The reason for the dramatic revival of regional integration initiatives is that globalisation is a double edged sword.[3] Optimists herald it as a source of investible resources, managerial expertise and technology that would impact positively on the development endeavours of hitherto developing countries. On the other hand, pessimists contend that it engenders social exclusion, immiseration, marginalisation and alienation.

It is against these changing perspectives on international economic order that the paper attempts to appraise the viability of SADC as an economic regional entity. The analysis pays particular attention to the institutional capacity of SADC to steer the member countries into at least meaningful integration into the potentially hostile globalising world economy. The paper also examines the implications of overlapping membership to regional integration initiatives, which are at different stages of development and have incompatible policy goals and targets.

The paper is divided into three sections. Section I reviews the relationship between regional integration and globalisation. It sets the conceptual framework for the rest of the discussion in the paper. Section II briefly outlines the historical development of SADC and the Common Market for Eastern and Southern Africa (COMESA) as examples of regional integration initiatives. Section III highlights the problems and prospects of SADC in the context of its declared policy goal, that is, to establish a development community vis-à-vis the dictates of the globalising world economy. We offer concluding remarks in section IV.

Regional Integration and Globalisation

If we are to adequately appreciate the current primacy of regional integration in the light of globalisation, it is quite imperative to situate its evolution in a proper historical context. The aim is to provide a benchmark for understanding the perceptual oscillations that have taken place over the years regarding the viability of regional integration as an economic policy instrument. It is thus important to restate here that regional integration is not at all a recent terminology in cross-border trade transactions. Efforts at regional integration on the continent date back as far as 1958. Outside the continent, the idea of regional integration was floated as early as 1932.[4] This paper distinguishes two phases of regional integration, namely, the old and the new wave of regionalism.

The Old Wave of Regionalism

The performance track record of these regional trading blocs particularly in the developing world has been extremely disappointing. Most trading blocs have not lived up to the optimism they generated three or so decades ago.

period and ensure that non-members are not unduly discriminated.[13] Additionally, the regional bodies should have the institutional capacity to foster compliance from the partners. Adjustments, often undesirable from the point of view of the partners, in regional and domestic environments are inevitable. The partners should also demonstrate strong political will towards the regional integration initiatives. It is virtuous in the sense that it renders credibility to the regional initiatives in the eyes of foreign investors, international institutions and international interlocutors. The operative environments for these initiatives must be politically stable. Political instability, at whatever scale, would engender massive capital flight but more importantly scarce potential foreign investment, which is needed to augment meagre domestic savings. There is, finally, need for at least adequate resources, namely, physical, financial and human to sustain the momentum towards the creation of viable regional trading blocs.[14]

Of particular concern in our case, therefore, is how SADC, as a regional integration initiative, strategically positions itself in order to maximise the potential benefits and minimise the imminent costs of globalisation. Does it have the requisite institutional capacity to proactively steer the economies of member states afloat in the face of globalisation? Is its operative environment generally supportive to the success of SADC as a regional integration initiative? These are some of the issues that are addressed in the remaining sections of the paper.

The State of SADC and COMESA as Regional Integration Initiatives

The historical origins of SADC can be traced back as far as 1975. It initially started as a grouping of front line states, namely, Angola, Botswana, Mozambique, Tanzania and Zambia whose aim at that time was to secure the liberation of Zimbabwe.[15] The imminent independence of Zimbabwe rendered the group more or less redundant. It is against this background that invitations were, in 1979, extended to the other Southern African countries to join the grouping and redefine the mandate and therefore justify its continued existence. The result was the launch of the Southern Africa Development Co-operation Conference (SADCC) in April, 1980.[16] Much as this body that brought together ten Southern African countries stood for several ideals, its primary emphasis was, however, on the region's reduction of economic dependence on the then apartheid South Africa.

The operations of SADCC were, since its inception, constantly reviewed. The 1987 review exposed considerable structural and institutional hitches that constrained its performance as anticipated. The review prompted states to confer on SADCC a legal status, which paved the way for subsequent institutional and organisational reforms. Moreover, the demise of apartheid in South Africa made it increasingly irrelevant. The efforts saw the ratification of a declaration and treaty that transformed SADCC into the Southern African Development Community (SADC) in August 1992. The transformation also meant the regional body graduated from performing merely a co-ordinating role of sectional projects to facilitating trade integration and co-operation efforts. SADC's mandate did not at all envisage integrating markets.[17] The membership of SADC has progressively expanded, South Africa joined in 1994 and Mauritius in 1995. To date, SADC's membership has expanded to include the Democratic Republic of Congo (DRC) and Madagascar.

The goal of SADC is to create a development community. A trade protocol came into effect on 1st January 2000. Its aim is to establish a free trade area by 2004 and bring down the level of tariffs to zero percent over an eight-year time frame after January 2000.[18] The specific clauses of the SADC Trade Protocol are:

• To further liberalise intra-regional trade in goods and services on the basis of fair, mutually equitable and beneficial trade arrangements;
• To ensure efficient production within SADC, reflecting the current and dynamic comparative advantages of its members;
• To contribute towards the improvement of the climate for domestic, cross border, and foreign investment;
• To enhance the economic development, diversification and industrialisation of the region;
• To establish a Free Trade Area among SADC member states.

SADC is not the only regional integration initiative that has been attempted in Southern Africa. Others include Southern African Customs Union (SACU), the Cross Border Initiative (CBI), the Common Market for Eastern and Southern Africa (COMESA) and the Indian Ocean Community (IOC).[19] However, COMESA deserves particular mention to enable us to put into perspective some of the potential, and prevailing bottlenecks that have thus far impeded the smooth operation of SADC.

COMESA was established in 1995. Until sometime in 1999, it used to be a twenty-three member regional body. Tanzania has withdrawn its membership. It superseded the Preferential Trade Area (PTA) which was established in 1981. Its aim is to reduce tariffs by 70% and to erect a Common External Tariff (CET) in order to protect industries in the region against foreign competition. It intended to establish a Free Trade Area in the year 2000 and a Customs Union in the year 2004. No specific date for the establishment of a Customs Union is given.

Problems, Prospects and Challenges for SADC

In this section we attempt to catalogue the problems, prospects and challenges that SADC faces as a regional entity in the new millennium. The most serious potential threat to SADC as a regional entity is its institutional inadequacy generally compounded by the demands of variable geometry. This is a situation that comes about when countries belong to at least two regional initiatives, which are, however, at different stages of development.[20] The impact of variable geometry or multi-speed approach to regional integration is debatable though. Those in favour of the strategy argue that "countries have to move at speeds which they can sustain and that progress towards integration is not determined by the slowest moving state".[21]

The resource paucity and institutional capabilities of most SADC member states make it difficult to reconcile the conflicting demands imposed by competing regional initiatives that are at distinct levels of development. The majority of SADC member states have acute deficits of skilled personnel let alone adequate resources to ensure that competing regional initiatives do not overlap, minimise duplication and waste of resources, and contain unnecessary conflict.[22] The problem is that multi-speed integration engenders a waste of scarce administrative and financial resources. The capacity of secretariats to effectively steer regional integration efforts is, as a result of multiple membership to regional initiatives, invariably curtailed.

The cases of SADC and COMESA, therefore, demand closer scrutiny. These two regional bodies have totally different time frames for achieving particular stages toward regional integration. COMESA has lower tariffs and more flexible rules of origin than SADC. For SADC only those products that have a value added component of up to 35% compared to 25% for COMESA qualify for free trade under the recently concluded trade protocol.[23] The parallel existence of these blocs is likely to create uncertainty and confusion in the ensuing trade transactions within the region. When COMESA forms a Customs Union, for instance, SADC member states which are also party to the COMESA treaty may not be in a position to extend zero tariff preference to SADC member states which are not COMESA members. This may confirm Chipeta's scepticism that the multi-speed integration strategy would "divide the sub-region into smaller groups each with its own vested interests it would try to protect against other groups."[24]

The trade protocol is likely to register dismal performance because it is not committed to wholesale liberalisation. It champions selective and gradual liberalisation of trade among the member states.[25] This particular approach makes it exceedingly difficult to achieve multilateral consensus, which anchors the success of regional integration initiatives. Ideally, regional integration initiatives ought to aim at full liberalisation of trade among member states and should apply to almost all traded goods within a reasonable time period.[26]

The paradox is that almost all SADC member states save for South Africa are not really prepared for the competition inherent in the new global economic order. Malawi is a particular case in point. Even within the ambit of the restrictive SADC Trade Protocol, Malawi's Garment and Textile industry is unprepared to face the likely competition embodied in the protocol.[27] It craves least developed country status in order for the industry to be classified as infant to allow it grow before it is subjected to outside competition within the region. This sort of reluctance, unjustifiably so, constrains progress. But the exposure to the competitive forces within the region would force domestic producers to improve their products as well as competitiveness as quickly as possible.

Unless, therefore, regional integration initiatives are pursued with high levels of commitment, domestic industries of the co-operating member states will hardly graduate into internationally competitive enterprises. It is imperative that SADC, if at all its relevance in the contemporary economic order has to be justified, has to revisit and possibly refine those prohibitive clauses within its Trade Protocol which came into effect at the dawn of the new millennium. SADC member states must realise with swiftness, that *cetirus paribus,* regional integration remains a useful tool for learning to adapt to the challenge of integration into the aggressively competitive global economic community.

Another cause of concern is that most SADC member countries have not fully utilised the preferential market access that they enjoyed to EU markets. Nearly all the countries have reportedly registered substantial decline in the volumes of trade with EU countries.[28] With the competitive global economic environment christened by the conclusion of the Uruguay Round Agreements, the volume of their trade with EU countries is destined to further plummet. It is, therefore, imperative that SADC member states have to reorient their excessive trade dependence on EU countries to other global markets but this could only be possible if the countries are competitive enough to penetrate alternative markets.

The resultant differential impact of the reduction of tariffs on the co-operating member countries is yet another hurdle that stands in the way of SADC's ultimate success. There is a high degree of differentiation of SADC member states in their dependence on custom revenue. Hess points out that customs revenue accounts for close to half of government revenue in Lesotho and Swaziland and about a third in Mauritius.[29] It is less significant in Zambia and South Africa. To enlist total commitment and enduring co-operation from member states likely to be adversely affected would therefore be problematic. There is thus need to put in place fiscal instruments to cushion the probable revenue losses. If the anticipated hitches in the financial health of the affected member states are not addressed, efforts to transform SADC into a viable regional entity will prove futile.

Not all is, however, lost. Opportunities abound which SADC can capitalise on in its quest to become a functionally viable regional bloc in the face of globalisation. The region is politically stable and the majority of the member states have gone through fairly successful democratic transitions. Apartheid was successfully dismantled in 1994; civil war in Mozambique ended in 1992; some member states have just held their first democratic elections since independence, and quite a good number have held two consecutive democratic elections.

The only countries which are politically volatile are Angola and the Democratic Republic of Congo. Civil wars rage on without an apparent end in sight. It is nonetheless not an exaggeration to contend that these unprecedented changes have created a political milieu that is congenial to political accountability and transparency, respect for human rights and good governance, security and peace. These are essential prerequisites for sustainable political, economic and social development. Potentially, therefore, the SADC region should be a fairly attractive and competitive investment and foreign aid destination. The relative stability and the democratic changes sweeping across the region are very critical assets. They give it an edge over other regions, which are engulfed in relentless civil strife. Not only does political instability engender excessive capital flight from a region, it also scares away potential foreign investment.[30] Stable democratic regions improve the image of the host region both among foreign and domestic investors. The challenge for SADC is simply to fine-tune its inherent institutional limitations. It would be fairly easy for it as a regional entity to court large scale foreign investment.

Concluding Remarks

The paper has analysed the salience of regional integration in the wake of globalisation. The relative political stability the region enjoys and manageable divergences in social, political, historical and economic heritage hold promise for a successful regional integration initiative. The onus is on SADC to rectify the apparent institutional shortcomings that threaten the efforts to ultimately achieve a viable development community.

Given the current institutional limitations, we propose that SADC could benefit from the establishment of Regional Information Centres (RICs) and Regional Development Agencies (RDAs). The RICs would play a very critical role in gathering information on global opportunities and technological development. The RDAs would, on the other hand, assist SADC member countries to explore strategies on how to link up with universities and align part of the research agenda of relevant university departments and research institutes in order to promote both regional and national development. Networking is particularly crucial to exploit trust and reciprocity at regional level. National, transnational and international partnerships thrive on their abilities to keep abreast with the reigning best practices, global policies and trends. The fact is that regional blocs have to think globally but act locally.

The eventual success of the regional integration initiatives, however, is greatly dependent on the existence of quality leadership. Rugumamu aptly sums up the requisite leadership stature when he writes, "there is need for quality leadership that is democratic, people oriented, visionary in the sense of being conscious of what direction to follow and what goals to seek as well as capable of inspiring and mobilising citizens for development".[31]

Notes and References

1   C Chanthunya, 'Regional Integration', in C Chipeta (ed), *Trade and Investment in Southern Africa: Towards Regional Economic Co-operation and Integration*, Harare: SAPES Trust, 1998; M Matsibula, 'SACU and SADC: Strategic Optimism for the Future', in C Chipeta (ed), *Trade and Investment in Southern Africa: Towards Regional Economic Co-operation and Integration*, Harare: SAPES Trust, 1998.

2   Chanthunya 1998.

3   D Rwegasira, 'From Recovery to Accelerated Development: Some Key Issues for 21st Century Africa', *Journal of Development Assistance*, vol 5, no 1, 1999; S Rugumamu, *Globalisation, Liberalisation and Africa's Marginalisation*, Harare: AAPS, 1999.

4   E Grill, 'Multilateralism and Regionalism: A Still Difficult Coexistence', in F Riccardo and E Grill (eds), *Multitateralism and Regionalism after the Uruguay Round*, London: Macmillan, 1997; Chanthunya 1998.

5   S Sideri, 'Globalisation and Regional Integration', *European Journal of Development Research*, vol 9, no 1, 1997; Rwegasira 1999; Grill 1997.

6   C Chipeta, 'An Overview of Governance, Trade and Investment in the SADC Region', in C Chipeta (ed), *Trade and Investment in Southern Africa: Towards Regional Economic Co-operation and Integration*, Harare: SAPES Trust, 1998; Rwegasira 1999; Grill 1997.

7   R Hess, 'SADC: Towards a Free Trade Area; Implications for EU-SADC Trade Relations', *SAPEM*, vol 12, no 4, 1999; Rwegasira 1999; Rugumamu 1999.

8   C Clark, *Globalisation and International Relations Theory*, London: Oxford University Press, 1999.
9   Sideri 1997, p 70, emphasis added.
10   *Ibid.*; P Hirst and G Thompson, 'The Problem of Globalisation: International Economic Relations, National Economic Management and the Formation of Trading Blocs', *Economy and Society*, vol 21, no 4, 1996; UNCTAD, *World Investment Report*, New York: United Nations, 1997.
11   M Moore, 'Politics against Poverty: Global Pessimism and National Optimism', *IDS Bulletin*, vol 30, no 2, 1999, p 35, emphasis added.
12   Sideri 1997; Grill 1997; Rwegasira 1999.
13   Grill 1997; Hess 1999.
14   Matsibula 1998; Chipeta 1998.
15   Matsibula 1998.
16   The founding members of SADCC included Angola, Botswana, Lesotho, Malawi, Mozambique, Namibia, Tanzania, Zimbabwe and Zambia.
17   Matsibula 1998; Chanthunya 1998; Hess 1999.
18   Chanthunya 1998; Matsibula 1998; Hess 1999.
19   The Members of SACU, established in 1969, include Botswana, Lesotho, Namibia, Swaziland, and South Africa.
20   Chipeta 1998; Matsibula 1999.
21   Matsibula 1998, p 77.
22   Chipeta 1998; Chanthunya 1998.
23   Chanthunya 1998; Hess 1999.
24   Chipeta 1998, p 13.
25   Chipeta 1998; Chanthunya 1998; Hess 1999.
26   Grill 1997; Sideri 1997.
27   *Daily Times*, 23 August 1999.
28   Chipeta 1998.
29   Hess 1999.
30   Matsibula 1998; Rugumamu 1999.
31   Rugumamu 1999, p 16.

Regional Integration and Sustainable Development in Southern Africa: Lessons from the Migrant Labour System

SN-A Mensah

The influence that the economic activities of countries could have on each other's growth and development performance has, for a long time, produced a variety of reactions: competition, protection, integration, co-operation, and so on. The serious world-wide economic depression of the late 1920s and early 1930s has been attributed to some of these reactions. Because of the lessons learnt from that depression, including the realisation that 'beggar your neighbour policies' could make beggars of every country, efforts were made after World War II to discourage protectionism and promote competition in international trade, as a way of preventing another slide into depression. These efforts took the form of international agreements on procedures for trade and the establishment of supervisory international institutions such as the International Monetary Fund (IMF), the International Bank for Reconstruction and Development (World Bank) and the proposed, but never established, International Trade Organisation (ITO). The place of the ITO was later taken by the General Agreement on Trade and Tariffs (GATT), which has now given way to the World Trade Organisation (WTO). It was thought then that these institutions and the policies they represented would promote and ensure sustainable growth and development throughout the world, through competitive production and trade.

But soon came the Treaty of Rome in 1957 and the formation of the European Community – perhaps in response to Viner's pioneer work on custom unions.[1] And since then trade liberalisation drives (which, together with improved flows of information and finance, have been given the name globalisation since the 1990s) have moved simultaneously with "a rapid spread of regionalism across the world".[2]

The boost that advances in computer technology gradually gave to globalisation – "the widening and deepening of international flows of trade, finance and information" – over the last 40 years did not slow down the drive toward regionalism.[3] During that period, Europe progressed from a free trade area of six countries, through a customs union and a common market to an economic union – "the most complex form of economic integration" – of 15 countries.[4] With the Euro going into circulation in 2002, a political union, the last stage in the integration-co-operation spectrum, now seems quite possible. These developments in Europe have consistently presented the region "as an integrated economic powerhouse", and so have encouraged similar groupings all over the world – though none of these has attained the same degree of unification.[5]

North America has produced the North American Free Trade Area (NAFTA) and Central America, the short-lived Central American Common Market (CAMC). South America is still working on various groupings: the Latin American Free Trade Association (LAFTA) of the 1960s has now grown into the eleven-nation Latin American Integration Association (LAIA). Other sub-groupings are still emerging within LAIA. Argentina, Brazil, Paraguay and Uruguay have formed the Common Market of the South (MERCOSUR); and Bolivia, Ecuador, Colombia and Peru are moving in the same direction. Then there is the Enterprise for the Americas Initiative (EAI) launched in 1990, "which envisages an eventual move to free trade in the Americas with the inclusion of Latin American nations".[6] Recent summits show how determined they are to deal with the obstacles to integration of the Americas.

Asia has not officially established an exclusive economic space, yet the formation of the Association of South East Asian Nations (ASEAN) shows that the Asian-Pacific region has not been left out in the drive to regionalism. The Middle East also has the League of Arab States.

Africa has also produced similar economic groupings. These include the Economic Community of West African States (ECOWAS), the recently revived East African Common Market of Kenya, Uganda and Tanzania (Tanganyika), the Preferential Trade Area (PTA) for East and Southern Africa, and the Economic Community of Central African States (CEEAC). The Southern African Development Community (SADC) is also an effort at regional co-operation and integration. As noted by Motete, the objectives of SADC include "the creation of a genuine and equitable regional integration".[7] Areas of co-operation identified so far include transport, communication and meteorology, mining, education and training, tourism, shared watercourse systems, energy, and combating illicit drugs and smuggling. Within SADC, however, a strong economic bond, akin to loose integration and co-operation, has existed between South Africa and Botswana, Lesotho and Swaziland (the so-called BLS countries) for over a century.[8] This chapter scrutinises the labour migration component of this bond in the hope of drawing lessons that could assist in strengthening the bond and in helping to direct further efforts at regional integration and co-operation within the SADC.

Regional Integration and Regional Co-operation

The literature on regional integration does not often distinguish between economic integration and economic co-operation, but is almost unanimous on the understanding and progression of economic integration.[9] Kindleberger's position on integration, though quite informative, is one of the few exceptions in this respect; but the disagreement is not major.[10] Economic integration and economic co-operation do not always refer to the same arrangements between countries. The focus of economic integration, on the one hand, is trade liberalisation so that, initially, goods and services, but later factors of production also, could flow freely among a number of countries. On the other hand, as a community, the member countries are protected against competition from the rest of the world. In connection with this latter point, economic integration becomes a useful vehicle for promoting industrialisation, because of the wider market provided and the possibilities for specialisation and economies of scale in production in an environment of reduced competition with the rest of the world. Economic co-operation, on the other hand, is not so focused; "it denotes any combined action by nations to promote the interests of the parties involved".[11] These interests, although often economic, may also be social or even political and cultural. Economic co-operation may therefore be in the areas of education (as in the case of the now divided University of Botswana, Lesotho and Swaziland), infrastructure or environmental protection, for instance. So, while regional integration is always within the framework of regional co-operation, the reverse is not always the case.

Economic integration, as defined above, is a process that begins with a free trade area and may end with an economic union, a monetary union, or even a political union, depending on how far the countries involved want to go. From its very beginning, integration requires the removal of barriers that discriminate between domestic and foreign goods and services within the bloc, and later factors of production are also allowed to move freely. The free movement of labour, however, is often a thorny issue in integration arrangements. The SADC member countries, for example, have signed protocols in various areas which are dependent on the free movement of labour in the region. Yet the governments of the SADC member countries have not signed a protocol on the free movement of labour.

Integration usually begins with the formation of a free trade area, where member countries eliminate tariffs within the area, but each country maintains its individual tariff system with the rest of the world. Due to the problem of trade deflection, trade may not really be free and so the member countries may decide to adopt "a common tariff nomenclature and identical tariff rates with the rest of the world".[12] The free trade area then becomes a customs union, such as the Southern African Customs Union (SACU). Customs unions do not provide for free movement of factors of production between the member countries. This restricts the scope for customs unions to facilitate the transfer of skills among the labour forces of the member countries and the location or relocation of industries within the region to minimise costs. The distribution of factors of production and of demand for goods and services within a customs union could however suggest possibilities for location or relocation of industries to achieve greater production efficiency, lower production costs and better profit levels – all of which are important for sustainable development. Economic rationality, therefore, often opens the way for the free movement of factors of production to follow in the trail of free movement of goods and services. When this happens, then the customs union has become a common market.

Once factors of production could move freely, economic rationality again suggests further levels of integration. For example, the free movement of capital would require identical policies among member countries for the regulation of money and capital markets, for determination of interest rates and foreign exchange rates.[13] Soon economic expediency would suggest common macro-economic policies, especially fiscal and monetary policies, as a way of diminishing competition and reinforcing co-operation. By the time common macro-economic policies are being adopted, the common market would have become an economic union. Monetary unification improves cohesion and so strengthens an economic union, and it paves the way for political unification. The USA and UK are examples of regions that have pushed integration to the last stage of political unification.

Economic integration, at whatever stage in the free trade area/economic union spectrum, makes possible a strange coexistence of elements of competition and free trade with elements of greater protection. On the one hand, by ensuring that production is carried out by the most efficient firms using the most suitable factors and in the most suitable locations, integration could increase trade in goods and services and movement of factors of production among member countries. This promotes efficiency in production and exchange. The effects of production efficiency on prices could also improve efficiency in consumption. On the other hand, integration tends to restrict trade and competition with the rest of the world, which could introduce inefficiency and thus reduce world output and distort regional prices and consumption patterns. This negative aspect is the price that has to be paid to correct the uneven development of the regions of the world. And the theory of the second best, which deals with sub-optimal situations, provides adequate justification for this.[14] The main point of this theory is that when one of the necessary conditions for a Pareto optimal situation to prevail cannot be fulfilled – which makes welfare maximisation unattainable – then the maximisation of attainable welfare (i.e., the second best) would require violation of other Pareto conditions. When applied to economic integration, this means that regional blocs could improve their welfare levels by violating other Pareto conditions such as by integrating the region to protect it against competition from the rest of the world.[15]

Kindleberger differs slightly from the understanding of economic integration presented above.[16] In his schema, integration is attained only at the final stage in the economic relations between countries. Economic relations then take the form of a progression from free trade area through customs union, common market and economic union to complete economic integration. He defines economic integration as that arrangement between a number of countries that allows for "factor-price equalisation". From this definition, any policies or situations that interfere with trade, whether by tariffs or transport costs, would prevent the prices of goods, and therefore factor prices, from being equalised, and would therefore make integration difficult to attain. This may explain why most countries that have been successfully integrated have been contiguous. This view of integration requires that the arrangement between the countries should ensure that their wage rate-price and interest rate-price ratios tend toward equality. This equalisation could be achieved through trade, without factor movements, through factor movements, without trade, or through some combination of the two. As Kindleberger realised, this definition of integration gives a standard of measurement that may never be reached.[17] By this definition, neither the provinces in South Africa nor the states in the United States are economically integrated since the interest rate-price and the wage rate-price ratios vary in different provinces or states in these countries. The practical relevance of this definition, however, lies in its implication that, for a customs union like SACU to move towards complete economic integration, the policies of the member countries should ensure that factor-price differences between them are narrowed.

One problem with Kindleberger's view of integration is that it is possible to attain factor-price equalisation without having economic integration. For example, because each BLS country trades extensively with South Africa, it is possible for "factor-price" ratios to tend towards equalisation. But this would not mean that the BLS economies are "integrated". By promoting wage-price ratio equalisation, the free movement of labour between the four countries could play an important role in ensuring true "integration".

It should be clear from the foregoing that while some regional co-operation arrangements may not constitute economic integration, all integration arrangements are efforts at regional co-operation. As examples of co-operation in the Southern African region, du Plessis *et al* have cited labour agreements between South Africa and Botswana, Lesotho, Malawi, Mozambique, and Swaziland, and the agreement between Lesotho and South Africa on the Lesotho Highlands Water Project.[18] This listing shows that conditions already exist in the region, but especially between South Africa and the BLS states, that are conducive for integration and co-operation.

Conditioning Factors for Integration and Co-operation

The South Africa-BLS sub-region has both historical and geographical factors that are conducive to integration and co-operation. This sub-region could therefore be used as a model or test case from which lessons on integration and co-operation could be drawn for the regional exercise.

All the BLS countries are contiguous with South Africa, and this is important in reducing the transport cost problem and therefore in aligning factor-price ratios which, in Kindleberger's schema, facilitates integration. This observation also applies to Namibia, Zimbabwe and Mozambique. However, these countries are excluded from the analysis here.

The histories of the BLS states and South Africa have been intertwined for a long time, not only because they are contiguous, but also because of the High Commissioner Territory arrangement of the colonial era which placed BLS administration under South Africa. This common history is responsible for the similarity in educational systems, the formation of the SACU and the CMA (although Botswana is no longer in the CMA), and the pattern of flow of investment funds. These institutional arrangements give the sub-region some of the characteristics of an economic union. The common currency ensures a permanently fixed exchange rate between Lesotho, Swaziland and South Africa, which also contributes to factor-price equalisation. Even though Botswana has moved out of the CMA, its currency (the Pula) is linked to the Rand and so its value cannot deviate significantly. As pointed out earlier, a tendency towards factor-price equalisation does not indicate considerable integration among the BLS countries, but reflects their bilateral ties with South Africa. However the CMA is an important conditioning factor for future integration and co-operation. In fact, it is like having a monetary union in the sub-region before an economic union.

Capital moves with little difficulty from South Africa to the other three countries in the sub-region in pursuit of maximum returns. This could be seen from a listing of the commercial and manufacturing firms in the four countries. This free movement of investment funds is important in aligning the interest rate-price ratio in the four countries – another important condition for integration in the Kindleberger schema.

The CMA limits the capacity of the central banks in Lesotho and Swaziland to formulate and implement monetary policy for the management of their economies. This makes their monetary policies and the determination of their interest rates, for all practical purposes, the responsibility of the Reserve Bank of South Africa. This is the usual situation in a monetary union. The countries in Europe that have adopted the Euro are approaching this stage of unification.

The BLS states also have a uniform educational system, and at one time shared a common university. This common educational system blends in quite smoothly with the South African educational system. During the apartheid era many black South African studied in BLS educational institutions, and many BLS students now study in South Africa, either for the Joint Matriculation Board examination (after their Cambridge Overseas School Certificate), for university degree programmes, or for Honours programmes or other higher degrees. The basis, therefore, has already been established for co-operation in education and training between the BLS countries and South Africa. It should be stated, though, that a second look ought to be taken at the assumed superiority of the South African Joint Matriculation Board examination over the BLS Cambridge Overseas School Certificate examination. Exchanges of students between South Africa and the BLS countries may be all it would take to clear this obstacle to a unification of the education system in the sub-region.

A comparison of the BLS-South Africa situation above with that of the United States – a completely integrated region of some 50 states – reveals that the sub-region already has in place some of the important factors that facilitate integration and co-operation. While the BLS-South Africa sub-region has the advantage of linguistic contiguity – all the BLS languages spill over into South Africa – the USA has the advantage of free labour movement. But as shown by the long existence of the migrant labour system in the region, geographical and linguistic contiguity promotes labour mobility.

The Migrant Labour System

Labour migration is one of the three major kinds of labour market investments workers undertake. And so migration will always take place if it is expected to produce acceptable returns and the law does not proscribe it.[19] The free movement of workers within a region of many sub-markets, as is the case in Southern Africa, promotes multi-market equilibrium, which has been shown to be a prerequisite for efficiency and equity in such a market system.[20]

The pace of internal migration in the BLS states quickened with the development of urban centres as places of employment. However, the experience with external migration spans over a century, during which both men and women have oscillated between their homesteads and the mine towns and agricultural fields in South Africa where they worked.[21] This movement of non-South African blacks in and out of South Africa for work was supported and even promoted by the South African Chamber of Mines (COM), successive South African governments, and the governments of the sending countries.

The COM supported the labour migration system not only because it helped to ensure a steady supply of black labour, but also because the migrants, by virtue of the vulnerability of their status, pushed beyond the average effort. This is why the COM would want to keep them for as long as possible. Towards the end of the apartheid era, efforts were made to persuade the COM and its agents to employ more black South Africans and fewer foreigners. These efforts were resisted on the basis that foreign workers were important to the very survival of the mining industry as they "comprise a reservoir of skills, experience and work discipline, which the industry could not do without".[22]

Past governments of South Africa supported the migrant labour system because they would not take the risk of making the most important industry in the country dependent on the very militant and highly politicised black workforce, who saw the mineral deposits of South Africa as their birthright. Migrant workers, on the other hand, were politically less deviant.[23]

On coming to power and with the adoption of a people-centred approach to policy, which meant formulating "policies that will restructure the lives and material well-being of South Africans", the newly democratic government had to confront two labour-migration-related realities it had inherited.[24] The first was the labour market situation in South Africa: the unacceptably high unemployment rate among black South Africans, and the declining growth rates of GDP and employment. The second was the fact that there was a large number of foreigners in the South African mining sector whose jobs the "massive and highly visible army of unemployed South Africans" would willingly accept.[25] The direction of government employment generation policy in such a situation should be clear, despite the assurance of ex-President Nelson Mandela that foreign mine workers in South Africa would not have to worry about their jobs, as long as market conditions allowed it.[26] The reality, however, is that the decline in the number of foreign miners which started in the late 1980s has continued in spite of changes in product market conditions.[27] Thus the labour migration system in the region that has lasted for over a century with the support of various governments is now under threat.

Another government action that would adversely affect the labour migration system in the region is the question of giving permanent residence status to some migrant workers. In October 1995, the South African government, bending to pressure from the National Union of Mineworkers, accepted a proposal that mineworkers who had been working legally in South Africa for a period of at least five years could apply for a South African Identification Card, which would make them permanent residents. This would give the migrants several privileges: voting rights, the choice to move their families to South Africa, unemployment insurance, subsidised health care, subsidised education for children, old-age pensions, employment in other sectors, and so on. At a time of job uncertainty in the mines, this could not have come at a better time for the migrants. However, because of its implication for remittances, this was a new source of concern for the governments of the sender countries, even though the actual numbers that would want to take advantage of the concession could not immediately be determined. It turned out that between November 1995 and November 1996, just over 48 000 foreign African migrant workers applied for permanent residence, and these came from Lesotho (32 150), Mozambique (8 608), Botswana (3 538), Swaziland (3 228) and Malawi (449).[28]

The BLS governments, like others in the region, have supported the migrant labour system because of the benefits their economies derived from the remittances of miners. In Lesotho, for example, an estimated 48% of the population depended on migrant income in 1989.[29] Table 1 gives an idea of the contribution of migrants to the functioning of the Lesotho economy, and the situation with Swaziland is quite similar.

The government also benefits, by using the remittances of migrants to fill the gap between imports and exports. The importance of this can be seen in Table 2 below.

Both Botswana and Swaziland used remittances of miners in the same way. Botswana has, however, been having balance of trade surpluses since bcoming a mineral exporting country and so no longer needs the remittances of miners to pay for imports. In fact, with the development of local mines in Botswana, external migration has lost its attraction. Mogalakwe and Siphambe have demonstrated that, in terms of magnitudes, internal migration has become more important than external migration in Botswana.[30] The importance of this finding is that market forces would be able to regulate labour movements in the region for efficient utilisation. And so governments in the region should endeavour to strengthen the

Table 1: Number of Basotho Mineworkers, Wages and Remittances

Year	Average number of mineworkers	Percentage change	Average annual wage	Percentage change	Remittances (Thousands)	Percentage Change	Rate of Inflation
1981	123 538	–	2 520	–	26 982	–	–
1982	117 641	– 4.8	2 985	18.5	51 004	89	–
1983	115 327	– 2.0	3 436	15.1	74 207	45	–
1984	114 041	– 1.1	3 927	14.3	82 923	12	–
1985	116 223	1.9	4 452	13.4	92 675	12	13.3
1986	121 450	4.5	5 136	15.4	104 776	13	18.0
1987	125 934	3.7	7 160	39.4	124 354	19	11.8
1988	124 781	– 0.9	7 598	6.1	166 127	34	11.4
1989	126 733	1.6	8 679	14.2	190 900	15	14.9
1990	125 786	– 0.7	10 069	16.0	231 100	21	11.5

Year	Average number of mineworkers	Percentage change	Average annual wage	Percentage change	Remittances (Thousands)	Percentage Change	Rate of Inflation
1991	122 188	- 2.9	11 350	12.7	130 900	-43	17.9
1992	119 596	- 2.1	12 440	9.6	91 800	-30	17.0
1993	116 129	- 2.9	13 359	7.4	94 100	3	13.9
1994	112 722	-2.9	14 562	9.0	85 900	-9.	7.9
1995	103 744	- 8.0	16 801	15.4	104 600	22	9.6
1996	101 237	-2.4	18 476	10.0	174 676	67	8.5
1997	96 541	- 7.9	21 193	10.5	127 386	- 27	7.8

Sources: Fifth Five-Year Development Plan, 1991/92-1995/96, p 7; Sixth National Development Plan, 1996/97-1998/99; Central Bank of Lesotho, Annual Report, Several Years; Ministry of Labour and Employment, 1997, p 31.

Table 2: Merchandise trade – 1985-1997 (in millions of Maloti)

Year	1985	1986	1987	1988	1989	1990	1991	1992	1993	1994	1995	1996	1997
Imports c.i.f.	-751.0	-807.4	-954.8	-1328.4	-1614.8	-1808.3	-2320.2	-2638.3	-2952.1	-3119.6	-3718.0	-4465.6	-4884.9
Exports f.o.b.	50.0	58.0	94.7	144.9	172.6	153.7	186.2	310.9	438.9	509.3	580.6	812.1	899.0
Trade gap	-701.0	-749.4	-860.1	-1183.5	-1442.2	-1654.6	-2134.0	-2327.4	-2513.2	-2610.3	-3209.4	-3653.5	-3985.9
Growth rate of trade gap	-	6.9	14.8	37.6	21.9	14.7	28.9	9.1	8.0	3.9	23.0	13.8	9.1
Exports as % of imports	6.7	7.2	9.9	10.9	10.7	8.5	8.0	11.8	14.9	16.3	15.6	18.2	18.4

Source: Compiled from Central Bank of Lesotho, Annual Report, Several Years.

institutional structures that improve the functioning of the labour market. Their fears about displacement of their nationals from employment would then be taken care of in a more efficient way.

Lessons for Regional Integration and Co-operation

Regional integration and co-operation are bred from the mutual concern of nation states in a region for their advancement. And there is evidence of such concern between South Africa and at least the BLS countries. Ex-President Mandela is reported to have said in Maseru in 1995 that, "A state of affairs in which there was a vibrant South African economy alongside increasing poverty in neighbouring countries could not be sustained".[31] Labour migration is one of the main channels for spreading development in the region. Thus, one of the major challenges facing decision-makers in the region now is to make labour migration – the region's longest economic heritage – proceed in a way that would release its fullest potential in contributing to regional development through integration and co-operation. The uneven playing field onto which the era of globalisation has been ushered and the uncertainties of the global economic environment should make regions in the Third World see the need for joint efforts in addressing their common social and economic problems. A united front would also enable them to acquire the strength required in obtaining fair deals with the rest of the world. If SADC as a unified regional bloc should negotiate a free trade agreement with the EU, the outcome would be more favourable than what South Africa has negotiated alone. The same would be true of any individual country in the region. And so the economic integration and co-operation among the SADC countries is not an option, but a necessity in tackling the region's share of the complex problems of the world economy.

The view expressed in this chapter is that the labour migration system that the region has had for over a century furnishes vital lessons that should be learnt and applied for regional integration and co-operation.

One reason why the migrant labour system has lasted for so long is the mutual benefit to all the countries in the region that participated in it; even though the distribution of the benefits was highly skewed in favour of South Africa. The lesson from this observation is that integration should start by identification of areas where most of the countries in the region would benefit. As argued above, a progression from the old migrant labour system, with its many control mechanisms, to the free movement of labour, would speed up the rate of development and improve its distribution in the region. Myopic political considerations that create obstacles to the free movement of labour would produce only short-term gains. The

United States, for example, provides evidence for policy-makers in SADC that in the long-term the improvement in productivity that increased labour mobility in the region would generate would influence the workforce in all countries in the region. The change in work ethics that increased mobility would bring about, for example, is not only an important condition for sustainable development in the region, but also an important condition for a more even development. As argued below, even development in the region would eventually reduce external migration.

The history of the migrant labour system shows that voluntary migration generally takes place only when migration is expected to provide better returns than work at home. For example, the discovery of diamonds in the Northern Cape Colony in the late 1860s and the employment opportunities it provided for Black labourers did not immediately draw migrant workers from Lesotho. Instead, the concentration of paid workers in the Northern Cape increased demand for grain and wool from Lesotho and brought prosperity to the Basotho, who were mainly farmers. This prosperity in turn created demand for more livestock and for manufactured goods, including guns. Ironically, this taste for imported goods and the binding land constraint were among the factors that eventually "pushed many Basotho to the diamond mines of the Cape Colony", though many only looked for temporary employment during the lean season.[32] The lesson from this observation about labour migration in the region is that the free movement of labour could initially increase the volume of migration. However, since migration in the long run improves labour's efficiency and income, remittances of migrants would increase. The remittances could be mobilised for investment and development throughout the region; and this would eventually reduce the volume of external migration.

Botswana's experience with external and internal migration is quite instructive in demonstrating how economic development in a country could affect external migration. As shown by Magalakwe and Siphambe, improved economic performance in Botswana has, with time, shifted the emphasis from external to internal migration.[33] We could therefore generalise these findings and state that, as national economies benefit from free movement of labour within the region and are strengthened, migration would tend to be more national than regional. In fact, with respect to the migrant labour system – as distinct from 'brain drain' – the bulk of the migrants from the BLS countries have come from the unskilled and semi-skilled categories because of difficulties with employment at home. The BLS economies have been able to absorb their skilled, technical and professional workers and so proportionately few in this category migrate. This should allay the fears of politicians who expect net in-migration to be a constant feature of free movement of labour in the region and are therefore concerned about the labour supply effects of free movement of labour on employment opportunities, wages and on the welfare of their nationals.

Because of South Africa's position in the global mining market and because most BLS migrants in South Africa are absorbed into the mining sector, the bilateral monopoly model could approximate the market for migrant labour. On the supply side is the National Union of Miners, which tries to influence the conditions under which mine labour services in South Africa are sold. On the demand side, the Chamber of Mines uses the Employment Bureau of Africa as its recruiting agent. Because of the indeterminacy of this model, market forces cannot, even in theory, determine equilibrium employment and wage rate, which makes negotiations between employer and labour an important feature of such markets. However, in the case of South Africa, the COM consistently puts pressure on the South African government to maintain a maximum average wage system in the mining sector, which requires mining companies to have a collective agreement not to pay average wages in excess of a certain very low maximum.[34] This interference with the labour process in the South African mines has affected incomes and remittances and, therefore, also interfered with the potential of the migrant labour system to contribute to the development of the sending countries. In this era of liberalisation and globalisation, therefore, the production process in the region should be allowed to operate optimally by employing the most suitable workers, irrespective of national origin, and by rewarding all factors optimally. This is one way to co-operate for the development of the region as a whole.

The migrant labour system also provides lessons in how not to go about regional co-operation and integration. For example, when the pace of industrial and agricultural development in South Africa reached a stage when the demand for labour of black workers could not be met from domestic supply and voluntary in-migration, the methods used to induce more migration from the neighbouring countries were anti-co-operation. In the case of Lesotho, the white farmers realised that the main factor restraining the active participation of Basotho in the South African labour market was the availability of land. To secure Basotho labour, "the Boers decided to force the Sotho to live within such narrow limits that it would become impossible to subsist on the produce of agriculture and livestock and [so] be compelled to offer their services to the farmers in the capacity of domestic servants and labourers".[35] Such forced migration promoted conflict, not co-operation, in the region. The HIV/AIDS pandemic, too, is causing such devastation in the region, especially in South Africa, that the prospect of serious labour shortages in the near future cannot be ruled out.

Instead of the old way of forced migration, the free movement of labour now would provide the basis of dealing with labour shortages in the future in a spirit of co-operation.

Notes and References

1   J Viner, *The Customs Union Issue*, New York: Carnegie Endowment for International Peace, 1950.
2   SPJ du Plessis, BW Smit and CL McCarthy, *International Economics*, Johannesburg: Heinemann, 1996, p 143.
3   UNDP, *Human Development Report 1997*, Oxford: Oxford University Press, 1997.
4   M Chacholiades, *International Economics*, New York: McGraw-Hill, 1990, p 225.
5   Du Plessis *et al* 1996, p 144.
6   *Ibid.*, pp 144–145.
7   L Motete, 'The Review and Rationalisation of the SADC Programme of Action', Paper presented at a workshop on "The Review and Rationalisation of the SADC Programme of Action", Maseru, 18–20 February, 1998.
8   TM Shaw, 'Introduction to Southern Africa as a Regional Subsystem', in TM Shaw and KA Heard (eds), *Co-operation and Conflict in Southern Africa*, Nova Scotia: Centre for African Studies, Dalhousie University, 1977, p 2.
9   Du Plessis *et al* 1996, p 135; Chacholiades 1990, pp 222–242.
10 CP Kindleberger, *International Economics*, Homewood: Richard D. Irwin, 1973.
11 Du Plessis *et al* 1996, p 135.
12 Kindleberger 1973, p 174.
13 *Ibid.*, p 181.
14 Chacholiades 1990, pp 226,227.
15 *Ibid.*, pp 227–228.
16 Kindleberger 1973, p 182.
17 *Ibid.*, p 182.
18 Du Plessis *et al* 1996, p 136.
19 RG Ehrenberg and RS Smith, *Modern Labour Economics: Theory and Public Policy*, New York: Addison Wesley Longman, 1997, p 268.
20 FR Marshall and VM Briggs Jr, *Labour Economics: Theory, Institutions and Public Policy*, Homewood: Richard Irwin, 1989, pp 124–129.
21 CM Cockerton, 'Less a barrier, more a line: The migration of Bechuanaland women to South Africa, 1850–1930', *Journal of Historical Geography*, vol 22, no 3, July 1996.
22 J Crush, 'Mine Migrancy in the Contemporary Era', in J Crush and W James (eds), *Crossing Borders: Mine Migrancy in a Democratic South Africa*,

Cape Town: Institute for Democracy in South Africa, 1995.

23 GM Malahleha, 'Dissonance and Class Conflict in Post-Apartheid South
    Africa', in B Oden and H Othman (eds), *Regional Co-operation in Southern
    Africa: A Post-Apartheid Perspective*, Uppsala: Scandinavian Institute of
    African Studies, 1989.

24 Crush 1995.

25 *Ibid.*

26 Central Bank of Lesotho, *Emerging Trends in the Migration of Basotho Miners*,
    Maseru: Government of Lesotho, 1996, p 16.

27 S N-A Mensah, 'Labour Markets, Migration and Lesotho's Economy', Paper
    presented at a workshop on "Labour Markets and Migration Policies in
    Southern Africa", SARIPS, Lilongwe, 12–13 July 1999.

28 K Matlosa, 'Basotho Migrant Miners in South Africa and Lesotho's Future',
    in L Sachikonye (ed), *Labour and Migration in Southern Africa*, Harare: Sapes
    Trust, 1998, p 39.

29 Mensah 1999.

30 M Mogalakwe and H Siphambe, 'Economic Performance and Labour Market
    Trends in Botswana', Paper presented at a workshop on "Labour Markets
    and Migration in Southern Africa", SARIPS, Lilongwe, 12–13 July 1999.

31 Central Bank of Lesotho 1996a.

32 J Gay, D Gill, T Green, D Hall, M Mhlanga and M Mohapi, *Poverty in
    Lesotho: A Mapping Exercise*, Report prepared for the Food Management
    Unit, Maseru: Government of Lesotho, 1991, p 2.

33 Magalakwe and Siphambe 1999.

34 Gay *et al* 1991, p 3.

35 T J Keegan, *Rural Transformations in Industrialising South Africa: The Southern
    Highveld to 1914*, Johannesburg: Ravan Press, 1986, p 9.

Containing Local Conflicts from turning into Civil Wars

Rhoda Cynthia Bakuwa

Every country is made up of groups of people with different interests, values, traditions and religious beliefs. These differences make people pursue different courses of action in order to satisfy their divergent interests. At times, as one group pursues its course of action, another group might perceive that action as being meant to frustrate some of their concerns or interests. Hence you may have tension between the concerned groups which can lead to conflicts.

According to Gordon, conflict refers to antagonism or opposition between and among people.[1] Conflict is the result of incongruent or incompatible relationships between individuals or groups. It is a process that begins when one party perceives that the other has frustrated, or, is about to frustrate some concern of theirs. Thus conflict occurs when mutually exclusive goals or values exist in fact or are perceived to exist, by the groups involved; when interaction is characterised by behaviour designed to defeat, reduce or suppress the opponent, or to gain a mutually designed victory; when the groups face each other with mutually opposing actions and counter actions; or when each group attempts to create a relatively favoured position vis-à-vis the other.

In many countries world-wide, local conflicts between groups of citizens of the same country have at times escalated from non-violent to violent confrontations at which point dangerous weapons such as guns have been used. In this way, local conflicts degenerate into civil wars. However, in countries such as Angola, Mozambique and Rwanda, where civil wars have occurred, the people have experienced many devastating consequences such as the loss of innocent lives, displacement of people, and destruction of the country's infrastructure and economy. Due to such negative consequences of civil wars there is a need to find ways of containing local conflicts so that they should not degenerate into wider conflicts, and even wars. Based on experiences drawn from some countries in Africa, this chapter discusses the factors that cause local conflicts to degenerate into civil wars and how to contain such conflicts.

Causes of local conflicts

There are several specific reasons why local conflicts between citizens of the same country occur. The first of these is related to political factors.

Political causes

Politics can be defined as competition among people trying to influence government decisions towards different outcomes.[2] In many countries, different political parties are formed and usually these parties have different philosophies or ideologies. The political parties compete with one another to form a government so that they can then influence the government outcomes in line with their own philosophies. At times, this competition is so strong that it leads to conflict.

Indeed, most of the intense conflicts in Africa have occurred because of political differences and/or political intolerance between and amongst political groups since political opponents see each other as political foes and not as colleagues with different points of view. For example, in Angola the Popular Movement for the Liberation of Angola (MPLA) has fought a civil war for many years with the Union for the Total Independence of Angola (UNITA); in Malawi, the United Democratic Front (UDF), Malawi Congress Party (MCP) and Alliance for Democracy (AFORD) are old enemies; and in Mozambique, there was fighting for a long time between the Front for the Liberation of Mozambique (FRELIMO) and Mozambique National Resistance (MNR or RENAMO).

Moreover, the concept of democracy in Africa has really complicated matters. Democracy means rule by the people and, according to democratic theory, the primary means by which citizens put in place a democratic government is through voting in free and fair elections.[3] However, elections in many African countries have been associated with numerous problems which have led to intense conflicts amongst political parties. Some of the problems associated with elections in Africa include the election of electoral commissions, technical shortcomings, and political leadership.[4]

The appointment of a national electoral council or commission is usually the first point of controversy. Political groups, especially those in opposition, are rarely convinced of the impartiality of members of the commission. Indeed, there are times when the work of the electoral commission leaves a lot to be desired, as their independence is often questionable. At times it appears that the members' activities reveal some bias in favour of the ruling party's line.

In addition, political parties sometimes contest the fairness of the campaigning process, the validity of voter registers, mechanics of voting and even vote counting itself. This was a major issue of contention in Malawi's 1994 general elections when there were accusations and counter accusations between the Malawi Congress Party and the United Democratic Front about fake registers, people being denied the right to vote, as well as inflated vote figures. In Zimbabwe, the campaign for the 2002 elections led to a significant increase in political tension.[5] In fact, recent polls in the country have been marred by violence between opposite camps' supporters.

The response of leaders of contesting parties to either victory or defeat also plays a major role in determining what happens next. The problem is that some leaders of political parties are overconfident to the extent that they do not seriously contemplate the possibility of losing elections. Of course, it is not wrong to be confident but in any contest, especially elections where it is difficult to precisely predict the behaviour of voters, one can either win or lose, and one should be prepared for anything. Everything being equal, when these overconfident leaders lose the elections, they find it difficult to accept the results. A case in point is that of Jonas Savimbi of Angola: "when he discovered that he did not like losing he took up arms again".[6] In Malawi, too, the leader of the opposition MCP/AFORD alliance was quoted during the 1999 general elections as saying that there was no question of losing the elections. But when the election results were announced, the ruling party leader received 51% of the vote, whilst the opposition leader had to settle for just 44%. The opposition did not accept the results and went on to file a petition with the Malawi High Court – a case which dragged on for months.[7]

All these problems with elections in Africa fuel conflicts in the countries concerned since losing parties do not accept the results. In Lesotho, for example, after the 1998 general elections won by the Lesotho Congress for Democracy, three of the five opposition parties called for the annulment of the elections due to alleged severe election irregularities and fraud. In Zanzibar, the islands have been in political turmoil since the opposition Civic United Front (CUF) rejected the CCM's (Revolutionary) party victory in the 1995 elections. The CUF again disputed the October 2000 elections and demanded a re-run of the vote which it alleged was rigged. Even Commonwealth observers described the October 2000 polls in Zanzibar as a "shambles" and recommended that they be repeated, but the Tanzanian government rejected the call.[8]

There is also the problem of poor governance in many African countries which has led to a large number of political conflicts. Opposition parties have at times accused ruling parties of not having the welfare of the people at heart and failing to distribute the country's resources fairly. For instance, the Sudan People's Liberation Army (SPLA) launched the civil war in 1983 seeking autonomy for the ethnically Christian south which it alleged had suffered decades of neglect and discrimination at the hands of Al-Bashir's government.[9] In the Democratic Republic of Congo (DRC), Laurent Kabila's forces rose against the government of Mobutu Sese Seko, but the Congolese Rally for Democracy (RCD) later protested against the undemocratic behaviour of Kabila's government, especially his inability to hold national elections after overthrowing Mobutu.

Last but not least, some political leaders in Africa are blinded by their greed for power. Once they are in power they would want to stay in power even when the country's constitution states otherwise. Recently, there was a high-profile campaign in Zambia to amend that country's law so that Frederick Chiluba, who ousted founding president Kenneth Kaunda in the 1991 pluralist elections, could extend his stay beyond the constitutional two five-year terms. He later capitulated. Instead of the leaders stepping down gracefully at the end of their term of office and taking pride in retiring to their private lives like Julius Nyerere of Tanzania, Nelson Mandela of South Africa or Kitumile Masire of Botswana did, they prefer to go on until they are forced out.

Religious Reasons

In any country, there is a variety of people with different religious beliefs. In some cases the beliefs are so divergent to the extent that as one group pursues its beliefs it might be in direct conflict with those of the other group(s). Furthermore, there are times when religious groups want to dominate and show that theirs is the true worship; such practices often lead to conflicts. Each individual is of course theoretically free to drop one faith and embrace another, but in practice aggressive conversions may bring about bloody conflicts. In Algeria for example, thousands of people have been killed by people who say they are promoting Islam, whilst in Sudan – during the 18 year old civil war – in broad terms, the mainly Arabic Islamic north is pitted against the mostly Christian south.[10]

Race and Ethnic Reasons

At times conflict might occur simply because of racial differences. Some groups may feel oppressed or exploited by government on the basis of racial discrimination and this can lead to the sufferers becoming frightened or angry and eventually their attitudes or feelings can influence their actions. For example in South Africa, the way the black people were treated during apartheid led to protest matches, strikes and a great deal of violence.

Ethnicity might also be the cause of conflicts in some cases. In Rwanda, the current minority Tutsi government led by Paul Kagame came to power when "the Hutu government was toppled after the 1994 genocide in which an estimated 800000 Rwandas were killed" and in Burundi, fighting between the main ethnic Hutu rebel groups and ethnic Tutsi government rages on.[11]

Foreign Support

Sometimes foreign countries or even neighbouring countries may fuel conflicts in another country by providing support to groups which are sympathetic to their ideologies. For instance, it has now been demonstrated that in Angola, the USA supported Jonas Savimbi in his fight against Eduardo Dos Santos. In turn, the civil war in the Democratic Republic of Congo (DRC), began in 1998 after Rwanda and Uganda, Laurent Kabila's biggest backers in his successful 1996-97 campaign to oust president Mobutu Sese Seko, turned against him and supported rebels trying to topple him. While Rwanda and Uganda reinforced their pre-existing military presence in the east, several governments, including Angola, Zimbabwe and Namibia, sent in their own troops to defend Kabila's regime. Each of the foreign powers has its own interests –often economic – in the DRC. Rwanda, for instance, plans to remain in eastern Congo as a matter of self-defence until the perpetrators of genocide in Rwanda are disarmed and the border is secure. Uganda also insists that its forces remain in the DRC to protect its borders against its own foreign-backed rebel groups and to dismantle their bases. On the other side, all foreign forces say they are defending a sovereign government against foreign invaders.[12]

Print/Electronic Media

In modern life, news of any disorder or violence can be communicated almost immediately worldwide. Usually, trouble only erupts in one area where a potentially explosive situation exists. However, the mass media may act as an instant fuse so that disorder in one part of the country might spread elsewhere in a series of 'copycat' situations.[13] This was the case in Malawi soon after the 1999 election results were announced. Trouble erupted in the northern region and eventually spread to the other parts of Malawi once it was reported on Television Malawi and in some newspapers. In Rwanda, three journalists are among those accused of inciting mass slaughter in that country's 1994 genocide. The three are being charged with conspiracy and incitement to commit genocide and crimes against humanity. It is strongly believed that Rwanda's media played a large part in the 100-day slaughter.[14]

Positive effects of moderate conflicts

Life would be boring if everybody thought in the same way and agreed to everything. A fair amount of healthy conflict can provide ways of coping with life's problems. Some of the positive effects of moderate level of conflict will be discussed below.

Conflict brings hidden issues to the surface

Conflict gives people an opportunity to examine problems and solutions that may otherwise have been ignored. In Malawi, for instance, before the dawn of multi-party politics, if no one had plucked up the courage to challenge or oppose the one-party system of government, most Malawians would not have known that there was a problem with the one-party system of government. Thus, after conflict a new leadership or government may be brought in. This is a rare, albeit, important function of conflict. Furthermore, disassociating elements in a situation may be removed and unity may be re-established as in common parlance, "a good fight helps clear the air".

Conflict encourages creativity and innovation

As a result of conflict, people might do new things and behave in new and perhaps better ways because of the greater diversity of viewpoints. Each group may develop an increased understanding of its own position, since conflict forces people to articulate their views and bring forth all supporting arguments.

Conflict leads to better decisions

Perhaps during a disagreement a group may come to hold a different perspective on an issue or learn that a perception or information had been inaccurate. Hence old goals or beliefs may be modified or replaced by more relevant goals or beliefs as a result of conflict. As conventional wisdom would have it, everyone sees truth from a different angle and when all the angles are brought together one sees the whole picture.

Negative consequences of intense conflicts

Although certain conflicts are beneficial, too much or intense conflict can nonetheless overpower the people and lead to the collapse of society and even complete chaos. One major negative effect of too much conflict is civil war. Leeds points out that as conflict escalates it moves from non-violent to increasingly violent methods, e.g. from verbal disputes to the use of guns.[15] Indeed, a critical look at many of the civil wars that have erupted in countries in Africa, like Angola, Mozambique, Burundi, the DRC, Rwanda and Sudan, reveals that the civil wars were as a result of intense conflicts between divergent groups in the countries concerned. However, there are both humanitarian and economic costs of civil wars. For instance, the oil and diamond rich Angola has known little but wars since it won independence from Portugal in 1975. An estimated one million people have been killed and millions more displaced over that period.[16] There are similar sad experiences in Mozambique, Rwanda and the DRC. There are also the economic costs in the sense that conflicts of a highly intense nature usually result in the misallocation of the country's resources. People waste valuable time and money in carrying out their internecine warfare. As such, scarce resources are diverted from health, education and poverty relief activities to sustain the war effort.

Strategies for containing local conflicts

There are a number of strategies that can be used to contain local conflicts from turning into civil wars and where there is a cease-fire, to prevent a renewal of the conflict. The first of these is free and fair elections.

As discussed earlier, most of the conflicts that have occurred and are still occurring in many countries in Africa are political in nature. If democracy is to survive in Africa there is a need to promote free and fair elections. This can be done by, for instance, levelling the playing field and also ensuring the independence of the electoral commission. All contesting parties need to have a fair share of resources available for campaigning purposes. For instance, they should have reasonable access to the electronic and print media so that they can effectively communicate their policies, philosophies, and values to the masses for the voters to make informed choices during the actual voting exercise. There is also a need to provide election materials in all voting centres on time – even those areas where the opposition parties have a very large and strong following. Furthermore, measures have to be taken to ensure that the electoral commission is indeed an independent and neutral entity, by for example requesting major contesting parties to nominate at least one representative to be a member of the commission so that the views of different parties contesting can be represented. All this can be done to ensure that only genuine democratic governments reflecting the choice of the majority of the citizens are elected.

The responsibility of containing conflicts should be on the leaders of political groups as well. After elections, supporters take their cues directly from their leaders. Those who have lost, must demonstrate clearly whether they have accepted defeat. In 1991 in Zambia, the nature of Frederick Chiluba's response to victory and Kenneth Kaunda's to defeat, and in Malawi in 1994 the response of Kamuzu Banda to defeat played a major role in securing the success of the elections in the two countries. When Kamuzu Banda honourably accepted defeat through a radio statement his supporters did not find any justification for any form of violence. Indeed, political leaders need to understand that in any democratic elections you either win or lose. When they lose they should honourably accept defeat to diffuse possible conflict from their supporters.

Leaders therefore, should provide appropriate leadership to their supporters. Even those leaders that have won the elections can assist in containing conflicts soon after the elections by extending a hand of reconciliation to the losers so as to counter the alienation of defeated parties. Those who have lost can for instance, be given influential positions in the government. For example, in South Africa, the leaders of the two main opposition parties were invited into the Government of National Unity after the 1994 elections, as a deliberate attempt at reconciliation and nation-building. In Malawi, Bakili Muluzi invited the defeated Chakufwa Chihana to join his cabinet. Such actions can really assist in defusing an otherwise tense situation.

In addition, leaders should refuse efforts by foreign countries to influence the course of events in their countries, as they are sovereign states. It should also be noted here that leaders sometimes need to use force to contain conflicts. Although this may create feelings of resentment and mistrust that might lead to further conflicts at a later stage, the threat of or actual use of force may compel those with opposing views to revisit their stand. The aim is not to stifle freedom of expression, but rather, to ensure that people do not take democracy and freedom of expression beyond a point that is good for the country.

In turn, peacekeeping, according to Leeds, takes place when an individual or a group helps to keep antagonists apart or separate, maintain peace when a dispute has ended and to prevent a renewal of a conflict. Peacekeeping might even involve an invitation to an international force to intervene between two opponents in which case the role of the peacekeepers would be one closer to policing than soldiering.[17] The United Nations has deployed a small force of peacekeepers to the DRC, and one to Burundi for just such purposes.[18]

The hope is that the presence of the peacekeepers would help in the creation of peaceful and stable conditions that could make it easier for the leaders of conflicting sides to get together and solve their dispute. However, if no effort is made to identify the root causes of the conflict, relations between former antagonists may remain unfriendly with both sides harbouring grudges and waiting for a chance to reopen hostilities because of the continuation of an unresolved problem. Hence, even though peacekeeping may not solve the conflict as such, it may simply freeze the conflict and this can prevent the emergence of a civil war.

Peacemaking, in contrast, involves measures to solve a conflict permanently to the satisfaction of the various groups or individuals involved.[19] To permanently solve a conflict requires the identification of the underlying causes of the conflict and open discussion of all the relevant issues. Of course it may take time before a peacemaker finds out the causes of the conflict and helps the concerned groups to settle their differences because groups might be unwilling to disclose their real problems and interests to outsiders. But if the peacemaker has the relevant knowledge, experience and skills in handling others and is effective, peace is indeed the result.

As noted earlier, all groups fighting in DRC have their own vested interests. As such, to effectively deal with this conflict it means all these interests have to be addressed somehow. That is why in any peacemaking effort there is a need to involve all groups involved in a conflict in one way or the other. In Burundi, the 2000 peace deal brokered by former South African president Nelson Mandela did not include the main ethnic Hutu rebel groups. As such, it failed to end the bloodshed, while a later, more inclusive peace agreement has been more successful.[20] Moreover, Paul Kagame of Rwanda initially refused to attend a summit to revive the 1999 Congo peace accord in Zambia: "The summit can and may go ahead without him ... The problem is that Rwanda will refuse to be bound by anything it might agree on".[21]

There are different forms of peacemaking, including arbitration and mediation. Both forms call for outside neutral parties to enter the situation and assist in resolving the conflict. *Arbitration* is the process in which a conflict between parties is submitted to an independent third party to make a binding decision. The parties agree in advance that the arbitrator's decision would be final. *Mediation*, on the other hand, is a process in which an independent third party is asked to facilitate communication between parties in conflict. Thus the mediator can only suggest, recommend and attempt to keep the parties in conflict talking so as to reach a solution. Mediators and arbitrators can be well-known individuals in the world (working either officially or unofficially) or they can be drawn from international organisations such as the Organisation of African Unity (OAU) and the United Nations (UN).

To contain the conflict in Mozambique between FRELIMO and REN-AMO a number of people were involved including Lonrho's 'Tiny' Rowland, Zimbabwean president Robert Mugabe, Italian mediators and observers from France, the UK, USA and Portugal.[22] In Burundi, former president Mandela facilitated the peace process; for the DRC, the mediators include the previous Zambian president Frederick Chiluba and Masire of Botswana. If in a country there has been a civil war before, peacemaking entails full demobilisation and disarmament. Otherwise, groups may take up arms again if they are not satisfied with whatever is happening – as was the case with Jonas Savimbi of Angola, when he lost the country's multiparty elections. At the end of it all, parties in conflict should be committed to the peace process. Otherwise, the whole peacemaking effort will be in vain. Therefore, peacemaking is another strategy that can be used to contain local conflicts.

The electronic and print media can also be used to contain conflicts by emphasising the negative consequences of intense conflicts and the benefits of peace in any country, so that people can be more enlightened on such issues. At times people act out of ignorance, as they do not really know the consequences of their actions, but through responsible journalism people might learn to exercise judgement and say no to actions likely to fuel conflicts.

Conclusion

There are a number of factors that lead to conflicts in many countries in Africa, which can be grouped into the categories of political factors, religious differences, race and ethnicity, as well as the willingness of foreign countries to render support. Countries can of course benefit to a certain extent from moderate levels of conflicts. But too much conflict is harmful, especially if it escalates into civil wars. Looking at the experiences in Angola, Mozambique, DRC, Rwanda and Burundi, the devastating consequences of civil wars are laid bare before our eyes. The need, therefore, is to understand the causes of local conflicts and then develop constructive measures to contain such conflicts.

Amongst the various strategies available to contain local conflict from turning into civil wars in Africa, free and fair elections and appropriate leadership stand out. Free and fair elections in any country would help usher in genuine democratic governments reflecting the choice of the majority of voters. Other strategies, like peacemaking, peacekeeping and responsible news reporting, would not be effective if leaders of different groups – be they political, cultural, religious, or otherwise – do not tolerate one another and are not ready to work together for the good of the country. If leaders are not committed to securing and maintaining peace, then conflict is the result. Indeed leaders should provide the appropriate leadership since followers take their cues from their leaders.

Notes and References

1   J Gordon *et al*, *Management and Organizational Behaviour*, Massachusetts: Allyn and Bacon, 1990, p 532.
2   J Goldman *et al*, *The Challenges of Democracy: Governments in America*, New York: Houghton Mifflin, 1987.
3   *Ibid*.
4   *Africa Confidential* vol 33, no 23, 1992.
5   Misanet, February 2001.
6   *Africa Confidential*, vol 33, no 25, 1992,
7   *BBC Focus on Africa*, vol 10, no 4, 1999.
8   *Daily Times* (Malawi), 12 February 2001.
9   *Daily Times* (Malawi), 23 February 2001.
10 *Daily Times* (Malawi), 14 February 2001.
11 *Daily Times* (Malawi), 12 February 2001.
12 *The Nation* (Malawi), 6 February 2001.
13 C Leeds, *Peace and War*, Cheltenham: Stanley Thornes, 1987, p 20.
14 *The Nation* (Malawi), 31 January 2001.
15 Leeds 1987.
16 *Daily Times* (Malawi), 16 February 2001.
17 Leeds 1987, p 159.
18 *Daily Times* (Malawi), 16 February 2001, p 10.
19 Leeds 1987, p 162.
20 *The Nation* (Malawi), 27 February 2001.
21 Reuters report quoted by *The Nation* (Malawi), 13 February 2001, p 3.
22 *Africa Confidential*, vol 33, no 16, 1992, p 1.

The Quest for Peace and Security: The Southern African Development Community (SADC) Organ on Politics, Defence and Security

Bertha Z Osei-Hwedie

Southern Africa is striving to promote both good governance and economic development in the region, but political and economic development is only possible when political order and stability prevail. Political instability and civil wars, which characterise some of the states in the region, make peace and security urgent necessities, hence the need for collective regional security. A security regime is important for the region because threats to peace and security arise partly from disagreements on the proper form of political governance within states, and partly from animosities between neighbours.

This chapter examines the SADC Organ on Politics, Defence and Security as a co-operative mechanism for collective security and peace in the region. The aim is to explain the nature of the Organ by examining its origin, objectives, and structure, and to assess its effectiveness as an institutional framework for the security regime that co-ordinates the efforts and influences the behaviour of member states to resolve common problems of peace and security. The effectiveness of the Organ is evaluated with reference to two 'test' cases: The 1998 Lesotho instability and the civil war in the Democratic Republic of the Congo (DRC). In this respect, the Organ is discussed within the context of a redefined conception of security. Regime analysis is utilised to understand its formation, maintenance and change, and how the Organ articulates expectations, encourages international co-operation and influences the behaviour of its members. Problems and limitations of the security regime in Southern Africa are also analysed.

Security Regime: Theoretical Considerations

The Organ should be understood as part of efforts to deepen and extend co-operation among member states beyond the realm of economics, particularly trade, which is the predominant relationship in SADC, to the realm of security. Regional security co-operation is feasible because states realise that individually, each cannot resolve security problems within its borders, or those which transcend national borders.

Good governance and peace and security are ideals which are sought after by every state and region in the world. Regional security institutions have increasingly become prominent in solving problems of peace and security within their respective regions partly due to the desire of regions to manage their own affairs, and partly as a result of the incapacity of the United Nations. However, regional security institutions are expected to work in close co-operation with international bodies like the UN and other regional bodies like the Organisation of African Unity. Similarly, contemporary regional security organisations, unlike traditional ones, deal with threats emanating from within respective member states, in the form of rebellions, insurgencies, coups, civil strife, and international criminal activities. These post-independence security problems require not only a security regime but also a redefinition of security that focuses "on internal rather than external threats". It includes not only defence of incumbent governments against threats but also the pursuit of democracy, sustainable economic development, social justice and environmental protection.[1]

A redefinition of security is particularly relevant to the Southern African region because states achieved their independence relatively recently and are still in the process of development. In addition, most states are transitional, 'Third Wave democracies' with problems of consolidation of democracy, and hence, the need for a security regime. The current problem of ethnic and border conflicts prevalent in some countries, like the DRC, is a product of unequal development and undemocratic regimes which give rise to "economic, political and ecological refugees".[2] The intention by SADC members to promote peace and security arises from their realisation that peace, security and development are intertwined and can only be achieved if members share a common political orientation through adopting and implementing democratic principles. This objective is particularly poignant in the current global situation where democratic institutions and practices are associated with peace, security and development. Democracy is usually accompanied by market-driven economies. Thus, the twin institutions of democracy and the free market economy, vital elements of neo-liberalism, are the basis of peace, security and development. This is exactly what the Organ is expected to achieve.

Regime Analysis

Regime analysis, that of reciprocity and hegemony, is used to explain co-operation and conflict within the Organ and its effectiveness. Ruggie defines an international regime as a "set of mutual expectations, rules and regulations, plans, organisational energies and financial commitment, which have been accepted by a group of states".[3] Krasner defines regimes as "sets of implicit or explicit principles, norms, rules and decision-making procedures around which actor expectations converge in a given area of international relations".[4] Thus, to Krasner, principles are beliefs of facts, while norms are standards of behaviour based on rights and obligations. Rules are prescriptions for action, and decision-making procedures are practices for making and implementing collective choice. According to Keohane and Lake, international regimes are instruments of state craft and are created to facilitate co-operation by providing a legal framework, reduce transaction costs, and minimise uncertain and irresponsible behaviour by providing information to members.[5]

The reciprocity theory of international regimes argues that a regime is created and maintained to fulfil some function; that of achieving the common interests of members such that there is mutual benefit. Therefore, the self-interest of each member is the driving force for international co-operation. Conversely, when a regime loses its functional utility of promoting the common interests of its members, it is likely to falter or dismantle, as in the case of the Organ. The Organ was founded on the belief that members can make or adopt and implement common and coherent policy actions to solve political and peace and security problems within each member state and within the region as a whole.

The aim of the Organ as a security regime, therefore, is to pool resources so as to reduce costs in the security area for mutual benefit of members in terms of guaranteeing the national interest of each member. National interest is defined broadly to include guarantee of sovereignty, proportional distribution of benefits and equal sharing of the burdens of collective action. Such a balance between respect for sovereignty, and equal sharing of benefits and burdens would reduce disputes between members and thus ensure smooth functioning of a regime. This is important because demands of regional co-operation divert resources away from domestic requirements. However, when some members resort to unilateral foreign policy actions with little or no consultation and without consideration of other members' interests, disillusionment and disaffection set in. When this happens, the "myopic self-interest" has overridden common goals.[6] This underlies the inability of the regime to regulate and influence the behaviour of its members, as in the case of the Organ with respect to the DRC civil war.

Regime analysis based on the hegemony is more relevant to explaining the problems and limitations faced by the Organ of making and implementing collective choice and action to resolve security problems in the region especially in relation to the DRC. Hegemonic analysis helps to explain the conflict within the Organ and its eventual dissolution, and especially the struggle between South Africa and Zimbabwe which prefer negotiations and a military solution to the DRC war, respectively. Hegemony rests on the premise that the existence of a single dominant actor in the international or regional system results in international co-operation, order and stability. A hegemonic leadership consists of a single dominant state which is willing to bear the costs of providing public or collective goods beneficial to all members, including small ones. Conversely, the absence of a hegemonic state would mean a lack of international co-operation, and instability.[7] This means that hegemonic theory sees the equality of states as not being conducive to the successful functioning of the regime as in the case of the Organ.

Origins and Structure of the Organ

The Organ is one of the organisational units of SADC to which all 14 members belong. SADC, which replaced the Southern African Development Co-ordinating Council (SADCC), was created by the Treaty of 1992. The Treaty is the foundation of co-operation in various areas, but the ultimate goal is regional integration. Article 21 (3) of the Treaty outlines several areas of regional co-operation including peace and security, which the Organ is responsible for.[8] Previously, the states in Southern Africa formed the Front Line States (FLS), composed of Heads of Government and States to make regional policy and co-ordinate their efforts in the area of politics, peace and security. In particular, the FLS decided on how best to achieve independence for the remaining parts of Southern Africa still under colonial rule. The FLS opted for providing assistance to some liberation movements.[9] The independence of South Africa in 1994 signalled the end of the FLS as it had accomplished its mission. With the demise of the FLS, members felt the need for another security regime to make policy, co-ordinate their efforts and behaviour to tackle post-independence problems of peace and security for sustainable development. Hence the formation of the Organ. The Organ was established in June 1996 in Gaborone, Botswana, after extensive consultations on its role, organisational structure, operational mechanism and responsibility for its operations. The SADC Council of Ministers of Foreign Affairs, Defence and Security undertook extensive deliberations after 1994, postponed a decision on its establishment on several occasions, and subsequently made the final decision for its establishment through a recommendation to the Heads of States Summit in 1996.

Initial suggestions for a new organisation to replace the FLS centred on establishing two different units: a Sector on Politics, Diplomacy, Defence and Security, and the Association of Southern African States (ASA). However, to avoid duplication of functions, the Council of Ministers decided to create one organisation to carry out both functions.[10] The extensive search for an appropriate institutional mechanism to deal with the issues of politics, peace and security extended to the study of the Organ for Security and Co-operation in Europe (OSCE). The idea of a troika, meaning a team of officials drawn from various member states with joint responsibility for a particular task, was borrowed from the structure of the OSCE.

Three institutional frameworks were proposed and evaluated by the Council of Ministers as follows: The first suggestion was for one member state of SADC to assume overall responsibility, on a permanent basis, for the establishment, co-ordination and maintenance of regional politics, peace and security. Thus, one state was to establish a Sector Co-ordination Unit to undertake all functions in this area. The second option provided for rotational responsibility among all member states for the Sector Co-ordinating Unit. The third proposal, based on the FLS structure, centred on the creation of an Organ at the Heads of States level. The Chair of the Organ would be elected by Heads of States and held on a rotational basis among all member states so that each Head holds the Chair for 24 months.[11] The Council of Ministers chose the third option, with some modifications, which they recommended to the Summit of Heads of Governments and States for formal adoption. Thus, the Organ is based on a combined structure of the FLS, which it replaced, and the OSCE's troika system, with a very broad mandate covering two areas of co-operation in politics, and peace and security.

The Organ operates at the Summit, ministerial and technical levels.[12] Organisationally, the Organ exists at the Summit level because the Chair is the Head of State, elected by the Summit of Heads of Governments and States, after consultation. The high level the Organ occupies shows the importance attached to the security regime by members. According to the Terms of Reference, the Chair is held on an annual rotational basis and is based on a troika system. The Summit selected President Mugabe of Zimbabwe as the first Chairman of the Organ in 1996. President Mugabe promised all Heads that he would work closely and co-operatively with all member states and consult them on all issues dealt with by the Organ. Consultation is important since it is the Summit which appraises the political, peace and security situations in the region through reports from member states. This suggests that consultation is the basic mode of decision-making and implementation of collective action by the Organ.

Operationally, the major instrument of the Organ is the Inter-State Defence and Security Committee (ISDSC). But the Organ was given the mandate to create other committees whenever necessary to carry out its duties.[13] Although the ISDSC has no permanent structure, it is chaired by a Defence Minister of a SADC country on a rotational basis, and functions through meetings. The ISDSC is composed of a ministerial council with three sub-committees on defence, security and intelligence. Below the level of defence sub-committee, there are three functional committees, namely the Operations Sub-committee, the Standing Maritime Committee and the Aviation Committee. Thus, the composition of the ISDSC indicates that the Organ has concentrated on dealing with issues of peace and security. This means that all departments of Foreign Affairs of member countries are not represented in the ISDSC and are, therefore, currently excluded from the operations of the Organ. Similarly, non-governmental organisations (NGOs), which would be relevant to the monitoring of human rights in member states, are not included in the ISDSC.[14] In addition, there is provision for the Organ to function independently of other SADC structures, such as the Summit and the Secretariat. Such autonomy is necessary for flexibility to effectively and promptly respond to any threats to regional peace and security, and to decide on political issues.

In reality, the Organ has functioned primarily at the Summit level. To some extent, it has also functioned at the ministerial level through the ISDSC, but not at the technical level.[15] It is the Summit which has been most active in appraising the political, peace and security situation in the region through reports from member states tabled at the Organ's meetings. The first of these meetings of the Organ was held in Luanda, Angola in 1996.[16]

Objectives and Strategies of the Organ

The Terms of Reference of the Organ stipulate several principles upon which the security regime is based, and objectives which must be achieved. The primary principle is that of sovereign equality of all member states. The objectives of the Organ are a mirror image of the objectives contained in Article 21 of the SADC Treaty. The Article lists diverse areas of co-operation among which are politics, peace and security, which the Organ is responsible for. For analytical purposes, the Organ's 16 objectives are divided into five major categories: military and defence, crime prevention, intelligence, foreign policy, and politics and human rights.[17] Such a categorisation does not mean that the objectives are exclusive; rather, they are mutually overlapping to the extent that they can be further reduced to two broad objectives: politics, and peace and security, elements of a redefined conception of security.

The first, then, is the objective of military and defence. The Organ is mandated to develop co-operation in the fields of military and defence to provide protection against any form of instability through the development of a collective security capacity, a regional peacekeeping capacity, and the formation of a mutual Defence Pact to deal with external threats. The second objective is crime prevention, which is expected to be accomplished through co-operative efforts of the police and security services to deal with cross-border crime and to build a community-based approach to security issues. The third objective is intelligence. The aim is to co-operate in intelligence and early warning systems as pre-emptive measures against conflict within and between member states.

The fourth objective is foreign policy, with the intention to develop a common foreign policy on issues of interest to members and to adopt a regional position at international forums. Other intentions of foreign policy are to co-operate on regional security and defence through conflict prevention, management and resolution, and to mediate in inter-state and intrastate disputes and conflicts and to co-ordinate the participation of member states in international and regional peacekeeping operations. Foreign policy also aims to encourage and monitor ratification of the UN and OAU and other international conventions and treaties on arms control and disarmament, human rights and peaceful human relations between states.

The fifth objective relates to politics and human rights. The Organ is mandated to develop democratic institutions and practices within member states, and to encourage the observance of universal human rights in accordance with the Charters and Conventions of the OAU and the UN. Thus, the Organ has to ensure the application of democratic principles in member states. This objective underlies the redefinition of security arising from the fact that member states view democracy as critical to sustainable political stability, and a necessary condition for development, regional co-operation and eventual integration of the region. Indeed, common political values of democracy among members would make co-operation relatively easy, as they would most likely agree on common policies, such as economic ones. Moreover, the adoption and practice of democracy would mean that the region would be portrayed favourably in the international arena where democratic values are the predominant and preferred norms.

A two-pronged strategy has been used by the Organ to deal with problems of peace and security. Emphasis and priority are given to peaceful methods, including negotiation and arbitration, to settle conflicts between and within states. This means that whenever diplomatic efforts fail to resolve disputes, the use of military force is seen as a viable alternative. Members are required to reach a consensus on the use of force, which can only be used after it has been endorsed in a protocol on Peace, Security and Conflict Resolution.[18] This essentially means that the use of force is a last resort.

Responses to Peace and Security Problems: Test cases

The Organ has so far concentrated its efforts on the first objective, that of military and defence, primarily responding to threats to incumbent governments: political instability in Lesotho in 1998; and the civil war in the DRC. Here, the chapter attempts to analyse the extent to which the Organ has been successful or has failed in its duty to promote peace and security in the region, and to explain the different outcomes of the two crises, with relative success in Lesotho, and failure in the DRC.

The Lesotho Conflict

The Lesotho crisis arose from the 1998 general election results, which awarded the election to the Lesotho Congress for Democracy (LCD). Three of the five opposition parties – the Basotho Congress Party (BCP), Basotho National Party (BNP), and Moremo-Tlou Freedom Party (MFP) – did not accept the results, and called for the annulment of elections due to alleged severe irregularities and fraud, the dissolution of the LCD government and the formation of a Government of National Unity (GNU). When these demands were not fulfilled, the opposition organised protest marches and strikes and occupied the Royal Palace.[19] These anti-government protests culminated in violent confrontation between the government and opposition forces, hence the political instability, and rumours about an impending coup d'état. The inability of the government to contain the disturbances forced it to request military assistance from other SADC member states to restore order and stability.

The Organ, through the Allied Forces, composed of South African and Botswana defence forces, managed to restore order and stability by suppressing the opposition to the incumbent government. However, the Allied Forces were criticised for the military intervention in Lesotho. First, the controversy centred on the opposition parties' and citizens' claims that their country's sovereignty had been violated by the Allied Forces' intervention in Lesotho, and claims that the request for military intervention originated from an inappropriate authority in Lesotho. Claims of violation of Lesotho's sovereignty lack any foundation, as the intervention was at the request of the ruling Lesotho government. Similarly, the fact that the Prime Minister, Head of the Lesotho government, rather than the King requested military intervention from the SADC Allied forces led to questions being raised regarding the legitimacy of the SADC Allied Forces' intervention. Although the King, as a symbolic figure, has the legal responsibility to request foreign assistance as the Head of State, real power lies with the Prime Minister, the executive Head of Government. Moreover, since Botswana, South Africa and Zimbabwe had intervened in a previous incident of political instability in Lesotho in 1994, the 1998 intervention by the Allied Forces merely regularised their assistance.[20]

The second criticism centred on whether their intervention was sanctioned by the Organ. The intervention by the Allied Forces of Botswana and South African armed forces was sanctioned under the SADC interstate security agreement, the Protocol on Politics, Defence and Security which commits member states to collective security whenever a legitimate government is under threat. Collective security is not only intended to restore domestic tranquillity but also to safeguard the peace and security of neighbouring states. In accordance with the Protocol on Peace, Security and Conflict Resolution of SADC, member states unanimously agreed to military intervention as the most appropriate response to the deteriorating political situation in Lesotho. More importantly, President Mugabe, was consulted both as the Chair of the Organ and a member of the presidential troika of Botswana, South Africa and Zimbabwe, and he gave his approval to the military intervention in Lesotho.

The third criticism stemmed from the consequences of the military intervention, particularly South Africa's. The intervention had two main shortcomings. Lack of co-ordination between Botswana and South Africa resulted in the former being the first to arrive in Lesotho and the latter coming two days later. A more serious error, which was detrimental to the South African forces, was the fact that South Africa miscalculated the strength of the resistance to the LDC government and lacked accurate information as to the whereabouts of the rebel forces. Instead of a weak opposition, the South African forces were confronted with a well-equipped and committed Lesotho Defence Force and armed civilian groups. As such they had to fight the rebellion which resulted in the loss of South African and Basotho lives and the destruction of the city. The Botswana Forces provided only peacekeeping services, for which they are renowned.

The handling of the Lesotho crisis presents a classic case of a successful security regime that co-ordinates and organises a united behavioural response, and is capable of restoring peace and stability and preventing spill-over of the conflict to neighbouring states. Moreover, the SADC Allied Forces' intervention in Lesotho did not create tension within SADC and specifically between the Chair of SADC and the Chair of the Organ. The same is not true in the case of the DRC. SADC, through the Organ,

remained united in its intervention in Lesotho partly because the intervening Allied Forces of Botswana and South Africa had a common interest in
Lesotho. Primarily, the safety of the ruling government, historical ties and
geographical proximity motivated the intervention. Apart from South
Africa's interest in the Lesotho Highlands Water Project, there was not
much economic stake in Lesotho as compared to the DRC. The absence of
the involvement of external, non-SADC forces also made it relatively easy
for SADC forces to restore order and stability in Lesotho, thereby preventing the spread of instability to neighbouring countries. The success of
the intervention can be measured by the fact that it was of relatively short
duration and that it paved the way for mediation. The compromise by the
LDC government led to the release of those involved in rioting and the
attempted coup d'état. However, the national elections, which had been
scheduled to take place in the year 2000, were postponed until 2002.

The DRC Civil War

The civil war in the DRC has proven to be more complex and intractable
for the Organ than the political instability in Lesotho. The civil war broke
out in August 1998 between the Kabila government and the rebel forces,
which as an Alliance of Democratic Forces for the Liberation of the Congo
(ADFL), had overthrown the government of Mobutu in May 1997. The
rebel coalition forces, named the Congolese Rally for Democracy (RCD),
were fighting to protest the undemocratic behaviour of Laurent Kabila's
government, which once in power was unable to hold general elections
after ousting President Mobutu. The governments of Uganda and Rwanda,
which once supported Kabila and the ADFL, turned their support to the
RCD, ostensibly to protect their national interests and border security.

Kabila's request for military assistance from the Organ to safeguard the
survival of his government was responded to by three SADC countries:
Angola, Namibia and Zimbabwe sent their troops to the DRC. Similarly,
Chad, a non-SADC country, extended military support to the Kabila
regime. It was only in September 1998 that the Summit of the Heads of
Governments and States endorsed the military intervention of Angola,
Namibia and Zimbabwe in support of the Kabila government. As a result
of the prolonging of the war and the military stalemate between the three
rebel groups and the government troops, SADC's members' efforts were
directed at negotiations. The 1999 Lusaka Peace Accord to which the
Kabila government and rebel forces were signatory offered some prospects
for a peaceful solution to the war. In particular, provisions in the Accord for
a dialogue among contending parties offered good prospects for national
reconciliation, permanent peace and political stability. However, negotia-

tions for a peaceful solution to the war and implementation of the Lusaka Accord proved difficult due to disagreements between the rebel groups as to which of them was the legitimate opponent of the Kabila government; reluctance by both sides to abide by the Accord; military support for the Kabila government by Zimbabwe, Angola, Namibia and Chad; and military support for the rebel forces by Rwanda and Uganda, non-SADC members.

The inability to resolve the DRC civil war exposed the weakness of the Organ as a collective security regime as members failed to present a united front and solution, thus failing to end the civil war or protect the Kinshasa government against its opponents. There has been a lack of consensus among SADC members on how to resolve the DRC civil war. Two positions can be discerned within the Organ: member states which prefer negotiations instead of a military solution are led by South Africa, while the other group of members, led by Zimbabwe, together with Angola and Namibia, favours a military solution to the DRC war.[21]

The stand-off between members who support peaceful negotiations and those for a military solution to the war handicapped the functioning of the Organ and signalled the end of collective action and its eventual dissolution. This led to the formation of an alternative security arrangement, the New Defence Pact, by Zimbabwe's Robert Mugabe. Mugabe, frustrated by SADC's reluctance to endorse a military solution, his inability to use his position as the Chair of the Organ to rally SADC's support for his military option, and SADC's disbanding of the Organ, initiated the formation of a New Defence Pact. The Pact incorporated four countries, namely, Angola, the DRC, Namibia and Zimbabwe, thus leaving out the remaining 10 SADC members. Its primary goal was to eliminate rebels in Angola and the DRC, and to protect each Pact member's national interests.[22]

Angola and Namibia have valid reasons for supporting the Kabila government, to prevent the rebel forces, especially the RCD, from forming a government because of its alliance with the *Uniao Nacional para a Independencia Total de Angola* (UNITA). Angola and Namibia realise that should Kabila's side lose the war, an RCD government would allow UNITA's use of the DRC as a launch pad to attack the *Movimento Popular de Libertaçao de Angola* (MPLA) and South West African Peoples' Organisation (SWAPO) governments in Angola and Namibia. UNITA has been fighting the MPLA government since independence in 1975 and has had hostile relations with SWAPO, an ally of the MPLA, since the start of the liberation war during the pre-independence period. A victory for the MPLA government over UNITA is critical to the preservation of statehood. Therefore, the military intervention by the national defence forces of Angola and Namibia can be seen as pre-emptive attempts at maximising their own security.

The intervention by the Zimbabwe defence forces, however, can only be explained by factors other than the security interests of Zimbabwe. The belligerence by Zimbabwe and the stand off between pro-negotiation South Africa and pro-military solution Zimbabwe in the DRC can be explained by two factors: a power struggle for regional hegemony and a battle for control of the DRC's natural resources. Mugabe's belligerence should be seen as a challenge to the predominance of South Africa and especially former President Mandela in the region, and in the context of attempts to carve out a prominent role for Zimbabwe and himself within the region. There is no doubt that South Africa is the most dominant state, especially economically and militarily, in the region. Such a stalemate could also be explained by the inability of South Africa to assume a hegemonic leadership position as in the case of the USA in relation to the North Atlantic Treaty Organisation (NATO). The USA has shouldered the cost of military security of Western Europe and Japan as a result of the perceived threat from the former Communist bloc. This, therefore, suggests that the failure of the Organ in the DRC could be explained by the absence of a hegemonic leadership to ensure international co-operation among all member states of the regime and ensure stability within the region.

Similarly, the stand-off between South Africa and Zimbabwe could be seen in terms of the struggle for control of the abundant natural resources which the DRC has been unable to develop because of a lack of capabilities. Therefore, the two contenders for regional hegemony have made their national interests the basis for the different postures they have adopted towards the solution of the DRC war. It is the country's natural resource endowment which influenced SADC's admission of the DRC as a member in 1996. South African economic interests in the DRC can be identified in six principal areas: energy in the form of hydro-electric power from the Iringa Rapids, clean and renewable water from the Congo River Basin, arable land for South African farmers, minerals including copper, cobalt, tin, zinc and uranium, a large market for manufactures, and attractive investment prospects for South African firms.[23] For Zimbabwe, too, the DRC offers a good investment area, a market, and mineral resources, which it is assumed, would be used to rejuvenate Zimbabwe's ailing economy. There are allegations that Laurent Kabila signed over "huge mineral concessions and offering other financial guarantees to keep his allies loyal", particularly Zimbabwe and Namibia.[24]

In addition, the Organ's lack of a common regional position and action on the DRC war has not only created difficulties for a negotiated settlement to the war but has also caused tensions between Organ members. For example, Zambia, which was selected as SADC's mediator in the DRC between Kabila's government and the three rebel groups, was initially spurned by members of the New Defence Pact. Angola questioned President Frederick Chiluba's neutrality as he was alleged to be a supplier of arms to UNITA. The 1999 bombings in the Zambian capital by Angola aimed at punishing Zambia for its support of UNITA and dissuading it from supporting UNITA, and testify to the uneasy relationship between the two countries. The strained relationship between Angola and Zambia also indicates the primacy accorded to national interests rather than collective regional security, and points to the recurrence of old animosities between the Zambian government and the MPLA government. Similarly, Zimbabwe viewed Zambia's role as a mediator with suspicion after Zambia refused the request for the use of its territory as a transit route by Zimbabwean soldiers destined for the DRC to support Kabila's army.[25] Thus, national interests continue to be paramount preventing international co-operation in peace and security matters.

Internal divisions within the Organ, between members preferring negotiations and those for a military solution, and divisions resulting from different patterns of alliances with the outside world explain the lack of a common regional stance against non-SADC members' intervention in the DRC and the lack of a common foreign policy by the region in international forums like the UN, or regional ones like the OAU.

Problems and Limitations of the Security Regime

The Organ was important for the sake of creating preconditions for political and socio-economic development within the region. However, the Organ faced enormous problems and limitations to its efficient operations, especially to realise the objectives of peace and security. These arose partly from inherent organisational flaws and partly from the national interests of member states which prevent them from adhering to a comprehensive approach to peace similar to that of the OSCE.

Organisational defects of the Organ account for its inability to realise the goal of peace and security. This was primarily due to the undefined relationship between the Organ and SADC, the mother body, especially the unclear relationship between the Chair of the Organ and the Chair of SADC. Since the Organ operated at the Summit level, some confusion was created by the existence of two Chairs without clarification of the appropriate role and relationship between the Chair of the Organ and the Chair of SADC. In such a situation, it was unclear who of the two had to Chair the meetings of the Organ and who should assume the leadership role in resolving problems of peace and security in the region. Hence, there was a possibility of tensions between the two Chairs as had been the case in the DRC war. Neither is there provision in the Treaty on the Organ for the resolution of any tensions and conflicts that might arise between the two Chairs. Rather, mutual understanding between states was expected to cover any shortfall of the Treaty. This demonstrates a lack of clear guidelines as to how the troika system is to be operationalised, which has had negative consequences for the effectiveness of the Organ. Malan and Cilliers conclude that confusion as to the leadership role made it difficult for the region to respond to extra-regional threats which might have affected peace and security within the region.[26]

The lack of capacity also handicapped the performance of the Organ for it relied on members' contributions. Unfortunately, members have limited resources and those members who were capable of assisting the Organ were either unwilling to shoulder the costs or did so for their self-interest. For example, SADC has not been able to raise sufficient funds for a Joint Military Command for peacekeeping in the DRC to implement the anticipated ceasefire after all warring parties in the DRC signed the Lusaka Peace Accord. Even South Africa, which is militarily superior to all other SADC members, is unwilling to assume the hegemonic leadership role and absorb the cost of policing the region or guaranteeing regional peace and security. Zimbabwe tried to assert itself as a leader but met strong opposition from other members. The New Defence Pact of Zimbabwe, Angola and Namibia lacked legitimacy because it represented the self-interest of only three states of the region and thus failed to present a regional position. As a result of resource limitations, the lack of a hegemony, and self-interest, SADC prefers a UN peacekeeping force, which is still small. Similarly, the Organ has done relatively little to resolve the Angolan civil war which has been raging for more than two decades. In the case of Angola, too, SADC has opted for UN peacekeeping missions, the last of which, the United Nations Verification Mission (UNIVEM) III, wound up without resolving the war.

Resource limitations help to explain why the Organ achieved relatively little in the area of peace and security, but also why the Organ had done nothing much to realise the other objectives it was expected to accomplish. More importantly, just as the Organ members could not agree on the appropriate common response to the DRC crisis, it was unclear whether all states agreed on all objectives or attached the same importance to all objectives for which the Organ was responsible. For example, with respect to democracy, members of the Organ have diverse political values and institutions, ranging from long-established democracies like Botswana and Mauritius, to 'Third Wave' democracies with diverse characteristics and problems of consolidation of democracy, including South Africa, Zambia and Malawi, as well as authoritarianism and some democratic elements in Zimbabwe and Namibia, and undemocratic traditional monarchy in Swaziland, and a mixture of monarchy and democracy in Lesotho. These divergences made the Organ's task of promoting common democratic values and institutions in all member states extremely difficult. Therefore, the chance of establishing democratic governments as bases for sustainable peace and security for the development of the region is highly questionable. Furthermore, diverse political systems automatically mean different policies, and different interpretations of policies and resolutions of regional problems, as has happened in respect of the DRC. Also, the Treaty is unclear as to how these democratic values and practices are to be promoted by the Organ without contravening the principle of sovereignty.

The principle of sovereignty severely weakened the ability of the Organ to perform its role as guarantor of regional security. Whereas sovereignty provides a framework for co-equal states to facilitate co-operation, it also hinders international co-operation when member states invoke it to protect their national interests or a leader's ambitions regardless of the consequences for regional peace and security interests. For example, the DRC has dishonourably failed to honour the Peace Accord it signed; members of the New Defence Pact have stubbornly continued to militarily support the Kinshasa government in spite of the consequences; and South Africa and Zimbabwe continue to struggle for predominance in the region, all in the name of national sovereignty. Papp argues that "national sovereignty – the insistence by individual countries that they themselves have the right to determine their own courses of action and defend their own interest", has been the major obstacle to successful operations of international institutions responsible for peace and security.[27] In a similar vein, Swatuk and Vale also argue that "the creation of the Westphalian state form is at the heart of regional insecurity".[28] Therefore, sovereignty acts as a stumbling block to the Organ members' belief in the importance of international co-operation and collective decision-making and implementation. Consequently, the Organ was short-lived, operating for less than a year. The operations of the Organ were temporarily suspended pending the review of its mandate and restructuring to improve its functioning in the future. A committee, consisting of the Heads of Governments and States of Malawi, Mozambique, Namibia and Tanzania, was set up in 1997 to review and recommend appropriate and mutually beneficial authority relationship between the Organ and SADC.[29]

Future Prospects of the Organ

Organisational defects and national sovereignty constrained the effective performance of the Organ, hence its review by a Committee of SADC's Heads of Governments and States. The form the 'new' Organ might take is open to discussion. What is clear is that there is a need for flexibility and democratisation of the Organ to enhance its functioning. Malan and Cilliers make commendable proposals for improving its structure and operational capabilities.[30] In particular, they focus on resolving the problem of the dual Chairs, the need for a practical and workable troika system and a formalised structure rather than the current loosely designed format. They propose changing the tenure for the Chair of the Organ from one to three years to match that of the Chair of SADC. This would pave the way for a troika of Heads of Summit to avoid a dual leadership. The troika of Heads of Governments would consist of the Chair of SADC, the vice-Chair of SADC and the incoming Chair of SADC, who is also the Chair of the Organ. This basically means that there is one Chair for both the Organ and SADC on a rotational basis as is currently the practice.

To enhance the operational capacity of the Organ, Malan and Cilliers propose the establishment of the Political Co-operation Council of Ministers of Foreign Affairs to replace the ISDSC.[31] Such a Council would draw on the expertise of ministries of Defence, Security and Intelligence depending upon the issue being dealt with by the Council. Other proposals include the establishment of two committees, one on defence and crime prevention, to replace the defunct sub-committee of the ISDSC on defence, crime prevention and intelligence, and the other on conflict prevention, management and resolution, drawn from ministries of Foreign Affairs and Intelligence. These suggestions would ensure that the security institution operates simultaneously at the Summit, ministerial and technical levels as opposed to the defunct system operating at the Summit only. They also recommend the establishment of a Multinational Secretariat to undertake administrative tasks, including networking with other organisations like the OAU and the UN.

In addition, it is important for a restructured Organ to provide for participation of civil society, especially in cases involving crime, defence and democratic rights. In this respect, Malan and Cilliers make two provisions: the involvement of non-state actors in areas of human rights and democracy, particularly NGOs to monitor human rights situations in member states, and the establishment of an Institute for Democracy and Human Rights as an information generating and research machinery.[32]

However, much more than restructuring is needed to make the Organ effective and inter-state co-operation a reality. These largely depend on member states having the political will to bury their historical animosities, reduce competition and downplay the principle of sovereignty to allow for an effective system of collective regional security. Since national sovereignty remains the most significant threat to international co-operation or organisation, a reorientation away from the primacy of national interests to that of regional concerns is required for a successful and functioning international security regime. Such a reorientation would pave the way for a commitment to allocate sufficient resources by members to allow a restructured Organ to accomplish its objectives within the context of a new security orientation.

Conclusion

The Organ is an important tool for international co-operation and collective action to resolve problems of peace and security internal to member states and those of the region as a whole. Regime analysis helps us to understand both co-operation in the Organ, especially the successful resolution of the political instability in Lesotho in 1998, and the conflict arising from within the Organ due to the dual Chairs, national self-interest, competition for dominance, lack of a hegemonic leadership, and recurrence of old historical hostilities among members. Moreover, the continued civil war in the DRC points to the priority of national over regional interests. Unless member states acquire the political will to reorient their priority from national to regional interests, accept a redefinition of security, come up with a practical authority structure, and rise to the challenge of regional co-operation, the prospects for an effective and functioning security regime will remain elusive.

Notes and References

1   T Shaw, 'The Marginalization of Africa in the New World (Dis)Order', in R Stubbs and G Underhill (eds), *Political Economy and the Changing Global Order*, London: Macmillan, 1994, p 392; L Swatuk and A Omari, 'Regional Security: Southern Africa's Mobile "Front Line"', in L Swatuk and D Black (eds), *Bridging the Rift*, Boulder: Westview Press, 1997.

2   Shaw 1994, p 393.

3   J Ruggie, 'International responses to technology: Concepts and trends", *International Organization*, vol 29, no 3, Summer 1975, p 570.

4   S Krasner, 'Structural causes and regime consequences: Regimes as intervening variables', *International Organization*, vol 36, no 2, Spring 1982, p 186.

5   R Keohane, *After Hegemony: Cooperation and discord in the world political*

economy, New Jersey: Princeton University Press, 1984; D Lake, 'British and American hegemony compared: Lessons for the current era of decline', in J Frieden and D Lake (eds), *International Political Economy: Perspectives on global power and wealth*, London: Routledge, 2000.

6   Keohane 1984, p 99.

7   M Williams, *International economic organizations and the Third World*, New York: Harvester Wheatsheaf, 1994.

8   SADC, *Declaration and Treaty of the Southern African Development Community*, Gaborone: SADC, 1993.

9   BZ Osei-Hwedie, 'The FrontLine States: Cooperation for the Liberation of Southern Africa', *Journal of African Studies*, vol 10, no 4, Winter 1983–84.

10   SADC, *Terms of Reference for the SADC Sector on Political Cooperation, Peace and Security: Meeting of SADC Ministers Responsible for Foreign Affairs, Defence and SADC Affairs*, Gaborone: SADC, 18–19 January 1996a; SADC, *Press Release: SADC Ministers Meet in Gaborone*, Gaborone: SADC, 1996b.

11   SADC 1996a.

12   SADC, *Communique: Summit of Heads of States or Governments of the Southern African Development Community (SADC)*, Gaborone: SADC, 1996c.

13   *Ibid.*; SADC, *The SADC Organ on Politics, Defence and Security: Meeting of SADC Ministers Responsible for Foreign Affairs, Defence and Security*, Gaborone: SADC, 18 January 1996d.

14   M Malan and J Cilliers, *SADC Organ on Politics, Defence and Security: Future Development*, Pretoria: Institute of Security Studies, 1997.

15   *Ibid.*

16   SADC, *Communique of the Summit of the SADC Organ on Politics, Defence and Security Held in Luanda, Angola*, Gaborone: SADC, 2 October 1996e.

17   SADC 1996c; Malan and Cilliers 1997.

18   SADC 1996c.

19   J Akokpari, 'Theoretical perspective on prospects for democratic stability in Lesotho', *Lesotho Social Science Review*, vol 4, no 2, December 1998.

20   L Swatuk and P Vale, 'Why democracy is not enough: Southern Africa and human security in the twenty-first century', *Alternatives*, no 24, 1999, p 371.

21   *Mail and Guardian* (Johannesburg), 25 Sept–1 Oct 1998.

22   *Mail and Guardian*, 16–22 April 1999.

23   L Swatuk, 'Tapping Congo's Wealth', *African Agenda*, no 15, 1998.

24   C Simpson, 'What Price Congo Peace?', *Mmegi*, 2–8 July 1999.

25   *Mail and Guardian*, 16–22 April 1999.

26   Malan and Cilliers 1997.

27   D Papp, *Contemporary International Relations*, New York: Macmillan, 1994, p 80.

28   Swatuk and Vale 1999, p 363.
29   B Tsie, 'Regional Security in Southern Africa: Whither the SADC Organ on Politics Defence, and Security', *Global Dialogue*, no 33, December 1998.
30   Malan and Cilliers 1997.
31   *Ibid*.
32   *Ibid*.

Conflict Management in Africa: Diagnosis and Prescriptions

Severine M Rugumamu

In the realm of peace and security in Africa, the 1990s witnessed dramatic and profound changes throughout the continent. With the conclusion of the Cold War, some of the major tensions between East and West over the African battleground were markedly eased. South Africa and Namibia installed democratically elected governments. Relative peace and stability was established in Mozambique after three decades of confrontation between warring parties. Several dozen African countries held democratic elections. Unquestionably, all these are positive and significant signs towards peace, stability and development. However, while many parts of the world moved towards greater stability and political and economic co-operation, Africa remained one of the cauldrons of instability. Political insecurity and violent conflict became increasingly persistent realities of the development scene. Internal strife with deep historical roots surfaced in many countries on the continent. Ironically, while the international community paid less and less attention to African security affairs, the continent's institutional and organisational capacity to manage its pervasive conflicts was not developing at the same pace as conflict escalations. Against such a backdrop, peace and peace-making in Africa emerges as a critical issue in global politics.

Widespread societal conflicts in Africa are often played out against the backdrop of deep poverty, illiteracy, and weak systems of governance. Undermined by unfavourable terms of trade, indebtedness and administrative failures, most states in Africa have not responded adequately to the critical social needs of their citizens. In the most extreme cases, Africa's insecurity has been reflected in traumatic episodes of collapsed and collapsing states. Almost invariably, state collapses are products of long-term degenerative politics marked by a loss of control over the economic and political space. As would be expected, collapsed states in Africa have had harmful spill-over effects on neighbouring countries. The overflow of refugees, heightened ethnic tensions in some cases, and the resulting diplomatic conflicts, have engaged substantial resources and efforts from the relatively stable countries that share borders with collapsed states.[1] In the process, what were once thought to be mere domestic conflicts, out of the purview of international organisations like the United Nations (UN) and regional organisations like the Organisation of African Unity (OAU), have now been internationalised. External actors have been drawn into what was technically civil war in order to restore peace and security. It has become increasingly apparent that Africa should develop the capacity to deal with its own growing domestic security problems.

This chapter has several objectives. First, it seeks to describe and explain the nature and character of African conflicts. Second, it provides the changing national and international context within which violent conflicts in Africa are managed. Finally, it examines various third-party intervention strategies that are needed to manage conflict as well as to create a sustainable environment for positive peace-building.

Essence of conflicts and conflict mapping

From antiquity to contemporary times, competition and conflict have been regarded as inherent phenomena in both nature and society. Latent social confrontations have long been considered as the *primum mobile* for social change and transformation. Arguments to support this proposition are that conflicts and competition are inevitable and ubiquitous in all societies at all times. Similarly, in the best of circumstances, conflicts and competition are bounded and circumscribed. Contending groups of people and rival nations get involved in violent conflicts either because their interests or values are challenged or because their needs are not met. The deprivation of any important value induces fear, a sense of threat, and unhappiness. Whether contending groups in a particular society are defined by ethnicity, religion, ideology, gender, or class, they have, by definition, different needs, interests, values and access to power and resources. Such differences necessarily generate social conflicts and competition. What is at issue, therefore, is how to manage and resolve inherent social conflicts before they degenerate into violent expressions and massive destruction.

It is not always possible to distinguish a cause of a conflict from its consequences. In fact, as a conflict emerges, cause and consequence tend to blend. Hostility might be a consequence of one phase of a conflict and a cause of the next. Perceived goals and interest incompatibility are perhaps the most basic causes of social conflict. Identity defence is also common, particularly in the contemporary world where group awareness and rights have assumed high visibility. Cultural differences, and particularly language, are yet other sources of separateness and difference. They create a sense of self and self-defence, which is probably another primary motive for conflict. It is thus important to distinguish clearly between the contending goals and interests of each party.

Once conflicts escalate into violence, the major concern of neighbouring states, civil society, and the international community is to intervene in the conflict in order to facilitate the mediation process and to help transform structures that produce insecurity and structural violence into positive peace.[2] We should hasten to point out that conflicts in which the state is an effective arbiter do not present particular difficulties since they are manageable within the national framework. The problem arises when the state itself is a party to the conflict, for under those conditions, external involvement becomes necessary. It is argued in this chapter that a solid foundation for effective organisation and enabling institutions is a necessary precondition for sustainable and enduring peace-building. For the purposes of this chapter, institutions are understood as sets of rules governing the actions of individuals and organisations, and encompass the interactions of all relevant parties and negotiations among participants. Specifically, countries as well as societies need institutions that strengthen organisations and promote good governance, whether through laws and regulations, or by co-ordinating the actions of many players, as in international treaties. Rule-based processes increase the transparency of policies designed to create desired outcomes, and of organisations used to implement them.[3]

International context of conflict management in Africa

During the bipolar era, Cold War competition and rivalries between two ideological blocs largely shaped the security environment of Africa states. On the one hand, this internationalised otherwise local conflicts. The superpowers' competition for global influence exacerbated and prolonged local and regional conflicts in an extensive bipolar rivalry. Each superpower, fearing the other might provide decisive support and thereby gain political advantage, was driven to assist one or the other party. By the same token, the bipolar structure of the Cold War allowed local disputants to manipulate the superpowers to advance their respective interests.[4]

On the other hand, the superpowers also restrained local African conflicts out of fear of escalation. In their spheres of influence, each superpower suppressed conflicts, concerned that open disputes would create opportunities for the other to intervene in its politically sensitive backyard. By whatever means, the superpowers did exercise a degree of management to counteract increased regional tensions and keep conflicts within bounds, occasionally even imposing settlements. They restrained their client regimes by stationing troops, extending security commitments, rejecting or limiting the shipment of advanced offensive weaponry, applying political pressure, and using economic rewards and threats of punishment to elicit certain behaviour. In the process, foreign powers imposed an artificial and tenuous stability on the continent by propping up regimes of client states. Unquestionably, this is one of the major ways in which numerous dictators in the Third World in general, and in Africa in particular, were born, bred, and sustained. The blind support by Cold War warriors of many unpopular and oppressive African regimes inevitably led aggrieved groups to carry out coups d'état, and to start secessionist and irredentism movements, and rebellions against the state. So powerful were the Cold War dynamics that they set in motion serious internal conflicts that have long outlasted the Cold War itself.[5]

Once the Cold War ended, and communism was no longer considered a serious threat to Western global interests, Africa's intrinsic significance to its former allies declined irretrievably. This led, in turn, to the relaxing of vast networks of alliances, obligations, and agreements that bound most African states to competing global security systems. The ensuing break-up of alliances, partnerships, and regional support systems exposed weak African states to systemic instability. Predictably, the hollow nature and character of the African state and the unfinished agenda of state and nation-building became manifestly obvious. Slowly but inexorably, foreign powers began to withdraw their automatic support from authoritarian African regimes, and the concomitant financial, military and political assistance that accompanied that support. In fact, states that had been overly dependent on Cold War patronage, such as Angola, Mozambique, Ethiopia, Zaire, Somalia, and Liberia, soon began to disintegrate thereafter. Not surprisingly, old conflicts, which for a long time had been buried under the cover of the Cold War, started to re-surface with greater virulence as states grew weaker, and small arms and mercenaries became readily available. The realities of the new situation have encouraged African leaders and intellectuals to examine the norms of external intervention and sovereignty for the purposes of settling domestic disputes.[6]

It is important to note that during the Cold War period, the division of labour between the roles of the sub-regional, regional and international organisations was clear. While the traditional role of the UN was to mount peacekeeping operations, and to deploy political missions, regional and subregional organisations concentrated largely on preventive diplomacy. However, such operations were few and far between. Since the early 1990s, the UN has engaged in a number of simultaneous, larger, and more ambitious peace operations such as those in Angola, Bosnia and Herzegovina, Croatia, Mozambique and Somalia. The financial, personnel, and timing pressure on the UN to undertake these massive short-term stabilising actions impaired its overall ability to ensure timely and effective intervention measures. Worries about the Security Council's ability to effectively address serious threats to international peace and security increased. The Security Council's credibility as the dominant actor for assuring international peace and security began to be questioned.

In recent years, a new international security management paradigm seems to be emerging. It consists essentially of regions and sub-regions accepting co-responsibility and sharing the burden of policing themselves and, consequently, a dilution of the central responsibility of the UN in this regard. This agenda is primarily driven by the United States. It is demanding co-operation and burden-sharing by all others. The most recent, and arguably most important indication of this trend is US support for the greater "European defence identity" as opposed to a "Trans-Atlantic identity". In fact, this is a harbinger of what is evolving as a generalised global security management doctrine. The commonly repeated phrase that calls for "African solutions to African problems" seems to be aptly capturing the new mood.

It bears repeating that with the conclusion of the Cold War, Africa's importance and relevance in global politico-strategic concerns of the West has diminished markedly. As Barry Buzan aptly argues, Africa's geo-strategic significance has become marginal to the vital interests of the West.[7] Europe, in particular, seems to be gradually diverting its attention away from Africa in favour of those regions of the world with which it has closer cultural, economic and strategic connections. The European Union's intense preoccupation with the security problems of the former Yugoslavia compares unfavourably with its relative inattention to the crises in the Democratic Republic of Congo, Liberia, Rwanda, Burundi, Somalia, Guinea, and Sierra Leone. By the same token, the Mediterranean states are likely to receive more EU attention and security resources in the years to come. To be sure, these states are closer neighbours to Europe than the sub-Saharan African countries. European security concerns stem from the flow of illegal immigrants into Europe from North Africa as well as from the spectre of political Islam in Algeria and Egypt. Not surprisingly, European military bases in sub-Saharan Africa are fast closing down, and Africans are constantly counselled by the West to fend for themselves.[8]

An implicit policy has thus emerged which encourages so-called "layered responses" to African conflicts: local and national organisations are expected to respond initially, followed by responses at sub-regional and regional level, and ultimately at the level of the broader international community. According to the architects of this policy, the aim is to encourage African initiatives that seek African solutions to African conflicts. Accordingly, in recent years, the OAU as well as its sub-regional organisations have taken bold steps to develop their organisational capacities for managing regional conflicts. It is little wonder, then, that instead of the familiar UN blue helmets, peacekeepers in Sierra Leone fought under the banner of the Economic Community of West African States (ECOWAS). By the same token, when the warring parties in the DRC gathered in Lusaka, Zambia, in July of 1999 to sign a ceasefire pact, they endorsed an agreement initiated and mediated by the Southern African Development Community (SADC), with the UN playing a secondary role. In fact, Africa is the only continent being called upon by its former Cold War allies to set up its own international force for peacekeeping and humanitarian assistance.[9]

In theory, the emerging international security management concept has several advantages. First, member states in regional and sub-regional security arrangements are the ones who are likely to suffer the consequences of instability in their region most directly. Their nations will bear the cost of caring for refugees, and providing sanctuary for insurrectionist actions; African regions will have to spend more on defence, and will bear the cost of reduced economic growth. It is therefore in the interests of regional organisations to preserve their regional peace, security and stability. This vital interest ought to translate into greater political will to ensure that stability is secured. Secondly, members of a regional or sub-regional security organisation are likely to be more in tune with the conflict at hand as they share the same cultural background and often speak the same language. In some cases, personal relationships have developed among the leaders, which undoubtedly result in a greater understanding of the situation, and may result in fruitful dialogue based on personal trust. Thirdly, regional organisations, being in tune with their own areas of interest, may provide timely responses based on better intelligence of a looming crisis. But, more often than not, the willingness to maintain sub-regional security is rarely matched with the ability to do so.

Conflict management in Africa

Causes and Cycles of Conflict

Most of the contemporary violent conflicts in Africa underline the reality that the security threats to the state and the population are less external to the continent and less military than they are economic, environmental and social in nature. Since the beginning of the 1990s, the African continent has acquired the dubious honour of being number one in hosting the largest number of armed conflicts and complex emergencies. In his 1998 Report to the Security Council, UN Secretary General Kofi Annan lamented Africa's insecurity situation:

> Since 1970, more than 30 wars have been fought in Africa, the vast majority of them intra-state in origin. In 1996 alone, 14 out of 53 countries in Africa

were afflicted by armed conflicts, accounting for more than half of all war-related deaths world-wide and resulting in more than 8 million displaced refugees, returnees and displaced persons. The consequences of these conflicts have seriously undermined Africa's efforts to ensure long-term stability, prosperity, and peace for its people ... Preventing such wars is no longer a matter of defending states or protecting allies. It is a matter of defending humanity itself.[10]

As this quotation aptly demonstrates, intrastate conflicts in Africa can no longer be considered temporary deviations from a stable national or regional security pattern. To some cynical observers, the complex emergencies of Africa seem to arise from chronic, insoluble problems. Be that as it may, we do not intend to rehash the causes of violent conflicts in Africa. Suffice it to mention that the sources of the continent's conflicts are complex and multifaceted, involving many actors, thus making it impossible to ascribe the conflicts to a single cause or source: local, national, regional and international forces have combined to fuel almost every war on the continent.

To explain why violent conflicts happen, most theories distinguish between structural causes of conflict (or "root causes" or "imbalance of opportunities"), and accelerating or trigger factors. Structural factors include political, economic and social patterns such as state repression, lack of political participation, poor governance, the unequal distribution of wealth, the ethnic make-up of a society, and the history of inter-group relations. They increase a society's vulnerability to conflict. Accelerating or trigger factors often consist of political developments or events that bring underlying tensions to the fore and cause the situation to escalate. They can include new radical ideologies, repression of political groups, sharp economic shocks, changes in, or the collapse of, central authority, new discriminatory policies, external intervention, and weapons proliferation.[11]

The OAU's Record so Far

Although one of the primary objectives of establishing the OAU was to manage conflicts among member states, it has played a more reactive role in addressing threats to national and regional security. For a long time, the organisation was constrained by its Charter from intervening in internal conflicts. The Charter's preference for sovereignty and non-interference in the internal affairs of member-states rendered it powerless to address situations of poor governance and the gross abuse of human rights. Furthermore, until recently, the institutions mentioned in the original OAU Charter were either considered irrelevant or simply ineffective as instruments to end or manage armed conflicts. The Commission on Mediation,

Reconciliation and Arbitration, which was established in the 1960s, appeared to have been doomed from the start, as it was not designed to deal with internal conflicts. Nor was it mandated to prevent the outbreak of conflicts. This legal mechanism was created to encourage member states to submit their disputes for regional arbitration. Its lengthy and costly judicial process made the Commission unattractive to many would-be clients. In fact, the Commission was never used. It was dissolved in 1977, with the OAU opting for other methods of conflict management. Above all, the Defence Commission, envisioned under Article XX of the OAU Charter, was never established.

For well over three decades, therefore, various *ad hoc* commissions and committees of OAU member states undertook the responsibility of managing conflicts in Africa. Under the rubric of preventive diplomacy, the OAU and later sub-regional communities have extensively deployed the good offices of some prominent heads of state, the Secretary General, and elder statesmen to mediate conflicts. They included mediating disputes over border and territorial claims, allegations of subversion by member states against other member states, and, in a few cases, civil wars. A few successful mediation efforts include, notably, resolving the border disputes between Algeria and Morocco, Ethiopia and Somalia, and recently between Ethiopia and Eritrea. However, more often than not, these efforts were of limited lasting impact. This was, in part, because the OAU had no credible enforcement instruments – it could only appeal to disputing parties to adhere to the organisation's principles. It was also, in part, because of the Organisation's limited capacity to mount successful independent peacekeeping, peace enforcement or peace-building operations, as was clearly evidenced by the Chad fiasco in the early 1980s, as well as by its inherent inability to restrain both Uganda and Rwanda from continued occupation of the north-east provinces of DRC from the late 1990s.

As the rate of intra-state conflicts skyrocketed in the 1990s, it became increasingly apparent that the *ad hoc* conflict management arrangements of the 1970s and 1980s were not up to the task. At the 1993 OAU Summit in Cairo, African heads of state agreed to establish the Mechanism for Conflict Prevention, Management and Resolution. The Mechanism was charged with anticipating and preventing conflicts, and engaging in peacemaking and peace-building activities. In cases of severe conflict, there was provision for OAU co-operation with the UN in the development of a peacekeeping strategy. Although the OAU principles of respect for sovereignty, territorial integrity and non-intervention in internal affairs were forcefully re-stated, the Mechanism was also charged with the task of dealing with internal conflicts in circumstances of gross human rights abuses and atrocities. The emphasis on anticipatory and preventive measures expressly aimed at obviating the need to resort to the complex and resource-demanding peacekeeping operations that Africa could ill afford. As OAU Secretary-General Salim Ahmed Salim remarked, "given that every African is his brother's keeper, and that our borders are at best artificial, we in Africa need to use our own cultural and social relationships to interpret the principle of non-intervention in such a way that we are able to apply it to our advantage in conflict prevention and resolution".[12]

Most of the successful regional integration and collective security initiatives world-wide have thrived on a strong and willing leadership which Robert Keohane describes as the "theory of hegemonic stability".[13] The presence of a regional core or nucleus has the capacity to serve as a positive force for developing and nurturing a viable collective security arrangement. At the maximum, leaders are expected to assume a disproportionate cost burden of a collective security project as well as serve as the paragons of compliance to the regime's rules, norms, and procedures. Their commitment, reliability, and capability are expected to be beyond reproach. At the minimum, hegemonic leadership entails being able and willing to provide a mix of incentives and disincentives to members of the security regimes in order to ensure compliance. The hegemonic leader's economic strength and political stability, for instance, would bolster the region's economic vitality and political stability. It would also champion the cause of co-operation by pulling the less willing and less able member countries along, as it may not be possible for all countries to move at the same pace. Arguably, the hegemony-centred regional or sub-regional security order would be more workable and effective than a larger body. It would provide the necessary *leadership consensus* on crucial issues such as "entry points" in conflict management, modalities for action, and co-operation and co-ordination with OAU partners. Such rules of procedure would reasonably make the larger body effective.[14]

As a practical matter, equality among sovereign entities has always been a convenient international relations fiction. It has never been backed by realities because some powers have always been more dominant than others and therefore have been explicitly or implicitly charged with the responsibility for enforcing the agreed-upon norms of behaviour. The role of the United States in NATO, Germany in the European Union and South Africa in the Southern African Customs Union are excellent success stories of hegemony-centred co-operation arrangements in recent times. By the same token, South Africa, Nigeria, Egypt and Angola have the capacity to play this strategic role within the OAU as permanent members on the Central Organ as well as on the security and defence organs in their respective sub-regional organisations. It is simply common sense that countries which bear the burden of peace operations should have disproportionate decision-making powers.

Understandably, in the absence of a strong collective will and requisite intervention capacity within the OAU system, sub-regional organisations and even some African governments have not hesitated to by-pass the cumbersome and usually indecisive OAU Mechanism for Conflict Prevention, Management and Resolution. Recent peace enhancing initiatives include uninvited interventions by some African governments in neighbouring countries in order to restore constitutional government, end threats to peace, or achieve peace enforcement; these are a clear testimony of the OAU's inherent institutional incapacity. Furthermore, in the absence of a strong decision-making organ at the centre, the OAU has remained virtually powerless in intervening in relatively bigger countries such as Angola, Sudan and the DRC. In fact, it has failed to articulate credible plans for conflict management in these three conflict-ridden countries.

The Secretary General of the OAU and the Conflict Management Centre (CMC) serve as the Secretariat of the Mechanism as well as its implementation agency. The CMC was established to serve not only as the research arm of the Mechanism but most importantly, to strengthen the OAU's institutional capacity for conflict management. In this regard, the Centre recruited about a dozen consultants through foreign-funded projects with a view to enhancing its analytical capacity. Furthermore, in order to facilitate the work of the CMC, the Mechanism sanctioned the establishment of a continent-wide Early Warning System. When fully operationalised, the system is expected to provide reliable and accurate early warning information on developing conflicts, and help experts to suggest various modes of response. Early warning and information management systems at the OAU will have to be harmonised and co-ordinated not only with those at the sub-regional levels, but most importantly, conflict management networks on the continent must be comprehensively structured in order to synchronise and synergise collective efforts and responsibilities. However, we should hasten to add that prompt and decisive responses to crisis situations in Africa would largely depend on how the Central Organ is composed and structured.

Besides the establishment of the CMC, the Mechanism also created an OAU Peace Fund to support the organisation's efforts relating to conflict management. The Fund is made up of financial appropriations of 5% of the regular OAU budget, as well as voluntary contributions from member states, and from sources within Africa. Moreover, the Secretary General may, with the consent of the Central Organ, and in conformity with the principles of the OAU Charter, accept voluntary contributions from sources outside Africa. The question of the Peace Fund needs to be studied urgently in order to design a resource mobilisation strategy. Included in future plans should be a comprehensive costing for the reconciliation and reconstruction activities that are conspicuously absent in the current Peace Fund mandate.

Since the establishment of the Mechanism for Conflict Management, the OAU has taken a wide range of initial measures and initiatives aimed at anticipating and preventing conflicts on the continent. They include the development of an early warning system (still in rudimentary form) and an analytical capacity to provide the organisation with advance notice of impending conflict situations. Moreover, various preventive diplomacy efforts through the use of the OAU Special envoys to crisis areas (for example the Comoros, 1997; Congo-Brazzaville in 1993; Ethiopia-Eritrea in 1998; Côte d'Ivoire in 2000) as well as limited preventive deployments to contain conflict escalation have been mounted. However, as earlier pointed out, largely because of the OAU's institutional and organisational inadequacies, most of its conflict management initiatives have had limited success. Summarising the organisation's performance at the beginning of the 1990s, OAU Secretary General lamented, "Many times, we have looked around for the OAU to intervene constructively in a conflict situation only to find that it is not there, and when present, to realise that it is not adequately equipped to be decisively helpful".[15]

Disenchanted and frustrated by the UN and OAU record in peacekeeping and peacemaking efforts since the early 1990s, various African states, civil society bodies and international non-governmental organisations have assumed greater responsibility for conflict management as a means of creating an environment where peace, stability and democracy are the norm. At sub-regional level, economic co-operation and integration arrangements such as ECOWAS, SADC, and IGAD have increasingly assumed the role of security co-operation and conflict management. They have gradually revised their treaties and protocols to include the provisions for managing regional peace and security. Like the OAU, the sub-regional economic organisations have shifted from *ad hoc* arrangements for conflict management to systematic approaches and procedures. They vary enormously in both capacity and willingness to play a collective security role. Thus, through a process of learning, and indeed because of international political expediency, more controversial political issues have been brought into the field of co-operation and integration. This is what neo-functionalist integration scholars have referred to as "spill-over effects".[16]

Under the auspices of SADC, South Africa and Botswana successfully reversed a palace coup in Lesotho by applying diplomatic pressure, threatening economic sanctions, and staging a seven-month long intervention operation in an effort to deal with the deteriorating security situation in the SADC member state. Under the same umbrella, Zimbabwe, Angola, and Namibia intervened, with limited success, in the Democratic Republic of Congo. In turn, the Inter-governmental Authority on Development (IGAD) assumed the added role of conflict management by mediating between the government of Sudan and the Sudanese People's Liberation Army. However, as various observers have noted, sub-regional approaches to peace and security in Africa can bring only limited additional capabilities to conflict management. Regional and sub-regional alliances of willing and able African states do not have the necessary wherewithal to bring security to the continent without the continued engagement and support of the OAU and the international community.[17]

The way forward

While more internal armed conflicts have occurred in Africa in the post-Cold War era than in any other major world region, the continent is becoming increasingly marginalised in US and European foreign policy agenda. What can Africa do for itself? How can the OAU and the UN achieve a shared vision of active partnership, co-operation, and co-ordination in responding to the continent's needs for peace, security, emergency relief, reconstruction, and development? What complementary role can sub-regional organisations play in the maintenance of peace and stability in their respective regions? How can Africa's sub-regional organisations enhance their respective internal capacities to respond vigorously and pre-emptively to armed conflicts?

Early Warning Signals and Preventive Actions

Preventing conflicts is essentially a long-term process. It needs long-term strategies and policies whose impact will prevent the emergence of conditions that gave rise to conflict escalation in the first place. These strategies and policies are fundamental to all countries and societies that seek to minimise the possibility of conflict escalation in the long-term. It is vitally important to recognise the fact that carefully designed and co-ordinated actions to address the root causes of conflict should always be based on reliable and accurate early warning analyses. Effective early warning combines historical, social, political and humanitarian information in order to forecast the dynamics of a particular conflict, and the instruments necessary to address it effectively before it reaches crisis proportions. An effective early warning system requires overcoming two fundamental problems:

the informational problem of obtaining both the necessary quantity and quality of intelligence in a reliable and timely fashion; and the analytic problem of avoiding misperceptions or faulty analysis of the likelihood of diffusion and escalation of the conflict, the impact on interests, and the potential risks and costs of both action and inaction. The need for the necessary personnel and technology comes to the fore.[18] The OAU as well as sub-regional organisations will need to put in place not only quality personnel with adequate surveillance and analytical capabilities, but also, equally importantly, the right technologies to access space-based information.

Early warning analysis provides insights into developing conflicts, suggests modes of response, and feeds these analyses and suggested intervention responses to critical organs that are responsible for taking the necessary preventive actions. Because of the strategic importance of conflict mitigation, it is usually desirable to achieve a shared analysis of the main conflict issues and trends with a wide range of interested parties. Early warning may also serve as one form of preventive action when such a warning is shared with the protagonists to a conflict with the intent of tempering their conflict-generating activities, or when it is shared with a political decision-making body that can initiate prompt preventive action.

When crisis conditions become manifest, timely preventive measures must be considered and rapidly implemented. Appropriate and timely measures can counter potential triggers that might otherwise push the conflict towards open confrontation and mass violence. Under the rubric of preventive action, there is a wide range of instruments available for mediating and settling conflicts. Preventive diplomacy, mediation, and military measures are generally utilised for moderating conflicts. A third party mediator from outside the country often becomes necessary – a wise man or woman acceptable to all parties to the conflict. Humanitarian aid, where possible, is usually brought in to supplement all other efforts. In some extreme circumstances, it may be necessary to mount a comprehensive ceasefire so that humanitarian assistance for the war victims and displaced persons can be provided. Though short-term measures to de-escalation are important and necessary, long-term efforts at peace building should be intensified. Conflict prevention, peace-building, and resolution initiatives need to be closely co-ordinated, if they are to play an effective role in supporting other activities. In the final analysis, all efforts should seek to address the root causes of the conflict.

Violent Conflict, Mediation, and Peacekeeping

Once a conflict escalates into violent confrontation, intensive diplomatic pressure and other resources should be promptly expended to achieve early, and indeed decisive, conflict mitigation and peace. A key to third party intervention is the creation of a condition of "ripeness" in the conflict – a conflict management concept meaning that the conflict is ripe for resolution. Ripeness is most commonly achieved as a result of what is described in the literature as a hurting stalemate – the point at which the parties no longer feel they can use force to gain a unilateral advantage and become willing to consider other options. It is characterised by the combatants' perception that the costs and prospects for continued confrontation are more onerous than the costs and prospects of a settlement. Ripeness implies a basic power equivalence of the parties, even if their sources of power differ. When the power of each side can prevent defeat but not produce victory, the result is a hurting stalemate that favours conflict resolution. It is an essential condition that must be cultivated by a third party hoping to intervene successfully in a conflict.[19] However, a mutually hurting stalemate becomes more problematic in multi-factional, multi-dimensional conflicts such as those in Somalia and the DRC, because they provide increased incentives for defection. Genuine negotiations have proven possible when the fear of continued fighting exceeds the fear of compromising in an agreement.

As peace agreements are reached, implementation skills and political flexibility become more critical. Understandably, security fears reach their peak during the implementation phase. Negotiated agreements are often fragile and difficult to put into effect. Parties to the conflict suffer anxieties that opponents will cheat on their commitments. It is therefore important that mediators act imaginatively to encourage all parties to live up to the agreements, and therefore produce an environment that promotes credible commitment.

Peacekeeping operations are a practical mechanism to intervene in order to prevent conflict from escalating and to provide an environment for political settlement. According to Chapter VII of the UN Charter, peacekeeping operations may take essentially two basic forms: the military observer mission and the larger peacekeeping force. The former category usually refers to unarmed military personnel sent to an area of conflict to monitor and supervise the cessation of hostilities when warring parties have agreed upon a ceasefire. In the latter case, military or paramilitary operations are deployed in extensive peacekeeping tasks. Such forces, often with thousands of armed troops, are used for peace enforcement in establishing buffer zones between warring armies and to supervise and assist the withdrawal of invading forces from the territories that they might have occupied during the fighting. In some cases, the threat of the use of force may be sufficient to bring about a cessation of fighting, as was the case in the early Unified Task Force (UNITAF) intervention in Somalia. Moreover, peacekeeping operations require a clear and precise mandate for operations, which can be unambiguously translated into effective action on the ground in the pursuit of clear objectives. Mandates should take into account the need for peacekeeping operations to remain impartial in implementing their mission, and to operate with the consent of all parties to the conflict. They also need to be framed with a view to the quality and quantity of resources which the international community would be ready to commit. Above all, peacekeeping requires a combination of skills and expertise including restraint, negotiation, mediation and liaison.

There are no blueprints for rebuilding societies after a war. While the challenges faced by societies are disarmingly similar in most post-war situations, the political context and configurations of actors, and the quality and nature of relations between actors and institutions, are unique in each case. It is not possible to replicate policies that proved successful in one case in a new situation. However, it is possible to learn from past successes and failures. A comprehensively crafted peace-building process normally begins with the introduction of background discussions that seek to address the root causes of the conflict. A country and/or sub-regional strategic framework, stipulating a long-term orientation that addresses the full and integrated conflict cycle, must be developed. The framework sets the signposts for the long-term conflict transformation process. It involves a whole range of activities aimed at establishing and consolidating peace, by putting in place the necessary measures for bolstering a peace agreement in the aftermath of a conflict. It also involves transforming the political, institutional, social, and economic landscape that generated violent conflict. Once agreed upon and signed, co-ordinated international assistance is required to monitor the ceasefire, demobilise combatants, develop a civilian police, reconstruct the state administration and create mechanisms for participatory governance, re-establish the rule of law and a legitimate, effective judiciary, strengthen civil society, and assist in economic and psychological reconstruction. At the core of the peace-building process is the initiation and sustenance of a broad-based national political dialogue that seeks to address critical issues of representation, power sharing, social healing, and government and community structures.

Reconciliation, Reconstruction and Peace-building

The process of reconstruction and reconciliation is usually long, arduous and expensive. The new government is likely to reign over a traumatised populace, a wrecked economy, easy availability of small and light weapons, a disassembled state structure, and a territory often heavily land-mined.

Mending relations and restoring trust have been identified as two of the primary challenges of the post-war societies. Relations must be mended between the present, the past and the future to prevent bitter memories of the past from poisoning visions of the future. This does not mean restoring the past. It means defining new roles and sound relations between people, ethnic or religious groups, and the authorities. It also means working out a new, common order of social norms and values. The challenge of a society rebuilding itself, if approached as a common task, can heal relations and restore dignity, trust, and faith in the future as people learn together to cope with the past.

Reconciliation is a highly problematic concept, which means quite different things to different people. Nonetheless, there are distinct activities that have become associated with it in Africa. In Mozambique, villagers have demonstrated their capacity to generate a culture of peace. South Africa and Rwanda have conducted various experiments in how to deal with war crimes and massive human rights abuses. Under the rubric of "traditional" reconciliation or conflict resolution techniques, social healing activities have included public hearings, ritual blessings, symbolic acts of forgiveness, corporal punishment, and material compensation awarded to an aggrieved party to be paid by the "guilty". In some instances, these activities have facilitated the building of understanding and consensus, but in others they have worked to benefit the office holder. What is particularly disturbing about traditional reconciliation practices is that the office holders are, almost universally, men. In addition, where these practices have been seen to work, they usually exclude women from active roles, and tend to be about peace-building between men. Women's needs tend to be completely marginalised and excluded. There is an urgent need to mainstream gender in all future peace-building processes in Africa.

The OAU Peace Fund is quiet on post-conflict reconstruction activities. In fact, the organisation's efforts are mainly focused on providing protection and humanitarian assistance to refugees and internally displaced persons. There is very little attention to post-conflict reconciliation and reconstruction in Liberia, Rwanda, Burundi or Mozambique. However, even if the Peace Fund were involved in post-conflict reconstruction, such efforts cannot make a dent without significantly mobilising international and multilateral financial and technical assistance. As the recent experience of Kosovo demonstrated, the Security Council mandated the World Bank and the European Community to co-ordinate the international effort to support the country's reconstruction and recovery. Under this mandate the two institutions were responsible for "co-ordination of matters related to the economic recovery, reform and reconstruction of the Southeast

European region" including mobilising donor support, providing economic analysis, developing appropriate conditions and implementing projects and programmes. To implement this joint mandate, an EC-World Bank joint office was opened in Brussels and a website providing information on the Balkans was launched. As the initial assessment report concluded, "the international community's immediate response to the crisis in the region has been swift".[20] Africa's post-conflict recovery experience compares unfavourably with that of Kosovo. The much-needed assistance has not been forthcoming, and when pledges are made, the disbursement process is often too slow to mitigate the effect of conflict on victims and facilitate a smooth shift from emergence to reconstruction.

It is important to point out that "quick impact" solutions such as infra-structure rehabilitation, social investment and the distribution of agricul-tural toolkits need to be integrated into long-term programmes for maxi-mum sustainability. In order to enforce compliance, peace agreements should categorically specify both incentives and sanctions. The future expansion and upgrading of such projects should be closely tied to full com-pliance with the fine details of the peace agreement. The end of the Cold War has brightened the prospects for success of sanctions against miscre-ant states and regimes. The perennial Cold War "black knights" problem has almost disappeared. There is a likelihood of a broad international coali-tion to support sanctions efforts, as was the case in Iraq (1990), Haiti (1991-94) and Yugoslavia (1992-95).

Conclusion

The recent move towards security regionalism is consistent with the post-Cold War concept of shared responsibility between the United Nations and regional and sub-regional organisations. The OAU and several sub-regional organisations have put in place institutional mechanisms for man-aging conflicts in their respective regions. Despite their initial glaring prac-tical shortcomings, such initiatives should be seen and understood as har-bingers of new global modes and institutions of regionally based peace-keeping operations. They need all the support that can be mustered. Institutions take time to grow, mature, and endure. If the record of the UN peacekeeping initiatives is anything to go by, then Africa's current security management efforts are on the right footing. And as earlier argued, they inject an important degree of predictability into social transactions. They also set the rules and boundaries, encourage compliance, and offer a sys-tematic way to punish transgressors. In order to properly restructure, strengthen, and equip these collective security organisations, we suggest that broadly based debates should be initiated in each African sub-region to define its security threats and propose strategies for how best to manage them. A consensus on the types and nature of the national and regional threats to peace and security should be sought, so as to arrive at the right strategies and institutional mechanisms for managing them. This strategy will also broaden, deepen and democratise the security policy management regime, which has historically been shrouded in secrecy. It would be prudent that a realistic collective security programme should start from a modest agenda that would be enlarged and strengthened over time. Such a strategy would prevent over-zealous politicians from chasing inappropriate and largely illusory goals.[21]

To strengthen the conflict management capabilities of the OAU and its sub-regional organisations, it is suggested that there is a need to redefine their respective organisational structures as well as to harmonise and co-ordinate various conflict management networks on the continent. It was further noted that the maintenance of collective peace and security in Africa is too sensitive to be left to the parochial politics of equality of member states and popular consensus. Much as the equality of member states is one of the highly cherished sovereign norms in international relations, it has often tended to bog down vital decision-making processes in sensitive areas of peace and security in Africa. We have therefore suggested the need to structure the Central Organ of the OAU along the lines of the Security Council in order to guarantee the principle of permanent seats for selected key member states which will largely shoulder the burden of maintaining peace and security on the continent in the emerging global security configuration. Similarly, it is also proposed that the decision-making and operational procedures of the Central Organ should reflect the inherent structural inequalities of the OAU member states. At the same time, it is noted that fears, sensitivities, and suspicions of hegemonic ambitions and the potential partiality of the relatively powerful member states in the organisation will slowly but inexorably be counterbalanced by the weight of numbers of non-permanent members.

It is further argued that even under the emerging co-sharing of security responsibilities, the UN retains its central and primary responsibility of maintaining global peace and security. At the same time, the OAU should negotiate mutually acceptable, yet realistic mechanisms to co-ordinate responses to African conflicts with the UN as well as its sub-regional organisations. As a practical matter, it would seem that a realistic and pragmatic approach would be for the OAU to address a limited set of critical areas of responsibility to prevent over-zealous politicians from chasing inappropriate and largely illusory goals. In this regard, the continental organisation should assume the lead responsibility of mobilising peacekeeping, peace-making, and peace servicing packages for African trouble spots. Such packages should identify modalities for joint peacekeeping, and specify and apportion responsibilities, according to relative comparative advantages, among various players including specialised UN institutions, the OAU, sub-regional organisations, and NGOs. Arguably, such packages and modalities would take advantage of extra-territorial powers by exploiting their moral authority, leverage, credibility, legitimacy and resources. By the same token, in order to participate credibly in large-scale peacekeeping in Africa, both the OAU and its sub-regional organisations should consider establishing the now much debated and controversial rapid peacekeeping force, to be deployed at short notice. Future peace enforcement actions in Africa will require the deployment of a force that would be overwhelming enough, both in numbers and in capability, to force the warring factions to comply with a ceasefire.

Finally and closely related to the previous argument, for any durable and sustainable peace and stability in Africa, nation-building and good governance should be brought to the centre stage of continental politics and international relations. Africa's national and sub-regional politics should be rooted in a process of pluralism and popular participation. This basic yet cardinal democracy prerequisite demands that governments are not only legitimate but also have the authority and capacity to rule. Such governments can be expected to promote not only respect for basic freedoms but, most importantly, can create the necessary conditions for durable and sustainable peace and security. Basic stability, law and order must be provided within the country that wishes to provide the same to its neighbours. Encouraging undemocratic weak states to assist other undemocratic weak states in the provision of security would be to promote political decadence in Africa. As Oboe Hutchful has concluded, "without acceptable standards of governance ... a regional security mechanism is liable to degenerate into a protection of racket autocrats".[22] In this broad sense, therefore, the ongoing economic and political restructuring in Africa deserves strong local and international political support.

Notes and References

1   IW Zartman (ed), *Collapsed States: The disintegration and restoration of legitimate authority*, Boulder: Lynne Rienner, 1995, pp 1–5.

2   Johan Galtung makes a clear distinction between "positive" and "negative" peace. Positive peace encompasses an ideal of how society should be. It requires that not only all types of violence be minimal or non-existent, but also that the major potential causes of future conflict be removed. Negative

peace is defined as the end of widespread violent conflict associated with war. It may include prevalent social violence and structural violence. For details, see J Galtung, 'Twenty-five years of peace research: Ten challenges and responses', *Journal of Peace Research*, vol 22, 1995.

3   World Bank, *World Development Report*, New York: Cambridge University Press, 2000, p 3.

4   S Rugumamu, *Lethal Aid: The illusion of socialism and self-reliance in Tanzania*, Trenton: Africa World Press, 1997.

5   D Lake and P Morgan, 'The new regionalism in security affairs', in D Lake and P Morgan (eds), *Regional Orders: Building security in a new world*, Pennsylvania: Pennsylvania State University Press, 1997.

6   E Keller, 'Rethinking Africa's regional security', in D Lake and P Morgan (eds), *Regional Orders: Building security in a new world*, Pennsylvania: Pennsylvania State University Press, 1997; G Hyden, 'Sovereignty, responsibility and accountability: Challenges at the national level in Africa', in F Deng and T Lyons (eds), *African Reckoning: A quest for good governance*, Washington DC: Brookings Institute, 1993; J Nyang'oro, 'Hemmed In? The state in Africa and global liberalization', in D Smith *et al* (eds), *State and sovereignty in the global economy*, New York: Routledge, 1999.

7   B Buzan, 'New patterns of global security in the twenty-first century', *International Affairs*, vol 67, no 3, 1991, p 435.

8   S Rugumamu, *Globalization, liberalization and Africa's marginalization*, Harare: AAPS, 1999.

9   G Clever and R May, 'Peacekeeping: The African dimension', *Review of African Political Economy*, vol 22, no 66, 1995.

10 K Annan, *Report on the causes of conflict and the promotion of durable peace and sustainable development in Africa*, New York: UN, A/52/871-S/1998/318.

11 E Azar, *The management of protracted social conflict: Theory and cases*, Aldershot: Dartmouth, 1990; E Azar and J Burton. *International conflict resolution: Theory and practice*, Boulder: Lynne Rienner, 1986; J Davis and R Gurr, *Preventive measures: Building risk assessment and crisis early warning systems*, Boulder: Rowman and Littlefield, 1997.

12 A Salim, *OAU report of the Secretary General on conflicts in Africa*, Addis Ababa: OAU, 1992, pp 11–12.

13 R Keohane, 'The theory of hegemonic stability and changes in international economic regimes', in O Holisti and A George (eds), *Change in the International System*, Boulder: Westview Press, 1980.

14 M Ayoob, *The Third World security predicament: State making, regional conflicts and the international system*, Boulder: Lynne Rienner, 1995; C Kupchan and C Kupchan, 'Concerts, collective security, and the future of Europe', *International Security*, vol 16, no 1, 1991.

15   Salim 1992.

16   J Caporaso, 'Encapsulated integrative patterns versus spillovers: The case of agricultural and transport integration in EEC', *International Studies Quarterly*, vol 14, no 4, 1970.

17   E Hutchful, 'The ECOMOG experience with peacekeeping in West Africa', in M Malan (ed), *Whither Peacekeeping in Africa?*, Pretoria: ISS, 1999; K Anning, 'Peacekeeping under ECOMOG: A sub-regional approach', in J Cilliers and G Mills (eds), *From peacekeeping to complex emergencies: Peace support missions in Africa*, Pretoria: ISS, 1999.

18   A George and J Holl, *The warning-response problem in preventive diplomacy*, Washington DC: Carnegie Commission for Preventing Deadly Conflicts, 1997.

19   IW Zartman, *Ripe for resolution: Conflict and intervention in Africa*, New York: Oxford University Press, 1989.

20   *World Bank Response to Post Conflict Reconstruction in Kosovo: General Framework for an Emergency Assistance Strategy*, http://www.worldbank.org/html/extdr/kosovo/kosovo st.htm, 15 July 1999.

21   M Malan, 'Debunking some myths about peacekeeping in Africa', in J Cilliers and G Mills (eds), *From peacekeeping to complex emergencies*, Johannesburg: SAIIA, 1999.

22   Hutchful 1999, p 81.

Civil Violence: A Challenge to Social Development in Africa

Lengwe-Katembula Mwansa

Civil violence has ripped apart many countries in Africa with telling consequences. Directly or indirectly, civil violence has dissipated the enabling environment for social development of many states in Africa such as Sierra Leone, Guinea, Liberia, Angola, Mozambique, Senegal, Morocco, Algeria and Sudan. More recently civil violence has erupted in Ethiopia, Eritrea, Somalia, the Great Lakes region (Uganda, Rwanda, Burundi and the Democratic Republic of Congo), Congo-Brazzaville, Namibia and Zimbabwe. The vortex of guns, bullets and 'pangas' has led to vicious civil conflicts that have increasingly sucked in ever larger numbers of citizens on the continent.

Quite obviously, civil violence has created untold misery for the poor innocent civilians especially the children, women and the elderly who cannot escape the vagaries of war. These have become victims of some of the worst military brutality. The scenes on television and in the print media of maimed children, orphans or child soldiers in Sierra Leone, Sudan, Rwanda and Burundi, to mention but a few, demonstrate the stark forms of barbarism of civil violence in Africa. It is common knowledge that most of these children come from harsh living conditions. So to subject them to even worse living conditions is simply imaginable. Such conditions simply destroy their capacity to function and make them easily succumb to fate. Perhaps the worst debilitating condition these children suffer is being deprived of their status as children. They are denied a chance to be children; to enjoy that stage of development. At a tender age when they most need guardianship, they are violently separated from their parents. They quietly suffer abuse and trauma every day they remain in a camp. They face the nightmare of living without parents and shoulder the burden of fending for themselves. Apart from the mental and psychological anguish they have to deal with every day in refugee camps, they live in conditions of squalor, without adequate water, sanitation, food, medicine or education. Malnutrition under such conditions has simply become a crisis, which usually leads to death and disability among children.[1]

Women are equally vulnerable to suffering: to abuse, rape, mental anguish and pain. They have to helplessly watch their children die of malnutrition. They too are vulnerable to malnutrition, especially before and during pregnancy and while they are breastfeeding. This is especially true because the conditions in which they live as refugees or displaced people do not provide for nutritionally adequate diets. The elderly suffer the indignity of living en masse without any privacy, and on handouts. The sense of being away from home and the lack of knowledge of what might have happened to loved ones or what tomorrow might bring simply take away their peace of mind.

In addition, due to the trauma of civil violence, ordinary people persistently suffer from a sense of insecurity, which induces fear. This perpetual fear brings about restrictions in movement, which in turn leads to a reduction in economic activities and ultimately poverty. Thousands of land mines, which have been indiscriminately planted, continue to torment civilians every day, including innocent children at play. For adults it is always a chilling experience to walk among the bushes in search of food or to cultivate the land knowing of the imminent danger of death by the landmines. Angola, for instance, is said to have over 10 million land mines planted all over the country. In Mozambique, even so many years after the war, people continue to be killed and traumatiaed by the land mines. The floods of 1998 simply exacerbated the mine situation in that country. The trauma or fear of death by land mines makes people unproductive. The destruction of infrastructure makes it doubly difficult for the people and government to launch meaningful efforts to realise their full potential and provide for their basic human needs.

Except for Namibia, the economies in such countries are in dire need of growth. Their export capacities have suffered negative growth and cannot therefore compete effectively on international markets. These economies are affected by the general circumstances of hyperinflation and stagflation, massive currency devaluation, rising unemployment and worsening terms of trade.[2] The deterioration of the economies has made the countries fail to generate resources for the social sector, while the debt burden has exacerbated the situation. By 1990, the total debt for sub-Saharan Africa stood at US $171.4 billion, up from US $55.6 billion in 1980. Within 10 years, sub-Saharan Africa's debt has increased by US $115.8 billion or 68%. Given this level of indebtedness, most African countries lack programmes of investment in the public or private sector that can generate resources for social development. However, as the debt burden grows, poverty increases to endemic proportions to create a vicious circle which in such circumstances makes it virtually impossible to break and which inevitably leads to a lack of social development. But the paradox of the situation is that instead of investing the meagre resources there are in development, they are directed to the purchase of weapons of war which destroy human life and infra-structure, disrupt production and distribution of goods and services and thereby negate social development.[3] Regional spending on military hard-ware in 1996 fell slightly lower than 1995 by 3% of the gross domestic product (GDP). But the fall is attributed to a reduction in South Africa's military spending and trading.[4]

Nature of the problem

Causes of civil violence in Africa, as elsewhere, are many, varied and com-plex. This is largely due to the fact that there cannot be a simple causal explanation for such a phenomenon. The multi-dimensional nature of the underlying causes of civil violence in Africa makes it even more difficult to identify a suitable theoretical framework or paradigm to explain with some objectivity where to locate the causes of civil violence. This perhaps, in some measure, explains why there are so many competing theories and paradigms that have been advanced which in many instances have tended to offer confusing evidence. There are those theorists who place the root of civil violence in people's actions, while others think it is embedded in the state, culture or in the international system.[5] In fact, some observers have categorised the dominant theories and paradigms as "a realist-state centric view of the world; a Marxist perspective, broadly defined; a periphery par-adigm, including dependence and related perspectives; and idealist-com-munitarian orientations, covering earlier functionalism, integration views and collaboration perspectives".[6] These contending perspectives deal with state behaviour and the political economy, making it difficult to distinguish between theories related to international relations and paradigms relating to political economy. The idea should be to delineate in simple terms the socio-economic and political causes of violence in order to be able to locate the causal factors that lead to civil violence in Africa. However, in this chapter, an attempt will be made simply to state those factors that enhance the propensity for conflict and violence.

According to Matlosa, the causes of violence include the tendency to control the state and its resources by a certain ethnic group, as is the case with the control of the diamond-rich areas of Angola, the Democratic Republic of Congo (DRC) and Sierra Leone.[7] Other causes include a lack of political intolerance, ideological differences (as initially was the case in Angola between Jonas Savimbi and Eduardo Dos Santos but is no longer the case), and a lack of transparency and accountability in the distribution of scarce resources.[8] Inequalities between groups create deprivation and insecurities not only in incomes but also in political participation (in parlia-

ments, cabinets, armies and governing structures as a whole), in economic assets such as land, human capital and communal resources, and in social
conditions such as education, housing and employment.[9]

However, some of the civil violence in Africa has been fuelled by the
developed countries either directly or through their proxies on the continent by providing financial and military support to the group that is seen to
uphold their interests. It is believed, for example, that the United States
supported Savimbi against Dos Santos.[10] Other types of civil violence are
simply a by-product of the arbitrary colonial division of geographical areas.
These divisions were drawn without attention to tribal, ethnic or national
needs or practicalities.

But the easy access and availability of armaments on the continent has
also become a serious destabilising factor in Africa. This is especially true
of the light weapons and small arms which account for the majority of the
continent's arms trade. These are the arms used in the trouble spots
because they are widely available, easily acquired and easy to operate. But
some of the disputes which have led to civil violence are embedded in historical antecedents, as in the case of Rwanda and Burundi.

The issues of arms and ethnicity are considered paramount as causes of
civil violence in Africa. These, therefore, merit some brief consideration here.

Ethnicity

With very few exceptions such as Lesotho, Swaziland and Somalia, most
countries in Africa are heterogeneous, consisting of diverse ethnic groupings.[11] The term ethnicity is a difficult concept to define simply because of
its vagueness. According to Ottaway this is further complicated by the
misuse of the idea of tribalism.[12] Ethnicity has manifested itself in various
forms in Africa and I believe elsewhere. In its simplest state it can be
defined as conscious and unconscious processes fulfilling a deep psychological need for security, identity, religious or traditional, common culture,
and sense of historical continuity.[13] Ethnicity carries two particular forms:
positive and negative. In the positive form, ethnicity provides cohesion, an
expression of unity or the feeling of "we-ness", and a sense of a distinct
identity and continuity. Seen from a positive standpoint, ethnicity can be a
source of great inspiration, internal solidarity, and strength without necessarily generating ill feeling, hatred, unhealthy competition, hostile attitudes, domination or control of other ethnic groupings.[14] In this form, ethnicity can be employed as a rallying point to combat exploitation and press
for fundamental changes in living circumstances. Different ethnic groups
can overcome differences to become "rainbow groups" and form strong
alliances without necessarily losing their own individuality. Most urban

groups such as trade unions or political parties carry this feature. Members of the trade unions or political parties from various ethnic groupings come together to forge a united front to fight for a common cause. Ethnic groupings can thus still get along in harmony with other groups, because they all owe allegiance to higher sets of values, norms and laws.[15] In Africa, ethnicity can be used as a vehicle of liberalisation, democracy and transformation. Despite being identified with conflict, ethnicity can be used as a positive force to give people confidence and a positive self-image to attain social development.

On the other hand, ethnicity can be a negative force. Although it provides a basis for social identity, cohesion and continuity, ethnic rivalries have characterised social interaction among many tribes in Africa.[16] This constitutes a serious and persistent threat to social existence in many situations in Africa. In fact, ethnic rivalries in their worst forms have become a serious threat not only to national but regional and continental peace as well, and ultimately to social development efforts. It is a social problem that requires an urgent and lasting solution. As a social problem, ethnicity manifests itself in many forms such as social tensions, vicious conflict and violence, and perpetual hatred which creates barriers to social development. In the precolonial era, tribal warfare was fuelled by ethnic sentiments. Such warfare led to the enslavement of the conquered tribes. It was not uncommon to witness tribal violence, for example, in the mining areas of Zambia, but on a limited scale. Such tribal feuds occasionally claimed lives while others resulted in the heavy beating of the victims by ethnic mobs.[17] De Ridder describes a similar experience in South Africa.[18] To this day, ethnic rivalries exist across Africa to the detriment of development.

Ethnicity is currently at the heart of most of the ugly civil violence in Africa. The genocide in Rwanda of Tutsis at the hands of the Hutus illustrates the extreme negative form of ethnicity as a force. Despite countless initiatives, peace continues to elude the continent. The warring parties that are involved in violence identify themselves principally with one ethnic group which becomes not only a reference point but also a source of support and legitimation. In such situations, the biggest danger lies in the fact that ethnicity and violence tend to reinforce each other. The warring parties continue to reinterpret and thereby reinforce their long-standing prejudices, hatred, stereotypes and myths to justify the violence perpetrated by one group against the other.

The situation in Rwanda and Burundi, as complex as it is, could be explained by examining the historical antecedents, political system and control of the means of production and distribution of goods and services during the pre-colonial, colonial and post-colonial periods. It is important to seriously examine these periods to avoid trivialising or glossing over the essential features of ethnicity in any situation in Africa. The pre-colonial period will provide historical antecedents of the circumstances of living before the white man came, while the colonial and post-colonial (including the neo-colonial) legacies will provide the influence and effects on the current living circumstances of the indigenous tribes.

Civil violence existed in Africa well before the coming of the white man. However, the onset of colonialism brought about fundamental changes to the existing tribal rivalries to basically transform its nature and complexion.[19] Critical analysis, therefore, should provide cogent information on how the onset of colonialism and neo-colonialism transformed the nature and magnitude of ethnic consciousness into a negative force. For example, for a long time the Hutu and Tutsi tribes have lived in perpetual distrust and fear of each other, harboured hatred, and sought control and hegemony over each other, but never to the same magnitude as experienced in the genocide of 1994. The presence of a third force, the colonialists, playing one group against the other, has complicated the situation in both Rwanda and Burundi. Each of these tribes has sought superiority or domination over the other. These ethnic sentiments of domination and hegemonic motives to acquire and control the state and national resources such as land have fuelled violent resentments by the other tribe with disastrous consequences.

In both Rwanda and Burundi, the colonialists adopted a policy of "divide and rule" as was the practice in practically all African colonies. This policy was devised as a mechanism to control the diverse populations of Africa.[20] In simple terms, this meant that one group was favoured over the other so as to secure the loyalty of the favoured group. Essentially, therefore, the diverse ethnic groups could not forge unity against colonialists, neither could they develop a sense of unity.[21] The favoured group became paramount and enjoyed considerable privileges to reduce other groupings to a subordinate position. This inevitably led to the birth of an ethnic superiority complex, and the desire to dominate, manipulate and control other ethnic groupings. Obviously, this was a recipe for vicious ethnic civil violence as we have seen it unfold today. The colonial force manipulated an already existing rivalry between the Hutus and Tutsis in both Rwanda and Burundi by supporting the former ethnic group who were the minority.[22]

Accessibility and Availability of Arms

The easy acquisition of arms is also a key factor, as it makes the conflicting parties quickly resort to violence instead of seeking peaceful resolutions to their conflicts. But there are also great difficulties in regulating the arms trade within the areas of conflict due to opportunistic and economic reasons.[23] There is also the mercenary factor, either directly sponsored by the internal elements or externally funded by outside forces to carry on the war. These are proxies waging war on behalf of external forces. Notably, from the past Cold War period to date, the international arms market has gone through various phases. In the 1960s, for example, arms acquisition was largely done by states through certain arrangements such as credit facilities or grants.[24] This continued through the 1970s. But later on, the situation rapidly changed to the effect that any person could procure arms as long as he or she had the means. This means that while there is very little arms transfer in the form of grants, greater amounts of arms are transacted in direct cash payments. Since then, the amounts of money spent on the weapons have tremendously increased.

The arms trade is a profitable and lucrative economic activity. This explains the growing importance attached to the manufacture and sale of armaments in the economy. For example, South Africa's arms production was US $0.204 billion in 1970, US $0.607 billion in 1980 and was projected to grow to US $0.797 billion in 1990.[25] Of course, consideration should also be given to both the forward and backward linkages which add further attractions to military production for the economy. Given the substantial economic spin-offs such as job creation, further stimulation of economic growth, skills formation through the use of advanced technology, the creation of effective demand from civilian systems and, above all, as a source foreign exchange earnings, arms production becomes an extremely attractive industry to form the basis of the economy. The trouble spots in Africa offer a ready market for the disposal of such arms including those in the experimental phase. With diamond money available, for example, Jonas Savimbi of Angola and the rebels of Sierra Leone have continued to acquire arms either directly or indirectly from various sources through intermediaries both in Africa and abroad to wage relentless, savage guerrilla warfare.

The interesting aspect of the civil violence in Africa is how quickly those involved in conflict acquire arms. Shortly after the declaration of war, for instance, the rebels fighting the DRC government acquired arms. In fact, it was as if someone with arms was simply waiting in the wings for the declaration of war to be made before the arms could be delivered. However, retroactively, the linkage of Uganda and Rwanda to the conflict provides a better explanation of such immediate availability of arms to the rebels. Furthermore, the quick acquisition of arms is greatly enhanced by the improved electronic technology and efficient distribution and transportation network throughout the world. These include countries in Africa which are distributors of weapons from Eastern Europe, the USA, China and South

Africa, among others. Such countries easily supply weapons to civil war zones. South Africa is not only a producer but a supplier of arms in Africa.

Efforts to control weapons in Africa are being undermined by the presence of military companies or mercenary outfits. Defence is a major sector which is increasingly being privatised and international military companies are proliferating. These companies are involved in arms supply and other activities. For example, Executive Outcomes and Sandline International and military professionals Resources Incorporated offer military and training services to governments and large corporations. Such companies have been quite active in Africa. The difficulty lies in the fact that since they are private companies, they cannot be publicly controlled or regulated. As private organisations, they are only accountable to those who pay for their services. Both domestic and international efforts to limit mercenary activities have been ineffective.[26]

The economic aspect of the arms trade requires serious attention if control and peace are to be attained. There is a need to turn such economies from arms production to peaceful economic activities that will ensure the promotion of peace in Africa or at least provide no source of arms to any country in Africa. The massive imports of armaments into Africa have not only increased the debt burden but created violent conditions that have made social development almost unattainable. The easy availability of weapons has also destroyed the chances of seeking other peaceful alternatives to conflicts by the warring parties. Parties to the conflict easily resort to war rather than negotiating peacefully, thus destroying the will and the opportunity to resolve conflict peacefully.

Social Development

The Copenhagen Declaration and Programme of Action of the World Summit for social Development declared an enabling environment a *sine qua non* for social development to take place. In particular, social development is clearly linked to the development of peace, freedom, stability and security, both nationally and internationally. The desire to achieve better living conditions for the people by better harnessing human potential and natural resources will require increased solidarity not only within but across states in Africa. In fact, genuine solidarity within and among states will reduce intolerance, xenophobia and all forms of discrimination that are counter to the values of social justice and that make the achievement of sustainable social development possible.[27]

Social development in its comprehensive state aims at the progressive reduction and elimination of the negative conditions of human life that inhibit people's ability to realise their full potential and to function socially. It therefore seeks to attain the maximum possible human development through the creation of suitable social services that will eventually eliminate malnutrition, disease, illiteracy, squalor, unemployment and all forms of inequality and discrimination.[28] People's participation and self-reliance are central in this approach. It is assumed that for sustainable social development to take place, it has to be locally motivated and inspired. People, based on their existential experience through various processes of transactions and interactions and social institutions, have to decide on their needs, take action and evaluate their efforts. Social development should not merely be seen as the provision of social services. It is a process of planned institutional change with the involvement and participation of the people to bring about better conditions of human life in the economy, health, education, civil liberties, social policies and programmes. There is a constant dialectical relationship between the micro and macro levels for the necessary changes to take effect.

Various sub-units or interests in society have to engage in dialogue; they have to participate and co-operate to bring about a desired outcome. Who participates and how the processes of participation and co-operation are undertaken become important considerations. Sustainable social development should allow for the citizen and civil society to have a say in the whole process of how policies and programmes for change are conceived and executed. Citizens through various institutions have to interact with each other in order to arrive at amiable solutions that are non-discriminatory but inclusive. The dialogue therefore becomes necessary so as to discuss the allocation and distribution of resources. These resources can be tangible or intangible. They can include land, employment, mineral wealth, political power, housing, education and opportunity. So questions about who gets what, how much and when are of critical importance to the egalitarian principle embedded in the social development. According to Osei-Hwedie, this egalitarian principle also implies giving attention and emphasis to the most vulnerable and disadvantaged in society.[29] Children, women, the elderly and people with disabilities are given special attention to ensure that their needs are met in the most humane way.

Dialogue, participation and co-operation, it must be emphasised, can only take place in a congenial and peaceful atmosphere free of intimidation and violence. The conditions necessary for mutual co-operation must be deliberately developed and sustained to create the enabling environment for social development. Civil violence that has swept across Africa has undone the dialogue, participation and co-operation, all essential for social development. Instead, civil violence has brought about destructiveness with heavy human costs; the loss of life, misery, orphans, disease, starvation and the displacement of thousands of people throughout the continent. The disruptive effects of civil violence continue to haunt the people in the aftermath, making them psychologically unstable and less productive in pursuit of their daily routines.

Civil violence, especially that which is ethnically motivated, depersonalises and brutalises both the victim and the perpetrator. Perhaps more importantly, it violates and denigrates humanity and the principles of egalitarianism, mutual co-operation and respect, with disastrous consequences for the wellbeing of all people. Essentially, civil violence militates against building a just and democratic society in which all people enjoy their freedoms. Moreover, the consequences of civil violence destroy the development that has already taken place to place the people at the disadvantage of starting over again. Since World War II, Europe, the USA and Japan have not looked back to start all over again to construct their societies.

Civil violence is therefore a challenge that needs to be completely resolved for the continent to move forward in social development. Civil violence can be prevented if the continent adopts a common value system. Clough suggests that "the single most uniform characteristic of all cultures is that they have basic values about what the people want to get out of life".[30] The centrality of shared values in human activities therefore provides a starting point, that must be exploited. Secondly, a common value system must be appreciated at two levels: individual and society. At the individual level, it will serve to conscientise individuals towards developing an ethical sense and commitment to work towards unity. A central value system will also stimulate a sense of self-responsibility and commitment towards the realisation of the common good. Individuals have a moral responsibility towards self and society.[31] At societal level, citizens will develop a sense of mutual respect and tolerance for other groupings.

In addition, adopting a common value system will enable us to create a common supreme authority with the necessary power to enforce the general will and common good of the continent. The Organisation of African Unity (OAU) comes close to this suggestion. But in its current form, the OAU lacks authority and power. At best it simply serves as a "talk shop" without the ability to enforce anything at all. There is thus a need to strengthen the continental body, so that it has both the power and authority to act when necessary. The central value system embodied by the OAU could serve to provide a reference point out of which a consensus will be derived to guide its decisions and dictate actions. A common value system should bring all ethnic groups together to engage in society building. There are no illusions that this is a simple process. It is quite evident that there is bound to be a great deal of disagreement about this proposition due to differences in the dominant value base. But the proposition is borne out of deep-seated conviction that the continent needs a rallying point that will drive the resolution of civil violence. The lack of a common reference point, it is suggested, remains a major obstacle to peaceful co-existence and tolerance on the continent.

Conclusion

Various factors have been suggested to account for the lack of social development in Africa. But the availability of small arms, and the enduring problems of ethnicity have been identified as some of the major factors that have contributed to the glaring absence of social development in the continent. Various countries in Africa are experiencing persistent economic difficulties, stagnation in overall exports, declines in per capita food production, as well as crop production, leading to episodes of famine. The easy acquisition of arms has posed a grave problem for these fragile economies. These difficulties are excerbated by civil violence, which will continue to make social development elusive on the continent. At the same time, there has been a clear failure in Africa to manage ethnic pluralism, which has led to ethnic tensions – with disastrous consequences, as was the case of the genocide in Rwanda in 1994.[32] Civil violence has created instability in many places in Africa and led to numerous almost insurmountable problems of refugees and displacement. It is suggested therefore that a central value system be adopted that will help not only to diffuse ethnic tensions and rivalries but bring about a sense of compromise and accommodation to create a peaceful environment for social development.

Notes and References

1   UNICEF, *The State of the World's Children 1996*, London: Oxford University Press, 1998.

2   United Nations Development Programmme (UNDP), *Human Development Report 1999*, New York: Oxford University Press, 1999.

3   D Eade and S Williams, *The Oxfam Handbook of Development and Relief*, Oxford: Oxfam, 1995, p 841.

4   International Institute for Strategic Studies, *The Military Balance*, London: Oxford University Press, 1997/98.

5   N Choucri and R North, 'Roots of war: The master variables', in R Vayryne, D Senghaas and C Schmidt (eds), *The Quest for Peace: Transcending collective violence and war among societies, cultures and stores*, London: International Social Science Council, 1987, p 204.

6   *Ibid.*

7   K Matlosa, 'Globalisation and regional security: Southern Africa at the cross-
    roads', Paper presented at a SARIPS Annual Colloquium on "Peace and
    security in Southern Africa: challenges and opportunities", Harare, 26–30
    September 1999.

8   JK Akokpari, 'The challenges of sustainable democracy: Southern Africa in
    the twenty-first century', Paper presented at the 21st Southern African
    Universities Social Science Conference, University of Malawi,
    29 November–4 December 1999.

9   UNDP 1999, p 36.

10 *Africa Confidential*, vol 40, no 9, 24 September 1999, p 1.

11 *World Social situation in the 1990s*, New York: United Nations, 1994.

12 M Ottaway, 'Ethnic conflictual security in Southern Africa', in EJ Keller and
    D Rothchild (eds), *Africa in the new international order: Rethinking state sov-
    ereignty and regional security*, Boulder: Lynn Rienner, 1996.

13 *Ibid.*; OJM Kalinga, 'Colonial rule, missionaries and ethnicity in the North
    Nyoma District, 1891–1938', *African studies Review*, vol 28, no 1, 1985;
    WC Cockerham, *The Global Society: An introduction to sociology*, New York:
    McGraw-Hill, 1995.

14 MM Munyae and MM Mulinge, 'The centrality of a historical perspective to
    the analysis of modern social problems in sub-Saharan Africa: A tale from
    two case studies', *Journal of Social Development In Africa*, vol 14, no 2, 1999;
    Eade and Williams 1995.

15 M Bloom, *Introduction to the drama of social work*, Illinois: FE Peacock-
    Publishers, 1990.

16 Munyae and Mulinge 1999.

17 AL Epstein, *Politics in an urban African community*, Manchester: Manchester
    University Press, 1973.

18 JC de Ridder, *The personality of the urban African in South Africa*, London:
    Routledge, 1961.

19 Munyae and Mulinge 1999.

20 Cockerham 1995.

21 Kalinga 1985.

22 Munyae and Mulinge 1999.

23 *Africa Confidential*, vol 40, no 9, 24 September 1999.

24 S Deger, *Military expenditure in Third World countries: Their economic effects*,
    London: Routledge, 1986.

25 *Ibid.*, p 157.

26 UNDP 1999.

27 *The Copenhagen Declaration and Programme of Action: World Summit for
    Social Development*, New York: United Nations, 1996.

28 A Lombard, ML Weyers and JL Schoeman, *Community work and community development perspectives in social development*, Pretoria: Haum, 1991; G Meier, *Leading issues in economic development*, New York: Oxford University Press, 1976.

29 K Osei-Hwedie, *A search for legitimate social development education and practice models for Africa*, Lewiston: Edwin Mellen Press, 1995.

30 S Clough, *Basic values of western civilisation*, New York: Columbia University Press, 1989, p 213.

31 A Morales and T Sheafor, *Social Work: A professional of many faces*, Boston: Allyn and Bacon, 1989.

32 PR Baehr and L Gordenker, *The United Nations in the 1990s*, London: Macmillan, 1992, p 87.

The Aid Regime Factor in Civil/Regional Conflicts and Challenges of Public Security in Southern Africa

GS Maipose

The primary objective of international development aid is poverty alleviation and economic development, while military assistance focuses on ensuring peace and political stability. Addressing the problem of governance is increasingly seen to be at the heart of the development challenge and of much signficiance for enhancing aid effectiveness and long-term peace. A large body of literature has attempted to explain the factors that cause civil wars, political instability and dismal economic performance. The problems associated with a variety of external shocks (such as the terms of trade and debt crisis) that affect economic performance in developing countries are widely acknowledged and cannot be underrated. On the other hand, a poor governance record, corruption, and economic crisis are among the leading internal factors for economic crisis and political instability.[1] In fact, they are the main justifications for civil disturbances and whenever the military seizes power. The same factors loom high in explaining why aid has been largely ineffective and why the African region has failed to attract more foreign direct investment.

Broadly examining development and military assistance, this chapter attempts to illuminate the significance of the Aid Regime factor in Africa's economic crisis and, most importantly, in domestic and regional conflicts – both directly, by taking sides, and indirectly, through aid fungibility, which has made development efforts problematic in Southern Africa. It is acknowledged that changes in aid policy and measures for debt relief are necessary. But, it is argued, the impact of the overall development effort will remain largely ineffective unless concerted efforts are directed at reducing the costs of aid fungibility and the severe socio-economic costs of civil and armed conflicts, by diffusing the causes of internal insecurity and regional conflict, including the use of force against the worst offenders or support for one warring side against the other as the only viable route to hasten the end of conflicts.

Context and underlying issues of the aid regime

To put the underlying issues in proper perspective, it is imperative to reflect on the context and underlying issues of the aid regime factor in regional wars and challenges for public security and regional stability. Fighting poverty by supporting economic growth and development in the least developed countries has been and continues to be a major objective of development aid, while military aid, by and large, tries to enhance peace and stability.[2] Many African countries are aid-dependent and unfortunately the impact has been generally disappointing.[3] In spite of aid, most countries in the SADC region have become increasingly poorer, and "genuine" liberation wars have been replaced by civil wars or civil insecurity perpetuated by poor governance and emergence of what are now recognised as "warlords" or the elements that benefit from civil wars and instability. There is a growing belief that foreign aid must be changed considerably if it is to be effective in promoting Africa's development in a less intrusive and directive manner.[4] Ironically, aid dependence, according to Lancaster and Wangwe, "appears to have contributed to poor economic performance" in a number of African countries.[5]

The evidence is overwhelming in Africa as a whole and the SADC region in particular. SADC is composed of some of the least developed countries in the world – such as Mozambique, which may be contrasted with the potentially richest but mismanaged economy on the continent, that of the Democratic Republic of Congo (DRC). SADC also houses Africa's longest civil war in Angola and the region's greatest surviving "war criminal", Jonas Savimbi of UNITA. Foreign intervention is conceived as military aid in the ongoing DRC civil war and a form of regional networking for "profit" which undermines peace-making initiatives. Another misfortune of modern African states and SADC member states in particular, is that when the international community declared World Refugee Day in 1970, nearly all the refugees in the region were political refugees – freedom fighters involved in the wars of liberation against white-dominated ruled states in Zimbabwe, Angola, Mozambique, Namibia and South Africa. Ironically, the number of refugees nowadays has increased tremendously – mainly composed of political refugees, displaced citizens and "economic refugees" from independent African states due to civil conflicts and bad governance problems.

Economic crisis and political disorder have had direct implications for the international aid regime and two opposing trends are worth noting. Economic and political misfortunes initially led to a tremendous increase in the level of aid for development, military and humanitarian purposes up to the peak of the Cold War, and this was supplemented by aid in support of economic and political "reforms" up to the mid-1990s, which was followed by a subsequent decline in aid flows as donor countries increasingly questioned the effectiveness of aid and a feeling of "aid fatigue" set in.[6] Moreover, economic misfortunes and conditions for how aid is used have led to other inter-related problems. Save for a few exceptions, aid-receiving counties have tended to slide into domestic or regional conflicts as well as increasing aid dependence over the years with little, if any, achievements in the field of development. A good number of these countries are in political and economic crisis – fuelling their political instability, civil insecurity and crime, thereby rendering aid generally ineffective. Ironically, many of these aid recipient governments spend a significant amount of their resources on defence and some offer or receive military assistance in regional conflicts. The "warlords" who benefit from the crisis have no interest in ending the wars and do everything possible to fuel the regional and civil wars – all at a severe economic and social cost.

In addition to aid, which in some cases has been specifically donated for military purposes and sustained by the "warlords", development assistance can directly or indirectly enhance recipients' capacity to finance military and defence expenditure. In a subtle manner, aid helps to sustain governments that otherwise might not have survived or have done little to defuse civil conflicts and enhance civil security. But the onset of political instability, derived from civil wars and macro-economic instability, can frighten off foreign investors and engender a vicious economic cycle with precipitous decline in security. What valuable lessons can we learn from the policy-based aid experience in Africa, and Southern Africa in particular?

Fundamental changes in aid policies, such as the introduction of structural adjustment lending and debt relief measures, have been called for to enhance the impact of external development assistance. Given the level of civil and regional wars and crime in many Southern African countries, the international community also has to recognise the threats of insecurity and instability to socio-economic development. Again, for all the emphasis on good governance and the need to attract foreign investment, there has been little attention to enhancing national and civil security, without which good governance and the flow of foreign investment are impossible. How aid is given, especially what aid finances, has been an issue of controversy over the years. While many donors would categorically refuse to support agencies of defence – widely seen as draining external development assistance into the "bottomless pit" of the Third World – the same cannot be said of donors funding agencies for civil security, for instance to enhance police professionalism. Despite their enormous impact on the poor, their extraordinary cost to business and their potential to destabilise public order, civil insecurity and crime have received little attention and aid in this sector has been minimal.

In addition, it has been increasingly recognised in recent years that foreign aid can unintentionally create some impediments to development.[7] Donor governments and international organisations have often provided aid for bureaucratic, political and commercial objectives that have overridden (and at times undercut) development concerns, leading to ineffective aid from a development standpoint. Foreign aid, when it is large and continuous, can have unintended, negative impact in recipient countries. For example, it can appreciate the exchange rate (and so discourage exports) and ratchet up the government budget. Relatively large and poorly managed amounts of aid can also have an impact on the incentives that affect the behaviour of political and economic agents – potentially inducing misuse or diversion of aid or public funds released by aid for personal use through the regime's own corrupt patronage networks. This is not a new development, especially where aid is not provided to fund a coherent set of priority activities. It was reported in 1947 already that, "When the World Bank thinks it is financing an electric power station, it is really financing a brothel".[8] The observation questioned the extent of aid fungibility – the extent to which donor funding changes the spending priorities of recipient governments such as diverting own resources for personal use (a clear case of corruption) or spending money on consumption or low-priority projects. This interpretation, when collaborated with the evidence, has led to a critical analysis of the impact of aid, coupled with a general feeling in key donor countries that aid is "a futile process of pouring resources in a bottomless pit of the Third World countries".[9] This feeling is one of the main reasons for so-called donor fatigue. Indeed, any diversion of aid for defence spending or use of own resources for personal benefits clearly constitutes misuse of resources. However, one might wonder whether donors see aid to public security sector as going down the drain as well. This, in our view, should be one of the critical areas of concern for aid to support – that is enhancing one of the most important functions of the state, domestic law enforcement and civil security.

In many southern African countries, the ability of governments to ensure security through traditional means has declined. Civil insecurity and crime have escalated dramatically, especially in urban areas. The situation is more or less the same even in countries like Malawi where civil security was rated high under the authoritative Banda regime. Indeed, one of the great challenges for new democratically oriented governments, especially in South Africa, Zambia and Malawi, is to rebuild the working relationship between the people and the police.

Crusades for debt forgiveness are made in good faith and are legitimate concerns with increasing momentum. Debt relief initiatives have so far delivered too little relief, too late and for too few countries. It is also imperative to come up with workable and effective ways of ensuring that the proceeds of debt relief go to fight poverty and improve civil security, law and order – not going down the drain in bureaucracy or spent on military arms.

The issues of domestic and regional conflicts and rising defence spending in aid recipient countries have attracted the attention of many observers, including donors. But very little has been done to explore the linkage with the international aid regime and areas of possible intervention. National defence and civil security are important functions of government. Security from external threats and the maintenance of law and order contribute to socio-economic development. But peace and security cannot be attained in the conditions of abject poverty that are prevalent in Africa today. Security is no longer confined to preventing invasions, but should be built on a firm foundation of sustainable development. Member states should draw lessons from past crises including the failure to anticipate and prevent the genocide in Rwanda and the inability by UN Security Council and SADC to end the crisis in the DRC. It must be stressed that peace and development are two sides of the same coin – without development, the causes of conflict will not be eliminated, and without peace the conditions for development will not be met. However, high levels of defence spending burden the economy and may impede growth, while civil insecurity and crime can aggravate the problem by frustrating economic activities and making the country almost ungovernable. It need not surprise us that Africa – the continent with the least economic progress – has produced some of the greatest conflicts.

Provision of national and civil security is a fundamental responsibility of the state, without which both good governance and economic growth or positive economic returns on investment (which donors emphasise) are impossible. It has long been established that "a capacity to govern is the capacity to budget".[10] Government budgeting involves fundamental questions about conflicts, decision making, and "who gets what" in society, when, how and what difference it makes.[11] Does the same question apply when a significant amount of money or almost all the expenditures (capital and recurrent) are being funded by donors? Does aid play its envisaged "gap filling" role, and what are the potential conflicts? It is imperative to analyse the extent of aid fungibility and its role in conflict.

Does aid constitute an additional or fungible resource?

The question of whether aid constitutes an *additional* or *fungible* resource is crucial to explore if a realistic case is to be made to illuminate the significance of external development assistance in civil and regional conflicts. External resources are fungible if the recipient, under any circumstances, would have financed what the external contribution is used for, but they are additional if they are used for activities that would not have been financed by government. Mainly because of their very low savings rate, it is perhaps instructive to note that empirical results on the extent of aid fungibility in sub-Saharan Africa have concluded that aid has not been fungible.[12] This is probably true, but little has been said about the extent to which aid or donor funding can change the spending priorities of the recipient governments. Fungible external contributions can allow an aid recipient government to finance lower priority activities. The actual or net impact of the external contribution is thus to allow the implementation of lower priority activity, as well as opening up the possibility of abuse or misuse of the donor resources. In practice, external contributions may be partly fungible, partly additional because a project may contain some activities that would have been financed and others that would not. For example, a recipient government can decide to spend on arms if aid is used to service foreign debt which would have been serviced (partly or in full) with the recipient's own resources. The same applies if aid is used for balance of payments support when a recipient had intended to spend a given amount of its own resources on fuel imports.

The level of fungibility is a direct function of the degree of leverage donors exercise on budgetary decisions of the recipient government and the degree of control that the recipient government has over the development process. Actually, the fungibility problem and the major worry depends much on how aid is given and how the recipient manages its resources against the backdrop of the quality or level of donor's confidence. The underlying problem is that if a project is financed which the recipient government would have undertaken, then the aid money is actually financing some other unidentified projects which the aid agency does not know about and most importantly might not like. Thus, donor funding may alter the recipient government's spending priorities – creating possibilities for abuse or diversion of its own public resources, or undertaking additional or different activities such as defence spending which the donors may not approve.[13]

The question of aid fungibility has a number of implications for the mechanisms used to deliver and also for evaluating the impact of aid regardless of its form.[14] Project aid, which has been the most common form of bilateral assistance, has been largely tied up in conditions, including how it is given and used, and it is, therefore, less fungible. In this way, project aid can create a (sometimes misleading) sense of certainty about the impact of aid on development. The same cannot be said about programme aid or balance of payments support and many forms of structural adjustment lending by the World Bank and the IMF. These forms of external assistance are not usually tied and are therefore more fungible, and can more easily be integrated into the recipient government's budget as just one of several sources of revenue. The disadvantage of programme aid, as seen by many donors, is that its fungibility allows recipient governments to escape their control and to pursue objectives they may not desire. It is thus perceived to be open to abuse. Donors have tried to lessen the fungibility of various forms of programme aid by accompanying it with conditionalities and an increasing preference for enclave projects and parallel management structures. For example, disbursements of structural adjustment lending are usually divided into several tranches, each of which is released only after the fulfilment of mutually agreed-upon reforms or levels of performance. In some cases new external support cannot be released, or negotiations for assistance may not even start unless certain conditions are met. The practice of relying on enclave projects, on the part of some donors, is motivated in part by the desire to control inefficiency, the diversion of aid resources and corruption.

Given this broad connotation of aid fungibility, we can explain the links between aid and defence spending or military intervention, focusing on what aid finances and the incentives, on the part of donor agencies, for tying aid to avoid abuse by recipient governments in Africa and southern Africa in particular. First, the question of what aid ultimately finances is interesting only if the preferences of the donor are different from those of the recipient. If they had identical preferences, then it would not matter if the aid were given for a specific project or as budgetary support.[15] When donor and recipient preferences differ, it is not always clear whether the presence of fungibility is good or bad, such as cases when donor funds or government resources released by aid are spent on viable projects. However, the presence of fungibility is clearly bad when resources released by aid for the government to spend are diverted to unproductive activities, such as defence or military spending. Second, rather than integrate their aid within ministerial administrations or contribute to a pool of aid which, along with the government's own resources, would finance the entire public expenditure package, donors may resort to various mechanisms and structures to demarcate their own activities – leading to the proliferation of stand-alone projects outside the national budgetary system.[16] The practice of relying on enclave project structures may be motivated by the desire to control the environment in which aid-funded activities take place (i.e. minimising the vulnerability of aid to the inefficiencies, resource scarcities or corruption of the recipient government). The problem is that the practice tends to undermine local project 'ownership' and capacity building, including questions about budgetary or fiscal prudence and the institutions necessary for effective governance.[17]

Ideally, governments are responsible for estimating and raising revenue, monitoring and controlling expenditure, managing public debt, directing resources toward developmental objectives, and ensuring accountability. High levels of aid dependence may take many of these functions out of government hands, either deliberately or by default, and make the budget cycle fairly meaningless.[18] Where governance is judged to be poor, donors may scale back their assistance or take over the design and implementation of aid-funded projects through parallel management structures, with adverse implications for local capacity building. Far from enhancing state management capacity, aid dependence has had a devastating institutional and governance impact. These include a loss of sovereignty, lack of policy ownership and an undermining of the role of public budgets as instruments for socio-economic management.[19] It is also important to note that conditionalities do not sufficiently address the issue of how recipient governments spend their own resources. Clearly, aid giving in both programme and project modes remains problematically fungible so long as recipient governments' (national) resources are not put to good use. It is for this reason that concerns about aid fungibility centre on what aid ultimately finances and the extent to which donor funding alters the spending priorities of recipient governments against the backdrop of the preference of the donor.

The debate on aid versus own resources

Given the above orientation, it is possible to see how aid can be used to finance wars and neglect civil security in the sub-region. From here, we can proceed to the debate over own resources vs. external assistance. The primary purpose of international regimes is to promote mutually beneficial co-operation among sovereign states, with the ultimate objective of promoting international stability and development. The international aid regime is similarly conceptualised, with the main objective of promoting rapid development in low-income countries by supplementing domestic savings or relaxing foreign exchange and institutional capacity constraints. Given the underlying issues on fungible or additional resources, it can be argued that an individual donor's assistance is, generally speaking, more fungible than the assistance of donors as a group. This is so for a simple reason: if one donor is not interested in financing a particular project, or withholds aid because of the recipient government's poor record on governance or perceived diversion of resources for defence, another donor may very well provide and even increase its bilateral aid. Wars or defence spending and unproductive ventures have continued to be financed from aid in this way.

On the other hand, there is the well-known tendency by donors to follow the same trend, leading to policy-based lending covering institutional development, governance, private sector development, etc. If all or most of the recipient countries' development expenditure is financed from foreign resources, the donors' "flock mentality" would influence development in the country very strongly. That is what happened to Zambia when it liquidated its loss-making national airline and when its rating on governance was poor.

Unfortunately, donors have not been able to use their leverage on defence spending until quite recently. For example, Zimbabwe was called upon to account for its defence spending before a World Bank loan was released, because of that country's involvement in what has turned out to be a regional war sparked off by what is essentially a civil war in the DRC. Even then it remained doubtful whether the state was going to be restrained in any way in its defence spending. In Botswana, by contrast, an increasing share of development expenditure, including large defence expenditure in recent years, is financed from domestic resources – already estimated for in the country's well-entrenched medium-term national development plan and put in motion through annual budgets. This makes the country less exposed to the effect of donor fads. The practice of the established systems of resource management – planning and budgeting – is quite transparent and this includes defence spending, which is "hidden" in many countries in the region. Botswana's military intervention together with South Africa in Lesotho to restore peace did not in any way amount to a diversion of aid money because no one would question its capacity to finance an external military intervention from its own domestic resources. If the donors leave certain priority areas, the Botswana government has the financial means to simply pick up the pieces, and financial aid remains quite insignificant in the country's total expenditure. Moreover, knowing the preferences, constraints and modus operandi of the different donors, the Botswana government tries as much as possible to match donors and projects in a way that optimises the net contribution of aid to Botswana while at the same time satisfying donor's interest.[20] In this way there is a general concurrence as regards the development objectives of Botswana and donor assistance, and Botswana's well-developed national development planning system is an important factor in this regard.

The extent to which aid can be said to finance defence spending or military intervention in some southern African countries is relatively easy to establish analytically. But it is not easy to get evidence because defence spending is confidential or disguised in many countries in the region. As already noted, the literature on aid fungibility centres on what aid ultimately finances and the extent to which donor funding alters the spending priorities of recipient governments. If foreign development assistance is used to build a primary school which the recipient government would have built anyway, then the consequence of this specific aid is to release resources for the government for other items, such as defence spending or even for abuse by corrupt government officials. Basically, more or less the same can be said about programme aid, such as balance of payments support. Thus, while the primary school may still get built or a government Land Rover imported, the aid is financing some other expenditure in recipient countries. Aid tying tries to minimise the chances for aid fungibility, while efforts to increase government "ownership" of aid projects or to integrate aid funds into national budgets may be increasing the chances of aid fungibility.

To start with, foreign policy objectives, irrespective of quality of governance, have been one of the leading motives for aid to some African countries. Throughout the Cold War, many US decision-makers, as was the case among other Western donors, viewed foreign assistance as a key foreign policy instrument in the struggle against international communism.[21] For example, key US allies in Africa, such as the former Zaire and Somalia, received a disproportional share of US aid to Africa.[22] The decision to provide a large quantity of aid was dictated by foreign policy concerns for stability in the region. In the case of Zaire, aid was made despite overwhelming evidence that the government would not manage aid resources well.[23] Similarly, France continued to focus its foreign aid programmes on its former colonies in Africa where it maintained an array of commercial, military, and foreign policy interests. The evidence about the significance of aid in civil or regional political instability is overwhelming in Southern Africa. For example, US aid served to defend and strengthen the UNITA rebels in the Angolan civil war, while the Soviet Union and Cuba funded the government side. Broadly justified as a struggle against the spread of international communism during the Cold War era, US aid clearly sustained rebel organisations such as UNITA, which might otherwise not have survived. It also reinforced the patrimonial elements in the state system, sustaining a situation in which key rent seekers or war lords have no interest in ending the wars. Relatedly, foreign policy concerns led donor governments to stress political stability and order in Southern Africa, sometimes at the cost of sustainable development, good governance and political and economic reforms. Consequently donors tolerated corrupt regimes and sustained incompetent and even venal governments.

The same can be said about aid to Africa's leading dictators, such as Kamuzu Banda of Malawi, and warlords such as Charles Taylor of Liberia and Savimbi of Angola. Controversy surrounding the World Bank-led international donor lending to Zimbabwe is a good example of how lack of transparency in the use of aid and government's own resources undermines national development. It is not a clear case of how aid can sustain incompetent and even venal governments, but a case of adverse consequences for a lack of transparency. Zimbabwe has tended to be cast out and then welcomed back into the financial fold of the IMF and several international donors, according to the pattern of disagreements over economic reform policy and its costly military interventions. The economic consequences of the lack of transparency demonstrate why the state's economic role makes government effectiveness essential to economic performance.

As can be seen from Table 1, the importance of foreign aid within African economies is overwhelming in the crucial macro-economic indicators – Gross Domestic Product (GDP) and Gross Domestic Investment (GDI). Except for a few countries like Mauritius and South Africa, the share of aid in GDI ranges from as high as 178% for Malawi, 133% for Mozambique, and 127% for Zambia, to as low as 17% for Zimbabwe and 8% for Swaziland. The explanation is partly due to the way African governments have managed their economies over the years, inability to make full use of their potential for taxable capacity, and partly because these countries, like many developing countries, have been prone to a variety of external shocks that have affected their economic performance. In many African countries, inappropriate economic policies and the inability to respond to exogenous shocks combined with external factors to undermine economic growth and accelerate macro-economic instability, which in turn undermined the government's ability to raise public revenue and implement policies effectively. This engendered a vicious cycle of poverty and low real wages which made public servants preoccupied with the need to make ends meet and to engage in corrupt activities. It is also the main cause of civil conflicts and increasing requests for aid and loans from the rest of the world, as many African governments tried to get what their own economies were incapable of supplying, and very few can do without aid. This all too often led to "strong" governments which either presided over chaos or used their powers to suppress the living standards of all except those who kept them in power through patronage networks.

Table 1: Significance of ODA in selected countries, 1993-1998

Country	Aid in GNP		Aid in GDI		Defence GDP		Govt Defence Budget	
	1993	1998	1993	1998	1993	1998	1993	1998
Angola	9.0	8.3	20.8	22.2	24.2	20.5	28.6	36.3
Botswana	2.9	2.3	11.7	10.6	4.4	5.1	10.3	13.4
Congo	7.5	3.9	21.8	9.4	3.0	5.0	16.1	41.4
Lesotho	12.9	6.2	27.1	17.2	3.6	2.5	10.5	6.1
Malawi	22.3	24.4	157.5	187.8	1.1	1.0	3.9	2.9
Mauritius	0.8	1.0	2.6	3.9	0.4	0.3	1.5	1.2
Mozambique	61.3	28.2	440.2	130.7	7.6	2.8	17.0	9.2
Namibia	5.5	5.7	35.0	30.7	2.2	2.7	5.6	7.3
South Africa	0.2	0.4	1.5	2.5	3.2	1.8	9.8	5.6
Swaziland	-	-	-	-	1.8	1.4	7.2	5.8
Tanzania	21.8	12.4	80.1	82.8	2.2	1.3	10.0	10.7
Zambia	28.9	11.0	177.0	72.6	3.3	1.1	9.3	3.9
Zimbabwe	7.9	4.7	33.3	25.7	3.8	3.8	10.1	11.9

Source: *World Development Indicators 2000*, Washington DC: World Bank, 2001.

Spending on military and the proportion of defence spending in the total government expenditures in many African countries go a long way towards vindicating the observation by Galbraith that "in the poor lands (of Asia, Africa and Latin America) the military power and its claim on resources is the greatest economic scandal and the greatest political tragedy of our age".[24] But the evidence is not easy to get and allegations cannot be easily collaborated with hard data, mainly because of the secrecy or lack of transparency in all forms of military or defence spending. The use of aid for military purposes need not be elaborated upon in the obvious cases where donors have directly supplied arms to the warring parties in civil wars in Angola, Mozambique, the DRC, and other parts of Africa. The less obvious examples relate to the fungibility of aid and these examples are also many. Despite the secrecy and lack of transparency surrounding official records, it is common knowledge that military spending in Africa has been and continues to be high and yet many of these countries cannot survive without aid.

One dimension is represented by the irreconcilable actions of visionary African leaders such as Julius Nyerere who, on the eve of his country's independence, questioned the need for a poor country to have an army, but subsequently built up a sizeable and relatively well-equipped defence force and used it against Idi Amin in 1979 – a move which had a crippling effect on the Tanzanian economy. Zimbabwe's military interventions, first in Mozambique and recently in the DRC, are in many respects justifiable. But the implications for the country's economy have been devastating, and while many observers acknowledge the need for land redistribution, many objective analysts and the international community have criticised the way the government has proceeded to seemingly allow lawlessness and land "invasions" by war veterans – leading to a deep sense of civil insecurity and aggravation of the economic crisis. Zambia has never been at war and has enjoyed peace and stability since independence in 1964. But the country's geo-political position and open-ended support for the liberation wars in Southern Africa inflicted a heavy toll on its economy during Kaunda's regime, while apparent systemic official corruption under Chiluba's administration has undermined the regime's legitimacy and donor confidence. For example, constitutional and statutory expenditure, under which defence spending was disguised and mixed with debt servicing in official reports, rose significantly from about 25% in 1975 to 42.3% of total expenditure in 1986; it reached a peak of 47.6% in 1988 and began declining modestly thereafter.[25] Within the total constitutional and statutory expenditure, the share of defence spending was more than twice as much as the share claimed by real expenditure for debt service from 1975 up to 1983 and thereafter the two competing items were almost even until 1986 when the debt-service share escalated.[26] The same government report makes it clear that "the defence expenditure, as a ratio of total expenditure items, continued to be much higher than other items (besides debt service) and in fact too high and an expenditure item of great concern".[27] Moreover, just as it became evident in the 1980s that potentially good projects often fail in a poor policy environment with each failure leading to authoritative tendencies, it has also become evident under the reform- minded Movement for Multiparty Democracy (MMD) government that policy reforms are less likely to succeed when public institutions and governance are weak. The problem of corruption in Zambia is increasingly seen to be at the heart of the development challenge.

Civil conflict in Southern Africa, as in many parts of the continent, is getting more complex and destructive, drawing outside forces with neighbours openly supporting one side or another or even intervening directly with their resources. The conflict in the DRC started as a civil war, and escalated into a regional war. The rebel factions, with military support from Rwanda and Uganda, started the civil war, while Angola, Namibia and Zimbabwe became directly involved following a request for assistance by Kabila's government. Civil disturbances in Lesotho forced South Africa and Botswana to intervene, lending military support to the government and remaining in that country for several months after peace and stability had been restored. The protracted civil war in Angola has compelled a UN peacekeeping force to pull out, and activated renewed allegations of Zambia's involvement in the rebels' supply line. The latter has been, to some extent, linked to political and civil instability and defence spending in Zambia. The point is that with increased conflicts in the region, military expenditure was bound to rise rapidly. The irony is that all the countries involved are aid dependent. However, the degree of dependence varies considerably, with Botswana and South Africa as the least dependent on aid, while Zambia, Angola, Uganda, Rwanda, and Zimbabwe can hardly survive without aid. The conflicts have certainly diverted budget resources (indirectly including aid) from human development related investment in health, education, community services and poverty alleviation. Given this scenario, the "savings" from the debt relief might not go to poverty-reduction programmes and the social sector. Thus, the aid that is not specifically given for military purposes is a matter of concern and that concern is about fungibility of aid or what aid ultimately finances.

Do we have any idea about how the same countries spend on defence? Figure 1 compares military expenditure as a percentage of combined Education and Health spending for the 1990-91 period. It is very clear that Angola and Mozambique spent more on defence than on education and health combined, while Zambia, Zimbabwe, the DRC and Tanzania spent at least 50% (on average) more on defence for the same period. We have no recent figures, for defence spending is taken as secret in many countries except for a few who have nothing to hide. However, we can get a rough idea from isolated reports. The protracted war in Angola has become more complex and destructive, drawing in outside forces with neighbours openly supporting one side or another or even intervening directly with their forces. Although we have no hard data, military spending increased dramatically in the DRC, Angola, Zimbabwe and Namibia. In Zambia, the MMD government, dazzled with enormous aid given as a goodwill gesture to a reform-oriented government, restored and extended subsidies for the defence forces (including beer and food). The increase in defence expenditure in Botswana "embarking on an accelerating and barely explicable arms build-up" (given the overall peace in the region), has raised internal and external eyebrows, and the country's military intervention in Lesotho was criticised even by some of its own back-benchers.[28] According to the Military Balance report for 1997/98, countries within the Southern African region were among the highest spenders on defence.[29] The same source reported that military spending in Uganda rose from US $81 million in 1994 to $131 million in 1996.

It is also interesting to note that countries involved in the civil war in the DRC are aid-dependent countries. Is aid enhancing the capacity to finance the war in the DRC? Countries that depend heavily on aid may have difficulties in justifying high defence expenditure. However, it must be noted that Africa is conflict ridden and the potential for conflict is still high given the high rate of unemployment, poverty, hunger, the lack of a democratic culture in a number of countries and the oppression of autocratic regimes which sow the seeds of civil war, and the fragile nature of some peace initiatives which could erupt into civil war and spill across borders.

Figure 1: Military Expenditure as a Percent of Combined Education and Health Expenditure, 1990-91

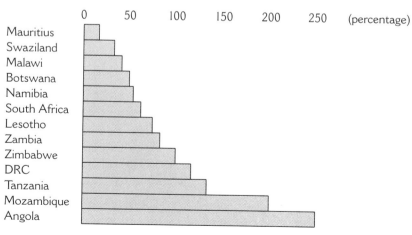

Source: *SADC Human Development Report*, Gaborone: SADC, 1999, p 32.

How peace and stability can enhance socio-economic development can be illustrated by the experience in Mozambique. The country was until quite recently one of the most conflict-prone countries in the region, spending more on military than on education and health combined, as shown in figure 1. However, with reduced military conflict following the signing of a peace accord and the end of the civil war, military expenditure has declined rapidly. In recent years, Mozambique's government and its development partners have shown more interest in conflict prevention, conflict management, and post-conflict reconstruction. The results have been clear: the civil war has ended and the national defence establishment is doing relatively well in terms of responsibility for national security and crime. The country has been able to attract private foreign investment and it has recently sustained one of the highest economic growth rates in the region. Thus, just as the national stability and civil security improved since the end of the civil war, so has the flow of foreign investment and economic growth.

Challenges of civil security

Many governments in the region seem unprepared to face internal security threats because of lack of funds and a breakdown of their public security structures or management systems. The protection of citizens does not seem to be a high priority; and most of the governments cannot afford much more. Unfortunately, international development agencies have been more concerned with cutting military spending than improving the professionalism of the internal security forces. Consequently, civil insecurity and crime have escalated dramatically. Almost all the countries in the region have experienced a rise in burglary, robbery, rape, murder, etc. These affect all classes, though it is crime against prominent people – politicians, businessmen, and tourists – which attracts newspaper headlines. Unfortunately, when a prominent politician is killed, government agents tend to be blamed for what are termed political assassinations, but rising crime is blamed when the victim is an ordinary person or a tourist – mainly due to unfair, biased or unprofessional reporting. Bureaucratic corruption and the complicity of police and customs agents allow criminal syndicates to gain a foothold, while the lack of other employment opportunities provide a ready supply of cheap recruits.

In many countries civil security institutions, especially the police, have not embraced the reforms in other branches of government and this has received little attention from development partners. Among the public security agencies, the police are underfunded, poorly run and lacking in accountability and transparency. Their ability to maintain vehicles and other expensive assets is inadequate. In many cases, they spend too much on personnel, but not enough on readiness. Even specialised police units function poorly. For example, internal intelligence organisations, which are important complements of the police forces, have in many cases lost sight of their fundamental mission. Far too many intelligence assets counter legitimate domestic political opponents of the governing regimes or do the bidding of the president of the day. Too few are devoted to the fundamental mission of understanding the development of security threats, while corruption and political patronage have further eroded their effectiveness. Due to the decline in professionalism and poor conditions of service, police are sometimes involved in organised crime or shoot and kill criminals on sight.

If this account is true, it is inconceivable that civil security has attracted so little donor funding. It is equally inconceivable that the independent press and human right advocates pay more attention to the plight of criminals, prisoners, and coup plotters than to general insecurity and rising crime. Across the continent, two major dynamics that influence violence are at work and the role of donors to contain the situation would be useful. First, the long economic crisis in most African countries has eroded the revenue base, the effectiveness of the state, and even its physical presence in outlying areas. Police and soldiers, with other public sector employees, are inadequately paid, equipped and trained. Second, the defence balance between state and society has been fundamentally altered. Security forces in the early years of independence, athough weak, could maintain order in part because the state controlled weapons and corruption was not widespread. Except for a few countries, the state now no longer has a monopoly on coercive power. Indeed, some governments find their police, and even their military, outgunned by criminals and rebels. Light weaponry is readily available with the dumping of stocks at the end of the Cold War, and the spillover from regional conflicts. Moreover, the trust between police and the citizenry – critical for law enforcement – has been severely undermined.

Due to the loss of confidence in the public security system, private companies have sprung up and their role has been increasing. Whatever their success in providing security in the short-term, private security companies are not a long-term solution to rising crime level. Relying on them may aggravate already difficult situations by further eroding the capacity of public institutions to ensure order, thus undermining the legitimacy of the state. However poorly some states have managed to ensure public security, it remains a goal to be striven for, not left by default to private providers. Aid too can help at least to improve the professionalism of the security forces. Unfortunately, it does not seem easy to ensure peace and security because conflicts have tended to result from bad governance and some foreign aid intended for peace has ended up escalating the conflicts. This is a complex situation indeed.

Aid for peace or political disorder for business

A number of African conflicts result from bad governance. Weak, corrupt and authoritarian governments, Stremlau contends, lack the institutional capacity to manage functional struggles and exclude majority or minority groups from power.[30] In environments where war has become a business and disorder is being deployed for political and profit purposes, the inadequacies of our present conceptual tools for resolving conflicts are glaringly obvious.[31] The unpalatable reality, according to Horace Campbell, is that "those who profit from war as a business will agree to peace accords while making mobilisations and troop movements for war."[32] The explanation is obvious. There were and are elements which do not want to end the conflicts. For these, war is more profitable than peace. Thus, the rebel leader in Angola, Jonas Savimbi, has been described as "Africa's greatest surviving war criminal" living on diamond rent. On the other hand, connectivity feeding off the conflict is "exemplified by the Dos Santos regime's own corrupt patronage networks built around Angola's lucrative oil industry". The bulk of the oil money bypasses the budget and goes straight into the hands of the presidency. Indeed, "for one particular year, the entire profit from the country's oil for the next three years had already been spent either on armament or to finance the super-rich life-style of the 'oligarchy' because the ruling and rebel elites appeared to accept indefinite war as a natural state of affairs".[33]

Similarly, the wars in the DRC and its neighbouring countries are a catastrophe in the heart of Africa. A form of regional networking, very often clandestine and illegal, has helped craft a regionalisation of conflict that undermines peace-building efforts. A recent UN Expert Panel has published a detailed report on the blatant and illegal exploitation of biological and mineral natural resources in DRC by Rwandan and Ugandan armies on the side of the rebels.[34] These are the "uninvited" combatants. The report concludes that these clandestine activities are helping to fuel the war. Taylor has also described the role of the "invited" participants such as Angola, Namibia and Zimbabwe as "equally involved in clandestine activities".[35] The Kabila regime tolerated the exploitation of the conflict for personal profit by a number of ruling elites from Zimbabwe, Angola, and Namibia in return for renting out their armies. It is close to what has been described as "Africa's Scramble for Africa".[36]

Some illustrative examples are in order. Zimbabwe's ruling elite has invested in timber, mining, army supplies and retail deals including the regional connectivity of the Zimbabwean company Osleg which buys diamonds and gold from the DRC. The Angolan government, which intervened to block a UNITA-friendly regime in the DRC, is connected through the business deals of its political elite in profitable oil marketing networks and diamond-buying operations.[37] There are allegations, too, against Namibia. If these bear any truth, then Taylor was on safe grounds to conclude that "much of the foreign intervention in the DRC is not only about preserving national security and defeating enemies, it is also about securing access to resource rich areas and establishing privatised accumulation networks that can emerge and prosper under the conditions of war and anarchy".[38] In this sense, war assumes the characteristics of a business venture, the beneficiaries of which are unlikely to give up the venture easily. Therefore, ending the war is not in line with the special interests of some actors who have tended to be key leading government officers and rebel leaders or warlords. Given these circumstances, the use of force against the worst offenders is not only justified but the only viable route to long-term peace.[39] In many cases support for one warring side against another is a valid response that can hasten the end of conflict and restrict the loss of life. It is for this reason that the peacekeeping role of neutral organs such as the OAU and UN needs to be strengthened. To be effective, these peacekeeping organs should be morally obliged to use force against obvious aggressors if military aid is to play its genuine peacekeeping role, complementing development aid.

Conclusion

This chapter presents evidence and debate over own resources versus external assistance in Southern Africa by exploring two inter-related issues as the main concern. First, it explores what governments are allowed to do and actually end up doing with the resources that are released by aid projects, and the extent to which aid increases the propensity to spend on defence or conflict resolution. Second, the chapter shows that regardless of what the recipients do with their own financial resources, aid fungibility and the role of foreign direct investment have important implications for how development and policy analysts evaluate the impact of foreign resources inflows, including aid, and implications for conflict management or productive investment. To the extent that aid is fungible, the development impact of aid-funded health clinics is not captured by the rate of return of those specific projects.[40] One can add, the development impact of debt relief will not come about by the amount to be forgiven but how recipient governments use the proceeds of debt relief in the fight against poverty. No one would want to see the money gained from debt relief go down the drain in bureaucracy or spent on military arms by the recipient government. Similarly, armed conflicts and a bad governance record have made it difficult to attract more foreign direct investment because of a lack of confidence among potential investors.

Most recent armed conflicts in Southern Africa have been internal conflicts, typically in states with poor governmental legitimacy and weak institutions. Civil insecurity and crime have escalated dramatically in most Southern African countries, especially in urban areas where some cities appear almost ungovernable. Civil wars and conflicts appear to be driven by competition for power and resources, while armed conflicts have fuelled civil insecurity and crime – breaking down law and order, militarising society, and inculcating a culture of impunity. Unfortunately, there are those who benefit from the conflicts or institutionalised political disorder. These have no interest in ending the conflicts, though some governments in the region seem unprepared to face internal security threats because of a lack of funds and a breakdown of their management systems or a decline in professionalism of their civil security agencies. This poses a dilemma for donors. Does their unwillingness to spend money on defence extend to helping build up coherent and effective public security structures in these countries?

The policy and development implications of the issues raised above are threefold. First, the existence of aid fungibility strengthens the conclusion that donors should be concerned with the quality of the overall public expenditure programmes of the recipient country – not just focusing narrowly on what aid finances. Given the fact that much of aid is tied, how recipient governments spend their own resources is crucial. Second, what also needs to be recognised is the fact that governments spend more on defence out of their own resources than they do out of aid resources at the margin. On the other hand, lack of good policies and bad governance frustrate economic growth and hinder the steady flow of foreign direct investment. But poor governance is the main cause of political instability. Third, the international community also has to recognise the threats of insecurity and instability and their adverse implications on economic growth and good governance. For all the current emphasis on good governance, there has been very little assistance for security and stability, or for finding concerted methods to punish warlords, without which good governance and socio-economic development are impossible.

To sum up, the problem of how aid is linked to domestic and regional conflicts and the leverage a number of donors can have suggests that further work on the cost of aid fungibility to recipients and their implications for domestic and regional conflicts and good democratic governance may be a fruitful area of research. Continued conflicts, which in Southern Africa are basically civil wars or domestic insecurity, are manifestations of struggles for power, resources or poor governance, including a decline in civil security. These to some extent are testimony to the difficulties of institutionalising democracy and holding in place coherent and effective public security structures after decades of authoritarianism.

Notes and References

1   J Stremlau, 'Ending African Wars', *Foreign Affairs*, vol 79, 1999.

2   I Serageldin, *Development Partners, Aid and Cooperation in the 1990s*, Stockholm: SIDA, 1993.

3   J Carlsson *et al*, *Foreign Aid in Africa: Learning from country experiences*, Uppsala, Nordic Africa Institute, 1997.

4   N van de Walle and T Johnston, *Improving Aid to Africa*, Washington DC: Overseas Development Council, 1996.

5   C Lancaster and S Wangwe, *Managing a smooth transition from aid dependence in Africa*, Washington DC: Overseas Development Council, 2000, p 4.

6   *Ibid.*; Carlsson *et al*, 1997.

7   Lancaster and Wangwe 2000.

8   S Deveranjan, S Rajkumar and V Swaroop, 'What Does Aid to Africa Finance?', Working paper presented at a workshop on Managing a Transition from Aid Dependence in sub-Saharan Africa, Nairobi, 4–6 December 1998, p 1.

9   PT Bauer, *Equality, the Third World and Economic Delusion*, London: Weidenfed and Nicolson, 1981; JC Wheeler, 'The critical role for Official Development Assistance in the 1990s', *Finance and Development*, no 26, September 1989.

10   D Axelrod, *Budgeting for Modern Government*, New York: St Martins Press, 1995; A Schick, *The Capacity to Budget*, Washington DC: Urban Institute, 1990.

11   H Lasswell, *Politics: Who Gets What, When, How*, New York: Meridian, 1958; A Wildavsky, *The Politics of the Budgetary Process*, Boston: Little Brown and Company, 1979.

12   H Pack *et al*, 'Foreign Aid and the Question of Fungibility', *Review of Economics and Statistics*, vol 75, 1993; Devarajan *et al*, 1998.

13   Pack *et al*, 1993.

14   T Feyzioglu *et al*, 'A panel data analysis of the fungibility of foreign aid', *World Bank Economic Review*, vol 112, 1998; P Mosley, *Overseas Aid: Its defence and reform*, Brighton: Wheatsheaf Books, 1992.

15   N Khilji and EM Zampelli, 'The Fungibility of US Military and non-military assistance and the impacts of expenditures of major aid recipients', *Journal of Development Economics*, vol 43, 1994.

16   Van de Walle and Johnston 1996, p 66.

17   D Brautigam and K Botchwey, 'The impact of aid dependence on gover-

nance and institutions in Africa', Paper presented at a Workshop on Collaborative Project on the Transition from Aid Dependence, Nairobi, 1998.

18   A Sekwat, 'Public budgeting deficiencies in Sub-Saharan Africa: A review', *Journal of Public Budgeting, Accounting & Financial Management*, vol 9, no 1, 1997, p 146; Brautigam and Botchwey 1998.

19   D Brautigam, 'Stale capacity and effective governance', in B Ndulo and N van de Walle (eds), *Agenda for Africa's Economic Renewal*, Oxford: Transaction Publishers, 1996; Van de Walle and Johnston 1996.

20   GS Maipose, GM Somolekae and T Johnston, *Aid Effectiveness in Botswana's management of external assistance and case studies of the US/Botswana Relationship*, Washington DC: Overseas Development Council, 1996; ST Dahlgren, A Duncan, P Gustafsson and P Molutsi, *SIDA Development Assistance to Botswana 1966–1993: An evaluation of 27 years of development co-operation*, Gaborone: SIDA, 1993, pp 53–88.

21   RS Walters and DH Blake, *The Politics of Global Economic Relations*, New Jersey: Prentice Hall, 1992, pp 152–159.

22   MG Schatzberg, *Mobutu or Chaos? The United States and Zaire, 1960–1990*, New York: University Press of America, 1991.

23   *Ibid.*; S Askin and C Collins, 'External collusion with kleptocracy: Can Zaire recapture its stolen wealth?', *Review of African Political Economy*, no 57, 1993.

24   Quoted in W Tordoff, *Government and Politics in Africa*, London: Macmillan, 1993, p 275.

25   GRZ, *The Zambian budget deficit and options for reducing it*, Lusaka: Government Printer, 1990, pp 3, 11.

26   *Ibid.*, p 10.

27   *Ibid.*, p 3.

28   K Good, *Realising Democracy in Botswana, Namibia and South Africa*, Pretoria: Africa Institute of South Africa, 1997, p 147; *Mmegi/The Reporter*, 8 March 1996.

29   *Mmegi/The Reporter*, 17–23 October 1997.

30   Stremlau 1999, p 118.

31   W Reno, *Warlord Politics and the African State*, Boulder: Lynne Rienner, 1998.

32   Quoted in I Taylor, 'South Africa's Foreign Policy and the Great Lakes Crisis', Paper presented at a Political and Administrative Studies Seminar Series, University of Botswana, 14 February 2001, p 5.

33   K Good, 'Autocratic elites and enfeebled masses: Africa and Botswana', Paper presented at a Political and Administrative Studies Seminar Series, University of Botswana, 5 April 2000, p 14.

34   *UN Expert Panel Report on the Illegal Exploitation of Natural Resources and other Forms of Wealth of DRC*, New York, UN Security Council, 2001.

35 Taylor 2001.
36 JM Weinstein, 'Africa's Scramble for Africa: Lessons of a continental war', *World Policy Journal*, vol 17, 2000.
37 J Collier and C Dietrich (eds), *Angola's War Economy: The role of oil and diamonds*, Pretoria: Institute for Security Studies, 2000.
38 Taylor 2001, p 8.
39 Reno 1998.
40 Deverajan *et al*, 1998.

Domestic Violence as a Violation of Women's Democratic and Human Rights

Gwen N Lesetedi

Democracy is a rather elusive concept that has mainly been defined with reference to the governance process. The emphasis is on representative government chosen through competitive elections.[1] Democracy, however, is much more than simple voting rights or the holding of multiparty elections every few years. A standard of any democracy is respect for the rights of all its citizens. In a liberal democracy, citizens should enjoy equality before the law and their rights should be protected through constitutional safeguards. This is why we speak of democracy and human rights in the same breath. As Sørensen put it, the concept of democracy means participation as well as civil and human rights and liberties.[2]

As utilised in this study, the term democracy does not emphasise the system by which citizens determine who and how they are to be governed. Rather, it refers to conditions existing at the family, state and interstate levels which either promote or frustrate participation in decision-making, an equitable sharing of responsibility and resources, and a recognition of individual autonomy.[3] These three elements are essential to the realisation of the UN goal of "building the smallest democracy at the heart of society".

The aim of this chapter is to analyse domestic violence within the framework of human rights and democracy. In doing so the chapter focuses on violence as a violation of (women's) democratic and human rights and as one of the often overlooked barriers to the realisation of truly democratic societies. The basic position is that the democratisation process has not been able to make an impact on the family as one of the core institutions of society. There is a growing international recognition that domestic violence is widespread in many societies around the world. The home, and the family for that matter, has become one of the most violent institutions in society.[4] Most violence against women occurs in the family, or in the community. Although anyone can be a victim of domestic violence, women and children are the most frequent victims. They suffer violence not only at the hands of strangers but at the hands of family members and acquaintances.[5]

Focusing on family or domestic violence does not suggest that it is the only indicator of a lack of democracy and respect for human rights at the micro-level societal institution of the family. Rather, domestic or family violence is treated as the ultimate pointer to the absence of the same. Indeed, the chapter acknowledges the existence of other indicators of a lack of democracy and respect for human rights at the family level including exclusion from decision-making and a lack of access to and control of important resources. But women's ability to achieve social, economic, legal and personal equality by participating in private and public life is severely inhibited by the procedure of widespread violence against women in society. Women who are denied their basic rights to security of person cannot fully participate in society. There is a need to promote and acknowledge women's self and collective empowerment and their contribution to politics, economics, social and community based activities. One of the ways of realising this is by eradicating domestic violence.

There are two major reasons why it is important to focus on the family as an entity in a discussion about democracy and human rights. First, a number of UN conventions that aim to improve the status of certain members of the family especially women (and children) have been ratified by African states. While these provide a commendable basis for the protection of certain family members, there exists an apparent potential for conflict between them. It is perhaps in light of this fact that the UN, in 1994, adopted a motto during the International Year of the Family (IYF) that stressed the need to build "the smallest democracy at the heart of society"; that is, the family.[6] It is this smallest democracy that is considered by this study to constitute the springboard for the democratisation of the rest of societal institutions. Indeed, it is the conviction of this chapter that unless the democratisation of the total society proceeds hand in hand with the democratisation of the family, true democracy and respect for human rights will never be realised. This is particularly true in light of the fact that democracy requires strong and democratic institutions and the family is one of the key institutions of society.

Second, the family today is confronted with unprecedented challenges that undermine its functions and it thus needs to be protected and supported. While family violence is the ultimate of these, there are other major challenges facing the family. These include the erosion of the extended family which acted as a source of economic or material, social and emotional support and the rising number of single parent families which is a consequence of either divorce or separation, or a decision especially by women to opt to start a family on their own.[7] In addition, the family is being undermined by rising divorce, separation and remarriage rates that produce blended families, the emergence of dual career families (which causes stress and strain between spouses), poverty, unemployment, disease – particularly HIV/AIDS – and armed conflict and civil wars. One of the surest ways, and indeed the beginning point, for salvaging the family is to make it more democratic.

The status of women's democratic and human rights

The Universal Declaration of Human Rights identifies three categories of human rights. The first is civil and political rights, which include freedom of speech, freedom of movement, and freedom of religion. These exist in most constitutions, are protected by the judiciary and are recognised as an indicator of a functioning democracy.[8] The second category comprises social, economic and cultural rights. These include the right to education, work, food, clothing, housing, and medical care.[9] The third category of rights includes the rights to development and solidarity. In this chapter, the three categories of human rights are not treated differentially. All are considered to be equally important. It is also argued that all human beings are entitled to human rights on equal terms. With respect to women's rights as political and civil rights, there is a need to create awareness about women who suffer general human rights violations as well as calling attention to the particular abuses that women encounter because they are female.

The gendering of human rights can be traced to various conventions and declarations passed by the United Nations and ratified by a large number of member states. While these aim to promote more equal rights, they lack the teeth of enforcement mechanisms. Four of such conventions are worth citing. First is the 1981 Convention on the Elimination of All forms of Discrimination Against Women (CEDAW) which had been ratified by 160 government by 1997. Second is the Vienna Declaration and Programme of Action passed in 1993. It is credited with being the most important step towards women achieving equal human rights. The Declaration went beyond the usually high sounding declarations of international agencies in that it insisted that the state bears responsibility for ending gender-based abuses. It was followed the same year by the adoption by the UN General Assembly of the Declaration on the Elimination of Violence Against Women. This constituted the first official United Nations step toward the prohibition of violence against females as a fundamental human right. This declaration is the first such international instrument to extend the domain of human rights from the public sector to the private sphere of the family. The conventions outlined above reflect government commitments to ensuring that the human rights of women are protected.

In principle they recognise the human rights of women to be "an inalienable, integral and indivisible part of universal human rights."[10]

In addition, there is the 1995 Platform for Action of the Fourth World Conference on Women. It is the Beijing Women's Conference that appears to have been the climax in the campaign for improved women's rights. It reaffirmed the principles set out in the Vienna Declaration that the human rights of women (and the girl child) are part and parcel of universal human rights. As an agenda for action, the Platform seeks to promote the full enjoyment of all human rights and the fundamental freedoms of all women throughout their lives. Article 13 of the Beijing Declaration states that "women's empowerment and their full participation on the basis of equality in all spheres of the society, including participation in the decision-making process and access to power, is fundamental for the achievement of equality, development and peace."[11] The Declaration guarantees women equal treatment and freedom from discrimination.

The international women's rights movement has succeeded in creating a climate in which it is becoming increasingly difficult for the state not to comply with international human rights norms. Pressure is now being exerted on the state from different directions to tackle violence against women head-on. This would not have been possible without international bodies like the United Nations taking the lead in this regard. Getting the UN to recognise and acknowledge gender-based violence as a human rights violation is a significant victory for women.

At a regional level, SADC has undertaken activities to promote the human rights of women and eliminate all forms of discrimination. Most of the SADC member countries – including Botswana, Malawi, Mauritius, Mozambique, Namibia, South Africa and Swaziland – have identified the elimination of violence against women as one of their national priority areas of concern. Based on the Gender and Development Declaration, SADC has moved to repeal and reform all laws, amend constitutions and change social practices which still subject women to discrimination.[12] The organisation also aims to enact gender sensitive laws. One may also note that five countries in the SADC region, namely Angola, Botswana, Mozambique, Namibia and Tanzania, have identified the promotion of human rights as a critical area of concern at national level and are in the process of amending their statutes to ensure equality and non-discrimination under the law. Furthermore, with the exception of Swaziland, all SADC countries have signed, ratified or acceded to the Convention on the Elimination of All Forms of Discrimination Against Women (CEDAW) as an effort to promote and protect the human rights of women. Most of these countries have set up legal reform committees. For instance, Lesotho has set up the National Law Reform Commission to work on the laws and narrow the existing gender gaps in all legal issues in the country.

Violence as a Violation of Women's Democratic and Human Rights

The family has been defined as "a set of people related by blood, marriage (or some other agreed-upon relationship) or adoption who share the primary responsibility of reproduction, caring for members of society".[13] Although universal, its organisation may vary from one culture to another. For instance, in a study conducted on family forms it was revealed that while conventional, male-headed family forms based on marriage remain common, other family forms such as female-headed families and co-habitants are on the rise.[14]

As a social institution, the family performs several functions for society that include reproduction, protection and socialisation; regulation of sexual behaviour, and companionship; provision of social status, emotional, social and economic support; and social security for all its members.[15] The traditional family also served a legal function. It formulated and enforced laws, settled disputes within the family and represented the family's interests within the community.[16] The tremendous transformations in the modern family due to economic and social restructuring taking place globally, however, act to undermine its capacity to perform these functions effectively.

Violence against women in its various forms is endemic in all communities and countries around the world. It is a phenomenon that cuts across class, age, race, religious and national boundaries. Family (or domestic) violence undermines the protection (social support), affection and companionship functions of the family. By domestic violence reference is made to "any act that results, or is likely to result, in physical, sexual or psychological harm or suffering to the victim, including threat of such acts, coercion or arbitrary deprivation of liberty, whether occurring in public or in private life".[17] Violence against women is understood to encompass physical, sexual and psychological violence occurring in the family, including battering, sexual abuse of female children in the household, dowry-related violence, marital rape, traditional practices harmful to women, non-spousal violence and violence related to exploitation. There is a tendency to deny the problem of violence against women. There are many myths surrounding the existence of domestic violence. Some of these include that women 'ask for it', that women invite sexual harassment by their behaviour or dress, that rape is a crime of passion, and that battery only happens in low-income families. These myths contribute to the secondary victimisation of women.

Violence against women has many causes including unequal power rela-tions between men and women, cultural patterns and lack of access to legal protection for women. At the broad level, the universality of violence in the family can be understood in terms of the entrenchment of socio-political and legal orientations that are still heavily grounded in patriarchy. Families teach boys and girls to accept a system of values based on male superiority. These values are in turn backed by laws that enforce men's privileges and women's subservience in families. While in principle most nations are founded on the notions of democracy and equal rights for all citizens, in practice men predominantly occupy most institutions of socie-ty and bring into their structures the perspective of male dominance and female subservience. Violence against women, especially in the domestic form, is the means by which men maintain control over their wives, part-ners or children. Most disturbing is the fact that in many communities, vio-lence is viewed – at least by men – as an acceptable way of exerting con-trol over women. Most men who abuse their partners feel that the women are their possessions and property to treat as they please. Women are also seen as inferior minors who must be disciplined. Ultimately violence against women is about power and control. Religion has also been instru-mental in determining relations between the sexes. Another factor respon-sible for escalating family violence is the reluctance of social agents like the police, lawyers, social workers and medical doctors to intervene in what is often termed a 'domestic matter'. This is a reflection of the tolerance of family violence by society.[18]

Another factor that plays an important part in violence against woman is their unequal status in society. Widespread violence against women must be seen in the context of legal change and its effect on the relative position and decision-making powers of men and women within society. While women's legal status has changed substantially, their social status remains relatively unchanged. As male dominance is threatened by the elevation in the legal status of women, men become insecure and may result to violence in an attempt to assert their position. All these threats to male social status are made worse by poverty and unemployment (that undermine men's tra-ditional roles as family providers) and high rates of alcoholism. There is evi-dence to suggest an inverse relationship between women's economic power and the extent to which they are victims of violence.[19] As women consoli-date their control of significant economic resources, men are less likely to abuse them.

The few studies that have been conducted in sub-Saharan Africa indicate that women experience alarming levels of violence primarily by their part-ners, but also by other family members.[20] For many years, violence against women received little or no attention in sub-Saharan Africa. It is only now, through the actions of women's organisations at national, regional and international levels, that the subject is emerging as a human rights issue of major importance. With specific reference to Southern Africa, general statistics indicate that violence is a great problem in southern Africa with figures showing that women, regardless of their race, class and geographical areas, continue to suffer violence at the hands of spouses and partners.[21]

In Botswana domestic violence or battering of women is the most common form of violence against women and it transcends education, class, income and ethnic boundaries. Although the extent of violence against women in Botswana is not adequately documented, violence against women by men with whom they have sexual relations, particularly husbands, is quite prevalent. It "involves the abuse of a woman not by strangers but brutally suffered at the hands of relatives, husbands and lovers".[22] Existing evidence shows that about 50% of all women murdered are killed by current or former partners.[23]

The lack of statistical information on domestic violence in Botswana can be explained in terms of the problems of crime recording in general. Most women do not report cases of family violence to the courts. Rather, they prefer to take them for arbitration and reconciliation by family members and, where this fails, to the customary courts. Where cases do reach the courts, many are withdrawn on the insistence of the women because they are related to or economically dependent on the abuser.[24] Cases are also withdrawn because of pressure from the perpetrator, his relatives or the family of the victim who may not want their family name tarnished. To circumvent the dilemma of economic dependence, which undermines the democratisation of the family, women's economic independence should be increased.

The police regard the family as a private affair. This view is grounded on the understanding that a man's home is his castle and that marriage is sacred and the family sacrosanct. As such, domestic violence is seen as a domestic affair between a man and his wife or partner rather than as a special category within the police crime recording systems.[25] The traditional notion of the family and of boundaries between it and the outside world still cause the police to be reluctant to intervene in cases of domestic violence. They tend to regard it as a waste of time to pay attention to the cries of abused women, who often fail to press charges. At times the attitudes of the officers handling the case discourage women from pursuing the case. And this interferes with the right of women to access justice.[26]

This experience is not only unique to Botswana. As elsewhere, violence against women is also a substantial problem in Zimbabwe.[27] Women are at risk of violence within their homes. Much of what occurs is not discussed outside the family, or reported to the police, social welfare or other organisations. Consequently, existing figures on the extent to which women are vulnerable to different forms of abuse remain incomplete and inaccurate. In a household survey conducted in 1996 in an attempt to obtain accurate figures, it was found that over one in three women had experienced some form of psychological abuse. In addition, more than one in three women had experienced economically disempowering forms of violence (e.g. being prevented from getting a job or going to work), while almost one in three women reported experiencing physical abuse since the age of sixteen. Only one out of every seven women interviewed did not report having experienced any form of violence.[28] The perpetrator of most of the above forms of abuse was found to be the woman's current or former partner; only in less than 2% of the cases was the perpetrator a stranger.

Similar trends obtain for South Africa where the dominant forms of violence include rape, child abuse, femicide and political violence. With reference to rape, reported cases are thought to have increased by 46% during the five year period from 1990 to 1994.[29] From 1993 to 1994 the rate of rape increased by more than 16%. This figure is rather conservative, given that police estimates indicate that only one out of every 35 cases of rape is reported. The increase in reported cases could be attributed to awareness campaigns by women's rights and health promotion organisation whose efforts have attempted to encourage women to report the offence and depart from self-blame so often associated with underreporting. However, the justice system has not initiated related developments in terms of the support structure for rape victims.

In Namibia, too, women find themselves in the midst of violence. They are the targets of personal violence, domestic violence, rape and femicide. However, there are no comprehensive statistics on the incidence of violence within the family because it is seldom reported to the authorities. The extent of domestic violence is also hard to measure because people treat it as a private matter and therefore not to be discussed with outsiders. Nevertheless one study shows that at least 50% of Namibia's women (and children) have been or will be victims of domestic violence.[30] With particular reference to rape, the number of reported cases have increased steadily over the last few years. For instance, during 1991 564 rape cases were reported and in 1994 there were 740 cases.[31] The existing violence in Namibia has been explained in terms of women's unequal social status in society, among other factors. It has been argued that women's legal status in Namibia has changed since independence but that their social status remains relatively unchanged. This divergence between legal status and social status is said to be responsible for the violence against women.

Family violence is seen by many international agencies including United Nations organs as a human rights issue. It constitutes a denial of women's rights to life and liberty on a large scale throughout the world. The most pervasive violation of females is violence against women in all its forms, from wife battery, incest and rape to female genital mutilation.[32] All too often these issues are ignored as trivial or seen as endemic to a culture and hence not subject to intervention. However, violence is not just personal or cultural. It is profoundly political since it results from the structural relationships of power, domination and privilege between men and women in society. Despite the recognition that family violence is a violation of the individual's human and democratic rights, little has been done by way of addressing it. Even where laws have been put in place to protect the victims of family violence, there is usually a reluctance to enforce them. Indeed, there is a clear gap between the articulation and implementation of human rights as it applies to women. From a democratic point of view, this gap can be understood in terms of the subordinate position occupied by women in most societal institutions.

Notice should be taken of other indications that women are denied their democratic rights within the institutions of society. These include lack of equal participation in decision-making at different levels of society including the family. Women are also denied access to and control of important resources. Virtually all SADC countries guarantee women the rights to hold key leadership and policymaking positions. Yet women are under-represented at all political levels. In Namibia, for example, only 16.7% of National Assembly members are women.[33] This is an improvement from 1989 where females comprised only 7.7% of the National Assembly. Only South Africa fares relatively better in this regard, having attained about a third female representation in the National Assembly.[34] However, at village and council level female representation remains low. This denies them active participation in development initiatives, resources and decisions that affect them. Although the political changes that have taken place in the country allow women to attend public (*kgotla*) meetings, entrenched patriarchy still prevents them from confidently voicing their opinions.

Concerning societal resources, women tend to have limited access to and control of important resources such as land, cattle, income, credit, education and employment.[35] Yet these are resources that bequeath economic, social and political power on the individual. To illustrate, in Lesotho to obtain credit a married woman must seek her husband's permission to enter into a contract. Consequently, women have had to adopt alternative means of obtaining credit such as group saving schemes and revolving funds.[36]

Discussion

The family is one of the most idealised of all society's institutions. It is generally supposed to be a safe haven, a refuge from the problems of the external world. International standards of human rights recognise the family as the natural and fundamental group or unit of society. Conception of the family as a unit connotes that the family is to be protected as a collective entity by the state and society. Although the existence of family violence suggests that state and society have avoided this responsibility, women are entitled to the equal enjoyment and protection of all human rights and fundamental freedoms in the political, economic, social, cultural, civil or any other field. These rights include the right to life, equality, liberty and security of the person, equal protection under the law and freedom from all forms of discrimination.

In most countries the responsibility for championing human rights has remained the exclusive preoccupation of select non-governmental organisations and women's groups. These have initiated extensive campaigns and advocacy all over the world which have brought the traditionally private issue of domestic violence to the forefront of public opinion. But in some countries governments have a tendency to dismiss such NGOs and women's groups as self-seekers and meddlers in the internal affairs of sovereign nation states who are driven by ulterior motives. While some governments have passed strong legislation to regulate the violation of rights within the home, it is becoming increasingly apparent that various anti-discrimination laws including even United Nations covenants are either premised on a male standard of equality or subsume identities of women as subjects of human rights.

In Botswana, for instance, it was not until recently that any consolidated effort was made to address the situation and rights of women and girl children. This of course is not due to the absence of violence against women in our society. The media report frequent incidents of forms of violence against women and girl children. Information on issues of violence, though scanty, is also available from previous studies. The low priority given to issues of violence against women and children in the country could be a reflection of the Botswana patriarchal attitudes and systems which generally view the rights of female persons as inferior relative to those of their male counterparts. The very notions of male superiority and female subservience, which are the foundation upon which the Botswana society is built, create a conducive environment for violence against females by males. The under-representation of women in democratic and other important institutions of decision-making (such as parliament and the judiciary) is also partially to blame. Not to forget that males by far dominate the decision-making processes at family level.

In South Africa, on the other hand, the response of the legal system to family violence has increased dramatically over the past few years and relevant legislation and the response of the courts and police appear to be adequate.[37] However, the continued escalation of family violence in the country suggests that many of these changes and their impact on everyday life are not known to the majority. It may also suggest that the system is still inadequate. What may be lacking is a strong legal system, long-term preventative programmes, support services for victims and perpetrators and a drastic public education campaign aimed at changing the attitudes and values that lead to violence. Greater commitment to law enforcement and equal access to legal services may also be required.

Some governments still treat family violence as a matter in the private sphere thus perpetuating the denial of the reality of the existence of the problem. There are contradictions as to what the nature of the relationship between the family and other institutions including the state should be. Generally speaking, whatever issues are classified private as opposed to public, the state would not intervene in such matters. The only arena in which the state may intervene is that of the public world. Consequently, many governments continue to view the family as the basic institution of organised social living and there should be clear boundaries marking off the private world of the family and the public world of the state and wider society. As such, the state has no right to intervene in whatever is taking place within the family including domestic violence. There are implications of the family being termed as private and these can be seen in two ways. First, family members have the right to say or do what they like within the confines of their own home without undue interference from outsiders. Secondly, this implies that families should be able to resolve their own problems without seeking any outside interference. This is regardless of how serious or even life threatening the experiences may be. This raises serious concern as to how the family can be in a position to resolve such problems.

There are two sides to state intervention in the private sphere. On the one hand it can be seen as being negative because it is intrusive, repressive and controlling. On the other hand, it can be viewed as positive in that it is enabling, empowering and protective. Those who view state intervention as repressive focus on how it might limit opportunity and potential while those who see it more positively focus on the potential to enable individuals or groups to reach their potential. There are those who stand somewhere in between. However, with specific reference to state intervention in the family, it has been acknowledged that one of the macro-systems most influential for family life is the state. Most economic and social policies formulated and enforced by the state have wide ranging effects on family life, for instance policies dealing with taxation, adoption and marriage.[38]

The notion that it is inappropriate for the state to intervene in the private world of the family presents serious problems for the individual woman being abused within the family. The concept of privacy encourages, reinforces, and supports violence against women. Emphasising privacy sends the wrong message that violence against women is permitted, acceptable, and part of the basic fabric of family life. What goes on in a violent relationship should not be the subject of state or community intervention. This is an individual, and not a societal problem, therefore not warranting any state intervention. It is argued here that the protection and promotion of human rights in all spheres of society including the family is a fundamental building block in the realisation of democracy. As such, it should be the full responsibility of any government that purports to support democracy.

It is only logical that the state intervenes in matters of domestic violence in order to regulate, reconstitute and if necessary punish both "malfunctioning" family relationships and "malfunctioning" families.[39] Indeed, cases of women seeking police protection for themselves and or arrest of the abuser represent an attempt to obtain state intervention in the private world of the family. State intervention in the domestic sphere should not be kept to the minimum in the name of preserving family autonomy. The family as a central institution in society should not be outside the legal regulation of the state. States should condemn violence against women and should not invoke any custom, tradition or religious consideration to avoid their obligations with respect to its elimination. They should pursue a policy of eliminating violence against women at all levels of society. This is consistent with the 1995 Platform for Action of the Fourth World Conference on Women.

The state should also assume the responsibility to educate women about their rights and the avenues available to them for redress. After all state intervention in the family is not alien. The state is involved in the constitution of the family by sanctioning and dissolving marital unions. To illustrate, marriages solemnised by state-recognised state or religious marriage officers receive the fullest recognition. They are registered and a marriage certificate granted. The legal consequences of such marriages are in general laid down by statutes or by common law as interpreted by judges. The state also participates in deciding on issues of inheritance and child maintenance. While a variety of family forms exist in reality, both the state and employers regard the nuclear family with a male head, a dependent wife and children, as the norm. Any state that is truly committed to democracy must start by building what the UN referred to as the "smallest democracies at the heart of society". These should be the initial foundations of the inculcation of a democratic culture in the populace.

By arguing for state intervention in the family, this chapter is not suggesting the state take over the family and its functions. Rather, what is being suggested is that the state can provide mechanisms for the support and review of the family where and when necessary. To illustrate, where a woman's rights are being violated as in the case of domestic violence, the state, being the custodian of all human rights, must intervene to protect the rights of the victim. That is, the state must accept greater responsibility for family members that are also its citizens. It is acknowledged that there are situations where state intervention may not work or may result in more harm than good. Nevertheless, this should not constitute a justification for the state to abdicate its responsibility of protecting all of its citizens.

Research findings indicate that, despite being patriarchal in nature, the family is the most accessible structure for conflict resolution.[40] Even when a woman feels that the family will not deliver justice, and decides to take the matter to other institutions, she would be frowned upon if she does not allow the family to deal with the matter first or just inform the family. However, the question that lingers on is whether the family has the capacity to police itself given its patriarchal tendencies. Also one may ask, is democracy possible in an institution founded on patriarchy like the family? As Albie Sachs puts it, strengthening the family and at the same time weakening patriarchy could be a daunting but not impossible task.[41] Charman agrees with the view that attempting to weaken patriarchy in the family is not easy. But he feels that since the family is one of society's most complex products, reform should start within the broader society within which the family is constructed rather than from within the family itself.[42]

While both Sachs and Charman have valid points, the position adopted here is one that harmonises their arguments. That is, changes in society should occur simultaneously with changes in the family. That way it would be possible to circumvent the type of dilemma witnessed in countries such as South Africa where legal reforms have not been accompanied by social changes that make the family more democratic. Social change should be accompanied by women's empowerment to enable women to acquire economic independence through government and other schemes. The general educational programmes that are supposed to sensitise the populace about participation in the democratic process and the human rights that are guaranteed them through the constitution should also be taken advantage of to spearhead change within the family. As indicated earlier, democracy is much more than simple voting rights, which all adult women the SADC region have, or the holding of multiparty elections every few years. It should also be about understanding and claiming our rights as members of macro and micro institutions in society and participating equally in decision-making at all levels including the family and the state. For women are the majority of voters and this has never guaranteed them equal rights and representation in the democratic process.

Conclusion

Women are increasingly using the legal system to exercise their rights but in many countries lack of awareness of the existence of these rights is an obstacle that prevents them from fully enjoying their human rights and attaining equality. As envisaged by the Beijing Platform for Action, the provision of human rights education is essential for promoting an understanding of the human rights of women, including knowledge of recourse mechanisms to redress violation of their rights. It is necessary for all individuals, especially women in vulnerable circumstances, to have full knowledge of their rights and access to legal recourse against violations of their rights. This is where the democratisation process fits in. In particular the process of voter education, which is usually conducted mainly by NGOs and in some cases electoral commissions, should not just emphasise voting wisely but also the democratic and human rights of the individual. It is recommended that the politicisation of the citizenry should be a continuous process that is not confined to election years. The knowledge imparted should integrate the specific human and democratic rights guaranteed through the constitution and enlighten the populace concerning other rights that they are entitled to but are not protected by law. Also it should teach them how they can demand those rights and the type of democratic institutions they should penetrate in society. This is possible given that experience in many countries has shown that women can be empowered and motivated to assert their rights, regardless of their level of education or socio-economic status.

The family should be a source of comfort for the mutual growth of its members.[43] While its importance as a social structure should not be underrated, excessive faith in its nurturing capacities may lead to efforts to sustain the family unit even where members are being victimised by other family members. Yet, the maintenance of the family as a unit should not take precedence over the interest of the individual as has tended to be the case in the past. To reiterate, the right to be free from domestic violence or the threat of domestic violence is a fundamental and universal human right. To protect such democratic and human rights at the family level calls for a multidisciplinary approach involving all parties concerned – social workers, police, justice system, the state and the community including the family itself. This is essential because the right to a private family life does not include the right to abuse family members. In addition, international and regional human rights instruments universally guarantee the right to a private life and to a home. Not to forget that at state level in the SADC region, governments have made commitments to promote the human rights of women and eliminate all forms of discrimination by signing declarations. Some have even gone a step further and have placed the elimination of violence against women as one of their priority areas of concern. But strategies are yet to be devised so that these declarations can filter through to the 'smallest democracy' in society – the family.

Notes and References

1   R Pinkney, *Democracy in the Third World*, Boulder: Lynne Rienner, 1997.

2   G Sørensen, *Democracy, Dictatorship and Development: Economic Development in Selected Regimes of the Third World*, London: Macmillan, 1991.

3   B Rwezaura *et al*, *Parting the Long Grass: Revealing and Conceptualizing the African Family*, Gaborone: WLSA Working Paper no 12, 1995.

4   MA Strauss, RJ Gelles and SK Steinmetz, *Behind Closed Doors*, New York: Bantam, 1980.

5   *We Won't be Beaten: A Guide to the Prevention of Family Violence Act*, Pretoria: National Institute for Public Interest Law and Research, 1996.

6   Rwezaura *et al* 1995.

7   A Adepoju and W Mbugua, 'The African family: An Overview of Changing Forms', in A Adepoju (ed), *Family, Population and Development in Africa*, London: Zed Books, 1997.

8   A Mogwe, 'Will basic human rights and individual freedoms continue to be protected, promoted and respected?', in S Brothers, J Hermans and D Nteta (eds), *Botswana in the 21st Century: Proceedings of a Symposium Organised by the Botswana Society*, Gaborone, 18–21 October 1993.

9   ZF Arat, *Democracy and Human Rights in Developing Countries*, Boulder: Lynne Rienner, 1991.

10   Commission on Human Rights, *The Vienna Declaration and Programme of Action*, Vienna: United Nations, 1993.

11   *Beijing Declaration and Platform of Action*, New York: United Nations, 1995a.

12   *SADC Gender Monitor: Monitoring Implementation of the Beijing Commitments by the SADC Member States*, Gaborone: SADC Gender Unit, 1999.

13   RT Schaefer and RP Lamm, *Sociology*, New York: McGraw-Hill, 1995, p 361.

14   *Botswana Families and Women's Rights in a Changing Environment*, Gaborone: Women and Law in Southern Africa (WLSA), 1997.

15   Adepoju and Mbugua 1997; Schaefer and Lamm 1995.

16   A Armstrong, 'Law and the family in Southern Africa', in A Adepoju (ed), *Family, Population and Development in Africa*, London: Zed Books, 1997.

17 *Women: Looking Beyond 2000*, New York: United Nations, 1995b.

18 N Hutchings, 'Sexism promotes violence against women' in KL Swisher, C Wekesser and W Barbour (eds), *Violence Against Women*, San Diego: Greenhaven Press, 1994.

19 RL Blumberg, 'Gender equality is human right, empowerment, women and human rights: Past, present and future gender equality and human rights', *INSTRAW News*, no 28, 1998.

20 C Watts *et al*, 'Women, Violence and HIV/AIDS in Zimbabwe', *SAfAIDS News*, vol 5, no 2, 1997.

21 SADC 1999.

22 M Tabengwa and IM Fergus, *Violence Against Women*, Paper Presented at the First National Crime Prevention Conference, Gaborone, 2–4 February 1998, p 1.

23 Metlhaestile Women's Information Centre, *Domestic Violence: It's a Crime*, Gaborone: Lentswe La Lesedi, 1999.

24 *A Report Submitted by the Police Task Force in Response to Cases of Domestic Violence*, Gaborone: Botswana Police, 1997.

25 *Ibid.*, p 46.

26 Southern African Research and Development Center (SADRC), *Beyond Inequalities: Women in Botswana*, Gaborone: Ditshwanelo, Botswana Human Rights Center, 1997c.

27 LL Lueker, 'Fighting for Human Rights: Women, War and Social Change in Zimbabwe', *INSTRAW News*, no 28, 1998.

28 Watts *et al*, 1997.

29 Southern African Research and Development Center (SADRC), *Beyond Inequalities: Women in South Africa*, Bellville: University of Western Cape, 1997a.

30 See Southern African Research and Development Center (SADRC), *Beyond Inequalities: Women in Namibia*, Windhoek: University of Namibia, 1997b.

31 *Ibid.*

32 Blumberg 1998.

33 SARDC 1997b.

34 SARDC 1997a.

35 WLSA 1997.

36 Southern African Research and Development Center (SADRC), *Beyond Inequalities: Women in Lesotho*, Maseru: WLSA, 1997d.

37 M Swarts, 'The Family: Cradle of Violence in South Africa', *In Focus Forum*, vol 4, no 5, 1997.

38 RE Dobash and RP Dobash, *Women, Violence and Social Change*, London: Routledge, 1992.

39 S Foreman and R Dallos, 'Domestic Violence', in R Dallos and

E MacLaughlin (eds), *Social Problems and the Family*, Milton Keynes: Open University, 1994, p 8.

40   *Chasing the Mirage: Women and the Administration of Justice*, Gaborone: Women and Law in Southern Africa, 1999.

41   A Sachs, 'The Family in a Democratic South Africa: Its Constitutional Position', *Agenda*, no 8, 1990.

42   A Charman, 'A Response to Albie Sachs: What is the family?', *Agenda*, no 8, 1990.

43   *Strategies for Confronting Domestic Violence: A Resource Manual*, New York: United Nations, 1993.

Liberalisation in a Fragile Financial Sector: Evidence from Lesotho

Rets'elisitsoe A Matlanyane

In the past few years, trade negotiations and arrangements have placed emphasis on trade in commodities. Lately, services are increasingly becoming an essential input into the production and trade in commodities. The development of trade in services is expected to have far-reaching impacts on economic growth. The General Agreement on Trade in Services (GATS) under the auspices of the World Trade Organisation aims to extend the rules governing trade in goods to trade in services by establishing a framework for liberalising trade in services.[1] Liberalisation in this regard requires countries to modify domestic regulations relating to trade in services and gradually relax restrictions on trade in service products.

The focus of this chapter is on financial services in particular. McKinnon and Shaw describe financial liberalisation as the process of breaking away from a state of financial repression.[2] Within the context of developing economies in particular, the state of financial repression is associated with government interventions in the financial system that are aimed at promoting developmental agenda within the framework of scarce resources. In many cases this is effected through high liquidity and reserve requirements, limitations on innovations of financial instruments, legal ceilings on bank lending and deposit rates, public ownership of major banks, entry barriers into the banking sector and restrictions on capital transactions with foreigners.[3] These however introduce distortions that lead to the inefficient allocation of resources in the financial sector and are usually reflected in low and sometimes negative real rates of interest. Because of this, financial liberalisation has been commonly associated with the liberalisation of interest rates. However, with the recent developments in the global economy, financial liberalisation has come to involve a wider spectrum of modifications. Besides elimination of high liquidity and reserve requirements as well as directed credit schemes, it entails the easing of portfolio restrictions on banks, changes in the ownership of banks, enhanced competition in the banking sector, integration of domestic banking institutions to international markets and changes in the monetary policy environment.

Currently, the financial sector of Lesotho is in a vulnerable state following a series of bank failures since the 1980s. This situation is the legacy of mismanagement, government intervention, the fragility of the legal system and hence lack of law enforcement, imprudence in the domestic regulatory framework, and weaknesses of the supervisory procedures. In these circumstances, there is a need to adopt appropriate regulatory and supervisory practices. However, evidence shows that financial sector liberalisation efforts often fail if undertaken in an unstable macro-economic setting and a weak regulatory framework.[4] This suggests that cautious liberalisation strategies have to be adopted. This is even more important for countries that are members of multilateral and regional trade and monetary arrangements. In the light of this background, this chapter therefore seeks to assess the prospects and likely costs and benefits to Lesotho of becoming part of an international agreement that liberates the market for financial services. The chapter begins by providing background on the nature of and developments in the financial sector of Lesotho. The theories on which the policy of financial liberalisation is premised are extensively explored, to provide an understanding of the conditions under which liberalisation can be expected to be successful. The likelihood of successful liberalisation in Lesotho is assessed on the basis of the current status of the financial sector and the conditions as prescribed by theory, and the regional dimension of liberalisation of the financial market is considered.

Background

Two main features of the financial sector of Lesotho make it particularly vulnerable to external shocks. Firstly, it features a dual currency system in which the South African Rand circulates alongside the local currency as legal tender at the exchange rate of one to one. However, the quantity of the Rand in circulation within the economy is unknown. Secondly, there is huge cross-border trade in financial services between Lesotho and South Africa. Because the South African financial sector is relatively more developed, and as a result of its close proximity, a large number of Lesotho residents perform their banking and other financial activities in South Africa. This is encouraged by the unstable political climate within Lesotho and the absence of capital controls within the Common Monetary Area (CMA). In addition, strong competition for corporate lending also exists between Lesotho and South African satellite companies whose parent companies guarantee coverage against risk. Although this trade is quite significant, there is no formal record of its volume owing to the tediousness of quantifying services given the degree of integration of the financial markets of Lesotho and South Africa.

The Financial Sector Prior to Reforms

At the time of independence the financial sector consisted of two British-owned commercial banks whose developmental role in the economy was minimal.[5] Shortly after independence the post office savings bank was established to cater for small savers. In 1982, the POSB was incorporated into the newly established Lesotho bank which was entirely government-owned and served to address the government's developmental agenda. Lesotho bank grew to be the largest bank in the economy, operating along-side the two foreign banks and two specialised financial institutions, which were established to serve financial needs of specific sectors.

The main objective of government at the time was to increase and channel domestic credit into local investments with particular attention to the industrial and agricultural sectors. This objective was, however, not fully achieved. Official statistics indicate that the government became the largest holder of domestic credit in the 1980s. Households and the distributive business sector, which relies almost invariably on imports, held the next largest share.[6]

Relatively free entry into the market was practised partly because most applicants have been renowned British and South African banks. It was perceived that because of cross-border banking that already existed, the usual exposure to risk in the initial period of operation was minimal and that new entrants were not developing a new client base, although they might have to change their policies in line with those of the new market.

The high degree of concentration in the sector resulted in very little competition among financial institutions in the country. The degree and nature of government intervention in the sector has worsened this. The tax policy, for instance, exempts government-owned banks from tax while their foreign counterparts are subject to tax. Although this policy seems to be in favour of the local financial institutions, it discourages competition as it provides an uneven basis for competition while it also weakens the concerned banks' ability to compete actively in the market and limits credit to other sectors. In addition, a policy of administrative determination of interest rates, which resulted in large spreads between lending and deposit rates, has been practised. In setting the interest rates, the South African interest rates were used as a benchmark to limit financial price differentials.

Although the CMA allowed free capital mobility among members, capital controls were put in place. Financial institutions were required to hold at least 85% of local liabilities within the country and no more than 15% abroad. This requirement was intended to ensure that financial institutions invested most of their assets locally. However, given the high risk associated with private sector lending in Lesotho, financial institutions hardly ever complied with this requirement.

Supervision was conducted largely on the basis of off-site surveillance. Inspection was carried out through monthly reports compiled by the financial institutions. Occasional on-site inspections were carried out to ascertain the accuracy and completeness of data submitted for off-site inspections and to evaluate capital adequacy, overall risk exposure, quality of management and other internal procedures.[7] Often, inspections revealed that financial institutions hardly complied with the capital controls nor the liquidity and reserve requirements.

Evidence shows that despite capital inadequacy and the failure to meet other requirements for entry into the South African financial market, local banks cannot successfully compete with their South African counterparts or operate in South Africa because of a bad reputation for fraud for which timely corrective measures have not been taken. In general the sector was backed by a weak and fragile legal system, which resulted in deficiencies in law enforcement and mismanagement.

Theoretical Framework

Financial liberalisation has two broad dimensions. The first involves the easing of restrictions internally while the other entails lifting restrictions on international financial transactions. The latter variant basically involves liberalisation of the capital account and becomes particularly important given the rapid and explosive growth and movements of capital. These changes have significant economic implications that call for intensified economic management strategies. In addition to domestic and global liberalisation, the puzzle is made more complex by the existence of countries' membership of regional integration bodies, which they enter into because of the various economic benefits that they promise. In the short run integration is expected to stimulate intra-regional trade and investment. In the long run the expectation is that the combination of larger markets, improved competition, a more efficient allocation of resources and other positive externalities will raise the growth rates of member countries. In this sense regional integration is almost tantamount to liberalisation as it involves the reduction of trade barriers and investment restrictions. However liberalisation can be defined broadly to imply globalisation. This distinction has brought forth a policy dilemma of whether economies should opt for global or regional integration.[8]

At a theoretical level there are basically two diverging views regarding the analysis of financial liberalisation policy. One view attests to the allocative efficiency promoting properties of liberal financial markets, which subsequently improve global welfare. On the other hand, there is a counter view that recognises the existence of information asymmetries, distortions and other problems that face financial markets world-wide.

From the classical point of view, international capital mobility allows for improved savings mobilisation and hence increased domestic investment while it makes it easy for investors to diversify their portfolios. In another dimension it tends to enhance inter-temporal trade. Capital flows from capital abundant countries into capital scarce countries are said to improve the welfare in both countries. This proposition is based on the assumption that the marginal product of capital in capital scarce countries is higher than in capital abundant countries.[9] A vast amount of literature provides evidence that open economies grow at a faster rate than highly protected economies because of technology and investment effects that result from more liberal policies.[10]

Theoretically, capital mobility also opens up opportunities for portfolio diversification, risk-sharing and inter-temporal trade. Economic agents can smooth their consumption patterns by borrowing abroad when incomes are low and making repayments when incomes are high. This cross-border lending and borrowing dampens business cycles because it relieves economic agents of the need to reduce their consumption and investment expenditures and hence domestic demand when incomes are low. The holding of foreign claims also allows agents to diversify risks that are associated with disturbances in the home country, thereby enabling them to reap high risk-adjusted rates of returns. It is these higher returns that encourage higher savings and investments and hence faster rates of economic growth.

International trade theory dictates that countries that have a comparative advantage in the production of financial services should be net exporters of such services. Capital mobility in this case will ensure that the global economy benefits from the efficiency gains created by specialisation. Increased production and hence competition in the financial sector will also ensure that domestic producers of financial services to adopt efficient methods of production, become more innovative and improve productivity.

However, despite the attractive potential advantages of such policies, caution has to be taken in their implementation. For instance, factors such as structural rigidities within the environment in which they are imposed, the legal frameworks that surround the markets, the market structures as well as the sequencing of the liberalisation strategies can hinder the success of liberalisation. Some of these factors are discussed below.

Certain characteristics of a financial system can be interpreted to have stabilisation properties, which in turn can be translated into the soundness of the system. These include the ability of the financial system to offer a variety of financial markets and a variety of intermediaries. Financial markets in developed countries are characterised by a range of markets such as government securities markets, markets for corporate securities, equities, mortgages, insurance, futures and options and other assets, and the spot and forward foreign exchange market. These are coupled with a variety of intermediaries such as securities dealers, mortgage and leasing companies, insurance companies and other intermediaries. It is the competition that results from the existence of these markets that improves efficiency in the financial system while deepening and widening it at the same time. This lays a foundation that is not sensitive to external shocks.

Weak regulatory frameworks have also been identified as one of the factors that are not complementary to financial liberalisation. According to Eichengreen *et al*, it is not financial liberalisation that is at the core of the problem, but rather the deficiency of prudential regulation and supervision whose consequences are intensified by liberalisation.[11] Adequate regulation ensures that institutions monitor their portfolios and guards against suspect loans and capital requirements.

An important feature of financial systems in developing countries that aggravates their susceptibility to both internal and external shocks is that they are prone to the problems of moral hazards, adverse selection and herding behaviour, which may lead to the inefficient allocation of resources and a decline in welfare. Because of the difficulty of ascertaining the success of liberalisation policies in the face of failure to meet the preconditions, it is recommended that policies that minimise problems that plague the financial sector should be implemented. These include prudential supervision and regulations, improved accounting and auditing standards coupled with a carefully designed lender of last resort facility.

The welfare improving properties of financial liberalisation may also be frustrated by the presence of trade distortions. Brecher and Diaz-Alejandro provide an analysis particularly reflective of developing economies.[12] Assuming a small open, labour abundant economy that has enacted protective measures against its capital intensive industries, they illustrate that intuitively, protection of capital intensive industries increases the rate of return on capital relative to that of labour. Under the circumstances, capital intensive industries will grow at a faster rate than labour intensive industries. Naturally the misallocation of resources will force the value of domestic production to decline at world prices. This will certainly be reflected in the reduced global welfare. This analysis can be translated directly to the nature and operations of financial markets in developing countries in which governments have a habit of guaranteeing or subsidising foreign loans to local financial banking institutions. This has the effect of encouraging capital inflows through capital intensive financial institutions in a labour abundant economy, hence welfare reduction. The reduction or removal of trade barriers can, in this case, be used to offset the welfare reducing effects of the relatively free movement of capital.

The sequencing of liberalisation strategies is an equally important factor that determines the final outcome of financial sector reforms.[13] According to Montiel, stable institutional and macro-economic environments are prerequisites for the success of the liberalisation.[14] The simultaneous restoration of macro-economic stability and the restructuring and liquidation of insolvent financial institutions is suggested as the first phase as it may take time. In many cases domestic and international financial liberalisation increase the probability of the occurrence of crises if not supported by robust prudential supervision as well as sound macro-economic policies. This should be followed by the removal of internal reforms and finally external liberalisation. Though the sequence provided above sounds reasonable, it is important to note that economic conditions and priorities differ significantly from one country to another. This makes it difficult for one to prescribe a standard procedure for liberalisation.

The Financial Sector During and After Reforms

Restructuring of the financial sector in Lesotho has been underway since the implementation of structural adjustment programmes in 1988 against a background of the deteriorating performance of the sector.[15] The main problems in the financial sector were perceived as a lack of competition and institutional flexibility, inadequate banking supervision, a weak legal system, distorted interest rates, high information and transaction costs, a high degree of segmentation in the sector and the underdevelopment of the sector. At the inception of the programmes, the broad objective of government towards the financial sector was to enhance financial intermediation through broadening the range of money market instruments available for policy consideration.[16] The government's basic objective has been to ensure closer regional and international linkages and to strive to keep up with the recent changes in the global financial markets. In a narrower sphere, the aims were to improve the mobilisation of savings; to switch from direct monetary controls to indirect ones; to strengthen the institutional capacity of the sector; and to encourage short-term lending to small and medium sized indigenous enterprises. It was envisaged that these would be achieved by adopting policies that would encourage and enhance cross-border banking with minimum restrictions in order to stimulate competition and efficiency within the CMA; establishing a CMA payments system; encouraging universal banking; discouraging segmentation in the financial sector; reducing or eliminating capital controls; introducing venture capital companies; and providing more support to development finance companies.

Significant improvements have been realised in a number of areas, including the development of a securities market and increased allocation of credit to the private sector. From a position of the largest debtor to commercial banks in the early 1990s, government is currently a net creditor to commercial banks. The participation of the non-banking private sector in the securities market has increased tremendously owing to the issuance of smaller denominations of securities. This implies a development of a much-needed additional monetary policy instrument at the disposal of government and a move towards a market-oriented sector.

Although improvements have been realised, the performance of the banking sector has deteriorated tremendously in recent years. The contribution of financial and insurance services to domestic output had been increasing moderately to a peak in 1991. In 1991 finance and insurance was recorded as the largest sub-sector under the broader classification of the tertiary sector. From a growth rate of 4% in 1990, the growth of the financial and insurance services sector registered 20% in 1991. Its share to domestic output increased from 10% in 1990 to 11% in 1991. However, since 1991 their share in output has fluctuated but with a generally declining trend. In 1992 the share of the sector to total domestic output had fallen to 8.4%. This trend continued to a remarkable 5% in 1996, showing the declining importance of the sector in total domestic output. Considering the banking sector alone, since 1987 the importance of commercial banks in output has been declining. From 55% in 1987, assets of the banking institutions as a percentage of GDP declined by twenty percentage points to 35% in 1996. The foregoing analysis shows that since the late 1980s the banking sector has drifted away from the key position that it held in terms of its contribution to output in the economy.[17]

This trend was also reflected in an accelerated series of bank failures during the reform period. In the late 1970s, the Lesotho Building Finance Corporation suffered serious management problems that originated from bad lending practices.[18] The institution operated on subventions from government, a policy which government could hardly sustain. Although the corporation was capable of raising funds through deposits, that option proved to be expensive since lending rates were not at commercial rates. The government regulated lending rates while the corporation had to compete for deposits with other financial institutions. Failure to eliminate weaknesses in the control of records, which was inherited from the past, jeopardised the prospects of recovery. The continuation of this trend led to a merger of LBFC with Lesotho Bank in 1993.

In the beginning of the 1990s, performance also showed signs of distress that continued to the latter part of the decade. In 1990 the bank suffered a reduction in net income by 6% from the previous year, while the operating costs increased by 1.4%. This situation was reflected in the continuous decline of its market share from 61% in 1985 to 39% in 1995.

This problem has seemingly precipitated failures among other local financial institutions. At about the same time, the Agricultural Development Bank was experiencing more serious problems, which eventually led to its closure in September 1998. The poor performance of the bank was a result of high operating costs relative to net income and the poor repayment record of customers. The problem of the malfunctioning of the financial system was exacerbated by the relatively rapid expansion of the bank to a number of areas, some of which were not efficiently used because of the low population served by such agencies. By the end of 1996, the LADB had eight branches and six agencies compared to nine branches and fifteen agencies in 1995. Once again, mismanagement and poor regulation played a key role in the demise of the LADB.

Liberalisation in an unstable Financial System

As Montiel notes, in many Latin American countries liberalisation was unsuccessful because it was undertaken in unstable macro-economic environments and under weak regulatory frameworks.[19] Moreover, because financial instability can easily be transmitted into other countries, globalisation carries a huge amount of risk. Given that the policy is well designed and monitored it has the potential of enhancing market discipline and promoting the soundness of the market. Knight notes that currently the financial systems of developing countries are plagued by information uncertainties and inefficiencies, which present a major hindrance to successful liberalisation.[20] Demirguc-Kunt and Detragiache verified the fact that financial liberalisation increases the probability of banking crises in a large sample of countries.[21]

Given that the financial sector of Lesotho has been subject to costly financial distress for almost two decades, it is obviously not robust enough to withstand external shocks that come with liberalisation. In most developing countries and in the particular case of Lesotho the financial system comprises only a few commercial banks and insurance companies. The non-existence of the element of variety is a hindrance to competition and therefore provides a weak base that is susceptible to shocks. This implies that the system is bound to be overcome by the heavy flow of capital that accompanies the liberalisation and globalisation of the market. The non-existence or malfunctioning of a key market adversely affects the ability of the financial system to resist shocks.

In the case of Lesotho, the malfunctioning of the existing markets is mainly a result of fragile regulatory and legal frameworks. This represents a significant gap in the structure of the financial system. The banking sector is the main conduit of monetary policy because it is overburdened with the tasks of being the major supplier of credit to finance capital formation as well as the clearing and payments mechanism and the foreign exchange market while it also has to assess the risk and returns of private sector investment projects. The competitiveness of the market holds a stake in determining the efficiency with which these functions are performed. In perfectly competitive markets, an individual bank can have its share of deposits at a constant cost. However, intermediation becomes costly and less efficient in imperfect and highly concentrated markets because less stock of credit is supplied at higher costs to borrowers, while depositors are offered a lower rate of interest as compared to that of the competitive case. This is precisely the case that is reflected by the financial market of Lesotho.

The foregoing analysis has two important implications. Firstly, lower levels of credit are supplied in an imperfectly competitive banking sector rather than in a competitive banking sector. Secondly, imperfect competition results in less efficient intermediation. This suggests that a non-competitive banking system responds to problems of non-performing loans by reducing lending while increasing the intermediation spreads. According to Knight, this response tends to depress economic activity and increases the probability of banking crises.[22]

Imprudent regulatory and supervisory systems are among the factors that have contributed to the financial crisis that the economy of Lesotho is experiencing currently. The condition was made even worse by the weak legal system. Off-site surveillance, as has been used in Lesotho, can hardly be adequate as a cornerstone of monitoring a financial system, no matter how small the sector is. Through this system it is hardly possible to detect risky activities until it is too late. This has enabled banks that are distressed to gamble for redemption and to assume unhedged exposures. Unfit financial institutions are basically allowed to expand risky activities at rates that exceed their potential to manage them. The analysis therefore suggests that liberalisation can increase the risk of or intensify financial crises in settings where it is not backed by rigorous regulatory and supervisory procedures. In addition, the external dimension of liberalisation expands cross-border activities. This has in turn increased the degree of international market dependence that requires increased vigilance since the domestic market is now vulnerable to financial disturbance originating elsewhere.

Regional Effects

The high probability that financial crises can spill over to other economies necessitates a consideration of their regional effects, especially for countries that are members of regional trade agreements. A common example is the Asian financial crisis, which started in Thailand in 1997 and spread to other countries in the region, pushing them into deep and economically costly recessions. The financial fragility that resulted from weak regulation and supervision and improper sequencing of the liberalisation strategy is identified as the main element that facilitated the accommodation of the crisis into the neighbouring economies.[23]

Lesotho is a member of a number of regional trade and monetary arrangements including SADC, SACU and the CMA. The usual recommendation in this setting is stronger and closer co-operation between the members. To avoid conflicts between regional and global arrangements requires the maintenance of effective global and regional trade rules as well as an institution to enforce them. Tiemeyer identifies three approaches available for participants in the global financial system to reap the benefits of free mobility of capital.[24] These entail identifying sources of problems in both national and international financial systems. Co-operation in this exercise allows the authorities to create a pool of quality information that could be used to evaluate domestic and global financial conditions. This will assist in the formulation of appropriate national, regional and global regulatory and supervisory strategies. The development of and adherence to international rules and standards of practice should follow this. This will ensure that gaps in standards and codes of conduct are identified and filled timeously. Co-operation and co-ordination between national authorities and international regulatory bodies is the key to the success of this exercise. Nations should then make arrangements for consistent and co-ordinated implementation of standards by financial institutions. The effectiveness of the above strategies will require improved supervision. This therefore calls for closer co-operation between national supervisory authorities.

Conclusion

The popularity of the policy of liberalisation has brought rapid changes in the global financial markets. However, theory and evidence show that successful liberalisation requires stability of the financial system and the macro-economic environment at large. In some developing countries, the failure of the policy has been attributed to a volatile macro-economic climate, while in others a fragile financial system could not withstand the burden. In other countries, liberalisation was undertaken with a combination of these two problems. This is typical of the particular case of Lesotho where liberalisation was undertaken within a distressed financial system and a weak macro-economic environment. The analysis shows that this exercise led to further distress in the financial sector. A combination of a weak legal system, lack of prudential supervision and regulation have been identified as the major weaknesses in the system. This further makes it extremely difficult for government to contain the situation. The analysis highlights the importance of robust supervisory and regulatory systems in local and world markets to maintain a sound macroeconomic environment. Slow adaptation to the rapidly changing rules and new environments carries huge risks for the local and global economies.

Notes and References

1   *Business Guide to the Uruguay Round*, Geneva: International Trade Centre and Commonwealth Secretariat, 1995.

2   RI McKinnon, *Money and Capital in Economic Development*, Washington: Brookings Institute, 1973; ES Shaw, *Financial Deepening in Economic Development*, New York: Oxford University Press, 1973.

3   PJ Montiel, *Financial Policies and Economic Growth: Theory, Evidence and Country-Specific Experience from Sub-Saharan Africa*, AERC Special Paper 18, Nairobi: AERC, 1995; PR Agenor and PJ Montiel, *Development Macroeconomics*, New Jersey: Princeton University Press, 1996.

4   Montiel 1995.

5   *The Economy of Lesotho*, Washington DC: IBRD, 1974; Ministry of Economic Planning, *Economic Options for Lesotho*, Maseru: Government of Lesotho, 1997.

6   World Bank, 1990; L Petersson, 'Structural adjustment and economic management in a dependent economy: The case of Lesotho', in M Blomstrom and M Lundaht (eds), *Economic Crisis in Africa: Perspectives on Policy Responses*, London: Routledge, 1993.

7   *Central Bank of Lesotho Annual Reports*, Maseru: Central Bank of Lesotho, 1990.

8   A Vamvakidis, 'Regional trade agreements versus broad liberalisation: Which path leads to a faster growth?', *IMF Staff Papers*, vol 46, no 1, Washington DC: IMF, 1999.

9   M Eichengreen *et al*, *Capital Account Liberalisation: Theoretical and practical aspects*, Occasional Paper 172, Washington DC: IMF, 1998.

10   Vamvakidis 1999.

11   Eichengreen *et al* 1998.

12   R Brecher and C Diaz-Alejandro, 'Tariffs, Foreign Capital and Immiserising

Growth', *Journal of International Economics*, vol 7, 1977.

13 M Eichengreen *et al*, *Liberalizing Capital Movements, Some Analytical Issues*, Economic Issues 17, Washington DC: IMF, 1999.

14 Montiel 1995.

15 *Economic Memorandum on Lesotho*, Washington DC: World Bank, 1983.

16 Ministry of Economic Planning 1997.

17 *Central Bank of Lesotho Annual Reports*, Maseru: Central Bank of Lesotho, 1996.

18 World Bank 1990.

19 Montiel 1995.

20 M Knight, *Developing Countries and the Globalization of Financial Markets*, IMF Working Paper WP/98/105, Washington DC: IMF, 1998.

21 A Demirguc-Kunt and E Detragiache, 'The determinants of banking crises in developing and developed countries', *IMF Staff Papers*, vol 45, no 1, 1998.

22 Knight 1998.

23 T Lane, 'The Asian Financial Crisis: What have we learned?', *Finance and Development*, September 1999.

24 H Tietmeyer, 'Evolving Cooperation and Coordination in Financial Market Surveillance', *Finance and Development*, September 1999.

Socio-political Aspects of Foreign Investment in South Africa: Investigating the Impact of the State, Trade Unions and Business on Foreign Investment

Dominic Milazi

In his State of the Nation address after assuming the presidency in 1994, former President Mandela spelt out his reform plans for South Africa. Economically he pledged that his administration would continue to fight inflation, reduce the budget deficit, and try to avoid a "permanently higher level of general taxation". Politically, he put in place a power-sharing cabinet, a white finance minister (who later resigned) giving him free rein in reassuring the business community, and the former head of the South African Defence Force, Georg Meiring, to command the new South African National Defence Force (SANDF). These interrelated politico-economic moves were intended to dispel the hesitancy of foreign investors – especially because of the country's protracted background of endemic violence, most of it criminal, and a battered economy. These two greatest threats to democracy in South Africa together made a compelling case for the West to see democracy prevail in post-apartheid South Africa – to aid the new government as generously as it was aiding Boris Yeltsin's Russia and the Palestine-Israeli peace process.

In any discussion of foreign investment, some cognisance should be taken of the mood of the country. Not only do people have high expectations in so far as the African National Congress (ANC) government is likely to address their basic needs is concerned, but spirits have been high since the demise of apartheid, and there has been a shift in the country's mood from fear to excitement, if not hope.

A somewhat different shift, at the level of government, has also occurred. With a shift from an apartheid to a democratic, non- racial dispensation, the new government took on a different approach – that of initially establishing a government of national unity (GNU), in an effort to include both the traditions of an Afrikaner community that had been dominant and the traditions of the freedom fighter who struggled against apartheid. Despite the sharp differences, the idea of the GNU was to concentrate not on "two people", but to resolve the gap as a team in the interests of democratic governance and transition to "a better life for all" (the ANC election slogan). On the one hand, there was the "the Revolution Chief" (President Nelson Mandela) and, on the other, "the Calvinist Reformer" (former Deputy President FW De Klerk), two strong-willed yet pragmatic men, at once autocratic and democratic, more adored abroad than at home, beholden to their respective power bases and professing party loyalty and yet with a penchant for reaching momentous decisions on their own. To some extent, the "pullout" of the Nationalist Party (NP) as one of the major stakeholders in the government of national unity was a reflection of the sharp differences that almost paralysed government (and foreign investment). Whilst leaders of government come and go, policy on how to govern continues. It is to this policy issue (largely responsible for the differences and break-up of the GNU) that the study now turns.

It would seem that with the break-up of the major stakeholders in the GNU, no longer did the old political model – with the main conflict occurring between the NP on the right and the ANC on the left – tell us what was really going on. Rather, much of what was really happening in the new South Africa – the vibrancy of democracy, economic growth based on a macro-economic strategy, redistribution and transformation – was to be found within the ANC-led government, the party itself and its alliance.

With the establishment of the new ANC government, debates and policy positions vis-à-vis foreign investment emerged largely between the nerve centres of the tripartite alliance of the ANC, Congress of South African Trade Unions (COSATU) and the South African Communist Party (SACP). We shall examine these debates and policy stances in broad terms – starting with COSATU, the labour wing of the ruling alliance. But, first, an important rider is in order.

In the interest of foreign investment, the new South African state significantly toned down its nationalisation approach and qualified its economic policies in accordance with objectives for growth and development. It offered special treatment to investors who meet certain needs, i.e. they earn the country foreign exchange, transfer technology and create jobs.[1]

Alliance Debates

What follows is a presentation of the key aspects of the intra-organisational and intra-alliance debates. It will be shown that these debates seek to address conflicting imperatives – the need for stability and transformation in the key institutions of the economy in order to foster foreign investment. What emerges, it will be argued, is a mixture of pragmatism, moral vision and attempts at mobilising and representing the immediate aspirations of millions who remain victims of the country's apartheid past. It is these tensions and hard choices between pragmatism, vision and immediate demands that are captured in the positions outlined below.

The COSATU discussion document on its alliance with the ANC and the SACP has evoked the expected response from the capitalist class controlling the country's economy and from foreign investors alike, branding the document, "socialist". From the said document comes a debate whose essence is the question: "How do we transform society so that we can provide food, shelter, and a real income to the majority of our population?"[2] Whilst everyone agrees with this broad objective, two diametrically opposed views have emerged on how to address society's major problems. One viewpoint has it that the government is a hindrance to, not the facilitator of, economic growth and that increased economic equality and economic accountability impede economic growth. According to this logic, a prerequisite for growth is the distribution of wealth to the rich. In their desire to make more money, the rich will then invest in factories and, in this way, the wealth will trickle down to the poor. Implicit here is the notion that the government must reduce its spending – failing which it will remove savings from the economy. Consequently, the rich will not have the money to build factories and interest rates will rise.

These kinds of policies are not new, but rather part of an international policy consensus based on a set of conservative principles. In countries where these principles have been implemented, successes recorded are those of increased profits and a drop in inflation, even if these are less successful in improving overall economic performance and even increasing economic inequality. Why this policy consensus continues to be propagated regardless of its failures is partly because the beneficiaries, although a minority, are a powerful group in every society, a class to which public officials and politicians ("the ruling elite") belong, and who have adopted these policies, gaining in the process praise for being "responsible" and thus rewarded by the markets.

It would appear that this orthodox policy consensus has crept into policy formation in South Africa. The situation evidenced by the official obsession with deficit reduction is a case in point. Even though the deficit is not acute by international standards, business (and to a lesser extent, government) continues to urge that the deficit be reduced. This ushers in the second policy position – an entirely different stance, to which COSATU subscribes. It is a position that advocates a leading role by government and government expenditure in kick-starting the economy. COSATU believes that the government must kick-start the economy by investing in infrastructure even if it means increasing the deficit – although the level must, of course, be a reasonable one.

On the economic front, COSATU chooses to focus on a crucial aspect: that of establishing a universal social welfare system based on national health-care, retirement income, and unemployment benefits. Implicit here is the idea of effectively putting a floor under minimum wages and conditions that will eventually cut costs to the employer. This is the policy position held by the major left-wing, socialist formation in South Africa, a formation closely associated with the ANC and SACP and one that has chosen the path to socialist development.

These two policy positions seem to suggest a struggle between the interests of an elected government and rule "by an unelected market" such that a *fait accompli* is now in place: the ANC-led government merely attempts to govern while the market rules. It is, as it were, a critique (which may not please the country's economic elites) of those who advocate the superiority of central planning to the free market, which implies carrying the logic of political democratisation into the socially arid economic domain.

Capitalist proponents argue that in the economic context, government can – and should – help to provide an environment conducive to the creation of wealth: to be the investors' friend and to intervene in the market in order to hasten growth consistent with macro-economic discipline. The ultimate aim, of course, is the integration of the country's economy with the international capital market. Implicit, here, is that to create "growth for all" and to declare war on unemployment, foreign investment is crucial.

Pursuant to this seemingly pro-capitalist approach, is the so-called "Mbeki discussion document" – an oppositional policy position that seeks to counter COSATU's adversarial approach to the macro-economic strategy. In this regard, it needs to be stated that Thabo Mbeki's role as *de facto* Prime Minister while Deputy President and subsequently as President has, in fact, driven the production of the macro-economic framework, a position which has earned praise across the globe for its vision of investment-led development, which is equally a political and economic vision in keeping with the new global environment. With the release of Mbeki's discussion document, *The State and Social Transformation*, a "policy" vision was created that levelled criticism at the ultra-left in a struggle over economic policy. Contained within the document was the first comprehensive explanation of how a co-operative relationship between the state and capital – read the government and business – is the most important precondition for the success of the

ANC's struggle for democratic and economic transformation. To arrive at this conclusion, Mbeki explained how the new government inherited massive fiscal constraints from the old order, most notably a debt which rose from R37 billion in 1985 to R280 billion – some 65% of GDP – in 1996.[3]

The net effect of this inheritance – and the changing global environment in which investment crosses borders with fewer fetters – has been to limit the state's ability to implement the democratic project on its own. This has led to what Mbeki calls an "oscillation" within the democratic movement between "the establishment of a democratic state" and "the wish to establish a state whose distinctive feature would be the total defeat and suppression of both the national and class forces responsible for the system of national oppression and class super-exploitation epitomised by apartheid". Put differently, the question has been whether the struggle should be limited to establishing democracy or extended to ushering in socialism. In the current practice of the ANC-led government, the ANC has long abandoned its socialist pretensions, adopting a pragmatic, sometimes socio-democratic, approach to economic policy.

As for the ANC worker, after pointing out that the black working class has "been freed of the disability imposed on it by its oppression", the argument in the Mbekist economic position is that this class "would be best poised to assume a stance that is developmental and transformative". That is, the working class needs to take part in the new economic programme. There is, then, no doubt that Mbeki's view of a co-operative relationship between state and capital will triumph over the alternatives. Indeed, the fundamentals of the government economic strategy, which the SACP and COSATU have criticised, are not negotiable. Having committed itself to attracting foreign investment, government, the argument goes, has found that what its leftist critics call "Thatcherite" policies are the only way to make headway in the global economy. The growth, employment, and redistribution (GEAR) underlying the government's macro-economic strategy has, however, brought some disenchantment as the government takes less than firm steps to implement it.

Indeed, analysts are of the view that foreign investors are "very unforgiving of any signs of dithering" on the government's continued pussy-footing around the issues of lifting exchange controls and privatisation. Therein lies the key to South Africa's misfortunes in the 1990s and beyond. Foreign investors are seemingly no longer as well disposed towards the country as in the 'honeymoon' years of 1994 and 1995. Initial scepticism in the market became a self-fulfilling prophecy during the years that followed.

One of the most controversial aspects of South Africa's macro-economic strategy was its call for wage moderation in the current circumstances of massive income inequalities. This strategy envisaged achieving wage moderation via a "social agreement" between business, labour, and government in which each partner would sacrifice something for the common good. In the present debate and meetings between business and labour, scant enthusiasm is emerging and resistance to the idea runs deep, largely due to "battle fatigue". However, the process must continue if the apartheid wage gap between top income earners and the lowest paid workers is to narrow. This will help counter the argument that workers cannot be expected to accept moderate wage increases if management does not also make sacrifices.

Conditions for Foreign Investment

What are the structural conditions that undergird the social fabric for foreign investment? For one thing, South Africa hits rock bottom, with the worst score of all, when it comes to what is termed the "people factor", meaning the mobilisation of human resources. A global survey ranked South Africa lowest among 14 countries in expenditure on education.[4] It reported that the country "least meets the needs of a competitive economy" – for example, adult illiteracy is worse only in India, Pakistan, and Indonesia of the countries surveyed – and has the lowest ranking in worker motivation, which is in sharp contrast to the dynamism shown by rivals such as Singapore and Taiwan. In sum, competitiveness in certain categories, including the adult literacy rate, skills, and labour productivity, is lower than the average for developing countries even though the country compares "relatively favourably" with developing countries in terms of scientific and technological capabilities and the quality of its infrastructure.

Another deleterious factor militating against a favourable social fabric for foreign investment is the South African mining and industrial corporations, which under apartheid exploited the cruel migrant labour system and made unabashed use of cheap black labour, actively peddling its availability as an advantage to international investors. Today it is gradually becoming possible to count the costs; such that, until the country has significantly addressed low levels of literacy and basic education, as well as some of the fundamental social needs of the labour force, it is unlikely that improvement projects will reap the required productivity levels. This implies the integration of technology education into the national school curriculum – a level of technology and science education that would contribute to the country's economy but also earn workers decent wages.

Historically, and particularly over the last few years of democracy, little has been done to ease the plight of the black population. With racial and gender inequalities still a depressing fact of life in South Africa and over 4.2 million people unemployed (30% of the economically active population), the black majority still lives in poverty, having little access to electricity, water, sanitation, and other household services.[5] This, however, is changing under the new democratic dispensation. There is a further economic consideration, that of a critical debate that is raging over the phenomenon of "jobless growth", the fact that the economy has been growing, but not creating new employment opportunities. Also noteworthy are the twin evils of crime and unemployment that continue to bedevil South Africa's fledgling democracy.

Besides the social factors that impact on foreign investment are, perhaps, the more serious pointers within the country's political economy. Whilst, it is quite conceivable that the demands of global competition will destroy the lower end of South Africa's industries such as clothing and textiles, because the country is unable to compete with the labour rates of the Indonesians, Indians and Chinese, to cite but a few examples, the most critical tendency in South Africa that militates against foreign competition is the hostility of big business to foreign capital, especially of companies that disinvested from the country at the height of black revolt against white rule. How to restore the South African economy, although still the powerhouse of sub-Saharan Africa, is in itself a mammoth task. It is towards measures taken thus far and some of the promising outcomes that this study now turns.

Measures towards a Global Economy

One of the new global frameworks, the Labour Relations Act (LRA), that has been negotiated by government, labour, and business, ushered in the dawn of a new era in industrial democracy. Following a period of decades of apartheid labour legislation served by the *dompas*, the colour bar, and restrictions on black workers and their trade unions, South Africans are finally governed by labour laws that are appropriate to a democratic country. For farm workers and domestic workers alike, the LRA is a victory reminiscent of a revolution. For the first time the workers have been granted the same rights, duties and protection while the law is no longer fragmented, and no longer excludes marginalised groups of workers who found themselves outside the large, well-organised factories.

Industrial bosses are no longer allowed to prevent trade unions from organising on their premises, mainly because the new law provides a statutory basis for the organisational rights of trade unions. Additionally, the collective bargaining system has been reformed to promote industry-level bargaining, which should help to close the wage gap as well as promote the extension of retirement benefits to more workers.

Despite the tripartite nature of the labour agreement, there have been some attempts by business to roll back the inclusion of worker's rights and accommodation of workers' interests in the LRA. In particular, business and the political party which best represents their interests (the Democratic Party), have questioned the constitutionality of the LRA – with, for instance, the South African Foundation's "Growth for All" document claiming that the law introduces unnecessary "rigidities" into the labour market. It remains to be seen whether foreign business will welcome the new labour law as being in line with "international trends". What is clear, however, is that half-hearted attempts at the implementation of its provisions could backfire on management. On the other hand, the idea of a "social agreement" seems likely to die a slow death as South Africa enters the global competition.

This ushers in the question of investment opportunities and some promising prospects. South Africa has vast commercial potential. Among a handful of the world's richest countries, it is the leading exporter of gold and diamonds. It also ranks among the largest exporters of coal and non-ferrous metals. It is self-sufficient in food and is potentially a larger exporter of non-seasonal fruits and quality wines, as well as having vast untapped tourist resources.

The economic and political significance of the country lies in the fact that as a result of its geographical position and mineral reserves, it is of great strategic importance. It controls the Cape of Good Hope shipping lanes through which leading trading countries navigate their ships. Over half of Western Europe's oil supplies and one quarter of its food imports are shipped via this route. South Africa is equally important as a major producer of minerals such as chrome, manganese, platinum, vanadium, titanium and antimony. Without these and other minerals, the First World would be unable to continue its industrial superiority or produce its sophisticated national defence systems. Foreign investors in South Africa are, therefore, mindful of these resources and the chance of buying into an exciting opportunity. They are keen to tie up with local companies in order to assist in bringing in research and development, access to international markets and thereby providing economies of scale to local industry – all, of course, for an acceptable return.

Against this background, investors have become keen observers of entrepreneurial opportunities and South Africa because of its infrastructure, macro-economic policies and solid range of industries presents an exciting scenario. But they have also posed investment-related questions for the ministries of finance and trade and industry, focusing on issues of tax, labour, fiscal and monetary policies, trade and tariff barriers, capital movements and privatisation. Needless to say, the latter issue – the question of whether to expand state involvement or to privatise and sell some of the assets and enterprises – depends not on ideological imperatives, but on the balance of economic necessity.[6]

Perhaps the big question for potential investors is exchange rates – the liberalisation of currency transfers but also privatising state holdings – implying state transfer of ownership to what will almost inevitably be foreign investors. The realisation of both imperatives most certainly would, after a while, encourage net foreign investment. However, until then, there remain huge gaps between intention and reality.

Notes and References

1   S Barber, 'Development aid or free tickets for the Gravy Train?", *Sunday Times* (Johannesburg), 7 May 1996, p 14.

2   Trade Union Research Project, 1992. *Our Political Economy: Understanding the Problem, Handbook for COSATU*, Johannesburg: COSATU, 1992.

3   T Mbeki, *International Perspectives: Abstracts from Addresses*, Pretoria: South African Institute of International Affairs, 1994.

4   M Chester, 'South Africa in Minor League', *The Star* (Johannesburg), 31 July 1992, p 11.

5   D Robertson, 'Democracy fails to wipe out History's Inequalities', *Sunday Times (Business Times)* (Johannesburg), 1 December 1996, p 1.

6   I Wylie, 'Investors set to back Democratic South Africa', *Guardian Weekly: Finance* (Johannesburg), 8 May 1994, p 21.

Information Technology Human Resource Sharing: A Regional Option

Mwangala M Bonna and Elizabeth Mukamaambo

During the opening session of Global Knowledge 97, an international conference held in Toronto on the information revolution and the developing world, the United Nations Secretary General Kofi Annan referred to the information revolution as being the key to ensuring democracy and wiping out poverty around the world. According to him, information has a great democratising power waiting to be harnessed to our global struggle for peace and development. Based on the utilisation of computers in modern telecommunications, the information revolution is transforming societies, improving quality of life, and fostering the global exchange of culture, knowledge, goods and services. New equipment, techniques and materials have greatly improved efficiency and productivity in agriculture and industry but at the same time they are demanding more educated and qualified labour. Such computer-based innovations are at the centre of developments in the global economy. Computers have changed the way people think, work and interact with one another. Apart from this, computers have assisted in introducing new and high quality products on the market. Thanks to computers, the specifications of products are easy to determine and produce and transaction costs can be reduced.

The Southern African Development Community (SADC) as a region aims to be economically and politically strong. The countries within the region aim to achieve this by promoting regional co-operation through various national and regional strategies. Through this international understanding, co-operation and support, it is hoped that the underdevelopment, exploitation and deprivation that plagues Southern Africa will be overcome. In the Information Technology (IT) driven economy, it will be through full utilisation and management of IT that SADC countries can achieve this.

Information technology in this chapter is defined as the use of modern technology, especially computers, to capture, process, store, retrieve or communicate information in the form of numerical data, text, sound or images. It involves the processing of large amounts of data relatively quickly for little cost. IT, as an instrument, holds great potential to improve various aspects of human endeavour as well as accelerating their socio-economic development. However, inadequate indigenous IT manpower in the SADC countries is one of the major impediments hampering efforts to ride the crest of this Information Revolution in the process of development. The IT skills capacity in the region needs strengthening or, where necessary, should be out-sourced within the region to facilitate the building of stronger links within the region and with the rest of the world.

This chapter advocates the building of a regional IT manpower base through co-operation and sharing in training and education with a view to attaining self-sufficiency in these still rare skills. It suggests ways of bringing large sections of the workforce into the information age to avoid situations where the workforce is declared redundant in favour of those who are more computer literate. One major constraint of this chapter is that there is no statistical data on the number of available IT personnel in the countries concerned. Thus, the issues are discussed without direct statistical justification. Although the authors are aware that other skills should receive similar scrutiny, the choice of IT is necessary because it cuts across all industries. There is no industry to date that has not been directly or indirectly affected by IT. As we enter the new millennium and more and more countries are faced by the need to be part of the global economy, the importance of IT becomes even more critical.

A discussion on regionalism cannot ignore the globalisation process, which encompasses economic, financial, technical, political and socio-cultural phenomena, and thus implies both opportunities and challenges.[1] The opportunities lie in the potential that is to be harnessed if countries prepare themselves adequately. One aspect of this preparation for globalisation and world trade is having qualified manpower to take advantage of the opportunities offered by globalisation. IT can be used to the fullest to achieve this if it is employed to play the vital role it has been designed to in development. On the other hand, the challenge of globalisation is that of integration into the world economy. This integration may not be an advantage for economies that cannot compete in the international market, as is the case with some markets within the SADC region which are not able to stand up to competition from more economically established countries. Some of these also lack the resources to take advantage of the benefits being brought by globalisation. Improved IT within the SADC countries will be a first step towards appreciating the importance of being part of the "global village". There is a legitimate fear that many developing countries will lose out unless they prepare themselves to take part in the global world. Globally, new services and products are also emerging which are moving away from original manufacturing bases to being information providers (that is, the information and service sectors) in which IT plays a major role.

Applications of IT

The importance of IT lies in the fact that all industries in the modern society use some facet of information technology, whether directly or indirectly. Some of these applications include the following:

- *In the home*: radio and television, telephones, washing machines, microwave ovens, and many other home appliances;
- *In the office*: The computer is revolutionising the office as many types of office tasks are being simplified;
- *Education and training*: multimedia learning materials, computers and educational software;
- *Law enforcement*: Computers are increasingly being used to fight crime by improving police efficiency;[2]
- *Transport and communications*: Communication signals, as in railways and aeroplanes, are dependent on IT; cars; Internet, facsimiles, and email;
- *Retailing*: Point-of-sale systems linked to banks;
- *Banking*: Automated teller machines.

Information and Communication Technology (ICTs), or the wider sphere of IT, is at the centre of developments in the global economy. In addition to the refinement of traditional hardware, many companies are branching out into networking systems, including totally digitised fibre-optic global communications networks and optical disk storage systems which allow for high volumes of information to be shared. New applications software include remote sensing systems, microwave technology and bio-sensors, artificial intelligence systems and significant improvements in satellite communications.

IT permits the rapid dissemination of ideas, values and processes and supplements education, science, healthcare and culture. It also has potential for exchanging information to learn about people's needs and how they manage resources, and provides data to facilitate the production and distribution of wealth. With specific reference to the SADC countries, the 21st century provides the opportunity for a renaissance in harnessing the potential of IT. The level of economic independence and effective productivity, which can be achieved via IT, is high.

Labour needs in SADC countries

Regardless of the general perception that computers replace human labour in the workplace, a huge workforce is needed just to support and maintain the massive network on which IT and related systems operate. This includes the basic hardware of computers as well as networking components and peripherals. For prospective participants in developing countries (like those in SADC) in this global information technology-centred world, the infrastructure and skills necessary for full integration are in short supply. Many well-meaning or high potential information systems are likely to fail if there is no adequate know-how on how to implement them. The high rates of computer installations that are under-utilised or simply abandoned in these countries show that few have succeeded in exploiting IT potential for their socio-economic development.[3] Indeed, a large number of computer-users mainly utilise them for typing purposes and as a result fail to appreciate the full potential of these devices.

The 14 SADC countries are experiencing a very high rate of 'brain drain' in almost all areas of human resources. The problem is more critical in IT-related fields where there is already a shortage of skills. The general shortage is due to a tendency for children to follow well-beaten routes into the areas of medicine, law, sociology and other well-established disciplines. Very few would-be trainees choose IT for training purposes because it is a relatively new field and many people are still intimidated by computers. At times where there are people available to provide IT services, the industry may not absorb them for lack of infrastructure, thereby creating an artificial problem which forces them to migrate to counties where their labour is not only appreciated, but also adequately remunerated. Once they are in a new country, the problems of job security arise, for, if these people do not perform to their full potential, they run the risk of antagonising the locals. Furthermore, once people move, they create a vacuum in the sending country, at the same time improving the services of the receiving country. This means that the countries concerned may not be performing at the same pace. There is a need to address this problem in a deliberate effort to develop a regional IT skills base. Only then can the full range of opportunities provided by IT be really appreciated. The first task would be to take stock of available IT skills in the region with a view to seeing how this can be utilised to benefit all the countries in the region without incapacitating those countries whose economies are not very strong.[4]

IT skills and the availability of computers vary from country to country within SADC. South Africa leads in terms of computer usage, followed by Namibia. But even within countries, the distribution is skewed in favour of multinational corporations, followed by government and parastatal organisations. The private sector has very few computers in general and where these are available, most of them are too old to be upgraded in view of new improvements in IT.[5]

Moreover, IT training is usually carried out by large companies. There are very few organisations that offer specialised training in IT in these countries and most people cannot afford the cost. Training provided by vendors is generally cheaper but aimed at financial gains more than a need to offer a necessary service. The training offered by government departments is rarely of good quality as a result of a lack of adequate skills.[6] The few persons who may be trained at government expense usually leave after such training because remuneration rarely improves. Since each of the countries may not have sufficient resources to tackle such shortages of manpower on its own, pooling of resources and other courses of action can be taken for sustainability. Co-operation and partnerships among countries could lead to the redesign of operations and functions within and between organisations leading to skills sharing and optimal IT usage.

In terms of the SADC Protocol on Education and Training, education and training is one area of co-operation for SADC countries. The need for such co-operation is considered essential for the creation and sustenance of a capable workforce in all levels of education – basic and secondary, teacher education, vocational and technical, as well as tertiary training. Member states have also agreed to the general objective of establishing centres of specialisation to build capacity for regional training institutions to offer education and training programmes in critical and specialised areas and thereby increase the stock of trained personnel in the region.[7] The protocol also agrees to promote co-operation amongst management development institutions, competency based institutions, universities and other institutions that run short courses, seminars and workshops for the purpose of imparting and enhancing skills and to acquaint workers with new technologies. Other objectives in this regard include imparting management and administration skills in these areas as well as promoting professional development through professional bodies. IT is one such technical area in which SADC as a region needs adequately qualified manpower. If skills, materials, management and access to IT are lacking, the opportunities and choices mentioned above will be limited and the effective amount and range of IT that can be delivered is severely lowered. This might seriously inhibit the participation of the region in the global economy.

There seems to be a school of thought that assumes that simply acquiring computers would lead to increased productivity. However, what is needed is much more, and should take into account the environments into which computers are introduced. At times, the use of IT in an organisation brings profound changes to the way in which business is conducted; these changes often come with unforeseen problems which are not always technical in nature, but which can hinder the successful utilisation of the IT systems.

In addition, in information systems, computers are only part of an overall system. This means that there are a number of sub-systems within an information system. One of these is the social sub-system, which includes the people involved, business processes, social structures and the culture.[8] Unless such fundamental facts are grasped by IT implementers, information systems will be viewed as appliances where information systems are treated as something you simply buy and then plug in like a refrigerator or a washing machine. Personnel and business processes should not be treated as after-thoughts to be retrofitted to a computer; instead it should be realised that personnel and business processes are inseparable from and interact with the technology in an overall information system. IT personnel should be aware of these important factors when designing systems. Hence, the need to have competent, well-trained implementers in all aspects of IT cannot be over-emphasised. Such adequately trained IT personnel are what are needed for the region so that information systems are taken through the proper life cycles of feasibility studies, design, implementation and maintenance to ensure their usefulness and sustainability. Even other professionals need to be made aware of the different roles IT plays in relation to their professions.[9]

What is needed is to build knowledge and raise awareness about IT, to maximise the potential of IT in order to become more competitive. There is also a need for a substantial overhaul of education and training so as to match the changes taking place in the information revolution as well as to keep pace with continuing technological development during the years to come. In order to manage the process of change, everyone has to be involved – employers, workers, public authorities at all levels, education and training institutions and business support services.

A sad reality is that while much investment has been made in education (including IT), the orientation of education and the trained manpower mix has failed to respond to the regional needs and aspirations. While millions of dollars are spent on experts from the developed countries, a large portion of the trained sons and daughters of the continent are serving outside the region.[10] The massive 'brain drain' that is depriving the region of very skilled personnel in favour of the more industrialised nations needs to be arrested. This could be done collectively by the SADC countries through the identification of critical areas of need and developing strategies for sharing the resources without crippling member countries. This may result in the liberalisation of IT-skilled labour movements so as to adequately share those available.

Building a Skills Base

The first step towards building a skills base in the SADC region would be to take stock of the existing complement of IT human resources to find out what the current strength of IT manpower is in the region. Only then can the utilisation of these skills be maximised. SADC governments can then co-operate with each other on issues of IT training, development and utilisation. The available resources could then be used to support regional efforts and programmes.

Laying the Best Foundations

The quality of education and trainers in basic education schools affects the quality and organisation of schools and education at that level. This is true of both pre-school and higher education. Therefore teachers and trainers need to be targeted to promote their professional development and consequently that of their audience. They would then be able to mount suitable programmes integrating IT. These can then help in supporting pools of skills by forming the foundations of such skills.

Teaching to Learning Institutions

Learning institutions need to be more responsive to the needs of business and industry. Ties between them need to be strengthened through partnerships. Since retention is higher among learners when utilising IT rather than simply reading or hearing, the potential for self-learning using IT is immense and if shaped correctly could be the key tool for closing this skills gap. This would also ensure that new and changing skills are made available.

Retraining instead of De-skilling

The employability of the workforce needs to be reinforced through training. Reintegration should start before people are unemployed. Financial resources could be focused on training grants and new skills. During the 4th international conference of IT entitled "Information Technology Utilisation in Developing Countries: A Need for Co-operation and Co-ordination", Selim proposed a course of action to alleviate the critical IT manpower shortage in developing countries. In his paper entitled, 'Co-operative Training of the African IT Workforce for a Computer Driven World', he suggested forming a co-operative with IT skills development.[11] This is in line with SADC's vision and agreed policies for training for capacity in skills that are lacking and the sharing of available skills.

According to Selim, there is a two-phase approach to first deal with more immediate problems of staff and to make sure that the supplies of IT staff could be sustained. A centre or a committee in any one country with links in all the others could be formed. This could comprise a software developer, a hardware engineer, training providers, an administrative manager, a business manager, technicians and secretaries. These co-operatives could then establish a pool of existing and emigrant IT personnel and spear-head efforts in IT training and development. A similar plan of action can be followed by SADC as follows:

Short-term Plan:

- Mount an IT survey to assess available resources, identify gaps and needs in the region and then build a database of IT resources;
- Provide information and advice on IT training and development matters;
- Offer low-cost support to individuals and small businesses;
- Provide low-cost IT training separately or in co-operation with other organisations;
- Work with other centres to help aid IT personnel's mobility and place-ments within the SADC region.

Long-term Plan:

- Train for future needs and re-train existing workforce where possible;
- Manage, operate, maintain and repair modern information systems;
- Build appropriate and customised software packages;
- Export computer-based services to generate foreign currency;
- Compile IT resources databases;
- Establish an integrated computer network for SADC;
- Organise training workshops and seminars.[12]

Conclusion

It has been established that employing IT greatly improves lives and fosters development. Heading towards the 21st century, IT is also gaining in importance as a tool for bringing about desired social and economic changes. If the SADC as a regional body aims to take its place in the glob-al economy by being strong politically and economically, IT has to be employed. However, this cannot be done without the necessary person-nel. Building this skills base has to be given priority. SADC already has poli-cies in place to address capacity building in technical areas, of which IT is one. Knowledge campaigns need to be launched to educate people on this new paradigm. Grass-roots development of IT needs be done right from pre-school. One way of educating the region is by targeting trainers and teachers. These impart their skills to their audience through their knowl-edge and this could be reinforced via the curriculum. They can then also become part of the pooled IT resources.

The de-skilled workforce could be retrained instead of retrenched as IT starts to play an even greater role in the workplace. Centres of co-operation in Information Technology could be established to spearhead this process. These could be concentrations of IT staff where a service and support are provided for all who need it and also a pooling and placement of IT staff for where such needs are identified.

Notes and References

1   *Human Development Report*, New York: United Nations Development Programme, 1998.
2   R Carter, *Information Technology*, London: Made Simple Books, 1996.
3   E Selim, 'Co-operation Training of the African IT Workforce for a Computer Driven World', Paper presented at the CISNA 93 4th International Conference on Information Technology, Gaborone, Botswana, 2–4 June 1993.
4   V Hoek, *The Migration of High Level Manpower*, The Hague: Mouton and Co, 1970.
5   L Stephen, 'Global Imperatives and Paradigms: Information Technology and Regional Inequalities', Paper presented at the BITWorld 99 Conference, Cape Town, 30 June 1999.
6   Selim 1993.
7   *Protocol on Education and Training*, Gaborone: SADC, 1997.
8   Green Paper on 'Living and Working in the Information Society: People First', http://ww.ispo.cec.be/infosoc/legreg/docs/peopl/st.html, 1999.
9   B Talal, 'Technology: Impact on Human Development', in *Change: Threat or Opportunity for Human Progress?*, vol 6, New York: United Nations, 1992.
10 E Kasongo, 'Some Factors undermining successful IT utilisation in Developing Countries', in Paper presented at the CISNA 93 4th International Conference on Information Technology, Gaborone, Botswana, 2–4 June 1993.
11 Selim 1993.
12 *Ibid*.

A Pilot Project for AIDS Affected Orphans in Botswana: Protecting the Democratic and Human Rights of Unfortunate Children

Gloria Jacques

Democracy implies the existence of the rule of law from which flows respect for human rights and fundamental freedoms.[1] Indeed, democracy demands respect for human rights which constitute the foundation of solidarity (a necessary condition for democratic governance).[2] Universal solidarity, developing out of local and historical realities, can only exist within the veracity of a people's shared experience.[3] Michaels emphasises the fact that the process of democratisation is like waves washing up on a beach and then receding which, as Holm avers, has been the experience of the Southern African nation of Botswana.[4] Yet, in that country the process does continue as democratic principles abide from the most basic level of human functioning. This so-called grassroots democracy (unlike elitist democracy) pertains to the efforts of the people themselves to build a humane society and it is this distinction which characterises the nature of the democratic process in Botswana.[5]

However, notwithstanding the commitment of society to democratic principles, processes, and structures (inherent in which is the belief that no group should be marginalised, stigmatised, or denied access to needed resources), there are those in the population who are not always afforded their basic human rights, as is currently happening across the African continent and, in fact, in the global arena. The reference in this regard is to HIV/AIDS sufferers and their potential (or actual) orphaned children who are amongst the most stigmatised groups, in contemporary African society especially, and in greatest need of advocacy to enjoy those democratic rights which are the right of the entire population.

Children in these circumstances, particularly, lack self-advocacy opportunities and the means to protect their position and entitlements. AIDS-affected families are, in many instances, rejected by the community and children of these families frequently have to care for ailing and dying relatives with little or no support. They may also suffer poor health themselves through deprivation caused by a lack of material resources and the risks associated with nursing infected family members. Ignorance of legal rights robs many people, especially women and children, of that which is their due and relegates them to poverty through abuse of inheritance procedures by others. Also, children who enter the world of customary foster care are sometimes subjected to the effects of negative perceptions of relatives based on the belief that they are a burden on already limited household resources. Others are reduced to living in child-headed households where they themselves may be the inexperienced and distressed head, or they may be forced to take to the streets where the risks of contracting the HI virus are greatly increased. Poverty is often, inevitably, a concomitant problem.

Instruments for addressing the Needs of Children in Botswana

The United Nations Convention on the Rights of the Child (1989), building upon the Geneva Declaration of the Rights of the Child of 1924, Universal Declaration of Human Rights of 1948, and United Nations Children's Declaration of 1959, reaffirms the fact that children, because of their vulnerability, require special care and protection, and places particular emphasis on the primary nurturing and protective responsibility of the family. It also stresses the need for legal and other safeguards for the child before and after birth, the importance of respect for the cultural values of the child's community, and the vital role of international co-operation in securing children's rights.[6]

After much deliberation, Botswana acceded to the Convention in 1995 and is in the process of ensuring that all articles are enshrined in the law of the land as well as being translated into services available to the vulnerable within its communities. Accountability for such commitment is inherent in the accession process.

In 1993, the Government of Botswana, through a Presidential Directive, prepared and adopted a National AIDS Policy for the country. The policy provides the framework for a national, multi-sectoral response to the HIV/AIDS epidemic. Although the Ministry of Health was to play a leading role in addressing the problem, the policy acknowledged and articulated the significance of the role of other sectors in HIV and AIDS prevention, care, and mitigation through the establishment of a multisectoral AIDS Council. The rights of sufferers were also addressed, with the emphasis on the illegitimacy of institutionalised marginalisation and discriminatory practice.[7]

A National Programme of Action for the Children of Botswana (NPA), covering a ten year period from 1993-2003, identifies categories of children in especially difficult circumstances, including orphans of AIDS-affected families and HIV-positive children. In order to address the needs of these children the Second Medium Term Plan for HIV and AIDS, formulated by Botswana's Ministry of Health, made provision for, *inter alia*, children affected by HIV/AIDS. With regard to orphans, policy development, institutional strengthening, and service delivery have been incorporated in strategic and operational planning through a multi-sectoral approach to the problem, spanning such areas as review and amendment of existing policies and legislation, including the Destitute Policy, the Children's and Adoption Acts, and the National Programme of Action for the Children of Botswana; support for community-based and non-governmental organisations providing material, psychological, and social assistance to children from AIDS-affected families; support for studies targeting the needs of families and children distressed by HIV and AIDS; and the provision of foster care and adoption services for orphans, counselling and support for distressed children, and education performance monitoring systems for children in difficult circumstances.[8]

Also in line with the National Programme of Action for children, a consultancy was undertaken during 1998 to formulate regulations for the Children's Act (1981) addressing the situation of children in need of care, specifically those from AIDS-affected families. This followed nation-wide consultations on the issue, with all sectors of society. The provision of alternative forms of care was incorporated into this draft legislation, encompassing strengthening of customary foster care as well as so-called child-headed household foster care; redefining and refining the concept of guardianship; enhancing the principle and provision of residential care and children's homes; reinforcing the need for schools of industry; updating and standardising arrangements for formalised foster care in caregivers' homes through related and unrelated placements; and, significantly, extending the notion of places of safety (including emergency foster homes) for children at risk or in immediate need of alternative care provision.[9] Cabinet has subsequently unconditionally approved these regulations.

The amended Adoption Act (1952) and Affiliation Proceedings Act (1970) have now also been passed, and a team of consultants is reviewing the Children's Act in its entirety. The Destitute Policy is also under review with special focus on assistance for families financially disadvantaged by HIV/AIDS (as a result of increased health-care costs and loss of income resulting from sickness and death of wage-earning, productive family members).

The Short Term Plan of Action on Care of Orphans in Botswana (1999-2001), formulated by the Social Welfare Division in the then Ministry of Local Government, Lands and Housing, flowed from the National Conference on the Implications of Orphanhood organised jointly by the Ministry and the Swedish International Development Agency (SIDA) in 1998 and the Rapid Assessment on the Situation of Orphans in Botswana conducted by the AIDS/STD Unit in the Ministry of Health during the same year. Terms of reference for action encompass support for orphans on the basis of the National AIDS Policy; identification of strategies for youth in difficult circumstances in line with the National Youth Policy (1996); extension of day-care centre facilities for pre-school children; formulation of a national policy for orphans; protection of orphans' rights; removal of orphans to places of safety if necessary; enforcement of deserting parents' maintenance of children; waiving of educational costs for needy orphans; facilitation of alternative care provision; establishment of an orphan and foster parent database linked to the home-based care programme; and identification and registration of orphans. Other strategies included facilitation of community-based initiatives for orphans; strengthening of existing safety nets such as kinship systems, churches, social groups (friends), and community organisations; and reinforcement of institutional co-ordination and management of the Plan of Action among the various stakeholders.[10]

In 1998/99 the Ministry of Education appointed consultants to review the Day Care Centre Policy and formulate recommendations for an enhanced programme of early childhood care and education (ECCE) for the children of Botswana. Although this exercise did not specifically target those from AIDS-affected families, the reality is that many recipients of these services will fall into this category. Day-care facilities can serve to ease the burden on parents and alternative care-givers and ensure that the children concerned acquire the foundation for a positive and constructive lifestyle which will assure them and society of sustainable future development. Recommendations included a two tier system of provision, embracing family centres in ECCE care-givers' homes for children from six months to three years, and more educationally oriented centres for those from three to six years of age. It is believed that enhanced day-care provision will serve as an adjunct to other services for children in especially difficult circumstances, whether they are living in their own homes with ailing parents, in child-headed households, in customary or statutory foster or adoptive homes, in the care of guardians, or in residential facilities.

Multi-sectoral project

The Tirisanyo Catholic Commission in Botswana (TCC) has been involved with HIV/AIDS issues and activities since 1989. This non-governmental organisation began its work in the AIDS field with a focus on education and awareness and in 1994, established a programme of home-based care for the terminally ill and their families in Mogoditshane Village, Kweneng District. In 1997 the incoming President of the Rotary Club of Gaborone vouchsafed to transform his vision of a programme for AIDS affected children into reality through the launching of a Club project especially designed for this purpose. In view of the alarming statistics on orphans of the epidemic and the call by government for partners in a multi-sectoral approach to address the issue, TCC and Rotary joined forces in this endeavour and were promptly reinforced by the participation of UNICEF, SOS Children's Villages, and the Department of Social Work at the University of Botswana. This combined initiative sought the development of a community-based pilot project for orphans, suitable for replication in other parts of the country, the region, and possibly globally, which would be sustainable and in line with the identified needs of the communities involved. The goals of the programme were related to the improvement of the quality of life of orphans, potential orphans, and their families and the prevention and reduction of HIV infection and transmission in Mogoditshane Village.

From experiential information obtained through the home-based care programme conducted by TCC, it was obvious that these goals were necessary and in urgent need of attainment. Through the offices of UNICEF and the Statistics Department in the Faculty of Social Sciences at the University of Botswana, TCC was enabled to carry out a needs assessment in the village to determine specific areas which required attention and, on the basis of the results, it was clear that the project needed to open up several avenues of opportunity and assistance. A consultant's report also identified potential components of the programme, supported in principle by the multi-sectoral Steering Committee which then proceeded to work towards the establishment of the project in developmental stages.

It was agreed that a multi-purpose centre be established, through the renovation of existing buildings belonging to the church and/or the construction of new premises on land to be sought from the Land Board with the assistance of the local tribal authority. This centre would provide support services to potential and actual orphans and terminally ill patients in Mogoditshane Village. Programmes offered would include day-care for the most needy children of pre-school age; after-school activities for school-going children and youth; educational, training, and recreational activities for out-of-school children and youth; and recreational and socialising opportunities for terminally ill adults. The needs of infected children would be accommodated, insofar as possible, by the programmes for children affected by HIV/AIDS. A supplementary feeding programme would be delivered through the facility to complement the nutritional requirements of children and adults involved in centre activities. The facility would also develop, in co-ordination with the District AIDS Committee and UNICEF, a computerised registry of orphans and potential orphans in Mogoditshane. Counselling services would be offered to care-givers and other household members living with terminally ill patients, with regard to appropriate physical care of the sufferers and psychological support, to increase family members' knowledge and enhance their ability to cope with their stressful situations. Community outreach services would inform residents of Mogoditshane generally of physical and psycho-social aspects of HIV/AIDS as a preventive and remedial measure in the fight against the disease. Research would be conducted into appropriate income-generating activities which could be undertaken at the centre and these would be developed as and when viable. A future development, as the needs of young participants become more obvious, was envisaged as a residential facility for those children who require short-term care in a place of safety as a result of the sickness or death of their parents or care-givers, or longer term nurturing in a family-style children's home setting. This additional provision would, ideally, be part of the original centre but might have to be a separate facility if the initial site proved to be inadequate.

Target population and scope

For the purposes of this study orphans are considered to be children and youth, below the age of 18 years, both of whose parents are deceased or, in a single-parent family where that parent is deceased or permanently absent. Potential orphans are defined as children and youth living with terminally ill parents. In certain situations where young people over the age of 18 are attending school and in demonstrable need of assistance, they will be helped through the project in line with the definition of youth according to the Botswana National Youth Policy which spans the ages of 12 to 29.[11] As this is a pilot project, designed for replication within and possibly outside Botswana, there is potential for reaching a more extensive target population in the future.

The activities of the programme will be directed at the most needy within the target population. It is envisaged that referrals will be made through the village health clinics, social workers, and government and non-governmental home based care programmes. The selection of actual and potential orphans will be carried out by a project task committee comprising representation from TCC, local authority and non-governmental social welfare services, the Village Development Committee, and the project Steering Committee. Terminally ill service recipients will be selected by a similarly constituted committee with the inclusion of a member from the village health clinic.

Strategies and Activities

The project will be implemented in phases. The care of orphans by extended family members is still feasible in Botswana, although they do require assistance. Studies and anecdotal evidence have demonstrated that children of relatives are, at times, less well cared for than the natural children of the family and this exerts additional pressure on social planners attempting to afford children in need of care viable options for support and nurture. Furthermore, the projected number of orphans in the near future will necessitate the provision of non-traditional, alternative care facilities as kinship networks become overburdened. In Mogoditshane this situation is fast approaching due to the fact that, like many villages and peri-urban areas in Botswana and other developing countries, it is characterised by a transplanted population which lacks extensive support systems within the village. The project will thus, in its early stages, focus on initiating activities to support the most needy children, adults, and their families or households through the establishment of the multi-purpose centre which will not initially include the alternative residential care model planned for the future. Strategies for the first phase encompass strengthening the coping capacity of actual and potential orphans as well as that of the households in which they live; creating an enabling environment for orphans and their families through addressing the stigma and discrimination associated with HIV/AIDS; monitoring the impact of the disease on actual and potential orphans and their families; and engagement in resource mobilisation.

The Mogoditshane programme will also help to ensure the care of vulnerable children during the day when household members are occupied with jobs, school attendance, and household chores or when care-givers are ill and unable to make appropriate provision for young children. This will especially benefit older siblings who may be able to maintain or resume their own educational activities. If they have to leave school to engage in income-generating projects to help support the family, the availability of quality day-care facilities will assist their endeavours. In the case of those caring for younger siblings as well as ailing parents the provision will give physical and mental relief from at least some of their care-giving obligations.

With the limited extended family systems of many households in Mogoditshane, the illness and orphaning of family members leads to substantial pressure on the care-giving household. The afore-mentioned lack of pre-school services means that families taking in orphans have been forced either to divert household income to private, fee-paying institutions or to provide care for the children in the home. The latter option often requires the involvement of female household members (whether foster parents or foster or natural siblings) and may necessitate the curtailment of income-earning activities. Constant supervision is required which can be taxing for informal foster mothers and for care-givers and members of families living with terminal illness. The pre-school project will thus address some of these concerns.

School-going orphans and potential orphans will benefit from after-school activities organised through the centre, including help with home-work and preparation for formal educational assignments. The children themselves will be involved in organising these activities with the assistance of community volunteers. Older children will be encouraged to serve as tutors to younger children which will create positive, caring relationships, and develop an ambience in which concern, support, and enhanced self-esteem (possibly lacking in their day-to-day lives) will be promoted. Overburdened household members and ailing parents are often unable to provide the physical, emotional, and educational assistance which constitute a basic right of all children in the process of healthy growth and development. Both the 1959 Declaration of the Rights of the Child and the 1989 Convention recognise that children have a human right to develop to their full potential in every functional aspect of their lives.

Out-of-school children and youth affected by HIV/AIDS will be enabled to receive skills training, access educational programmes, and participate in constructive recreational and leisure activities through day-care centre arrangements specifically designed for them. They will also receive counselling on community training programmes, advocacy on their behalf with the organisers and tutorial assistance to strengthen literacy and numeracy skills (involving those volunteers who help the school-going participants with homework assignments). This should result in enhanced functioning and opportunities for those who otherwise might resort to a life on the streets with the concomitant risk of HIV infection which would perpetuate the cycle of sickness, death, and orphanhood.

To further assist in strengthening the capacity of distressed households containing potential orphans centre staff will liaise with ongoing home-based care programmes of TCC and the District Multisectoral AIDS Committee to identify potential and actual orphans in need of assistance as well as terminally ill adults for whom day-care programmes will be established, providing social and recreational opportunities to enrich their lives and create a support system for addressing common needs. There will also be the additional benefit of alleviating the burden on caregivers in the home and providing respite services for them. A supplementary feeding programme will address the nutritional needs of children and adults who utilise centre services. This will help to ensure the maintenance of higher levels of health for those affected and infected by HIV/AIDS. The needs of children who themselves might be HIV-positive will be accommodated by the existing programmes at the centre, if they are well enough to participate. There will be no specific testing or screening but all children will be treated as if HIV-positive through institutionalising necessary precautionary measures.

Information, education, communication, and counselling services will be provided by staff and volunteers of the centre for the target population and their families. These will include teaching the appropriate physical care of terminally ill patients to make them as comfortable as possible and to minimise risks to care-givers and family members, as well as addressing the psychological aspects of coping with, caring for, and living with terminally ill patients, and of having a terminal illness. Counselling on the legal aspects of property and inheritance rights will be available through referral as a result of identification of voluntary professional services. One of the lessons learned from the Ugandan experience is that inheritance rights of orphans have to be carefully protected as unscrupulous relatives may appropriate property (ostensibly on behalf of orphaned children) which never finds its way to the legitimate heirs.[12]

A statutory foster care programme will be launched in Botswana in the near future and social workers in state and mandated non-governmental organisations will be training foster parents and monitoring placements. It is envisaged that some of these foster parents will utilise the services of the centre, especially the pre-school and other child and youth care programmes, and networking between the centre, the social workers, and the foster parents will become an integral aspect of the project. Community outreach will be effected by presentations to *kgotla* (customary community association) meetings, schools, political gatherings, conferences, workshops, and professional and commercial groups, and by liaison with other non-governmental and community based organisations by centre staff. It is anticipated that this ecological systems approach will ensure a goodness-of-fit between the programme and the environment in which it operates to the benefit of the target population and the community as a whole.

The second phase of the project, the provision of residential care, will include the training of house parents which will be carried out by the SOS Children's Village organisation. The latter has an international training programme for their own house parents which will be appropriate for the centre facility staff. The representation of SOS on the Steering Committee will facilitate the co-ordination of this function.

In order to continually monitor the impact of HIV/AIDS on orphans and potential orphans and their families, the centre will liaise with the Village and District AIDS Committees and with UNICEF (also represented on the Steering Committee) to develop and regularly update a list of indicators which will help to monitor the situation of target populations in Mogoditshane. A computerised database will be maintained by the director of the centre to provide current information on the changing needs of the community to inform programme planning and design. The identification of orphans and potential orphans and updating of information will be effected through home visits by family welfare educators (members of the District Health Team), the monthly health status monitoring of under fives carried out at the village health clinic, and liaison with social workers employed by the District Council Social and Community Development Department and relevant non-governmental organisations.

Resource mobilisation will be an ongoing challenge for the project and regular assessments of opportunities for income-generating activities will be carried out by centre staff. This will include determining types of activities in which terminally ill patients (health status permitting) and out-of-school children and youth could participate. Such activities would then be initiated at and through the centre. The involvement of older orphans and those terminally ill patients who are able to do so in the running of the centre's activities on a voluntary basis will provide a challenge to the participants which can enrich their lives and enhance their self-esteem at a time when feelings of hopelessness threaten to destroy morale. It would also have the additional benefit of keeping staff costs at a minimum. The Rotary Club of Gaborone, a partner in the venture, will solicit voluntary professional service, covering the whole spectrum of needs, from amongst its membership. Other resource mobilisation activities of centre staff will include soliciting individual and corporate sponsorships for the project as a whole, for specific activities, or even for support to individuals; researching and accessing sources of government and donor funding; and organising special fundraising events.[13]

Partnership roles and framework

Five organisations are involved in the first phase of this project and comprise the Steering Committee. Their roles and functions are complementary and mutually sustaining, providing consistent channels of support for and development of the programme. TCC will be the implementing agency, responsible for the day-to-day management and administration of the project, including establishing and maintaining procedures for monitoring and evaluating activities and financial accounting, and sharing the outcomes with other partners and stakeholders. The Commission is involved in the recruitment and supervision of the centre professional staff (a coordinator has already been appointed) and will provide or arrange for the training of community volunteers. TCC chairs the Steering Committee and acts as secretariat for the project.

The Rotary Club of Gaborone is represented on the Steering Committee by three of its members and, apart from mobilising professional assistance from within the local chapter, will also be able to access funds available through Rotary International. Fundraising at local level will be organised to support specific aspects of the project. Inner Wheel, an association of partners and relatives of Rotarians, will also participate in fundraising programmes and the donation of equipment to the centre.

UNICEF is a potential funding partner, particularly with regard to the purchase of equipment and the provision of training and technical assistance. For example, the proposed training of houseparents for the residential unit will be provided by SOS Children's Villages and funded by UNICEF. The agency will also provide computer facilities to support the maintenance of the orphan database.

There are currently two SOS Children's Villages in Botswana, located in Gaborone and Francistown. In-service training for houseparents will be provided by the organisation as will assistance with the monitoring and evaluation of their performance. This partner will provide valuable insights into the development of residential care facilities during the second phase of the project. Professional guidance in early childhood care and education will also be forthcoming as the Gaborone SOS Children's Village provides not only residential care but also pre-school facilities for residents and children from the community. The organisation will also assist with fundraising endeavours, either in an advisory capacity or through identifying possible non-governmental resource networks. This agency has access to bulk purchasing privileges and would share this opportunity with the project.

The Social Work Department at the University of Botswana liaises with other departments and assists in research and needs assessment for the project. The Department also provides the project with students who become involved in components of the programme through fieldwork, benefitting both the project and the University.

The Steering Committee, comprising membership of all these partners, provides overall guidance to the project, and will be an important vehicle for ensuring community involvement. As the project begins to unfold it is envisaged that the Steering Committee will be extended to include representatives of the Village Development Committee; community professionals such as social workers, teachers, health workers, and religious leaders; and community members with personal knowledge of the target group such as family members or guardians and project volunteers. Members of the Steering Committee will provide input in the selection of project participants.

Conclusion

The vision and mission of TCC and the Rotary Club of Gaborone involve provision for the needs of actual and potential orphans and their families in Mogoditshane Village. In line with national and international policies on orphans of AIDS and affected families and local needs assessment, the multi-purpose centre project has been formulated and adopted and initial steps towards implementation have been taken with a view to staged implementation.

UNICEF's vision is one of focus on the programme as a pilot project for replication in other parts of Botswana, the southern Africa region, the African continent as a whole, and globally where circumstances are similar and needs congruent with those of African communities. Thus the holistic approach to service provision is promoted within the scope of dual continua and bilateral dimensions, addressing local needs on the one hand and establishing a blueprint for alleviating suffering at a global level on the other.

The multi-sectoral nature of this undertaking underlines the significance of government's continuing dogma of multivariate organisational and institutional arrangements as vital to the success of programmes addressing extensive problematic issues and attempting to introduce order into crisis situations. AIDS and orphans are issues of such sensitivity that societies have constantly to be reminded that democratic practice and advancement of basic human rights must always take precedence over attitudes whose locus is fear, stigmatisation, denial, hopelessness, and unrealistic rationalisation. This will not necessarily be straightforward in traditional communities where cultural norms and taboos hold sway and where education alone might not ensure pragmatism.

The partners have agreed that there could be limitations and obstacles in the process of establishing such a project. The church buildings, which might have been utilised, are now deemed inadequate and the quest for a plot of land through the Land Board is proving to be complex and time consuming. There might also be a lack of community support, both in terms of individual and corporate donations and the inability to locate sufficient numbers of suitable volunteers. Inadequate funding, generally, could prove to be a major stumbling block to the success of the project. The centre might be under-utilised because there is not a felt need for the services offered or because of the stigma related to orphanhood and its association with HIV/AIDS (whether directly stated or implied).

Thus the cycle of denial of democratic human rights may be perpetuated even where the goodwill of service providers lays the foundation for operationalised concern. It is within the hearts and minds of ordinary people that the advocacy movement must progress if positive change is to be effected and sustained.

This pilot project will carry with it frustration and the need for modification of plans on an ongoing basis but will, it is envisaged, eventually produce a blueprint from which large numbers of other communities and individuals can benefit without many of the delays and question marks characteristic of pilots. By focusing on the needs of disadvantaged and disempowered children and ailing adults, and ensuring that their right to meaningful life and dignified death is upheld and sustained by community programmes designed specifically for them, those involved are ensuring that some of the challenges of democracy, regional co-operation, and security in southern Africa are not only confronted but transformed into attainable goals in a new millennium of hope.

Notes and References

1   K Frimpong, 'Some pitfalls in Africa's quest for democratic rule and good governance', in K Frimpong and G Jacques (eds), *Corruption, Democracy and Good Governance in Africa: Essays on Accountability and Ethical Behaviour*, Gaborone: Lentswe la Lesedi, 1999.

2   P Russell, 'Towards Democratic Governance: Controlling Corruption', Paper presented at the 20th Southern African Universities Social Science Conference, Lusaka, 1997.

3   D Smith, 'The corruption of democracy, human rights and development', in K Frimpong and G Jacques (eds), *Corruption, Democracy and Good Governance in Africa: Essays on Accountability and Ethical Behaviour*, Gaborone: Lentswe la Lesedi, 1999.

4   R Michaels, *Political Parties*, New York: Free Press, 1962; JD Holm, 'Curbing corruption through democratic accountability: Lessons from Botswana', in KR Hope and BC Chikulo (eds), *Corruption and Development in Africa: Lessons from Country Case-Studies*, London: Macmillan, 2000.

5   CF Cnudde and DE Neuber, *Empirical Democracy*, New York: Markham, 1969.

6   United Nations General Assembly, *Convention on the Rights of the Child*, New York: United Nations Organization, 1989.

7   Republic of Botswana, *National Policy on AIDS*, Gaborone: Government Printers, 1993.

8   Republic of Botswana, *Botswana HIV and AIDS Second Medium Term Plan (MTP II) 1997–2002*, Gaborone: Ministry of Health, AIDS/STD Unit, 1997.

9   G Jacques, 'Back to the Future: AIDS, Orphans, and alternative care in Botswana', Paper presented at the National Conference on the Implications of Orphanhood in Botswana, Gaborone: 1998.

10   Republic of Botswana, *Short Term Plan of Action on Care of Orphans in Botswana 1999–2001*, Gaborone: Ministry of Local Government, Lands and Housing, 1999.

11   Republic of Botswana, *National Youth Policy*, Gaborone: Government Printers, 1996.

12   WHO/UNICEF, *Action for Children Affected by AIDS: Programme Profiles and Lessons Learned*, New York: UNICEF, 1994.

13   R Belanger, *Proposal for an Orphan Project: Mogoditshane Village, Kweneng District, Botswana*, Gaborone: Consultant's Report to Tirisanyo Catholic Commission, 1998.

Youth development through Participation in the Informal Sector in the Sub-Saharan Region

Charles Malan and Tomas Fenyes

Inevitably most discussions on youth development in Africa start with the problem of unemployment. The subject of youth unemployment is reflected in all national youth policies in Commonwealth Africa. Most countries have identified this as a problem that needs to be addressed. However, national programmes of action fall short on how the growing levels of youth unemployment will be resolved. Even the most developed country in the region, South Africa, cannot hope to reach its targets of creating employment and the youth are increasingly forced to find alternatives to formal employment. In this chapter the nature and implications of these alternatives will be discussed within the general and regional contexts.

The International Development Research Centre lists several conditions, such as demographics and GNP, that make the plight of youth in Africa particularly challenging.[1] The IDRC's Sustainable Livelihoods research was spawned by a growing concern that significant numbers of developing country youth lack a solid institutional context for developing their life and employability skills, thereby leading to unemployment and poverty. One of the commissioned reports notes that

> Youths constitute 40 percent to 65 percent of the unemployed in African countries, and this figure has been rising. For instance, between 1986 and 1991 the proportion of youth who were unemployed in Zambia increased from 19 to 27 percent. At present youth unemployment in Zambia stands at 30 percent. Unemployment is particularly severe in the age group 12-19 years … in Africa many children at the age of 12 are forced to enter the labour force as they cannot continue in school for various reasons.[2]

Still, across the world the youth are amongst the sectors of society worst affected by problems related to unemployment. Unemployment and under-employment is a long-term persistent trend, affecting up to 30% of the global work force, some 820 million men and women.[3]

Even though international attention to youth policies is a relatively recent phenomenon, many international organisations have recognised the urgent need for youth empowerment and development. In a number of cases they have initiated action plans to address these issues. These organisations include the United Nations, and related bodies such as UNESCO, UNICEF, the International Labour Organisation, and the IDRC (especially with their ACACIA and ASPR programmes in Africa). The United Nations World Programme of Action for Youth opens with the following clause:

> Every State should provide its young people with opportunities for obtaining education, for acquiring skills and for participating fully in all aspects of society, with a view to, inter alia, acquiring productive employment and leading self-sufficient lives.[4]

The influential United Nations Conference on Environment and Development (UNCED), held in June 1992, paid specific attention to youth's participation in decision-making and their need for sustainable livelihoods: "Numerous actions and recommendations within the international community have been proposed to ensure that youth are provided a secure and healthy future, including an environment of quality, improved standards of living and access to education and employment".[5] Economic development is singled out and the report stresses that, as has been the historical experience of all countries, "youth are particularly vulnerable to the problems associated with economic development, which often weakens traditional forms of social support essential for the healthy development of young people". The report then lists some of the main related problems. Urbanisation and changes in social mores have increased substance abuse, unwanted pregnancy and sexually transmitted diseases, including AIDS. "Currently more than half of all people alive are under the age of 25, and four of every five live in developing countries. Therefore it is important to ensure that historical experience is not replicated."[6]

Youth livelihoods in sub-Saharan Africa

To a large extent the problems surrounding youth livelihoods in this country mirror those in the rest of sub-Saharan Africa. In 1997, the Assessment of Social Policy Reform (ASPR) program of the IDRC organised a series of diagnostic country studies in sub-Saharan Africa on youth livelihoods and enterprise development. In addition, ASPR undertook an extensive literature review in this area. The research and discussions revealed a number of important issues:

- Widespread under-employment among young men and women, particularly among early school leavers, and most evident in the accelerated increase in small-scale youth vending activities in the informal sector;

- Well-articulated skills development policy objectives related to the target group of early school leavers, with a severely under-funded and under-resourced policy implementation system;
- A non-formal training system with pockets of success but which lacks appropriate links to policy, the ability to build on the livelihood, enterprise and employment capabilities of early school leavers and to link these capabilities to viable livelihood opportunities;[7]
- A need to better understand the roles of government, civil society and the private sector in the non-formal training system and in facilitating the transition of young men and women into more viable livelihoods.[8]

Overall, the IDRC finds that government and donor responses to the livelihood challenges faced by early school leavers in Africa are muted and superficial. The reasons for this are complex and numerous. To begin with, youth-related development challenges are relatively recent phenomena, and among a myriad of seemingly more pressing, short-term challenges, they tend to be sidelined. Following the trend in South Africa, youth in general are perceived as a liability and a problem that needs to be managed or subdued. "This combined with weak advocacy, a lack of knowledge on how to approach the challenges, and the political vulnerability of youth, results in superficial and fragmented interventions, often geared to placate".[9]

There is thus a need to understand the livelihood characteristics and aspirations of early school leavers; their institutional support needs; the policies and programmes that are effectively addressing these needs and reasons for success; and the types of interventions that are necessary to expand effective policies and programmes.

The Role of Government

Certainly a formally constituted governmental base responsible for policy formulation and implementation is integral to the success of youth development, as Mwansa, Mufune and Osei-Hwedie conclude in their comparative study of youth policy in Botswana, Swaziland and Zambia.[10] But in this regard lessons have been dearly learnt in Africa. Mkandawire and Chigunta refer to the loss of illusion by large segments of Anglophone African society, particularly the youth.[11] One such illusion is that central government and its policies could protect the vulnerable. The youth have adopted self-reliant coping strategies in order to survive the devastation brought on by economic crises and the social harshness of the measures implemented to combat it. Many youths have stopped looking up to the state, and have begun adopting practical survival strategies. This has resulted in the rapid growth of the informal sector in the region.

The reality has to be faced that although the provision of jobs remains the best solution, for many young people it also remains wishful thinking. It has become essential that the scope be broadened for a larger range of solutions: from a focus on employment to the nature of sustainable livelihoods, from entrepreneurship training to the development of enterprise capabilities, from reliance on government intervention to private and informal sector involvement.

Recent comparative research in Southern Africa has shown that young people are in desperate need of information and guidance that could help them maintain a sustainable livelihood. They do not only need guidance for employment, but information that will help them to cope: life skills, entrepreneurship, health, etc. The research conducted is part of comparative analyses of policies and practices in three African countries (South Africa, Zambia and Malawi), with the main focus on sub-Saharan Africa.

In a number of Commonwealth countries there is a rather naive assumption that since one of the major hurdles to the creation of self-employment among youth is access to credit, then what needs to be put in place is a micro-credit programme to promote micro enterprise development. This is of course understandable, because there is a rather limited body of knowledge on the linkages between youth unemployment, and various policies and programmes in such interrelated areas as education, micro-enterprise development, vocational training, the informal sector, and so on. This chapter is based on the premise that one cannot address the problems of youth unemployment in isolation from the various linkages that impact on employment.

Alternatives to Formal Education

In Africa, many youths will leave school before completing secondary school. It is increasingly common for these young people to enter the informal economy. Although some may succeed in this environment, it is more likely that these youths will merely cope and, in the meanwhile, not develop any further skills that may improve their livelihood in the long run.

Those youths who are outside of the school system and the formal economy have limited opportunity to develop skills through academic study or in a workplace with formal or informal training systems. This inhibits the development of transferable skills that would allow young people to adapt to changing economic circumstances. Although there have been a plethora of non-formal training providers (often funded through developmental non-governmental organisations), the links between these providers and emerging employment opportunities are weak and therefore whatever skills are acquired in these settings may soon atrophy.

Given the fluidity of the economic situation, the challenge facing youth cannot be addressed by merely constructing stationary paths from school to the formal economy. Rather there is a need to understand the full complexity of under-employment among school leavers and create flexible systems to respond to their needs. This approach would recognise that part of the solution lies in the capabilities of youth to adapt to changing circumstances; part in the need to grow and modernise the informal sector; and part in improving the links between non-formal training and employment opportunities.

Against this background the IDRC investigation focused on two issues:
1. Understanding current youth livelihoods for school leavers;
2. Developing institutional mechanisms to improve the life and employability prospects through enterprise skills of school leavers.

Young people have benefited substantially from the processes of democratisation and policy development, including youth policies. When the focus turns to economic conditions and unemployment, however, research produces a far less optimistic picture. In their study of enterprise and entrepreneurship in African countries, Mkandawire and Chigunta describe the backdrop of development crises which most Anglophone African countries have been facing since the mid 1970s and that have over the years induced far-reaching economic reforms.[12] Designed to improve economic management and performance, the reforms entail undertaking painful economic restructuring. A major effect of the reforms is that the formal, largely urban-based sector is losing ground as an important labour sponge, much as the urban areas have slipped as a credible haven for the survival of people, especially the youth. The restructuring of both the public and private sectors in the region has worsened the condition of young people through retrenchments, liquidation of companies and labour market freezes and shrinkage.

In the face of this, Mkandawire and Chigunta believe the on-going economic reforms in Anglophone Africa have to a large extent shattered hopes for a better future among the youth.[13] However, seen from a more positive side, these reforms present new challenges and opportunities for the youth to go into potentially gainful employment through enterprises and entrepreneurship development. Already the urban informal and rural/agricultural sectors have grown in importance as sources of employment in the region. This reality must therefore underlie any effort to meaningfully and realistically search for solutions to the growing employment problem in Anglophone Africa.

In their discussion of development problems in the region, the IDRC believes Africa provides a good example of the opportunity to apply enterprise to youth livelihoods.[14] There exists a situation of acute and wide-spread poverty. Economies of the region are in the midst of significant structural adjustment juxtaposed with a burgeoning youth population. In this process, masses of young people are moving away from rural, agrarian-based economies to urban centres in the hope of improving their lives.

Reliance has traditionally been placed on formal education and vocational training systems to impart the skills needed for entry into the formal labour market. Reforms are in place to integrate enterprise skills development into vocational training institutions. However, the large majority of young people exit the formal education system before Level 7 and are unlikely to be in a position to access the training services which result from these reforms. Hoppers states that the two key reasons for children leaving school are: (1) poverty, forcing people to abandon school in favour of working to enable families to survive; and (2) the education system has not adjusted to the demands for knowledge, skills and aptitudes that young people need to look after themselves and their families.[15]

The decline of formal sector livelihood opportunities has resulted in increased informal sector activity, accounting for up to 80% of GDP in some African countries.[16] This, in large part, is explained by vast numbers of young men and women entering the world of work prematurely and coping with poverty by eking out a livelihood in the informal sector. Although economic adjustment holds out the possibility of a better policy environment for employment growth and enterprise development, the immediate effect has been a reduced capacity of the economy to absorb new entrants into the workforce.

The Livelihood, Enterprise and Employment Capabilities Approach

The notion of livelihoods looks beyond the conventional meaning of employment and seeks to understand the fullest range of ways in which young men and women survive. Young men and women are often the last to be employed in the formal economy. They often engage in a number of income-generating activities to survive, which draw on their full range of capabilities and resources. Under-employment (rather than unemployment) keeps individuals living at a subsistence level and forces them to under-utilise their abilities because of a lack of access to resources.

The World Commission on Environment and Development introduced the concept of sustainable livelihoods in 1987, to relate to ownership of and access to resources, basic needs and existential security, particularly in rural areas. The United Nations Conference on Environment and Development

(UNCED) of 1992 acknowledged the integrative value of the concept in Agenda 21.[17] It also introduced the concept of "sustainable livelihoods for all", making it applicable in developing as well as developed countries. The concept enables decision-makers to integrate decisions on socio-economic and ecological policy issues in a coherent structure, which is pertinent to a development policy.

There is currently much discussion regarding the definition of sustainable livelihoods and its relevance to developing countries. According to the IDRC's first phase research findings, the definitions that have the greatest connection to young people in Africa are those that reflect an understanding of the realities which influence their decisions.[18] For sustainable livelihoods to be relevant to the target group we have defined it must take into consideration poverty, the lack of formal employment opportunities, family obligations and the significant gap between their education, their inherent capabilities and the resources available to them. Chambers and Conway define sustainable livelihoods in the following manner:

> [A] livelihood comprises the capabilities, assets (stores, resources, claims and access) and activities required for a means of living; a livelihood is sustainable which can cope with and recover from stress and shocks, maintain or enhance its capabilities and assets, and provide sustainable livelihood opportunities for the local and global levels and in the short and long term.[19]

Livelihoods is therefore a broader category than "having a job" and more in line with the actual manner in which many young men and women in developing countries must organise themselves and their activities in order to survive. The key to generating a sustainable livelihood is adaptability and the utilisation of what Chambers and Conway describe as dynamic livelihood capabilities. Chambers and Conway consider that, "Most livelihoods of the poor will continue to be adaptive performances, improvised and versatile in the face of adverse conditions, shocks and unpredictable change".[20]

The UNDP believes that sustainable livelihoods should integrate all economic activities currently defined under employment as well as

> introduce the social dimensions of sustainability and equity ... What is proposed is an inclusive, rather than exclusive, concept of `sustainable livelihood` that is potentially applicable to any form of making a living which can be pursued independently, (i) without compromising personal security, (ii) is reasonably stable across significant periods of time (without, of course, any guarantee), (iii) is mutually beneficial to individuals and their immediate social grouping, as well as to the consumers of their products/services, and (iv) does not compromise the physical environment.[21]

Creating a livelihood is a necessity, making it sustainable is the challenge. Sustainable livelihoods always entail more than employment or economic empowerment, crucial as these aspects may be. Political, ecological, socio-cultural, educational and other factors all are important indicators of a reasonable means of living and well-being.

The notion of dynamic livelihood capabilities dovetails with a broader notion of enterprise and entrepreneurship. Chambers and Conway describe dynamic livelihood capabilities as "the ability to perceive, predict, adapt to and exploit changes in the physical, social and economic environment".[22] By enterprise is meant that set of knowledge, skills and attitudes (referred to here as enterprise skills) that allow a person to adapt to changing circumstances by taking control and initiative. When these skills are applied to business formation and expansion we call this "entrepreneurism" whereas enterprise skills may be applied to a wide variety of other life circumstances including coping with poverty.

Enterprising behaviour can have various manifestations. It can manifest itself in adapting to adversity in the traditional rural sector and in various forms of self-employment and income generation in the informal sector. A common manifestation of this behaviour is in vending and trading in the urban informal markets, which in many cases is considered an under-utilisation of a young person's potential. More productive manifestations of enterprise capabilities may come in the form of a self-employed clothing maker, bricklayer or furniture maker.

Entrepreneurship is seen as the application of enterprise skills or dynamic livelihood capabilities in the context of long-term business development. According to Loucks, "All entrepreneurs are self-employed, but all self-employed are not entrepreneurs if we interpret entrepreneurship as involving production or sale of a product or service and the person concerned takes a substantial financial risk and its success generates further employment".[23] Enterprise capabilities allow technical skills to find social and economic expression where formal employment opportunities are constrained. Many young people naturally work in a dynamic or enterprising manner despite the barriers that block their access to important resources. Many of these enterprising behaviours are actually a manifestation of failure in the employment market. It can be argued that these conditions predispose a larger number of young men and women to self-employment because they have been exposed to it through the inability of the formal market to absorb them.

In summary, there are clearly defined sub-groups of school leavers who face different challenges and who posses different enterprise capabilities. The assertion being made is that enterprise approaches to non-formal training can help alleviate the market failure by: (1) helping young men and women cope; (2) helping improve the role of self-employment in the form of micro and small enterprise development; and (3) helping to generate more formal employment opportunities by expanding the private sector through entrepreneurship development.

A Coherent Approach to Livelihoods, Enterprise and Employment Development

There are several non-formal training programmes in place in, for example, Malawi, Zambia and South Africa. These programmes are focused on developing the livelihood, enterprise and employment capabilities of young men and women. The programmes are often developed in isolation of each other, with a lack of detailed understanding of the livelihood contexts and capabilities of the target group and with few if any links to policy or a broader youth skills development strategy. Credit programmes are developed with little regard to training or links to training institutions, often undermining the ability of young men and women to develop sound planning, management and basic savings skills.[24] Training programmes tend to be geared towards young men, with little understanding of the livelihood contexts of young women, and offer skills acquisition in areas which offer women limited employment opportunities.[25] Little if any link has been established with private enterprise (particularly with larger firms) and the demand for goods, services and skills. Grierson maintains that this lack of demand-supply match is the single most influential factor contributing to the failure of most programmes.[26]

Viewing the situation from a development perspective, there is a vast human resource waiting to be tapped. The 1997 UNFPA report on the world population talks of the bulge in the working age population, largely attributable to the growth in the population of young people (ages 15-30), as the "demographic bonus", which "offers (developing) countries an opportunity to build human capital and spur long-term development".[27] Complementing this potential is a real demand by the private sector for skilled labour in the form of, for example, self-employed bricklayers, carpenters, computer service technicians and sales representatives.[28]

Finally, the study of micro and small enterprise development has produced an abundance of literature on financial and non-financial services for small business development, some of which is relevant to promoting youth enterprise and livelihood skills development.[29] The ILO, UNICEF and the UNFPA and a number of international NGOs and local community-based organisations have documented experience on youth life skills development related to self-employment. In addition, experience and literature is emerging on the appropriate role of micro-credit in micro-enterprise development and self-employment.[30] The lessons learned from these experiences, placed in the context of the livelihood conditions, circumstances and capabilities of young men and women, has the potential for the development of a coherent non-formal training programme framework for the development of youth livelihoods, enterprise and employment capabilities.

The need for a comprehensive and holistic strategy to address youth employment is widely recognised. The Co-operative Research Programme called for education and training to inform people of opportunities in these areas.[31] They suggest three specific ways to empower the unemployed:

1. Education should be used to help to eliminate the harmful effects of myths and stereotypes about the unemployed;
2. There is a need for direct support services for the unemployed through the family, which currently provides most of the social and moral security for its unemployed in its midst;
3. The unemployed should be helped to externalise blame for their being without work. Solidarity among the unemployed needs to be supported insofar as it can provide a positive reference group for these people.

Linking Non-formal Training Programmes to Education and Training Policy Objectives

The ideal point of entry for the development of employment skills is the education system. However, the current reality in sub-Saharan Africa is that most young men and women leave this system before the age of twelve. The skills development of early school leavers, in most cases, falls under the jurisdiction of the ministries of Youth, Gender and Community Affairs. In many cases (e.g. South Africa, Zambia), self-employment skills development policy objectives for this group do exist. These objectives are often well articulated and are based on sound reasoning and a good general understanding of the conditions facing young men and women. The problem is that these Ministries tend to be understaffed with limited financial resources to implement these policies. A more efficient non-formal training system, with relevant links to policy could provide the means to implement many existing policy objectives.

In summary, the institutional challenge is to improve the effectiveness of the non-formal training system. There is a need to develop an institutional mechanism to respond to market failures to mediate the latent potential of young people into productive social and economic activity, while understanding their current livelihood conditions and capabilities. In particular there is a need to:

- Identify what skills and services are in demand and who is demanding them;
- Identify the young men and women with the capabilities to fill this demand;
- Develop the targeted training to support the development of these capabilities and link the supply of trainees to the demand for skills and services;
- Link the intent of skills development policy objectives to the range of effective programmes which do exist, and where possible establish links with the formal education system;
- Identify the appropriate roles for government, civil society and the private sector.

Support structures in the community

In many countries in Africa some young people have sought political space through volunteering to work with local communities, including church organisations. Hence although not fully employed, the political and social space that is provided enables them to gain some degree of skills including confidence, a sense of work belonging and connection to their communities. This provides them with a useful springboard into future employment.

Social support structures are especially crucial for empowering young women. It comes as no surprise that Sharif finds that women entrepreneurs in sub-Saharan Africa, especially young women, lack equal access to economic resources, such as land, improved technology and government services (such as transportation).[32] They also have unequal access to formal education and lack training in management related and technical skills. In South Africa, the National Job Summit fully recognised women's marginalised position as entrepreneurs and adopted a range of proposals to remedy the situation. Before their situation is improved, however, they will have to rely heavily on community and family networks.

Governments usually do not want to give the informal sector too much recognition because it brings with it a lack of bureaucratic control, loss of tax revenue, and so on. However ways of accommodating and assisting young people in the informal sector have become an urgent necessity. Without these innovative approaches and policies many sub-Saharan countries might be heading for disaster.

Notes and References

1   International Development Research Centre (IDRC), *Sustainable livelihoods for youth: A multi-country proposal for action research and the establishment of the Africa Youth Livelihoods Knowledge Network*, Unpublished proposal, IDRC, October 1998a.

2   IDRC, *Youth enterprise and entrepreneurship development: Research towards sustainable livelihoods for youth*, Unpublished report, IDRC, 1997, p 16.

3   JP Grierson, *Where there is no job: Vocational training for self-employment in developing countries*, Geneva: Swiss Centre for Development Co-operation, 1997, p 1.

4   *Perspectives on contemporary youth*, New York: United Nations, n.d; 'United Nations World Programme of Action for Youth', in National Youth Commission, *Youth policy 2000: National youth policy*, Pretoria: Government of the Republic of South Africa, 2000.

5   United Nations Conference on Environment and Development (UNCED), *Proceedings of UNCED*, New York: United Nations, 1992.

6   *Statistical charts and indicators on the situation of youth: 1980–1995*, New York: UN, 1998.

7   Non-formal training refers here to skills development programmes that lie outside the formal education system. These programmes are commonly managed by non-governmental organisations and community based organisations (e.g. church groups) and are funded by the private sector, donors and government.

8   IDRC, *Sustainable livelihoods for youth: Draft report of the IDRC research findings to date*, Unpublished report, IDRC, October 1998b.

9   IDRC 1998a.

10   LK Mwansa, P Mufune and K Osei-Hwedie, 'Youth policy and programmes in the SADC countries of Botswana, Swaziland and Zambia: A comparative assessment', *International Social Work*, vol 37, 1994, p 261.

11   RM Mkandawire and F Chigunta, *The regional study on youth enterprise and entrepreneurship in Anglophone Africa in the 21st century*, Unpublished report, Lusaka: Commonwealth Youth Programme, 1997.

12   *Ibid.*

13   *Ibid.*

14   IDRC 1998a.

15   W Hoppers, *The promotion of self-employment in education and training institutions: Perspectives in East and Southern Africa*, Geneva: International Labour Organisation, 1994.

16   IDRC 1998a.

17   UNCED 1992.

18   IDRC 1998b.

19   R Chambers and GR Conway, *Sustainable rural livelihoods: Practical concepts for the 21st century*, Discussion Paper 296, Sussex: Institute for Development Studies, 1992, p 5.

20   *Ibid.*, p 6.

21   *Productive employment and poverty eradication: How can livelihoods be more sustainable?*, New York: United Nations Development Programme, 1997, p 5.

22   Chambers and Conway 1992.

23   K Loucks, *Training entrepreneurs for small business creation: Lessons from experience*, Geneva: ILO, 1988.

24   RM Mkandawire, *Sustainable livelihoods and self-employment initiatives research for South Africa, with specific reference to the Northern Province*, Unpublished planning document, 1998.

25   NR Sharif, *Youth livelihood choices and constraints in Sub-Saharan Africa: A gender perspective*, Unpublished IDRC report, 1998.

26   Grierson 1997.

27   *The state of the world population*, New York: United Nations Population Fund, 1998.

28   Grierson 1997.

29   *Ibid*.

30   Sharif 1998, Mkandawire 1998.

31   VZ Slabbert, C Malan, H Marais, J Olivier and R Riordan (eds), *Youth in the New South Africa: Towards policy formulation*, Pretoria: Human Sciences Research Council, 1994, p 137.

32   Sharif 1998.

List of Contributors

John K Akokpari is a lecturer in the Department of Political and Administrative Studies at the National University of Lesotho. He has published articles on various issues in African politics, including migration, democratisation, foreign policies and globalisation.

Kwaku Asante-Darko is in the Department of English at the National University of Lesotho.

Rhoda Cynthia Bakuwa lectures in the Business Administration Department at the Malawi Polytechnic, Blantyre.

Mwangala M Bonna is a consultant in Information Technology in Gaborone, Botswana.

Blessings Chinsinga lectures in the Department of Political and Administrative Studies at Chancellor College, the University of Malawi.

Tommy Fényes is a professor of Economics and Head of the Department of Economics at Vista University.

Charles Freysen is a professor of Public Administration and Dean of the Faculty of Management, Vista University.

Gloria Jacques is a senior lecturer in the Department of Social Work, University of Botswana.

Gregory H Kamwendo is based at the Centre for Language Studies, University of Malawi.

Ackson Kanduza is in the Department of History at the University of Swaziland. He is actively involved in OSSREA, the Organisation for Social Science Research in Eastern Africa.

Gwen N Lesetedi lectures in the Department of Sociology at the University of Botswana.

GS Maipose is a senior lecturer in political and administrative studies at the University of Botswana.

Charles Malan is a professor in the Department of Information Science at the University of Pretoria.

Rets'elisitsoe A Matlanyane is in the Economics Department at the National University of Lesotho.

S N-A Mensah is in the School of Economics and Management Sciences at the University of the North, Qwaqwa campus.

Dominic Milazi was a lecturer in the Department of Sociology, University of the North-West in South Africa.

Fewdays Miyanda is a lecturer at the National University of Lesotho, teaching Professional Translation/Interpretation from French into English and vice versa. He holds a Secondary Teacher's diploma in French and English, a BA in French and English, and an MA and PhD in Professional Translation/Interpretation.

Elizabeth Mukamaambo is a lecturer in population and sustainable development at the University of Botswana.

Munyae M Mulinge is a senior lecturer in the Department of Sociology at the University of Botswana.

Lengwe-Katembula Mwansa lectures in the Department of Social Work at the University of Botswana.

Naomi Ngwira is in the Department of Economics, Chancellor College, Malawi. She was a member of the Malawi Vision 2020 National Core Team.

Mamane Nxumalo lectures in the Department of Sociology at the University of Swaziland.

Bertha Z Osei-Hwedie is based in the Department of Political and Administrative Studies at the University of Botswana.

Severine M Rugumamu is Executive Secretary of the African Association of Political Science (AAPS), based in Harare, Zimbabwe.